Gainful Pursuits

The Making of Industrial Europe 1600–1914

Gainful Pursuits

The Making of Industrial Europe 1600–1914

Jordan Goodman
Lecturer in Economic History, University of Essex

and

Katrina Honeyman
Lecturer in Economic History, University of Leeds

Edward Arnold
A division of Hodder & Stoughton

LONDON   NEW YORK   MELBOURNE   AUCKLAND

First published in Great Britain 1988
Reprinted 1990

Distributed in the USA by Routledge, Chapman and Hall, Inc.
29 West 35th Street, New York, NY 10001

British Library Cataloguing in Publication Data

Goodman, Jordan
  Gainful pursuits: the making of industrial
  Europe 1600—1914.
  1. Europe. Economic development, 1600—1914
  I. Title   II. Honeyman, Katrina
  330.94'02

  ISBN 0—7131—6606—1
  ISBN 0—7131—6545—6 Pbk

Photoset in Linotron Sabon 10/11pt by
Northern Phototypesetting Co, Bolton, England.
Printed and bound in Great Britain for Edward Arnold, a division of
Hodder and Stoughton Limited, Mill Road, Dunton Green,
Sevenoaks, Kent TN13 2YA by the Athenaeum Press Ltd, Newcastle
upon Tyne.

Contents

Acknowledgements

The making of this book, like that of industrial Europe, has been a lengthy and multi-directional process. We are grateful to the many authors referred to in the text whose work has enabled us to substantiate some of our ideas on European industrialization. Alan Milward has consistently supported the concept of this work. We are very grateful to him. Nick Crafts and David Hebb read parts of the manuscript; we thank them for their helpful comments. We also benefited from the contributions of participants at Theo Barker's seminar at the Institute of Historical Research in London; in February 1987. Finally, we should like to thank our editors at Edward Arnold for their gentle but persistent encouragement to complete the book.

List of Maps

The maps are based on information presented in *The Times Atlas of World History*, 2nd edn.

Preface

This book is about the history of industrial Europe in the period from the beginning of the seventeenth century to the outbreak of the First World War. It is about the growth and development of European industries; their relationships to other economic activities; and their impact on the structure of the European economy and Europe's economic role in the international economy. It does not offer a comprehensive economic history of Europe, nor, for that matter, does it offer a comprehensive industrial history. The selection of industries is, however, reasonably representative and designed to illustrate and highlight various issues central to the concerns of the book.

This book differs from other accounts of Europe's economic past in the following ways. First, it does not focus, in any thematic or organizational sense, on the Industrial Revolution. Secondly, it covers a relatively long period of time emphasizing change and continuity rather than discontinuity. Finally, it focuses on industrial production, as its unit of analysis, rather than on geographical entities such as regions, nations and continents.

In some ways, the history of industrial Europe is synonymous with industrialization as long as the latter is defined broadly and covers a greater period than is commonly accepted. Judging from the ease with which the term industrialization is used by historians and social scientists alike, it is perhaps not at all surprising that there is little agreement on what industrialization means. Some scholars, for example, prefer to use industrialization in the sense of technical change, by which they usually mean a process synonymous with mechanization and the general increasing use of technology in production. Others, however, choose to view it in economic terms, considering industrialization as a process through which industry becomes increasingly more important to economic life, and defined as a secular rise in industry's share of the labour force, of total output, of capital, or of some other measure. Finally, there are those who adopt a broad social and cultural view of industrialization which is often hard to distinguish from modernization. While there may be disagreement about which of these definitions – and there are others – of industrialization is more accurate or helpful, on one point most writers would concur – industrialization began towards the latter half of the eighteenth century and was set in motion by the

Industrial Revolution.

It is our belief that industrialization, at least in the first two senses in which it is commonly used, has a longer and more complex history than is generally acknowledged. That history definitely does not begin with the Industrial Revolution. Industrialization was already in progress long before that date and includes guild-based urban industry, rural proto-industry as well as the more familiar forms of factory organization and other examples of concentrated production. It also includes many important technical advances made before the late eighteenth century as well as unmechanized but highly dynamic industrial activities. Moreover, the history of industrialization covers a period beginning in the sixteenth and seventeenth centuries when commercial capitalism made enormous strides in integrating commodity (as well as factor) markets worldwide. In order to avoid confusion with the fore-shortened definition of industrialization, we have decided to avoid the term and concern ourselves with the notion of industrial Europe as the subject of this book.

In our attempt to shift the focus entirely away from what we consider to be a historically narrow perspective, we have adopted a framework for analysing the development of industrial Europe which is both simple and broad enough to convey impressions of continuity and change. The framework consists of two parts. On a broad level, we are focusing on changes in the overall levels of manufacturing activity, in both absolute and relative terms, regardless of the reasons for it. This has a counterpart on an industrial level, where our analysis concentrates on changes in the degree of the interrelatedness of industrial production as well as in the range, type and availability of industrial goods. As far as its geographic space is concerned, the framework adopts a European-wide perspective.

The initial date for this book, 1600, was chosen partly to satisfy the belief that the making of industrial Europe needs to be seen in a global context. Specifically, we feel that European industry was significantly transformed by the growing integration of the European market and by the expansionary forces of European commerce and finance in Asia, America and Africa, initiated in the sixteenth century but only developing towards the beginning of the seventeenth century. The end date of 1914 is more arbitrary, but was chosen in order to capture the then prevailing national context of industrial activity.

We have rejected geographic and political units in our analysis of industrial Europe because we feel that this obscures the generality of the process we are examining. Instead, we have decided to approach the theme of this book from four directions corresponding to the four parts into which the book is divided. Part I is concerned generally with the changing structural relationships between industry and the agrarian, commercial and financial sectors. The development of a world economy, progressively linked to economic, social and political changes within Europe, demographic conditions and urbanization within Europe all receive close attention. In Part II, we trace changes internal to industrial production in general highlighting the organization of production, the role and development of technology and the division of labour. Part III concentrates on specific European industries and their products in an attempt to provide more detail at the point of production. Familiar activities such as textile production, iron and steel manufacture, the chemical industry and power engineering are all discussed in addition to industries which normally receive less attention in general accounts – clocks, armaments, bicycles, cars, ships, and machine tools. The choice of industrial activity as the focus of analysis was influenced by the fact that it is amenable to the kind of long-term approach we adopt. Other economic entities, such as capital flows or the labour market, would have been equally good, but lack the quantity of research which European industries have attracted. Part IV provides a view of industrialization based upon the previous chapters and examines the impact of this process on the European economy. Each part of the book covers the period in its entirety.

Above all else, this book is dedicated to the view that industrial Europe was a complex of organizations of production, of technology, of labour and of output. Any attempt to deny this complexity by forcing the history of industrial Europe into theoretical constructions or nation types is to ignore the enormous weight of recent scholarship.

References, Bibliography and Further Reading

References in the text are primarily to works that provide further details, suggestions for reading and bibliographical information, or point to areas of debate. In most cases these works also provide the supporting evidence for the arguments developed in this book.

The books and articles listed in the bibliography at the end of the book are predominantly those items referred to in the text. As far as possible these references are accessible, both linguistically and locationally, to English-speaking students. References in a foreign language have been kept to a minimum, and appear only when they are of particular significance.

Suggestions for further reading follow each chapter. These are confined to books, or exceptionally articles, which provide a deeper treatment or a wider perspective of subjects discussed in the text, and which themselves contain useful bibliographies and references. The same emphasis is placed on accessibility.

Introduction: Industrial Europe in 1600

It is not common to think of Europe at the beginning of the seventeenth century as industrial. Images of rural societies and economies come most readily to mind. The experience of living in Europe at this time is most often summed up in terms of rural classifications – France is the country of peasant and seigneur; England of the tenant and absentee landlord; Holland of the independent farmer; southern Italy of the sharecropper and Prussia of the serf and feudal lord. Production, distribution and consumption likewise refer mostly to the goods and services of a rural economy. The size of the harvest and the purchasing power of a bushel of wheat are considered fundamental indicators of economic well-being. The potency of the rural model, however, is not confined to mere description. The society and economy are commonly thought of as performing a balancing act designed to keep population and resources in equilibrium. The rules and responses available to the economy are those of a backward, fundamental agrarian world whose non-rural parts exist to supplement the rural foundations.

There is some truth to these images. In purely quantitative terms, the agrarian world dominated the economic and social landscape. Most of Europe's population derived its income from the land whether from wages, rents or profits; most of Europe's labour was employed on the land; and most of the capital was invested in the land. There were considerably fewer towns than there are today and most of them were very small by modern standards – no city in Europe had more than 1 million inhabitants and only eight cities had more than 100,000 inhabitants. Though precise figures do not exist, there is little doubt that the overwhelming proportion of Europe's wealth consisted of agricultural goods and services.

In qualitative terms, too, the preponderance of the agrarian world is evident. Social classes and the distribution of political power were, in formal and official terms at least, conceived in terms of the relationship to land. Agrarian property rights were fundamental to the legal and political system as anyone who has studied the political history of Europe knows.

It is important, however, to keep a sense of perspective. By focusing so much attention on the agrarian world there is the danger of exaggerating its function and its proportion, and ignoring wider involvements.

It is not easy to define industry in 1600. Industry was not distinguished clearly by its location, by the nature of its production and finance nor by the nature of its entrepreneurs and work force as it is in modern economies. Industrial production was carried on virtually everywhere in Europe. There were no areas that were purely industrial as there were no areas that were purely agricultural; any region in Europe taken at random contained industrial, commercial and agricultural activities, which differed in degree rather than in kind. Most rural households undertook some form of industrial work either for their own consumption or for sale in the market to supplement their income. Even in towns, artisans and industrial workers produced for themselves in addition to what they produced for the market. The industrial work force was not particularly distinct. Most of the labouring classes followed several occupations simultaneously and these might involve different kinds of work. Building craftsmen were often employed in some form of textile manufacture and agricultural work in addition to work in construction. In the countryside, employment often varied seasonally between agricultural and industrial work while commercial activities were usually unspecialized. Within one's lifetime, it was certainly more common to have changed occupations many times than to have remained tied to only one.

The flexibility and fluidity of the labour market was matched by that of the capital market. Industrial capital was indistinguishable from commercial capital. Not only were industrialists and merchants one and the same, but capital invested in industrial enterprises was organically similar to that invested in commercial enterprises. Moving in and out of industrial investments was relatively painless as fixed investments, except in specific cases, were small or even absent, and, in many industries, the workers owned the means of production.

Despite these inherent difficulties in distinguishing industry, it is possible to offer some general observations which will serve to locate the contours of industrial Europe at the turn of the seventeenth century. There is little doubt that a large proportion of Europe's industrial production originated in towns and cities. With some notable exceptions of cities whose main role was to serve administrative or ecclesiastical functions, most European towns contained significant concentrations of industrial activities. Recent estimates for several European cities at the turn of the seventeenth century suggest that at least 50 per cent of the employed population were engaged in some form of manufacturing (Clarkson 1971; Cipolla 1976; Clark 1976; Hohenberg and Lees 1985). Textiles and clothing was generally the single largest employer; metalwork, woodwork, and leatherwork followed closely behind. Even in port cities, such as Venice, Bordeaux, London and Hamburg, the industrial sector was still the largest employer, which is not surprising considering the substantial industrial demands made by shipbuilding, warehousing and transport (Hohenberg and Lees 1985).

Within the urban industrial economy, several organizations of production were well established by the beginning of the seventeenth century. The most widespread form of production was artisanal. Metal-working, woodworking, leather-working, a vast array of semi-luxury manufacture, clothing and some amount of textile production was organized in this fashion. In general, the skill content of the work was high and individual workers possessed a wide range of skills giving them command over many, if not all, of the stages of manufacture. Workers commonly owned the tools of their trade as well as the raw materials, and the finished goods were often sold direct, though it was not uncommon for merchants to become involved in the transaction. Within the artisanal organization, a hierarchical division of labour existed containing masters, journeymen and apprentices and in certain places and in certain industries, the work process was directly regulated by guilds. Work took place within the master's household where the division of labour included the master's wife and children.

Not unlike this form of artisanal organization was that of artisanal production concentrated in specific sites outside the household. This was most common in shipbuilding and construction in general, though in the seventeenth and eighteenth centuries, it was an industrial organization commonly found also in sugar refining, brewing, iron smelting, in state enterprises and in porcelain manufacture. A hierarchical division of labour organized the work process, but unlike the artisanal system described above, work took place outside of the home. Family members were therefore not directly involved in the work process of the head of the household, who was usually male. The labour demands of shipbuilding and construction could be enormous; at the turn of the seventeenth century, the Venetian arsenal was employing over 2,500 workers of which two-thirds were highly skilled craftsmen, and the building of St Peter in Rome required a workforce of a similar size and structure (Romano 1968; Goldthwaite 1980; MacKenney 1987).

Finally, there was production based on the putting-out system, a form of industrial organization found most commonly, but by no means exclusively, in textile manufacture. Unlike that of artisanal production, the putting-out system entailed a complex and highly segmented division of labour. Part of this division was technical; preparatory stages were separated from later stages of production; spinning was separated from weaving and dyeing and so on. Another part of the division was financial. Merchants purchased raw materials and sold finished goods while putting the work out to the labour force. Workers tended to own their own tools but it was not unusual for them to be rented. There was also a division between town and countryside. Typically, the preparatory stages and spinning were carried on in the countryside, though there were a few exceptions to this. The more highly skilled stages, or those which required significant capital input, for example, dyeing, were concentrated within the city walls. Finally, there was a division of labour by gender. Women were invariably employed in the preparatory stages and in spinning and, in some cases, in weaving and in other later stages of production; men, on the other hand, tended to be employed in those stages of manufacture which were in many respects artisanal in character. Men were thus weavers, dyers, combers, carders, and, needless to say, merchants. Most of the work in the putting-out system took place in the home.

Whether in artisanal or putting-out production, labour was certainly the most important factor in industrial production. Capital investment in the form of plant and technology was generally low and narrow. The most significant concentration of industrial capital was in the shipbuilding industry, but even here it was dwarfed by the investment in wages and raw materials. Other sizeable concentrations of capital could be found in silk spinning, iron smelting

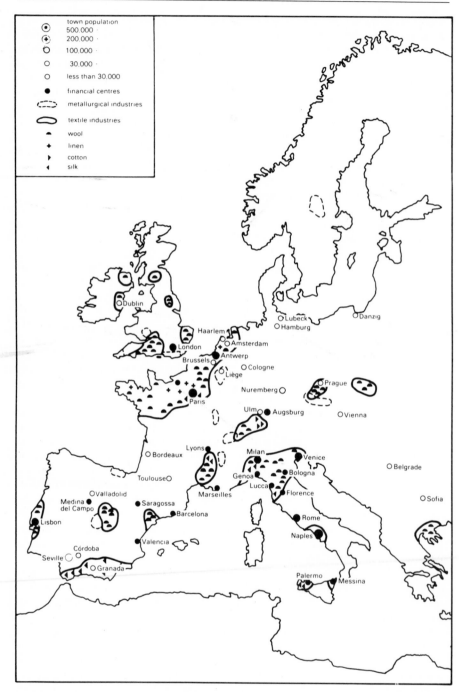

town population

⊙	500.000 ·
⊕	200.000 ·
○	100.000 ·
○	30.000 ·
○	less than 30.000
●	financial centres
⬭ (dashed)	metallurgical industries
⬭	textile industries
◣	wool
+	linen
▸	cotton
◂	silk

Dublin
Lübeck   Danzig
Hamburg
Haarlem
London   Amsterdam
Brussels   Antwerp
Liège   Cologne
Nuremberg   Prague
Paris   Ulm   Augsburg   Vienna
Lyons   Milan   Venice
Bordeaux   Genoa   Bologna   Belgrade
Toulouse   Lucca   Florence
Marseilles   Sofia
Valladolid
Medina   Saragossa
del Campo   Barcelona   Rome
Lisbon   Valencia   Naples
Córdoba
Seville   Granada   Palermo   Messina

1   Trade and industry in the sixteenth century

and glass-making, but these were exceptional. As far as technology itself was concerned, it would be misleading to suggest that it was neither important nor advanced. Technical change was an important factor of industrial progress and in certain areas was the chief determinant of industrial change. In the seventeenth century, this was especially true in most processes involved in ship-building, armaments production and in navigational and precision instruments generally.

But for most urban industrial activities, it was the quality of the labour and of the output which mattered the most. Since the early Middle Ages, cities had dominated industrial production and had developed various strategies to maintain quality and a share of the market. Some cities concentrated their efforts on a narrow range of goods for the external market. Lyons, Genoa and Geneva, for example, specialized in silk production; Florence, Norwich, Leiden and Lille concentrated on woollens and worsteds; Brescia and Liège were centres of small-arms manufacture. Other cities specialized in particular industrial processes; or concentrated on particular organizations of production, specializing, for example, in artisanal or small commodity output. In general, despite efforts to monopolize segments of the market, urban industries were incapable of maintaining their positions in the market. The most successful strategy adopted to undermine market power was by imitation and by attracting labour from competitors, either directly or by offering skilled labour a haven for refuge. By the turn of the seventeenth century, many industrial processes had diffused throughout Europe in this fashion. Geneva's silk industry was founded by Protestants who fled from Lucca where silk production had first become established in western Europe; Flemish emigrants had brought the techniques of producing worsted cloth to East Anglia; Huguenots helped to diffuse the manufacture of glass, silk and clocks to many parts of Europe. But this was just the tip of the iceberg. The migration of skilled labour was a constant feature of Europe's urban industrial economy. With every occurrence of the plague, of poor harvests, of a series of trade depressions, skilled labour would be found on the move and attempts by urban authorities to prevent the movement generally failed. The result of this mobility over the long term was that at the beginning of the seventeenth century, industrial technique and organization was remarkably uniform across Europe, and that competition in industrial production was intense.

The vast majority of urban industrial products that entered the market was destined for urban consumption. A complex network of commercial relationships and techniques existed to facilitate these transactions. There were seasonal fairs, established in particularly important centres of communication, where goods and services could be exchanged; there were other fairs at which only financial transactions took place; finally, there were private banks that cleared multilateral payments and arranged credits for the exchange of industrial goods. While the decentralization of these commercial and financial activities continued to some extent, a move to concentrate them in one city was firmly established. By the beginning of the seventeenth century, Amsterdam was fulfilling this role, having assumed this position at the expense of Antwerp.

By the end of the sixteenth century, urban industrial production was probably at the highest level it had been for several centuries and certainly since the middle of the fourteenth century. By all accounts, output had increased at a significant rate and across a variety of products. The range of goods available to European consumers was formidable. The variety of textiles available was particularly impressive. Simple cloths made from wool, cotton, silk and flax, were over-shadowed by complicated mixtures of basic fibres, of countless colours, weaves, designs and shapes – pattern books which survive from the period attest to the large numbers of variations available. All manner of leatherware, of metalware and woodworking was produced not to mention jewellery, coaches, musical instruments, glassware, ceramics and clocks and watches. With few exceptions, little was added to this range of goods produced in Europe before the nineteenth century.

In terms of European population, the labour employed in urban industry was relatively small. If we take a population of 5,000 or more inhabitants as defining a town, then at the turn of the seventeenth century, roughly 12 per cent of Europe's population was urbanized, of which only half were employed in industrial activities (de Vries 1984). Yet the wealth that this small proportion generated and the wealth which urban industry created generally was far greater than these figures might suggest.

Industrial production was not, however, confined entirely to the cities. The countryside was an important area of industrial production. In proportionate terms, more people were probably employed in industrial production in the country than in the city; and many activities were, by necessity, restricted to a rural location. Many industrial activities in the countryside were ancillary to agriculture. Every rural district had its blacksmiths, leather-makers, broommakers, ropemakers, thatchers and roofers and other craft workers. These were important skills not only for agriculture, but were potentially valuable in producing crafts for other markets.

Industries which were resource or energy intensive were often confined to rural areas. The iron industry was located generally in rural areas rich in water and forests and especially where there were iron deposits. In England, the primary iron industry was concentrated in the Forest of Dean and the Sussex Weald; in France, the favoured areas were the Dauphiné and the Franche-Comté; in Belgium, iron production was sited around Liège and in the district between the Sambre and the Meuse; in Germany, important centres of iron production were located in many areas such as Westphalia and Thuringia; other areas of iron production included the Basque region in northern Spain, Tuscany and particularly Sweden. In 1600, iron production throughout Europe was still heavily dependent upon charcoal as its chief energy source. It was for this same reason that many rural areas also supported glass production. This was true of the glass industry in the Black Forest region in Germany, in Champagne and the Nevers in France and in the Weald in England. Paper-making, flour-milling, and silk-throwing were also located in the countryside where sufficient water-power could be located.

By the beginning of the seventeenth century, and in several cases earlier than that, industrial production which was neither resource or energy intensive nor ancillary to agriculture spread in rural areas. This was especially true of linen and woollen manufacture, for which the market was usually distant from the centre of production. During the sixteenth century, rural industrial production grew alongside that of urban production. In some cases, production was organized on the basis of the putting-out system using wage-labour in a fashion similar to that found in the towns. Indeed, those organizing the work were frequently urban merchants. In other cases, however, production developed on the basis of small-commodity production where independent artisans would enter the market to purchase yarn and sell cloth. Such production was often perceived by urban authorities as direct competition to urban industry and attempts were made to check the development of rural industry, but generally to no avail. Industrial activities in the countryside could not be regulated because the institutions, such as guilds, of urban regulation were entirely absent in rural districts. To some extent, rural households had always engaged in industrial production, as one means, amongst many, of supplementing an agrarian income. Because of the development of European as well as overseas markets, however, rural industrial production in the sixteenth century began to develop a momentum whose results went far beyond satisfying the income demands of rural households. This can be seen clearly in the growth of Europe's linen industry, located in the flax-growing areas on the Continent extending in a broad arc from Britanny in the west to Silesia in the east. The main export market for European linen lay in the New World, but sizeable demand also came directly from the shipbuilding and outfitting industries. The manufacture of light woollen cloths received similar impetus from the opening up of the Levant and western Mediterranean market to northern European industrial products.

Industrial activities in the countryside around 1600 thus displayed a complex pattern ranging from goods manufactured for immediate consumption in agriculture or in rural households, through highly capital, resource or energy intensive production, to labour intensive manufacture of goods for export markets. We will probably never know how many rural inhabitants were engaged in industrial production, not only because the appropriate documentation rarely exists but also because much of rural work was highly seasonal. Nevertheless, recent research suggests that as much as 25–30 per cent of the rural population may have been employed primarily in non-agricultural activities as their main occupation (Wrigley 1985). Taken together with the previous estimates of the proportion of European population engaged in urban industrial activities, it is certainly possible that industry may have employed as much as one-third of Europe's inhabitants around 1600.

In terms of the organization, location and nature of production, it is clear that European industry at the turn of the seventeenth century was proceeding along several frontiers at about the same time. While the coexistence of several different industrial systems may seem perplexing to modern sensibilities, it is important to understand that each system had a rationale entirely its own and, perhaps more significantly was part of a single economic system with interlocking parts. For example, it may be surprising to learn that not all textile production in cities was organized on the putting-out system even though, on strict economic criteria and historical developments, this should be the favoured organization of production in the sixteenth century when markets were growing rapidly. Yet, in the woollen cloth industry in both Lille and Leiden, manufacturing was organized on the basis of small-commodity production where the draper or master weaver and not the merchant controlled the work process (DuPlessis and Howell 1982). This is not a case of the persistence of an inefficient organization. Rather, in both cities, small-commodity production was the economic solution to a political problem concerned with managing social relations in an urban environment. At the same time, the artisanal characteristics of woollen production in both cities could not have been supported without the substantial input of rural, largely female, industrial labour organized on the basis of the putting-out system which provided the necessary yarn. Only with hindsight would it become clear that the whole system would have run more efficiently, in an economic sense, if it were all based on putting-out.

As far as the technology of production is concerned, it would be highly inaccurate and misleading to describe the techniques of the period as primitive or backward. By 1600, European industry was already making significant use of a wide range of labour, capital and energy-saving devices, though the speed with which technology changed varied among industries. Textile production seems to have lagged behind other industries in the invention and adoption of new technologies. Spinning and weaving technology remained fairly constant even though small improvements were made to both. Of the two most important innovations, the stocking frame for hosiery manufacture and the water-powered mill for silk throwing, only the former could be considered a recent invention since the latter had long then been in use in Bologna for that purpose. Rather than advancing on the basis of new technology, textile production changed mostly by innovations in product lines. Besides adopting new mixtures of fibres, or expanding the manufacture of differently constructed cloths from previously used raw materials, such as innovations in producing worsteds rather than woollens, important innovations occurred in the dyeing process. Producing new colours, decreasing the cost of dyeing, or finding new ways of fixing colours to cloths which had not been successfully dyed were the most important areas of innovation in textile production.

The iron industry, by contrast, was an area witnessing frequent and significant changes in technique. The blast-furnace, for example, became quite common in iron smelting during the sixteenth century; water-powered forges and hammering mills were also being adopted widely. Beyond smelting, improvements were made in the rolling and drawing of iron such that by the end of the sixteenth century, wire could be produced in mechanized mills using water power. Casting was also improved significantly, not only for iron, but also for non-ferrous metals. These changes were particularly important for improving the production of cannon and cannon balls, for the manufacture of clocks, navigational aids and precision instruments in general.

Other notable achievements of the period were in the printing industry and in the production of inanimate sources of power. In the latter, significant innovations occurred in both water and wind-power. The Dutch, in particular, were successful in exploiting the potentialities and technologies of wind-power. Many basic processes were thus mechanized, the most outstanding achievement being perhaps the mechanization of the saw mill, which substantially decreased the costs of shipbuilding.

Judging from the nature of these, and other, technical advances, it can be argued that the focus of technological innovations lay in the area of mechanical engineering, especially in those sectors of the economy most closely related to commerce and to political power. Shipbuilding, armaments, printing and navigation were the primary recipients of advances in technology. Compared to textile production, these were small areas of the economy, but they were crucial to the period in which the growth of the centralized nation-state and the economic expansion of Europe overseas were most important (Cipolla 1965). As in more recent periods, technical change responded to wider political and economic developments and was therefore focused on specific problems the solutions to which may not have had any substantial nor immediate economic pay-off.

This discussion has sought above all to present an overview of industrial Europe in terms of its organization of production, its labour composition, its technology and its output. As such, it is merely a static description giving little guidance as to how the dynamics of the industrial system operated. For this, it is necessary to place the discussion in a wider context, especially that of the relationship between industry and other sectors of the economy.

It has become commonplace in most accounts of early modern Europe to focus on permissive and constraining factors in economic development. Historians seem to be of the general opinion that economic growth and development were contained within a system (known as the Malthusian system, after Thomas Malthus, the eighteenth-century English reformist who first articulated it) designed to ensure stability and stagnation in the long term. Changes in population and agriculture are deemed to provide the key to understanding the nature of industrial and commercial development. The whole economic system responded to changes in real incomes and the marginal productivity of labour in agriculture. Industrial growth could only occur when significant advances in agricultural productivity led to rising real incomes and a growing surplus of under- and unemployed agricultural labour who could be absorbed by the industrial sector without depressing agricultural output. By this analysis, historians have argued that the European economy operated within this system until sometime in the late seventeenth and early eighteenth centuries, and even then, only certain select parts of Europe managed to escape from its domination.

Many criticisms have been made of this approach to understanding the nature and growth of industrial Europe, but only two need concern us here: the issue of timing and the direction of causation. If we look at changes in the degree of urbanization, changes in the proportion of Europe's population employed in industrial activities and changes in the extent of the market, instead of at total population and agricultural prices, it becomes difficult to sustain the argument that in the sixteenth century, the European economy was operating under Malthusian rules (Hohenberg and Lees 1985). Between 1500 and 1600, urban Europe expanded substantially. The total number of cities having more than 5000 inhabitants grew by 13 per cent, while those having more than 10,000 inhabitants grew by more than 50 per cent. Overall, during the sixteenth century, the proportion of Europe's population living in cities exceeding 5000 inhabitants grew from 9.5 per cent at the beginning to just under 11 per cent at the end. The relative change for cities exceeding 10,000 inhabitants was much greater rising from 5.6 per cent to 7.6 per cent of the population. Over the following two centuries, urbanization in both categories of cities increased, though at a slower rate (de Vries 1984). Thus Europe's urban economy was growing relative to the rural economy and this, following the Malthusian model, could only be achieved by rising agricultural productivity. Further support for the latter comes from recent research which shows that during the sixteenth century, the proportion of the rural population in England, France and Holland engaged in non-agricultural activities was also rising (de Vries 1985; Wrigley 1985). The market for both agricultural and industrial goods was expanding not only within western Europe consequent upon urban development, but also in eastern Europe, principally in Poland and Russia; in Scandinavia; in the eastern Mediterranean; and finally, overseas, in Latin America and Africa.

Following the arguments of the Malthusian model, urbanization and a relatively growing non-agricultural rural population could only be achieved through rising agricultural productivity and rising real incomes. Yet, almost all the evidence we have on both these areas shows decisively that neither was rising, indeed both were falling. Clearly, either the evidence is faulty, which seems unlikely, or, the European economic system was, in its entirety, not behaving according to Malthusian rules. In other words, either the Malthusian model is in general inappropriate for the sixteenth century, or, it is appropriate only in certain parts of Europe. We are not yet in a position to decide which of these alternative interpretations is true, though it is beyond doubt that the Dutch Republic, northern France and southern England, at least, did not conform to the outlines of the Malthusian system.

As to the links between agriculture and industry, the same evidence suggests that the relationship was neither straightforward nor causally connected in the fashion prescribed by the Malthusian model. The demand for industrial goods was not simply determined by real incomes. In the first place, there is little hard evidence showing a strong correlation between changes in food prices and industrial demand, either in the sixteenth or in the following two centuries. Secondly, the supply and demand of industrial and agricultural goods need not come from the same source. The widening of the market during the sixteenth century clearly influenced Europe's supply of industrial products despite generally falling real incomes within Europe. Finally, the fall in real incomes during the sixteenth century varied by region as well as by social class, and therefore the generality of the process was disturbed.

Central to the Malthusian model is the primacy of agriculture over industry. During the sixteenth century, it might be more true to say that no direct relationship existed between the sectors, at least not in the way assumed by the Malthusian model. There were many developments which obscured the relationship, not least of which was urbanization and the expansion of European commerce overseas. The absence of a direct connection is seen once again at the end of the sixteenth century. While agriculture began to founder across many parts of Europe and population growth decelerated towards the end of the sixteenth century, urbanization and industrial production seem to have continued to increase. In other words, the agrarian sector was conforming to Malthusian rules while the industrial sector behaved differently. It may very well be, as the following section of the book argues, that the seventeenth and eighteenth centuries were periods in which towns and industries became the prime mover of agricultural change rather than the other way around. At any rate, there is sufficient justification for the view that industrial and agrarian Europe were not as intimately linked in 1600 as is often supposed.

The same cannot be said for the relationship between industry, commerce and finance. Here the evidence suggests that industry was subsumed within a commercial system but was not a critical component of it. Reference has already been made to the fact that, in so far as entrepreneurship and finance are concerned, there was no clear distinction between industry and commerce. This was especially true in putting-out industries, but less so in artisanal production. Judging from the scattered evidence on international trade in the late sixteenth century, it is clear that the vast majority of industrial goods which entered the market were the product of large-scale putting-out enterprises concentrating for the most part on textiles. In the latter half of the sixteenth century, for example, just over 90 per cent of the imports into the Low Countries consisted of textile products (woollen and silk cloths mostly) while 100 per cent of the exports were also textiles. Several decades later, the preponderance of textiles in the trade in industrial goods between France and the Dutch Republic was only slightly reduced (van Houtte and van Buyten 1977). It was rare for artisanal products to enter international commerce in the sixteenth century, though they were sold locally often directly from the workshop, and usually by the wife in the household. Women, in general, appear to have been most actively engaged in local commerce. In cases where artisanal products did move to distant markets, the specialized services of an international merchant were employed under specific conditions.

Industrial products for distant markets were not handled by those employed in the industries. The division of labour between industry and commerce was clearly drawn even though the industrial entrepreneur was more a merchant than an industrialist. International commerce itself was organized by merchants whose activities were wide-ranging. They would include commodity transactions, as well as financial services, banking and speculative ventures; the relative position of each function varied enormously not only among merchants themselves, but also from year to year. The international merchant looked upon industrial goods no differently than he did upon raw materials or foodstuffs or, for that matter, bills of exchange and other financial instruments. Consequently, there was little allegiance shown by the international merchant to the industrial products of any particular place. What mattered most was the best price he could obtain for whatever good in the market.

Europe's commercial system displayed remarkable dynamism and one which seems to have been generated without recourse to other sectors of the economy. Industry benefited from this in several ways. The opening of the Asian market to European merchants in the sixteenth century directly stimulated European industries. While the Asian market remained firmly closed to European goods, Europe's insatiable demand for eastern products had a pronounced effect on the demand for European goods within Europe. European goods flowed into Antwerp in the sixteenth century where they could be exchanged for pepper, spices and drugs brought from Asia by the Portuguese and the Spanish. The opening of the Baltic market had a similar impact on the redistribution of European industrial goods in Amsterdam towards the end of the sixteenth century.

European industry also benefited directly from the settlement of central and south America and from the successful incursion into the Levant market. Furthermore, the demand for European shipbuilding and armaments production and the ancillary industries such as iron, linen and wood grew from the expansion of commerce.

By 1600, therefore, European industry was being stimulated from several directions. Urbanization brought more consumers and producers into the market, and, undoubtedly encouraged the extension of industrial production into the countryside; Europe's expansion overseas brought both direct and indirect benefit to the industrial sector; and finally, the centralization of the state promoted the growth of certain key industries of the period. Industrial Europe was experiencing significant changes. What path it would take is the subject of the remainder of this book.

Part I
The Structural Context

Introduction

Even as late as 1914, Europe's transformation into an industrial economy was far from complete. Judging, for example, by the proportion of its working population employed in agriculture on the eve of the First World War, agrarian Europe might seem a more appropriate term. With the exception of Britain, Belgium and Holland, at least one-third of Europe's working population were employed in agriculture, making it the largest single employer of labour. In Italy and Spain the proportions reached 58 per cent and 71 per cent respectively, but even in Germany, generally considered as an advanced industrial nation, as much as 35 per cent of the working population were employed in agriculture in 1913. Other indicators, such as the sectoral distribution of gross domestic product point to a similar conclusion.

But as a reflection of a dynamic process, there is little doubt that the term 'industrial Europe' is particularly apt. In much of Europe, throughout most of the nineteenth century, the rate of growth of industrial production was consistently greater than that of agricultural production. In Germany, for example, the output of the industrial sector increased by 3.8 per cent annually between 1850 and 1914 while, at the same time, that of the agricultural sector managed no more than 1.6 per cent. In France, figures for the period from 1815 to 1913 show that gross agricultural output grew at an annual average rate of 0.7 per cent while gross industrial output achieved rates of 2 per cent or more. Figures for Britain and Belgium show comparable differences in the growth record of output during the nineteenth century. As a proportion of the total working population, employment in agriculture fell substantially during the nineteenth century. Between 1850 and 1914, agricultural employment in France fell from 53 to 37 per cent; in Belgium it fell from 32 to 17 per cent, in Holland from 37 to 28 per cent and in Germany from 52 to 35 per cent. The only exceptions to this trend were Italy and Spain where the proportion of the population employed in agriculture probably remained constant for most of this period, though the share of agricultural production in gross domestic product decreased significantly (Milward and Saul 1977, 1979; Mitchell 1975; Harrison 1978; Borchardt 1973).

What is reflected particularly in these figures is the inherent dynamism of

Europe's industry in the nineteenth century as well as the enormous possibilities available to the European economy by concentrating resources on industrial production rather than on agricultural production. But the relative strength of the industrial sector, as reflected in the employment structure of the European economy, was not a feature of Europe unique to the nineteenth century. Indeed, industry was continually attracting labour and capital away from agriculture from at least the seventeenth century, and by the nineteenth century, Europe's industrial strength was already considerably greater than it had been several centuries earlier.

The process of the disengagement of industry from agriculture was thus protracted and cannot, therefore, be understood in isolation from other long-term changes in the structure of Europe's economy. By 1914, it is clear that industry had become entirely distinct from agriculture, even in those parts of Europe, such as Italy and Spain, where agriculture continued to dominate many aspects of the economy. Industry had become organizationally and locationally distinct; it did not share its workers nor its capital with agriculture; its production cycle was independent of the agricultural season and it had its own commercial and financial institutions.

In Part II of this book, we will be looking at the process of disengagement in terms of changes in the organization of production, in the nature of the labour supply, its composition and qualities, and in the characteristics of technology. In this part, we will concentrate on how industry gradually became disengaged from agriculture partly through its own dynamism, partly by the nature of demographic changes and the process of urbanization and partly by the growth of Europe's participation in the world economic system.

1 Population, Agriculture and Urbanization

The transformation of Europe from an agrarian to an industrial economy is difficult to explain. Until recently, historians believed that the transition was reasonably well understood. They argued that before the eighteenth or nineteenth century, Europe's industrial economy was constrained by the powerful equilibrating and stagnating forces of a Malthusian system (Wrigley 1972, 1983). The system operated to ensure that population and resources would remain in balance in the long term. Any attempt by society to increase its numbers beyond some critical value would lead to a subsistence mortality caused by the failure of food supplies to grow beyond this point. Population levels would then fall back to a comfortable level. This positive check on growth was not, however, the only response possible. Society could also restrain its own growth by following a preventative check, such as by restricting its birth rate, or its marriage rate.

In this scheme, population change would occur independently of or in response to specific economic changes, but in either case, the limiting factor to population growth was the growth of agricultural productivity. The inability to produce ever-growing supplies of food not only constrained population growth but economic development in general. Without rising agricultural productivity, the agrarian sector would not be able to provide the economy at large with labour, investible funds, and taxes required to sustain industrial, commercial and urban growth; nor could it stimulate consumer spending on manufactured goods through a rise in real incomes and an enlarged market.

Because the agrarian sector seemed to be the lynch-pin of the economic and social system under which Europe existed before the eighteenth century, historians sought empirical evidence to confirm the critical role of agricultural change in Europe's demographic and industrial transformation. In demographic terms, there seemed to be little doubt that sometime towards the middle of the eighteenth century, European population growth entered a radical phase which had never been witnessed before. Not only did population grow at a much higher rate than in previous centuries, but more importantly, the growth was sustained, and historically new levels of population were reached. This growth was apparently supported by the rising agricultural productivity that had occurred in many parts of Europe from as early as the beginning of the seventeenth century, and in the exceptional case of Holland from as early as the late fifteenth or early sixteenth century.

Thus far, the findings confirm the vitality of the agricultural sector. The increases in agricultural productivity, however, were not as widespread nor as general as population growth. In Mediterranean regions, for example, population began to grow around the middle of the eighteenth century without any appreciable change in agricultural productivity; while in England, population seemed to grow most vigorously precisely at the point when advances in agricultural productivity were beginning to wane (de Maddalena 1974; Thomas 1985; Jackson 1985). It also appears that while a theoretical relationship between changes in agriculture and industry makes sense, the historical reality does not support it unequivocally. Industrial growth seemed to occur whether agricultural productivity was rising or not; and there seems to be little correlation, in comparative terms, between the extent of agricultural change and the degree of industrial growth. One recent investigation of the role of agrarian change in England in the eighteenth century suggests that agricultural developments did no more than set the scene for industrial developments, and that agriculture may well constitute an obstacle to rather than a precondition of industrial development (O'Brien 1985). In the case of England, the author concludes that as far as its role in widening the market for industrial goods is concerned, the agricultural contribution through rising real incomes and releasing labour to other sectors of the economy was slight. Of greater importance were the direct demands of industry for more labour and a wider market generated by technical changes within industrial production and developments in foreign trade.

It may be that historians have too readily accepted the rather narrow constraints of the Malthusian model (for recent criticism of the narrowness of the Mathusian approach see Weir 1984; Jackson 1985). The success of the English industrial economy in the eighteenth century cannot be fully explained by any particular demographic behaviour; nor can a narrow range of agrarian features illuminate the realities of the industrial and commercial world. One of the main drawbacks of the model is that it does not permit a broad geographic perspective. There is no reason why, for example, demographic development in one region needs to emerge from agricultural developments in the same region; nor is there any good economic reason why a particular region needs to supply its own food before it can embark on industrial development. In the sixteenth century, for instance, the Dutch Republic was able to achieve substantial economic growth because it could release its agrarian sector from producing low value-added essentials such as grain to producing high value-added products such as butter, cheese and livestock (de Vries 1974). The necessary grain was instead imported from the Baltic region where it was exchanged for manufactures as well as bullion and spices (Attman 1973, 1986; van Houtte and van Buyten 1977). While this agrarian change certainly contributed to Holland's unique economic experience in the sixteenth century, it would have been inconceivable without Holland's special economic relationship with the Baltic regions and its relative supremacy in bulk transport. England, likewise, ceased to be self-sufficient in agricultural products at a time of population growth. Between 1760 and 1801, domestic agricultural production failed to keep pace with the growth in population. The classic signs of a Malthusian downward cycle were developing, and prices for agricultural goods began to rise significantly as the terms of trade shifted against industry (Thomas 1985). Yet, the population did not stop growing; indeed, it doubled between 1801 and 1851. While English agriculture could not produce sufficient food, the industrial sector expanded and through the sale of industrial goods overseas England was able to import its food deficits allowing per capita consumption to grow. There is nothing sacrosanct about food – it is no different from any other commodity. As long as it is available somewhere, and as long as there are the means to get it and as long as there are goods to be exchanged for it, then it can be obtained. It is possible that no solution has ever really been found to the Malthusian problem as it has been defined in Europe. During the nineteenth century, for example, Europe exported massive numbers of people, as much as 25 per cent of the total natural increase. For the most part the emigrants settled in areas of the world which came to supply Europe with cheap food and industrial raw materials. It may be that had there been no out-migration, European agriculture would still have been able to cope with the numbers; but it may be that Europe's industrial and political supremacy permitted the continent to avoid the worst consequences of the Malthusian system and export it to other countries.

The Malthusian model is most applicable to an agrarian society with little access to trade (or to a wider world) with few urban centres and with little industrial production; but these were not the features of Europe of 1600. The making of industrial Europe was a long-term process in which changes in agriculture played a limited role both functionally and temporally. As far as industry was concerned, agriculture was a nuisance – industrial productivity could make little headway in the countryside as long as industrial production was connected to agriculture. Rural industrial work would continue to be affected by the agricultural seasons and the circulation of capital tied up in raw materials, wages and goods in progress would remain constrained by the demands of the agrarian calendar. The breakdown of this relationship heralded major changes in European industry but it did not emanate from within the agrarian system. The economic dynamic of the period from 1600 to 1914 lay in the city and in commerce and not in the agrarian countryside; but because European industry needed to disengage itself effectively from agriculture so that it could take advantage of the opportunities which a separate existence would offer, any discussion of the development of industrial Europe needs to take agricultural developments into account.

Before analysing the circumstances of the separation of agriculture and industry, it needs to be emphasized that there were several ways by which Europe could weaken the constraint of the Malthusian system, only one of which was to increase the productivity of cereal production. The Dutch solution of importing cereals from grain producing regions was one possibility; and another was to change from growing land-extensive crops like cereals to land-intensive crops such as potatoes; or to grow alternatives such as maize and rice. A third option was to increase the consumption of high-energy, low-bulk foods such as sugar, which was apparently the case in eighteenth-century England (Shammas 1984). Any of these options was possible after 1600.

Population Changes

While overall population development was not directly involved in the process by which industry disengaged itself from agriculture, it does provide the necessary context within which one can view the gradual weakening of the Malthusian system and the gradual separation of industry from agriculture. Demographic data before the nineteenth century are relatively scarce, and those which do exist are often difficult to interpret as the objective and method of counting was often for purposes other than simply knowing the total size of the population. In most cases, historians use demographic data which have been 'manufactured' from original data which are not truly demographic at heart. Thus, for example, historians construct demographic data from a source such as a listing of those paying a hearth tax, by multiplying the number in that list by an appropriate weight, namely the average number of people/size of family unit per hearth. It takes little imagination to see the problems inherent in such an approach, especially when it is used to construct time series or aggregate series, such as the population of a single country. While more sophisticated techniques have recently been applied to detailed sources, such as parish registers of births and deaths, problems of aggregation and time series remain. The difficulties inherent in more comparative data are even more pronounced. English demographic data for the early modern period, for example, are constructed using extremely detailed figures and the latest statistical techniques, while those for some other parts of Europe are more of the nature of estimates and guesses. Yet these data are often used to make quite explicit and definitive statements about comparative economic developments. There is therefore a good case for using data which are aggregated not at the level of the nation, but rather at the level of the region where the problems of construction and inference are minimized, and which make more historical sense.

Most economic histories of this period attempt to demonstrate the distinctiveness of the English economic and social experience (Wrigley 1983; Aston and Philpin 1985). Their starting point is typically demographic history which purports to show that while the population of continental Europe was struggling to increase, that of England was booming. Thus we learn that in the long eighteenth century (i.e. from 1680 to 1820) the population of England increased by 133 per cent while that of western Europe as a whole (including England) increased by only 62 per cent (Wrigley and Schofield 1981; Wrigley 1983). Moreover, with the possible exception of Spain, no other country in western Europe managed to increase its population by as much as the western European average. This kind of historical exercise makes a nonsense of history. In the first place, it makes the implicit assumption that somehow demographic regimes are bounded by nation states, or that there is a specific Italian, French or even English demographic experience. Secondly, the beginning and end dates are often chosen to highlight a specific and important period in the economic history of a single country, and are then applied to all countries without question as to their significance or relevance to these countries. Thus, the long eighteenth century may be more relevant to English social and economic history than it is to say, French social and economic history. Finally, the choice of countries and the indiscriminate lumping together of different countries are used to create the illusion of something different from the English case. For example, Belgium and the Dutch Republic are often combined to make a Netherlands aggregate, despite the difference of their demographic experience during the eighteenth century when Belgium experienced substantial growth while Holland's population size hardly changed at all. The result of aggregating the two figures is a compromise between rapid growth and stagnation – in other words, not the same as England. Finally, the overwhelming desire to find something distinctive about English population history obscures the crucial fact that the available figures on population totals show a remarkable similarity in general terms in demographic experiences across Europe, and that the so-called English distinctiveness was also apparent in Scandinavia, in Belgium and in regional areas similar in size to that of England.

Europe's demographic experiences during the seventeenth and eighteenth centuries, which was crucial to the overall economic development of Europe, should be interpreted in light of the above qualifications. Table 1.1 below contains generally accepted data on population levels of the countries comprising western Europe from 1600 to 1910.

Table 1.1: *Total population of Europe by country 1500–1910 (in millions)*

	1500	1600	1650	1700	1750	1800	1850	1890	1910
France	16.4	19.0	20.0	19.0	21.7	27.0	35.8	38.4	39.6
Germany	12.0	16.0	12.0	15.0	17.0	24.5	34.4	49.4	64.9
Italy	10.5	13.1	11.3	13.3	15.3	17.8	24.0	30.5	34.7
Spain	6.8	8.1	7.1	7.5	8.9	10.5	15.0	17.6	20.0
England & Wales	2.6	4.4	5.6	5.4	6.1	9.2	17.9	29.0	36.8
Belgium	1.4	1.6	2.0	2.0	2.2	2.9	4.4	6.1	7.4
Netherlands	1.0	1.5	1.9	1.9	1.9	2.1	3.0	4.5	5.9
Scandinavia	1.5	2.0	2.6	2.9	3.6	5.0	7.9	11.4	13.6
Portugal	1.0	1.1	1.2	2.0	2.3	2.9	3.8	5.1	5.5
Total	53.2	66.8	63.7	69.0	79.0	101.9	147.2	182.0	228.4

Source: J. de Vries *European Urbanization, 1500–1800* (London, 1984), 37; B. R. Mitchell *European Historical Statistics 1750–1970* (London, 1975), 19–27.

Several important features of European population history emerge clearly from this information. In the first place, Europe's population grew continuously from 1600 to 1910; by the latter date, Europe contained three times as many people as it did in 1600. Within this long period, demographic growth varied significantly over time as well as geographically. After the substantial growth experienced by every European country during the sixteenth century, Europe entered a period of at least 50 years in which there was virtually no growth or actual decline. By 1650, Europe's total population was significantly lower than it had been in 1600. Growth overall resumed after 1650 and from the beginning of the eighteenth century, no further signs of weakening appeared. As Table 1.1 shows, population growth accelerated everywhere after 1750 and reached unprecedented rates. Between 1750 and 1800, Europe added twice as many people to its overall population as in the years from 1600 to 1750; and the dynamic underlining these figures continued right through until at least the latter part of the nineteenth century. While the demographic pattern of the nineteenth century was radically different in its scale and speed, it should not be isolated from the earlier experience.

From the figures presented in Table 1.1 above, it is possible to calculate the rates of population growth of the various European countries. Overall, Europe's population grew at an annual average rate of 0.21 per cent between 1600 and 1800. Most of the European countries achieved growth rates near to or greater than this average. The Netherlands and Italy were the only countries whose growth rates were substantially below the average. On the same basis, the fastest growing parts of Europe were Scandinavia, England, Belgium and Portugal. France, Germany and Spain grew at about the same rate as the average. Growth rates varied across Europe, but size of population was certainly not an important variable. England's experience of above-average growth was also characteristic of several other European countries.

The dangers of aggregating population figures have been referred to above, but when Europe's population history is examined at the level of small administrative units (county, duchy or *généralité*), its features become both more complex and more revealing. France presents a particularly interesting case of the intricate nature of demographic change (Morineau 1977). During the eighteenth century, for example, the overall population of France increased significantly. Between the 1690s and 1780 (dates for which reliable figures exist), the population of France increased from 19.8 million to 24.3 million; that is an increase of 23.4 per cent over the period, or a growth rate of 0.23 per cent annually. Within France, however, the demographic profile was complicated by diverse regional experiences. Growth occurred in all but three *généralités*, but the pace of growth varied considerably. The fastest growing areas of the country were located in eastern France, in the region bounded by Metz in the north and Besançon in the south, in the region surrounding Lyons, in the regions surrounding Bourges and Moulins in the centre of the country, and in the region surrounding Perpignan in the very south of the country. The total population of these regions more than doubled during this period, from 2.1 million to 4.4 million inhabitants. In other parts of France where growth took place, the average increase was about 20 per cent.

Demographic data for counties of England and Wales during the eighteenth century reveal a similar pattern (Deane and Cole 1967). Total population grew from 5.8 million in 1701 to 7.5 million in 1781, an increase of 29.3 per cent for the entire period or a growth rate of 0.32 per cent per annum. Population grew in all but four counties, but while growth rates among the counties varied, the range of experience was not as great as in France. The slowest growing regions were to be found in the largely agricultural areas in the Midlands and in southern England; while the fastest growing regions were to be found in the largely industrial and commercial areas in the north and northwest of the country. The total population of Lancashire, Warwickshire and the West Riding of Yorkshire, almost doubled from 0.57 to 1.05 million during the period.

Eighteenth-century Italian population data also reveal interesting regional patterns (Felloni 1977). While the overall population of the Italian peninsula increased from 13 to 19 million inhabitants between 1700 and 1800, three distinct demographic zones – northern Italy, southern Italy and central Italy (between Naples and Bologna) – contributed differentially to the total growth of population. Growth was greatest in southern Italy where the population increased by 80 per cent between the beginning and the end of the century. The population of northern Italy increased by only 50 per cent over the same period, while the population of the central region increased by over 20 per cent.

The demographic experience of urban and rural Italy was even more distinct. The number of cities with more than 10,000 inhabitants remained constant during the eighteenth century (de Vries 1984). The total number of inhabitants living in such cities rose from 1,599,000 in 1700 to 1,768,000 at the end of the century, an increase of just 10.6 per cent. Italy's population growth was therefore greatest in the least urbanized areas, especially in the south of the country where only 20 per cent of the country's cities of 10,000 or more inhabitants were located.

Spain's population history also reveals a complex regional pattern. While total population grew by 44 per cent during the eighteenth century, that of Catalonia nearly tripled while in Valencia, population nearly doubled. By contrast, the population of Castile grew by only 40 per cent (for various estimates and recent debates see Mauro and Parker 1977; Ringrose 1983; Kamen 1980; Phillips 1987). In the Low Countries, the contrast is between a stagnant Dutch Republic and a growing region comprising the provinces of Belgium (van Houtte and van Buyten 1977). In the latter, it would appear that, in common with the experience in Italy, the rural areas grew rapidly, while the towns and cities in the country either stagnated, or, as in the case of Antwerp, actually declined in numbers.

Thus the European demographic system as it operated in the early modern period produced a complex mosaic-like pattern of regional experiences; yet many regions of Europe shared common demographic features. In the eighteenth century, for example, fast-growing regions included Lancashire, Warwickshire and the West Riding of Yorkshire in England; Catalonia and Valencia in Spain, Alsace-Lorraine, Languedoc and the Lyonnais in France; Brabant and probably Flanders in the Netherlands; and the Kingdom of Naples in Italy. Stagnating or declining regions, on the other hand, included parts of East Anglia, Westmorland, Cumberland in the north and Somerset and Devon in the west of England; the Soissonais, Burgundy and parts of Picardy in France; parts of the Papal States, Tuscany and some smaller duchies in the north of Italy; Castile and the Basque provinces in Spain; and Holland in the Netherlands. Moreover, the demographic experience of one region in one country often spilled over into a region of another country forming one economic and demographic trans-national region. Such was the case of Languedoc and Catalonia; the *généralité* of Lille in France and Flanders in Belgium; Alsace and Baden; and Liège and the Rhine Provinces in Germany. Contiguous regions of the kind described above became important in later stages of industrialization (Wrigley 1962, Pollard 1981).

While it is relatively straightfoward to describe changes in the overall levels of population in Europe, it is more difficult to explain them. The theoretical mechanics of population change are clear-cut. Populations grow, for example, by an excess of births over deaths adjusting for the difference between in and out migration. In the early modern period, changes in the birth rate (the number of births for every 1000 inhabitants) could be affected by any or all of the following (assuming for the moment that all births are in wedlock): the age and the extent of marriage and the spacing of births within the lifetime of the mothers. The birth rate was especially sensitive to the first two variables and was extremely important in determining long-term changes in population growth patterns (Wrigley 1969; Wrigley and Schofield 1981; Flinn 1981). The impact of a fall in the death rate could also be great. In the case of England in the period 1680 to 1820, it has been made clear that the actual fall in the death rate from 30.7 per thousand to 24.5 per thousand caused the population to grow by 0.5 per cent per annum, assuming all other rates were constant (Wrigley 1983).

The causes of population change were not consistent across Europe. In England, for example, although fertility increased and mortality decreased between 1680 and 1820, it was primarily the former that was responsible for the population growth during this period (Wrigley and Schofield 1981). The rise in fertility was principally caused by earlier and more universal marriage; and thus it was primarily changes in nuptiality which contributed mostly to the growth of the English population during the period under question. Within England, there were some important regional differences, and it is probably true to say that in the south, changes in both vital rates played equal parts in population growth, while in London, it was most likely that a fall in the death rate (leaving in-migration aside) was responsible for the growth in population of the capital.

Different mechanisms seem to have operated on the Continent though the techniques to which English population data have been subjected have not been systematically applied to other European data. The most recent synthesis of the demographic history of continental Europe argues that changes in overall population levels were primarily caused by changes in mortality and not in fertility (Flinn 1981). Indeed, most of the evidence which is so far available points to a fall, rather than a rise in the levels of fertility on the Continent. It seems that a rise in the age of marriage and a fall in the extent of marriage (the opposite of what happened in England) occurred in most of western Europe during the eighteenth century. At the same time, mortality levels were falling throughout Europe, mainly because of the reduced frequency and extent of mortality crises.

Mortality crises in the early modern period were of three types: those caused by famine; those caused by disease; and those caused by a combination of the two. Famines were fairly common in Europe during the period, though in most instances they were localized. Famines were caused by particularly adverse weather conditions when localized harvest failures were inevitable and unavoidable irrespective of the condition of the agrarian sector; or by a fundamental weakness in the nature of the agrarian economy which constrained production to the level of subsistence, and when even mildly adverse weather conditions could ruin the harvest. In both cases, the severity of the outcome depended on the means available to rescue the situation such as transport and accessibility. Disease, the second factor in mortality crises, was a frequent problem, and, in combination with a famine could wreak havoc over a wide area. The disease which has attracted the greatest attention from both contemporaries and historians is the bubonic plague, which remained endemic in western Europe until the first few decades of the eighteenth century (McNeill 1977; Biraben 1968).

While there is little doubt of its capacity to kill, the bubonic plague was part of a set of diseases including typhus, smallpox, measles and influenza which were particularly virulent during this period.

Historians of the early modern period have normally found that while it is relatively easy to pinpoint the timing of a mortality crisis, it is quite another matter to define its causes and the local nature of crises makes the task of generalizing very difficult. Most mortality crises, however, were caused by a combination of dearth and disease, and while some were the result of disease only, very few were caused solely by dearth.

Towards the end of the seventeenth century mortality crises in western Europe began to stabilize, mainly because of changes in the nature of disease, but helped by the fact that European agriculture was capable of feeding its population (Flinn 1974, 1981; Riley 1986; Kunitz 1983). By the end of the eighteenth century, a generalized fall in mortality began to take place in Europe, in a regional fashion (Lee 1979). In some parts of Europe, for example in Sweden, Belgium, the Netherlands, Britain and France, mortality rates were generally reduced by half between 1800 and 1910. In the Mediterranean countries as well as in Germany, on the other hand, mortality did not fall generally until after mid-century, but thereafter the rate of decline was relatively high. By 1910, mortality in Europe had fallen to about 50 per cent of the typical level found at the end of the seventeenth century, with much less variation than in previous centuries, ranging from a low of 14 deaths per thousand in Scandinavia to 20 deaths per thousand in Italy and Portugal (Lee 1979).

There is little doubt that over the long period from 1600 to 1914, the growth of Europe's population, despite short-term or specific changes in fertility and nuptiality, was the result of the long-term fall in the morality rate. Towards the end of the nineteenth century, population continued to grow in the face of a decline in the birth rate because falls in mortality were sustained (Lee 1979; Coale and Watkins 1986).

Agricultural Developments

Whatever the precise causes of the stabilization of mortality in western Europe, it is clear that the European agrarian system was capable not simply of feeding its people, but also of supporting a modestly growing population. Not all parts of Europe were equally dynamic, but sufficient agrarian regions were emerging during this period to provide the necessary support for Europe's population.

One of the most successful agrarian systems in western Europe in the early modern period was to be found in Holland (de Vries 1974, 1976). During the sixteenth century, while most of western Europe struggled to provide enough food for its rapidly growing population by traditional (and in the long run largely unsuccessful) techniques, Holland transformed its agriculture in profound ways. By importing its grain requirements, the Dutch agrarian sector concentrated its resources and factors of production on horticultural and industrial crops, especially dyes, dairy products and livestock where the benefits of convertible and alternate husbandry could most readily be achieved. Thus Holland avoided the worst excesses of the various subsistence crises which struck western Europe at the end of the sixteenth century.

By the end of the fifteenth century, Dutch merchants dominated trade between the Baltic region and western Europe. When grain production in the Baltic, particularly Poland, was stepped up at the beginning of the sixteenth century, the Dutch were thus well placed to purchase the surplus to satisfy the increased demand for grain from western Europe and Holland in particular. While exports of grain from Poland were modest at the beginning of the century, they had risen five to six times by the end of the century, and as much as 80 per cent of this trade was carried in Dutch boats for consumption in Holland. According to recent estimates, Baltic grain fed between a quarter to a third of the total Dutch population, which not only relieved resources from grain production, but also contributed to the high population density and specialized economy unique to Holland (de Vries 1974).

Not all of the imported Baltic grain was consumed in the Dutch Republic as considerable quantities were re-exported to western Europe; nor was Poland the only source of grain imports into the Dutch Republic – France and Russia both exported their surplus grain (Attman 1973). Nevertheless, the expanding European grain trade brought about by the increased supplies from eastern Europe and facilitated by innovations in Dutch shipping (see below, p. 65) was organized by Dutch merchants. By the end of the sixteenth century, Dutch ships laden with Polish grain had entered the Mediterranean and were largely responsible for averting the worst consequences of the famines which struck the western part of the Mediterranean in the 1590s (Clark 1985).

The Baltic grain trade continued to play an important part in providing western Europe with its food supplies until the mid-seventeeth century, when for a variety of reasons, western Europe turned to other sources of grain and to other food crops to supplement its grain diet (Bogucka 1980; Ormrod 1975; Collins 1984). Once again, the Dutch were at the forefront of this transformation. From the middle of the seventeenth century, the Dutch Republic imported its grain requirements from France, the southern Netherlands and later from England; and in the late seventeenth and early eighteenth century, the consumption of potatoes and rice increased to the extent that per capita grain consumption in the Republic was probably reduced by as much as half of its level a century earlier.

The experience of the Dutch Republic was largely replicated throughout western Europe. Europe's fundamental reliance on grain as the main foodstuff, for example, began to be undermined by the introduction of new crops imported from the Americas and Asia beginning in the sixteenth century (de Maddalena 1974). The most important of these were maize, rice and potatoes, and maize was particularly significant both in reducing the population's dependence on grain and affecting the nature of agricultural organization and production. Southwestern France, northern Spain, Portugal and northern Italy vigorously adopted maize as an essential component of total agricultural production towards the end of the seventeenth century (Hohenberg 1977; Goldsmith 1984; Coppola 1979). Rice was grown in the Po valley of northern Italy and in Valencia in Spain; and the potato played an important role in the agriculture of northern Europe, as well as in parts of southern and central Europe (Morineau 1970). These crops were crucial to the development of European agriculture during the early modern period (as well as in later centuries), and cushioned Europe's population from the kind of harvest disasters which had been commonplace in Europe in earlier centuries (Langer 1975). Not only could these crops be grown successfully on land unsuited to grain production, but their yields were commonly many times greater than that of grains, and they reacted differently to climatic conditions. Furthermore, growing these crops for local consumption released grain production for trade and thereby increased the circulation of grain in Europe to alleviate short-term local deficiencies.

Grain yields generally increased during the seventeenth and eighteenth centuries, particularly in the eastern counties of England, and in Holland, Flanders, Normandy and Picardy, where productivity gains were made through the diffusion of innovatory farming techniques such as convertible and alternate husbandry developed in Flanders and Holland (described fully in Slicher van Bath 1977; Turner 1982; de Vries 1974; Overton 1984; Jackson 1985). A sizeable proportion of English grain was exported to both southern and northern Europe, indeed English grain appeared to be replacing Baltic supplies as the latter were frequently shipped directly to the Atlantic coast and the Mediterranean.

The introduction of new crops especially into peasant production and the marked improvements in grain yields in areas of commercial agriculture especially in north and northwestern Europe brought a degree of stability in food production which had never before been achieved in western Europe (Weir 1984; Appleby 1979). From the early seventeenth century until the middle of the eighteenth century, grain prices fell throughout western Europe, reflecting the transformation of European agriculture (Braudel and Spooner 1967; de Vries 1976). Furthermore, the increasing diversification of European agriculture resulted in greater trade and in significant market integration; and indeed, it is clear that national grain markets were forming throughout Europe from the late seventeenth century regardless of the degrees of backwardness of the agrarian system and of transport systems (Braudel and Spooner 1967; Tilley 1971; Lenman 1977). There is also clear evidence of a convergence of international prices after 1700 and consequently of the emergence of a unified market. These profound changes together with the concentration of the European commodity markets in Amsterdam, the regular issue of printed price lists for a vast array of agricultural products, and more secure, cheaper and regular shipping throughout Europe's maritime region, meant that the spectre of widespread famine was clearly on the wane in the latter part of the seventeenth and eighteenth centuries (Flinn 1981; Post 1976).

Developments in the agrarian sector of early modern Europe were not, however, isolated from the rest of the economy. Although the agrarian sector was the largest component of the economy in terms of resources employed, it was part of a complex system involving profound industrial and social changes.

Urbanization

Urbanization provided a focal point for many of the industrial changes which Europe underwent in the period from 1600 to 1914. Cities were an integral part of the making of industrial Europe and although their functions and roles may have altered considerably, their position in the economic system was unassailable.

Recent estimates suggest that 7.6 per cent of Europe's population lived in cities with more than 10,000 inhabitants in 1600 (de Vries 1984). Europe became slowly more urbanized during the next two centuries and by 1800, the urban percentage had reached 10 per cent. Nineteenth-century urban growth was dramatic by comparison and by 1890, 29 per cent of Europe's population lived in cities.

With respect to the geographical distribution of urban growth, the most urbanized parts of Europe in 1600 lay in the Low Countries and in the Mediterranean region (Italy, Spain and Portugal) where the urban percentages were 21.5 and 13.7 per cent respectively. Elsewhere in Europe, less than 6 per cent of the population lived in cities exceeding 10,000 inhabitants. By 1890, the situation had changed. England and Scotland had become the most urbanized parts of Europe with an urban percentage of 61.9 and 50.3 per cent respectively while the urbanization of the Meditarranean region (22.2 per cent) and the Low Countries (34.1 per cent) had grown less impressively. In terms of the chronology of urban growth, wide variations were evident across Europe. In northern Europe, for example, urban growth was most rapid in the period from 1550 to 1650 and then stagnated for most of the first half of the eighteenth century. In the Mediterranean regions, by contrast, very little urbanization occurred in the seventeenth century; indeed Portugal and Spain actually suffered a decrease in the urban percentage of the population. Throughout the region, urban growth resumed during the first half of the eighteenth century, but until 1800, much of the growth entailed a recovery to the levels achieved by 1600. Interestingly, northern Europe's most active period of urban growth before the late eighteenth century occurred in a period of relatively little overall population growth while in the Mediterranean, that same period of demographic stability coincided with a stable or declining urbanization.

Most historians of urban development distinguish between urban growth before and after 1800 in terms of the quantity as well as the quality of the growth, and clearly, the scale of urbanization across Europe was wholly different in the nineteenth century from that experienced before (de Vries 1984; Hohenberg and Lees 1985). Before 1800, growth was most rapid in ports and capital cities, and, where capital cities were also ports, as in the case of London, Amsterdam and St Petersburg, growth was enormous. After 1800, though ports and capital cities continued to grow substantially, they were joined by rapidly growing industrial cities located in Germany in the Ruhr, in northern England, northern Spain and northern Italy. Those cities whose growth stagnated during the nineteenth century included commercial and administrative centres in predominantly agricultural areas and middle-sized port cities whose functions were being concentrated in other centres.

A recent study of European urbanization has emphasized the fundamental importance of these characteristics in understanding the nature of urban development as well as the wider economic developments (de Vries 1984). Throughout the period 1600 to 1914, Europe's urban growth was regionally based around a single unchanging dominant city. Changing economic circumstances stimulated regions differentially. Urban growth thus consisted largely of relative changes in the demographic experience of regionally dominant cities.

In 1600, the most important regions of Europe, in terms of the inherent economic and political power of their dominant cities, were located in southern Europe based on Naples, Milan and Venice, and in northern Europe based on Antwerp and Amsterdam, reflecting an intra-European urban system based on industrial and commercial strength. By 1800, both of these regions had given way to one which was essentially commercially based with a distinct Atlantic orientation. Between these dates, therefore, the relative decline of inland and Mediterranean regions reflected a shift in emphasis towards Europe's external relationships. After 1850 a new urban corridor developed which stretched from the Ruhr to northern Italy, this time based on rapid industrial growth without an Atlantic orientation (Crouzet 1964; Hohenberg and Lees 1985).

Over the period, therefore, there were important shifts in the fortunes of European cities as the general economic orientation of Europe altered. Yet within this complex development, the city remained the conduit for industrial change. While it is true that seventeenth and eighteenth-century industrial expansion progressed further in the countryside than in the cities, it was not strictly speaking an entirely rural phenomenon. The distinction between town and country, at least up to the nineteenth century, is both artificial and ahistorical. Rural industry was an extension of the urban industrial and commercial base and not separate from it (Hohenberg and Lees 1985). In the nineteenth century, when some industrial regions lost their industrial base, the dominant cities within them frequently declined as well. While much attention has been given to the new industrial cities of the century, especially those like Essen and Bochum in Germany, Bradford and Manchester in England, most of the urban industrial growth throughout the nineteenth century occurred in well-established industrial cities whose history stretched back to the Middle Ages (de Vries 1984; Pounds 1985).

Urbanization and the evolving urban systems were a context for, as well as a promoter of industrial change. In its quantitative aspects, urban growth increased the size of the consumer market; it also stimulated the transformation of the countryside to produce essential goods and services. At the same time, the growth of population in the cities led to a greater production of industrial goods for the urban market as well as an increased demand for service occupations. But urbanization also promoted industrial change by channelling and acting upon market information. The growth of Europe's Atlantic ports distributed an enormous amount of information about the nature of the overseas as well as the European market to producers throughout Europe. The widespread development of the linen industry in the seventeenth and eighteenth centuries, together with metalware, shipbuilding, and sugar refining were all consequent upon the concentration of market information in the ports.

Further Reading

Aston, T. H. and Philpin, C. H. E. (eds.) 1985: *The Brenner debate: Agrarian class structure and economic development in pre-industrial Europe.* Cambridge: Cambridge University Press.

Blum, J. 1978: *The end of the old order in rural Europe.* Princeton, N.J.: Princeton University Press.

De Vries, J. 1984: *European urbanization, 1500–1800.* London: Methuen.

Flinn, M. W. 1981: *The European demographic system 1500–1820.* Brighton: Harvester.

Hohenberg, P. M. and Lees, L. H. 1985: *The making of urban Europe 1000–1950.* Cambridge, Mass.: Harvard University Press.

Lee, W. R. (ed.) 1979: *European demography and economic growth.* London: Croom Helm.

Parker, W. N. and Jones, E. L. 1975: *European peasants and their markets. Essays in agrarian economic history.* Princeton, N.J.: Princeton University Press.

Post, J. D. 1985: *Food shortage, climatic variability and epidemic disease in pre-industrial Europe.* Ithaca: Cornell University Press.

Pounds, N. J. G. 1979: *An historical geography of Europe, 1500–1840.* Cambridge: Cambridge University Press.

Pounds, N. J. G. 1985: *An historical geography of Europe, 1800–1914.* Cambridge: Cambridge University Press.

Wrigley, E. A. and Schofield, R. S. 1981: *The population history of England, 1541–1871: A reconstruction.* London: Edward Arnold.

2 Europe and the Integration of the World Economy

At the turn of the seventeenth century, the European economy was dominated by the commercial world of transaction, exchange and finance. Interregional and international trade was widespread and commerce and finance affected many people's lives. International merchants of the stature of the Medici and the Fuggers were few in number, but the circulation of goods which characterized everyday life in seventeenth-century Europe stimulated a profusion of small-scale traders, connecting local as well as intercontinental markets.

The commercial system influenced the development of industrial Europe. It not only provided information and access to markets, but it also created demand for the products of industry. This applied equally to the output of the artisanal sector and to the output of the putting-out sector. As far as industry was concerned, the world was its market and merchants operated in a cosmopolitan fashion which is not always appreciated. What is now accomplished by the sales and marketing divisions of large industrial concerns was, in the early seventeenth century, the function of innumerable merchants (Ball 1977).

Industry was thus part of a complex economic system and, at the beginning of the seventeenth century, it could not easily be distinguished from commerce and finance. By the twentieth century, there is little doubt that in several key industrial activities, production had successfully disengaged itself from the commercial system. Not all industrial activities, however, conformed to this pattern. Throughout the period, many industrial enterprises continued to rely upon the merchant not only for the distribution of finished goods, but, more importantly, for the capital on which production was based. Across the industrial spectrum, throughout the period, the relationship between industry and commerce varied considerably.

This chapter will be primarily concerned with the development of the market in the widest possible sense between the seventeenth and twentieth centuries. An important part of this development consisted of the integration of world markets by European economies as well as the progressive integration of markets within Europe itself. We will be concerned, therefore, not only with the interaction of commerce and finance in the creation of a European market but, more importantly, with the growing dominance of world markets by European overseas expansion. The focus will therefore be on the structure of overseas trade, the global diffusion of staples production, intercontinental migration and capital flows.

The Role of Bullion in Market Integration

Most historians would agree that the voyages of Vasco da Gama and Christopher Columbus mark an important turning point in world history (for a recent discussion of the significance of this in a broad context see Scammell 1981). There is sufficient justification for this opinion. In the case of Vasco da Gama, his arrival on the Indian coast not only marked the end of a very long period of Portuguese exploration dating back to the fourteenth century, but more importantly, marked the beginning of a permanent European presence in a large, well established and highly advanced economic region. Before 1500 only a small number of western Europeans had ever been to the east, and these were mostly church officials, diplomatic envoys or as in the case of Marco Polo, an individual merchant. With the arrival in India of the Portuguese fleet in 1498, a presence was established consisting of permanent European institutions and personnel opening the way for future centuries of European involvement in Asian affairs. In the western hemisphere, on the other hand, Columbus's successful voyages marked the beginning of European colonization and economic exploitation in a region which was clearly economically backward in significant ways when compared to Europe and where there was little resistance to European intrusion. In both cases, the year 1500 also saw the maturation of specific European instruments and technologies of exploration, conquest and subjection which were fundamental in establishing the European presence in such distant parts of the globe; and this single-minded approach to extending European power overseas was the hallmark of the newly centralized states of Portugal and Spain (later followed by the Dutch Republic, France and England).

For sixteenth-century Europeans, the Asian economy clearly offered the greatest rewards from direct maritime contact. Asian products had long been in demand in Europe, and although the route to Europe was long and often circuitous, the European market was generally well supplied. Spices and silks were the most important commodities as both were capable of absorbing the relatively high cost and time of transport between Asia and Europe. Before regular Portuguese shipping between Asia and Europe began, both commodities entered the European market through Venice, which was traditionally the main gateway to Europe from the east (Lane 1973; Chauduri 1985). Despite the apparent advantages of a direct maritime route to Europe, this does not seem to have been the primary reason for the Portuguese interest in exploration; nor does it seem to have damaged the Venetian hold over the spice trade in the short term (Wake 1979). Whatever the costs of maintaining the Portuguese presence in Asia and whatever were the uncertain economic benefits of direct commercial contact, the Portuguese nevertheless rapidly established a trading empire which extended from the West African coast to Japan (for various aspects of the Portuguese empire see Boxer 1969; Magalhães-Godinho 1969; Verlinden 1970; Diffie and Winius 1977; Curtin 1984). This militant maritime empire was organized on the basis of fortified trading posts established en route, in part to protect Portuguese interests overseas, but more to provide commercial stations for exchange purposes and to enforce the policy of conducting trade by military means. Because of the nature of the trade which the Portuguese pursued, the most important trading posts were established strategically on the coasts of the Indian Ocean, beginning with Kilwa and Mombassa on the East African coast, to Hormuz at the opening of the Persian Gulf, extending to Goa on the western coast of India and finally to Malacca and the island of Macao. The choice of locations was made as much for military and strategic as for material supply reasons (Steensgaard 1974). The empire was theoretically administered and controlled by Lisbon, but increasingly, in practice, control was devolved onto the most important possessions such as Goa, Hormuz and Malacca. Commerce itself was conducted by private merchants under the protection and assistance of the Portuguese state and the Portuguese fleet (Scammell 1982).

From the point of view of the market, there was little difference in the nature of European–Asian trade either before or during its domination by the Portuguese. This trade was essentially one-way, that is, spices and silks were imported into Europe with no significant export of manufactured European goods in exchange (Magalhães-Godinho 1969; Steensgaard 1974). Within Europe, the Portuguese, like the Venetians before them exchanged Asian goods in European markets for those European raw materials and manufactured goods in short supply in their own country (van der Wee 1963). Within Asia, the Portuguese were comfortably accommodated within the Asian trading system, in which the trade with Europe accounted for a relatively small part. From the point of view of European capitalism, however, the Portuguese arrival and presence in Asia marked a fundamental break with the past. For the first time, Europe invested its capital, in the form of ships, warehouses, docks and buildings, overseas for the purposes of conducting exchange. The need to extract a constant return on this investment became the overriding concern in economic relations between east and west. In the case of the Portuguese, it was the state, rather than the commercial community which invested abroad; and the distinction between mercantile and state capital often meant that the purpose of participating in Asian trade differed between the two (Steensgaard 1974).

The Spanish pursued a rather different approach to overseas expansion in the Western Hemisphere (Parry 1966; Andrews 1978; Lockhart and Schwartz 1983; Meinig 1986). Unlike the Asian economic region which was rich in manufactures, raw materials and luxuries, the indigenous economies of Central and South America provided few goods of interest to the Europeans. The attraction took the form of bullion, initially seized from the Mayan and Incan empires. But within several decades of Columbus's voyages deposits of gold and then silver were discovered, and a programme of colonization was begun.

Most of the Spanish Empire consisted of territorial areas, but as in the Portuguese case, part of it was organized on the basis of fortified trading posts with a similar commercial system. The system extended from Seville to Vera Cruz and Acapulco and then across the Pacific to Manila, where it nearly joined with an extremity of the Portuguese empire. The economic basis of the Spanish empire was the extraction of precious metals which were used to pay for European manufactured goods and raw materials as well as the luxuries of the

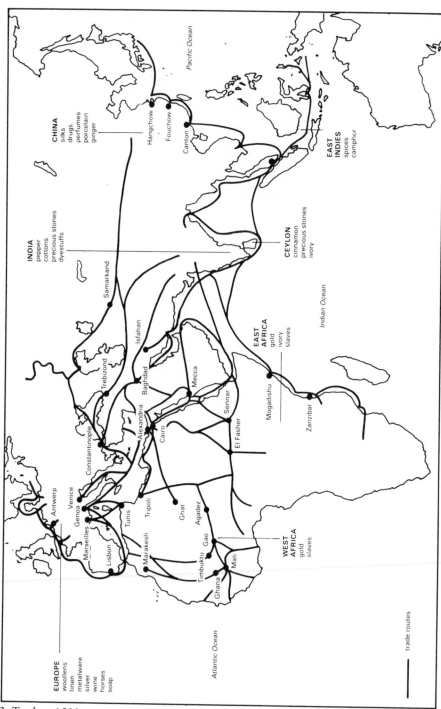

2 Trade *c.* 1500

CHINA
silks
drugs
perfumes
porcelain
ginger

EAST INDIES
spices
camphor

INDIA
pepper
cottons
precious stones
dyestuffs

CEYLON
cinnamon
precious stones
ivory

EAST AFRICA
gold
ivory
slaves

WEST AFRICA
gold
slaves

EUROPE
woollens
linen
metalware
silver
wine
horses
soap

Pacific Ocean

Indian Ocean

Atlantic Ocean

Hangchow
Fouchow
Canton

Samarkand

Isfahan

Trebizond
Baghdad
Mecca

Alexandria
Cairo
Sennar
El Fasher

Mogadishu
Zanzibar

Constantinople

Venice
Genoa
Antwerp
Marseilles
Lisbon
Tunis
Marrakesh
Tripoli
Ghat
Agadez
Timbuktu
Gao
Ghana
Mali

—— trade routes

Orient. Seville and Cadiz, like Lisbon, became important repositories for increasing quantities of European products during the ensuing three centuries. Though the nature of the European contact and presence in Asia and the Americas differed in significant ways, the external economies of these two regions became linked from the beginning by and through Europe. American silver, on the one hand, and the insatiable European demand for Asian luxuries, on the other hand, were the pillars of this integration. The worldwide circuit of American silver begun in the sixteenth century continued to define the essential characteristics of the international economy until well into the eighteenth century, despite the profound impact which the English and Dutch, in particular, had on the international commercial systems when they first appeared in Asian and American waters in the last decades of the sixteenth century (Chauduri 1978).

The arrival of the Dutch and the English in the Indian Ocean was not, like their Portuguese predecessors, preceded by exploration (for various aspects of the Dutch intervention see Furber 1976; Glamman 1958; Chauduri 1978; Curtin 1984). Commercial and political interests were at the very centre of their interest in this part of the world (Steensgaard 1974). The extent to which commercial and political motives dominated Dutch and English affairs in Asia can be seen directly from the way in which these two nations conducted trade in the area. In both cases, trade was organized by two very large incorporated companies – the Dutch East India Company (known as the VOC) and the English East India Company – who both began trading at the beginning of the seventeenth century. Being chartered by their respective states to trade in the east, these companies were from the outset monopoly enterprises and thus constituted a new form of co-operation between the state and merchant entrepreneurs (Steensgaard 1981).

The VOC and the East India Company were formidable organizations in Asian commerce. Not only were they much larger than any Asian trading concerns, but, more importantly, they were backed by superior naval power. European trading vessels were invariably well armed unlike their Asian counterparts that were either totally unarmed or, in some cases, inadequately provided with weaponry. The aim of the Dutch and the English to control both European–Asian and intra-Asian trade was thus facilitated by this imbalance. Unlike the Portuguese who adapted themselves to the Asian system, the Dutch and English attempted to change it. This was accomplished in a variety of ways depending on the area or products of trade. In the greater part of the Mughal Empire, until the eighteenth century at least, the Europeans were granted privileges which related largely to being exempted from certain customs duties and being granted special rates. In Ceylon and Indonesia, by contrast, the Dutch, in particular, acted as a territorial power. In relation to Asian products experience was equally diverse. In the pepper trade, for instance, forms of monopolies existed between the English and the Dutch; while in the cotton trade there was an open market consisting not only of the Europeans but also a host of Asian merchants. Nothing in Asia remained static, however, and changing economic conditions both in Europe and in Asia during the seventeenth and eighteenth centuries altered the nature of economic relationships between the two continents (Furber 1976).

Both companies responded actively to changes in consumer demand in Europe, and in certain cases may well have been responsible for generating this demand (Smith W. D. 1982; Chauduri 1978). The range of Asian goods which the VOC and the East Indian Company provided for Europe was far more diverse than that of the Portuguese. Besides pepper and other spices, which dominated the imports of the Portuguese, the Dutch and English imported coffee, tea, indigo, silk, and, increasingly during the latter part of the seventeenth century, cotton textiles (Glamann 1958; Chauduri 1978; Prakash 1985). Cotton textiles, the most important manufactured item exported from India, proved to be a highly profitable export, but subsequently provoked considerable political and economic problems especially in England after the middle of the eighteenth century.

In terms of exports from Asia, the companies were thus creative in marketing skills. In exports to Asia, however, the Dutch and the English were subject to the overwhelming commercial constraint which the Portuguese themselves faced, but were unsuccessful in breaking – namely, that the larger part of goods imported by the VOC and the East India Company had to be paid for by precious metals (Glamann 1958; Chauduri 1975, 1978; Gaastra 1983). This was true throughout the seventeenth and the first half of the eighteenth century, despite the efforts of the Dutch and the English to overcome the constraint. The increased participation of the VOC in intra-Asian trade was a reasonably successfully method of financing export products; and another, but generally less successful method was to sell European goods in the Asian market – here the attempt by the East India Company to dispose of English broadcloth in India is particularly noteworthy (de Vries 1976; Chauduri 1978). Nevertheless, a significant breakthrough did not occur until the second half of the eighteenth century when the East India Company assumed political power over Bengal (and to a lesser extent when the Dutch absorbed Java as part of their territorial empire), and when Europe in general, and England in particular began to alter the foundations of European–Asian trade by exporting cotton textiles to India.

As stated earlier, the economy of Spanish America and the external economy of Asia were linked directly to that of Europe through the export of bullion until the end of the eighteenth century (Cross 1983; Chauduri 1986). The three main European trading powers in Asia, England, France and Holland, all ran trade deficits with the Asian economies and the bulk of this was balanced by the export of bullion. Happily for Europe, South and Central America were able to provide the bullion in the form of silver and gold. Even as one source of supply dried up another took its place. This happened for example towards the end of the seventeenth century when Japan prohibited the further export of silver, a measure of great significance since the Japanese supply often exceeded the supply of bullion from the Americas (Kobata 1965; Atwell 1982; Yamamura and Kamiki 1983). Very quickly, however, gold production increased in Brazil and Colombia, as did silver production in Mexico, and the withdrawal of Japan from the bullion market was overcome.

Trade deficits between Europe and Asia from the late sixteenth to the end of the eighteenth centuries were superficially of little concern, so long as bullion supplies kept up with demand. Asia, however, was not the only major trading partner that ran up an export surplus; the same was true of the Baltic and the Levant (Attman 1986; Johansen 1986). There were many different ways in which the main European trading partners managed to acquire the amount of bullion necessary to clear the accounts, and this reflected the way each partner conducted its trade with other parts of Europe. The French and Dutch, for example, had large export surpluses with the Spanish, either through commodity exports, as in the case of France, or as in the case of Holland, as financial brokers and suppliers to the Spanish state of military needs. England, on the other hand, was able to procure some of its bullion needs in the form of gold bullion imported from Portugal in the eighteenth century (Fisher 1969).

As recent analyses of intercontinental trade in the seventeenth and eighteenth centuries have made clear, the supply of bullion and the European monopolistic control over it were the causes of, rather than the response to the expansion of east–west trade (Chauduri 1978; Prakash 1986). The Asian economies in general, but China in particular, were hungry for silver. When Europeans first appeared off the China coast, it was this fact which struck them most forcefully (Atwell 1982). Bullion that flowed directly from Mexico to China via Acapulco and Manila as well as smaller, but no less important shipments of silver from Bengal to China reflected this insatiable demand. According to one recent estimate, direct bullion shipments across the Pacific may have absorbed the greater proportion of total silver production in Central and South America throughout the sixteenth, seventeenth and eighteenth centuries (TePaske 1983). The VOC and the English East India Company, by contrast, may have been responsible for transferring no more than one-tenth of the output at the height of their activities (Richards 1983a). The flow of bullion and the economics of the silver trade ensured that in monetary terms at least the economies of Asia and Europe became integrated. Integration did not end there. The westward flow of Asian goods interacted with the flow of new colonial products from the Americas together with the migration of African slaves and Europeans to the New World. In the nineteenth and early twentieth century, market integration continued to evolve though the role of bullion decreased substantially while that of commodities and people increased sharply.

Europe and the Production of Staples

Between the seventeenth and twentieth centuries, Europeans encouraged the production of a large number of resource-intensive primary export goods, either for European consumption, or for the settlement of Europe's external commercial balances. These staple products can be classified as follows: industrial raw materials, including cotton, wool, rubber, timber, dyes, metals and fertilizers; stimulants such as coffee, cocoa, tea, and opium; foods such as rice, fish and sugar; and luxuries such as furs. Each staple had particular characteristics of location, organization and output, and interacted with the European economy in individual ways. This section will examine four staples – sugar, indigo, cotton and rubber – where the European imprint was most visible and where the processes of expansion and domination can be seen most clearly.

The commercial history of these staples followed a pattern determined largely by the history of European colonialism and industrial development. This pattern is not, however, consistent with any of the generally accepted stereotypes of European commercial and industrial involvement overseas. There was, for example, no clear distinction between the shaping of the sugar economies of the seventeenth and eighteenth centuries in the Caribbean and the rubber economies of the twentieth century in southeast Asia. Wherever possible, Europeans attempted to control primary production by the use of coerced labour in large organizations of production. Depending on circumstances, either labour was taken to the crops or crops to labour.

Sugar and indigo were, with tobacco, the principal staple products encouraged by Europeans in their colonies in the New World beginning in the sixteenth century. Tobacco was, of course, native to America, and demand for it was stimulated by its discovery there. Sugar and indigo, on the other hand, were developed because a demand for both already existed in Europe. Until the beginning of the seventeenth century this demand was largely satisfied by established supplies. Sugar came from the Atlantic Islands and the Mediterranean and indigo was imported from India by the Portuguese (Deerr 1949; Galloway 1977; Greenfield 1979; Mintz 1985; Alden 1965; Steensgaard 1974; Diffie and Winius 1977).

Between the seventeenth and mid-eighteenth centuries, European planters rapidly introduced sugar and indigo cultivation throughout the colonies using African slave labour, Indian labour and indentured white European labour. Sugar became concentrated in Brazil and in the Caribbean islands, whereas indigo made its greatest impact on New Spain and Guatemala, Saint Domingue and South Carolina. By the end of the eighteenth century, the production of sugar and indigo had become firmly established in the New World; and more than 90 per cent of world output of both products came from the Caribbean, Central America and South America (Deerr 1949–50; Alden 1965).

Within the colonial framwork, sugar and indigo were excellent staple commodities (McCusker and Menard 1985). They were both in great demand in Europe and had, within a few years of their cultivation in the New World, become the European mainstay in their respective fields. Sugar replaced honey as the universal sweetener and indigo became the preferred blue dye in European textile manufacturing, rapidly ousting native European woad (Mintz 1985; Alden 1965). Both crops, moreover, supported the colonial effort since their return on investment was substantial; and they were both well suited to the various labour systems exploited in the New World during the period. Both sugar and indigo were successfully cultivated on plantations using imported African slaves, and indigo could be grown commercially by smallholders. It grew very quickly and yielded as many as 7 harvests annually, and even though the capital equipment necessary to produce the dye from the plant was expensive, shortcuts could be taken or the harvest could be sold to larger producers (Davies 1974).

From ths second half of the eighteenth century, all of the major European colonial powers had their own sources of sugar and indigo, mainly in the New World, but the Dutch were also growing both in Java and output was responding smoothly to changes in demand. At the end of the eighteenth century, however, an abrupt change occurred. A combination of the loss of South Carolina by the British and Saint Domingue by the French resulted in a rupture of supplies of indigo from the New World (Deerr 1949–50; Alden 1965; Sharrer 1971). In the short term, the Spanish and Portuguese responded by stimulating the production of indigo in their respective colonies and in both Brazil and Venezuela output increased rapidly (Alden 1965). The British, however, achieved the greatest success. They encourged the cultivation of indigo in Bengal – recently conquered by the East India Company – through the migration of planters from the West Indies, and with considerable financial aid from the Company as well as agency houses in Calcutta (Mishra 1966). As a result, exports of Indian indigo soared to over 5.5 million pounds annually in the period from 1805 to 1814; and as the British captured the indigo trade, output of indigo in North, Central and South America slumped (Alden 1965).

The rapid increase in cotton textile production in Europe during the nineteenth century raised the demand for indigo considerably. During the first half of the nineteenth century, indigo represented as much as 25 per cent of India's export trade, and though its importance as an export commodity fell relatively during the second half of the century, in absolute terms it continued to grow. By 1890, for example, India was exporting more than 13 million pounds of indigo annually, rising to a record of over 19 million pounds in 1897 (Vetterli 1951; Chauduri 1983).

In 1897, however, BASF, the giant chemical concern in Germany, successfully synthesized indigo and it appeared on the market at a price competitive with the imported natural dye. Over the next six years, the price of synthetic indigo plummeted to less than one-half its original price, and the export industry of India and Java, as well as the minor producers still operating in Central and South America virtually disappeared (Vetterli 1951). Indigo imports into Britain which had exceeded £2 million per annum in the last quarter of the nineteenth century, were reduced to a mere £48,000 in 1913. Indian exports world-wide collapsed to a level of just over 1 million pounds in 1913 and as a proportion of total commodity exports, accounted for less than 0.2 per cent. On the other hand, Germany's exports of synthetic indigo soared from just over 1 million pounds in 1897 to 75 million pounds in 1913 when German production accounted for more than 95 per cent of the world's output of indigo (Tinker 1974; Haber 1958; Chauduri 1983; Hanson 1980).

From the sixteenth to the end of the nineteenth centuries, the fate of indigo as an industrial raw material lay entirely in European hands. Its commercial history illustrates the extent to which European colonial power directed global staple production and how that influence was finally broken by the familiar process of import substitution. The production of other dyestuffs followed a similar, if less dramatic pattern. The successful production of aniline and alizarin dyes in the second half of the nineteenth century, for example, affected the old colonial areas only marginally, yet, from the point of view of the global export of dyestuffs, aniline and alizarin dyes were crucial in increasing Europe's share of the world market in dyestuffs. In 1840, for example, Europe accounted for only 22 per cent of the world's total dyestuff exports; in 1860, after aniline dyes were first manufactured, that proportion increased to 27 per cent and with alizarin successfully produced in the 1870s, the proportion in 1880 stood at just over 66 per cent (Hanson 1980).

A similar pattern is evident in the commercial history of sugar production. At the turn of the nineteenth century, sugar production – all of it derived from cane – was concentrated in the Caribbean and to a lesser extent in South America

(International Sugar Council 1963). Towards the end of the eighteenth century, and the early years of the nineteenth century, several chemists and agronomists, principally in Germany, Hungary and France, had successfully demonstrated the practicality of deriving sugar from beets. By the first decade of the nineteenth century, production was well under way throughout Europe. France was the most determined to expand beet sugar production and by 1811, it was reported that France was producing over 7 million pounds of sugar from beets (International Sugar Council 1963). At this stage, however, the output of beet sugar was tiny compared to cane sugar production (Chalmin 1984).

Over the nineteenth century, the output of European beet sugar grew at a considerable rate, from a total output of 55,000 metric tons in 1840 to over six million metric tons in 1910, by which time over 80 per cent of the output came from Germany, France and Austria-Hungary (Chalmin 1984; International Sugar Council 1963). As a proportion of world sugar output, European sugar beet production rose from a level of 8 per cent in 1840 to a peak of 64 per cent in 1900. The proportion of the world's sugar produced in the Caribbean meanwhile fell from 81 per cent in 1800 to 48 per cent in 1840 and to 21 per cent in 1910 (International Sugar Council 1963). The European colonial powers, however, responded to the growing competition from European beet sugar producers by expanding production in the Pacific and Indian Ocean area, principally on the islands of Mauritius and Réunion, Hawaii, Queensland and Fiji, and in Java and the Philippines (International Sugar Council 1963). The workforce for these sugar plantations came from Indian, Chinese and Melanesian indentured labour and from East African slaves, a pattern of labour recruitment which hardly differed from that established in the old colonies of America (Marks 1984; Engerman 1986). By 1910, the plantations in southeast Asia, in Mauritius, Réunion and Natal province in South Africa accounted for nearly 30 per cent of the world's sugar cane output (International Sugar Council 1963; Albert and Graves 1984; Graves and Richardson 1980).

While indigo and sugar together constituted an important part of the framework of European colonialism throughout the period from the seventeenth to the twentieth centuries, cotton and rubber emerged as significant staples only after the first phase of colonialism was over. Cotton was, of course, used in European industry long before rubber, but until the end of the eighteenth century, it was not a particularly important staple. In the Americas, some cotton was grown in the West Indies from the end of the seventeenth century, and in Brazil from the 1760s, but strong competition for land from the other staples of the region, especially sugar and tobacco, ensured that cotton remained a minor crop (Davies 1974; Alden 1987). Until the end of the eighteenth century, therefore, European cotton manufacturers continued to draw on their traditional sources of cotton in the eastern Mediterranean and the Middle East for the greater part of their needs (Wadsworth and Mann 1931; Mazzaoui 1981).

The surge in demand for cotton in Europe did not come until the beginning of the nineteenth century, by which time the United States was emerging as the world's largest producer. In 1790, for example, American output was 700 metric tons, but by 1810, it had risen to 40,000 metric tons. Output grew at an impressive rate throughout the century and by the eve of the First World War, total American output of cotton stood at 3.2 million metric tons. On average, for most of the period from 1790 to 1913, United States exported over 60 per cent of its output, and, initially at least, Britain was the major recipient of these exports (North 1966). During the nineteenth century, however, demand for American cotton from continental Europe rose consistently, so that by 1900, it was at least as important as a buyer of American cotton as was Britain and, in the decade or more leading up to the First World War, the continental European cotton textile industry increased its share of American cotton exports to 56 per cent (Todd 1923; Mitchell 1983; Wright 1974; Hanson 1979, 1980).

Under the stimulation of the demand from the European cotton textile industry, output of American cotton soared and, at the same time, other regions of the world were encouraged to participate in the international market. Egypt, India and China were the main regions to undertake large-scale cotton production, and by the turn of the twentieth century, these three countries accounted for one-third of the world's output of cotton, the remainder being accounted for by the United States. Europe remained the main market for Egyptian cotton, but Indian cotton had a wider clientele including continental Europe and Britain as well as Japan which, by 1900, was India's single largest customer (Todd 1923; Chauduri 1983; Owen 1981; Kawakatsu 1986).

In the United States, the plantation system facilitated the rapid expansion of cotton production. Output increased more than 60-fold between 1800 and the outbreak of the Civil War, as production spread rapidly from its original base in Georgia and South Carolina to the southern states of Mississippi, Alabama, Louisiana, and as far west as Texas. It has been estimated that this expansion involved the forced migration of 835,000 slaves, the bulk of them being relocated between 1830 and 1860 (Wolf 1982). While the plantation system, at least in its use of slave labour, was extinguished by the Civil War, the basic tenets of the system were transferred to the newly emerging cotton regions especially in Eygpt and India. In both countries, under the stimulus of the export market, production rapidly shifted from peasant small-scale to large estate production where gangs of labourers were responsible for all the work. Cotton cultivation in Egypt, India and to a lesser extent China involved a transformation of an essentially peasant crop grown for subsistence or cash-cropping into a large-scale enterprise involving a distinct hierarchy of landowner and labourer (Wolf 1982; Owen 1969).

Rubber was known to Europeans from at least the beginning of the sixteenth century when early travellers reported that Amazon Indians extracted a liquid from certain trees which, when coagulated, produced a malleable, impermeable and highly elastic substance. Small amounts of this latex were imported into Europe from the Amazon region in the late eighteenth and early nineteenth centuries to waterproof cloth and produce a narrow range of articles. The demand for rubber was, however, restricted because the degree of the product's elasticity, and thus its usefulness, varied considerably with changes in temperature. The discovery, in 1839, of the process of vulcanization (where the rubber was treated with sulphur), overcame this problem; and gave rise to an immediate surge in the demand for rubber. Rubber production in the Amazon doubled between 1836 and 1840 (Weinstein 1983a).

In 1840, the Amazon was the only producer of rubber in the world, and its production depended on a traditional and complex network of tappers and traders seeking out concentrations of rubber-bearing trees. During the second half of the nineteenth century, the increase in the demand for wild rubber was considerable, and output, which in 1840 had amounted to 388,000 kilos, reached a level of 15 million kilos in 1890. This expansion was achieved with little change in the system of production (Weinstein 1983a).

In the 1890s, however, there was a surge of demand caused principally by the bicycle craze in Europe and the United States and output in Brazil had soared to over 26 million kilos by 1900. The unprecedented demand also stimulated the search for further sources of wild rubber, principally in Africa, but also in South America. Rubber extraction spread very rapidly in West Africa, Angola and the Belgian Congo so that by 1900, tropical Africa accounted for 36 per cent of the world's exports of wild rubber. Between 1900 and 1913, African wild rubber consistently accounted for at least 25 per cent of the world's exports of this commodity (Hanson 1980; Drabble 1973; Weinstein 1983a).

The bicycle boom of the 1890s was, of course, a prelude to the more expansive force of demand from the automobile industry. Following the invention of the pneumatic tyre and the subsequent increase in the demand for cars in Europe and in the United States, a change in the relations between the rubber producing and the rubber consuming regions occurred. Until the 1890s, demand for rubber was sufficiently broad that the rubber-goods industry had little interest in directly controlling production. As soon as demand became focused on a single commodity, tyres, however, interests in Europe and the United States were aroused. Attempts to monopolize supplies were made by a number of European and American firms in the Amazon, and by many British and French companies in Africa, but they were generally unsuccessful (Weinstein 1983a; Munro 1981, 1983). Production problems persisted as the existing relations of production failed to change, and figures on the output of wild rubber confirm the impression of production bottlenecks.

Between 1900 and 1913, total world wild rubber output increased from 20 million kilos to 30 million kilos (that is, a 50 per cent increase). The number of cars produced in Europe and the United States, by contrast, increased from around 10,000 units in 1900 to 600,000 units (that is, a 6000 per cent increase) in 1913 (the European share was 100,000 units). Clearly wild rubber could not and did not meet this concentrated demand (Drabble 1973; Foreman-Peck 1982).

Demand was met from cultivated rubber, and between 1900 and 1913 attempts by Europeans to increase the world supply of rubber proliferated. Particular interest had already been shown by the British authorities in the possibility of plantation rubber cultivation in their Asian colonies. Though seeds of the rubber-bearing tree had been illegally taken from Brazil by an employee of Kew Gardens and the India Office in 1876, it was not until the 1890s that the cultivation of rubber in Asia became a reality (Dean 1987; Drabble 1973). Growth in demand and rising prices encouraged production in many parts of south and southeast Asia, where the total acreage under rubber-tree cultivation grew from 7000 in 1900 to 2 million in 1913. By 1907, Malaya had overtaken Ceylon as the largest producer of cultivated rubber in Asia, and by 1913 accounted for 52 per cent of the Asian rubber acreage, with the Dutch East Indies a further 25 per cent. Initially, the Europeans controlled all the Asian rubber production, and although by 1913, Asian holdings totalled 43 per cent of the Malayan rubber acreage, they were much smaller elsewhere in south and southeast Asia (Drabble 1973).

The share of cultivated rubber in world exports overtook that of wild rubber in 1914, and by 1922, over 90 per cent of the world's rubber came from Asia. The expansion of rubber plantations in the colonies in Asia continued apace before 1914, even during the several periods of depression in the world market that caused violent fluctuations in the demand for wild rubber. Capital flowed into the plantations from Europe, and more than 260 companies were formed in the Malayan rubber trade between 1900 and 1913. There was also substantial investment from American tyre companies, many of whom purchased plantations (Chandler 1977). Expansion was further aided by cheap and plentiful migratory labour. Between 1900 and 1913, for example, more than 850,000 Indians migrated to Malaya, mostly to work on the rubber plantations, joining those from China and Java (Tinker 1974). Productivity was enhanced by continual improvements in the technology of rubber propagation, cultivation and processing.

Largely on account of the increase in production in Asia, world rubber output (wild and cultivated) between 1900 and 1913 soared from just over 20 million kilos to almost 55 million kilos. The single largest consumer of rubber in the world in 1913 was the United States, as it had been in 1900, but the combined consumption of Britain, France, Germany and Russia consistently overshadowed the American levels (Drabble 1973). While the colonial powers in Asia were being well repaid for their investments, the German chemical industry was attempting to produce a synthetic alternative. Important technical and scientific advances were made in this respect before 1914, but little production took place because of falling natural rubber prices. Only during the war did Germany manage to step up production of synthetic rubber which, while being at the time inferior to the natural product, nevertheless found enough uses so that its consumption accounted for as much as 10 per cent of the country's needs. Though far less successful than synthetic indigo, the case of synthetic rubber before 1914 demonstrates that no product, however much coveted by the colonial system, was immune from import substitution (Haber 1971).

The International Migration of Labour

Europe's impact on global economic conditions was reflected in the exploitation of the natural resources of indigenous civilizations. This led invariably to a greater integration of world markets. The primary products with significant exchange value which constituted the vector of this exploitation throughout the period 1600–1914 were labour intensive, and often required some form of labour coercion to ensure production. For the successful large-scale cultivation of sugar cane on the Atlantic Islands and the Americas, for example, it soon became evident to the conquerers and colonists that neither native labour (if available) nor imported European labour was willing to face the requisite conditions of work. The plantation system, using imported African labour under slavery became, in the late fifteenth century, a preferred solution to the economic dilemma facing Europeans overseas. Over the following centuries, the plantation remained the most important organization of staple production and coerced labour, though not always slavery, was generally the preferred response by planters to labour shortage.

The movement of labour from one part of the world to another, therefore, became inseparable from the economic exploits of the European nations throughout the period from the sixteenth to the twentieth centuries. This vast human migration included peoples of many cultures and from many countries. Although the familiar intercontinental migration of Europeans to North and South America, Australia and New Zealand is usually treated as a distinct phase in the history of migration, it is our intention to include this movement in the context of the long-term international migration of labour.

Until 1820, the greatest flow of intercontinental migration was between Africa and the Americas, destined largely for the plantation economies. According to the most widely accepted figures on the dimensions of this migration, 7,685,000 slaves were imported into the Americas between 1600 and 1820 (Curtin 1969; Lovejoy 1982; Eltis 1983, 1987). The Atlantic slave trade was initiated by the Portuguese in the latter half of the fifteenth century, partly to supply demand in Europe for domestic labour and partly to supply labour for the sugar plantations that the Portuguese had established in Madeira and Sao Tomé. Until the latter part of the sixteenth century, the export of African slaves was relatively small, especially when compared to the volume exported in later centuries. By the beginning of the seventeenth century, however, as sugar production began to increase substantially in Brazil, the demand for slave labour and the volume of slave exports from Africa expanded. The economic benefits of producing sugar for the European market quickly became evident in the West Indies; and as some islands shifted from tobacco to sugar production and others were colonized for the express purpose of producing sugar, the Atlantic slave trade responded with increased volumes (Davies 1974). By the end of the seventeenth century, slave labour began to be used in increasing amounts on tobacco plantations in Virginia and Maryland (McCusker and Menard 1985; Kulikoff 1986). During the seventeenth century 1.9 million slaves were exported from Africa, more than five times as many as had been exported in the previous 150 years.

During the eighteenth century, slave labour was extended to many parts of North and South America and the slave trade expanded accordingly. This was partly a consequence of an increasing demand for sugar and such products as indigo in Europe, which were best suited to plantation production; but it was also a reflection of the realization that slave labour could be cheaply employed not only on plantations, but also alongside other forms of labour, both indentured and free. By any standard, the eighteenth-century trade across the Atlantic was staggering – more than six million people were exported from Africa during this century, of whom more than 40 per cent were shipped by the English (Lovejoy 1982). The growth in demand for slave labour accounted for only part of this increase; the remainder was required because of the exceedingly high mortality experienced by slaves especially in the West Indies and in Brazil (Klein 1986).

During the period from 1600 to 1820, the Americas also received a

considerable influx of Europeans, though they were numerically far less important than the African migration. In total, North and South America became the
home for some 2,165,000 Europeans during the period, representing 22 per cent
of the total immigration. Twenty per cent of the European migrants were
indentured labourers; though as much as 66 per cent of the migration from
Britain until 1780 was of this type (Engerman 1986).

By 1820, therefore, the Americas had become demographically at least, an
extension of Africa, and economically, through staple production, an extension
of Europe (Eltis 1983). This structure helped to integrate the economies of all
three continents, but in the nineteenth century that structure became more fully
attached to the European economy as Europeans migrated in unprecedented
numbers to the American continents. At the same time, the process of staple
production diffused in Asia, which also encouraged substantial intercontinental
migration.

Just as staple commodity production and trade secured the integration of the
international economy with industrial Europe at the core, so the massive migration of Europeans during the nineteenth and early twentieth centuries reflected
the growing Europeanization of the world, and enhanced the relative strength of
the developed world at the expense of the less developed. From the 1850s
particularly, areas of surplus labour within the continent of Europe provided a
stream of skilled workers for areas of labour scarcity, particularly in the United
States, where the abolition of slavery left a great need for labour. Whatever the
costs and benefits of migration, and whatever its specific causes, the outcome
was a spread of European influence, predominantly to the Americas, but also to
South Africa, Australia and New Zealand. Skills, capital, technology and culture were transmitted with the nineteenth-century migrants, but because of the
geographical pattern of their destinations, the spread of knowledge was confined to areas with advantageous social and economic structures, and, therefore,
reinforced the relative backwardness of Africa, Asia and the Caribbean.

Between 1815 and 1914, around 50 million Europeans emigrated, which
represented around 25 per cent of the natural increase. More than half of this
total originated in Britain, Ireland and Italy; a further 20 per cent came from
Germany, Spain and Portugal, while the remainder – about 25 per cent of the
total – were Russian, East European, Scandinavian or from the Low Countries.
Within the century of emigration two distinct periods can be discerned. The first
wave took place during the middle decades of the nineteenth century, and has
come to be known as the 'old' migration. Those who emigrated at this time came
largely from Britain, Ireland and Germany, and moved either to escape famine
or to achieve social mobility. They were often skilled workers, they typically left
home in families and remained permanently in their chosen destination. The
second wave, which gathered momentum from the 1880s and is referred to as
the 'new' migration, originated largely in the south and east of Europe. These
migrants were characteristically unskilled single males, for whom migration
might be only temporary. Quantitatively, the emigration reached its peak in the
decades before the First World War when, because of the feedback mechanism,
most European economies had become involved in it. In both of the major
periods of emigration, the single most important destination was the United
States, where 70 per cent of nineteenth-century European migrants settled. Latin

America was also important, especially for Italian and southeastern Europeans late in the nineteenth century. Many British migrants also found homes in Canada, South Africa, Australia and New Zealand (Woodruff 1966; Gould 1979; Lee 1979).

Generally, the European migrants of the late nineteenth century had much to gain economically as they moved from areas of high to areas of low population density. The areas of new settlement were relatively spacious, and, with the help of new technology and cheap transport became highly productive. High productivity meant high wages in the short term at least, and while heavy migration eventually forced down wage rates, this was insufficient to deter further migrants for whom the feedback of positive information and significantly cheaper transatlantic travel provided substantial impetus to move. It is clearly impossible to make further generalizations about the reasons for the exodus of Europeans, but it seems likely that the early migrants, who encountered opportunities for mobility, informed potential successors, and for most emigrants, the decision to leave involved a balance between the expectation of the benefits to be derived from moving, and the expectations of the costs of remaining behind. After 1870, the decision to migrate was facilitated by the improvements in transatlantic transportation, by financial help from abroad – either from previous migrants or from prospective employers – and by increasing awareness of economic opportunities in the countries overseas. The extent of emigration built up through an incremental process, and by the end of the nineteenth century, new areas of departure had emerged. Between 1900 and 1914, massive numbers migrated, especially from the poorer parts of Europe, who perceived emigration to the United States or Latin America (especially Argentina and Brazil) as a means of escaping from a lifetime of poverty (Albert 1983). For this category, upward social mobility was less important than survival.

While much emigration in the nineteenth century was economically determined, its growth can be charaterized as a process of diffusion, which began first in north and west Europe and then spread to new origins in the Mediterranean and in southeastern Europe. By the end of the nineteenth century, therefore, the new sources supplemented the old, which continued to provide emigrants but at a far reduced rate (Gould 1980b).

Throughout Europe, emigration was influenced by previous emigration of family, friends and neighbours and was not only regional/local in origin but was also regional/local in destination. From the 1860s, the bulk of the emigrants moved along paths that had already been taken by friends and relatives. Return migration became an increasingly significant component of the European migratory movements. It rarely indicated failure, merely that the intention had not been to emigrate permanently. Emigrants who returned home – some not just once but several times (in 1904, 10 per cent of the Italian migrants to the United States were going for the second time) – were an important source of information to friends and relatives who were considering emigration for themselves. By the turn of the century, transatlantic migration in some cases became seasonal. Because of the large wage differentials that existed between the poorer regions of Europe and the United States and parts of Latin America, and because of the quicker and cheaper transport, temporary or seasonal migration might be financially worthwhile if physically and psychologically wearing. In some regions of Europe, where the opportunity costs of labour were very small and marginal farms could be run in off-season by women and children, it was not unusual for the adult male of the household to seek harvest work in South America. The international harvest thus emerged as a reality for those whose labour requirements were supplied by transcontinental migrants. Many migrants, therefore, left Europe temporarily to enhance their existing position, rather than to move out of it (Gould 1980a, 1980b).

Nineteenth-century European intercontinental migration partly served to redistribute the European population so that advantage could be taken of the plentiful land in the Americas, as well as in Australia and New Zealand, that had been very sparsely populated. The emigration also served to provide essential labour for the burgeoning industrial areas of the northeastern and central United States and selected areas in Brazil, Argentina and Uruguay. Thus, emigration resulted in a complex web of interrelationships, economic as well as social and political, which provided Europe with an unprecedented potential throughout the world (Denoon 1983).

It can be estimated that in the period from 1820 to 1920, Europeans accounted for over 90 per cent of the world's intercontinental migration (Engerman 1986). The remaining proportion consisted of several important flows. The first of these were represented by Africans migrating to the Americas, primarily sold into slavery but also with the addition of indentured servants. More than 2.3 million Africans migrated in this period, more than 80 per cent of them destined for the Americas. A second, important flow consisted of Indian and Chinese (and some Javanese) migrants, typically as indentured servants. Recent estimates place the level of this migration at over 2 million individuals, the bulk of whom were destined for the booming sugar, tea and rubber plantations developed by European colonial rule in Asia, Africa, Australia, as well as the islands of Mauritius, Réunion and Fiji (Engerman 1986).

The International Migration of Capital

The vast movement of European peoples especially in the nineteenth century was accompanied by an outpouring of European wealth and the joint action of the two processes served to heighten world integration with Europe at the core (Woodruff 1966; Pollard 1985). The great age of European foreign investment began around 1850 but accelerated after 1870 and its peak period coincided with that of migration. The export of European manufactured goods that swamped the world from the late eighteenth and early nineteenth century was enhanced at the middle of the century by expanding quantities of European capital, capital goods and factors of production.

Table 2.1 indicates the gathering pace of European foreign investment in the nineteenth century. Several European economies, of which the Netherlands is an example, maintained a steady but low level of capital exports throughout the nineteenth century. The major exporters, however, were Britain and France, and they had begun to invest abroad early in the nineteenth century. They added to their overseas stock significantly between 1875 and 1914, so that by the latter date, their joint interests accounted for 64 per cent of total world foreign investment. Germany, the third-largest European exporter of capital, only began to invest abroad in the 1880s, but by 1914, German investments accounted for 13 per cent of the world total.

On the eve of the First World War, after 30 years of consistent overseas investment, Britain's overseas commitments approached £4000 million – equal to 25 per cent of its national wealth – while France had invested almost £1800 million – or 15 per cent of its national wealth (see Table 2.2).

The massive migration of Europeans after 1870 clearly influenced the direction of European overseas investment. Table 2.3 presents the broad geographical distribution of foreign investment and shows that late nineteenth-century exports, more so than formerly, went mainly to areas of white (European) settlement. While much of Europe retained some investment in the non-white areas, only Britain continued to invest there significantly.

The export of European capital was clearly a new expression of European leadership and power in the world, and through it many parts of the world were pulled further into the European orbit. The world economy, with Europe at the centre, became more firmly established. Without doubt, exported capital was characterized by fixed investments in public utilities, especially in railways, but also in other infrastructure – docks, harbours, tramways – and in such utilities as gas, water and electricity supplies. Sometimes the exported capital was invested in large industrial and mining enterprises, in government stock and in

Table 2.1: *Cumulative growth of foreign investment from specified leading capital exporting countries (in £ millions)*

	1825	1840	1855	1870	1885	1900	1915
Britain	100	140	460	980	1560	2420	3900
France	20	60	200	500	660	1040	1720
Germany	—	—	—	—	380	960	1340
Netherlands	60	40	60	100	200	220	240

Source: W. Woodruff, *The Impact of Western Man* (London, 1966) 150–1.

Table 2.2: *British and French foreign investment 1870–1914 (£ millions)*

	Britain	France
1870–4	61.0	neg
1875–9	1.7	neg
1880–4	23.9	neg
1885–9	61.1	19.6
1890–9	45.6	23.5
1895–9	26.8	47.0
1900–4	21.3	
1902–8		55.0
1905–9	109.5	
1909–13		51.0
1910–13	185.0	
Total foreign investment in 1914	3763	1765

Source: H. Feis, *Europe, the World's Banker 1870–1914* (New Haven, 1930), 11, 44.

Table 2.3: *Geographical distribution of foreign investment Britain, France and Germany in 1914 (£ millions)*

To:	From:		
	Britain	France	Germany
Europe	210	820	500
USA	850	80	190
Canada	560	20	40
Latin America	740	320	180
Australia	340	20	—
Asia	710	250	140
Africa	490	180	100
Total	3900	1690	1150
% of world total	44%	19.9%	12.8%
Areas of white settlement	2700	1260	910
Areas of non-white settlement	1200	430	240

Source: calculated from H. Feis, *Europe, the World's Banker 1870–1914* (New Haven, 1930), 23, 51, 74.

banking and insurance companies. In the early 1840s, Britain privately financed the building of railway networks abroad, mainly in Europe but also in the United States. From the late 1840s, Britain's involvement in the most industrial parts of Europe fell away as those areas practised import substitution; and the focus shifted to eastern parts of Europe, especially Turkey and Russia, as well as regions outside of Europe, principally India and Latin America. Until about 1850, Britain was the major foreign investor in Europe. Most capital goods imported into France were of British origin, though some industrial enterprises were financed by Belgian and Swiss sources. After 1850, France became a sizeable capital exporter (except to Germany, the Netherlands and Scandinavia) and, indeed, in the period 1850–1914, France became the financier of Europe, having particularly close economic ties with Russia and southeastern Europe. Belgium also received some initial stimulus from British capital, as well as French and Dutch, but it too subsequently became a capital exporter, mainly to northern France and the German Rhineland, and later to Spain, Italy, Poland and Russia. Following the scramble for Africa in the early 1880s, some Belgian capital found its way to the Congo. Germany remained virtually self-contained until the last quarter of the nineteenth century. Britain had invested in the early German railways and some French and Belgian capital was invested in Rhenish-Westphalia mining and metallurgy, but this was short-lived, and German banks rapidly took over a considerable amount of industrial finance. Little capital was exported from Germany before 1880. Thereafter, it mostly went to Austria-Hungary, the Balkans, Russia and Turkey (Woodruff 1966; Feis 1930; Milward and Saul 1977).

The most important single item of European investment before 1914 was the financing of the American railway network. Capital continued to flow into the United States upon the completion of the network and by 1914, the value of

European investments in the United States had reached £1300 million, which constituted 14 per cent of international indebtedness, 22 per cent of European foreign investment and 91 per cent of total foreign investment in the United States. Britain was the major single foreign investor in the United States and even more overwhelmingly in Canada, which in per capita terms was the largest importer of capital. It was Latin America that attracted greater proportions of continental European capital.

By 1870, British investment in Latin America had reached £85 million, divided mainly between Argentina and Brazil. Latin America continued to attract funds to 1914 when total foreign holdings stood at £1800 million, of which Britain accounted for 42 per cent, France for 18 per cent and Germany 10 per cent. These European investments were directed mainly into public utilities, but also into manufacturing industries. German capital was largely responsible for the growth of the chemical and plastics industries of Brazil; and French and Belgian capital strengthened South American steel production. The cotton industry in Mexico received strong financial support from Spanish capital (Albert 1983).

The Asian continent was an important recipient of European capital, which historically had been utilized to develop trade with the west. Investment in infrastructure – railways and harbours – together with investments in plantations – tea, rubber, coffee and sugar – cheapened the goods Europe wanted to buy while at the same time ensuring a market for European manufactured goods. Britain invested heavily in Indian railways and ports, and in tea plantations and encouraged the production of cotton, opium and rice. Britain not only received cheap raw materials, but also found a solution to effect multilateral trade balances in the east as well as an enormous market for British cotton goods (Feis 1930; Latham 1978).

Before 1850, European capital in Africa was used to finance legitimate trade, precious metals and ivory, but subsequently, the gold and diamond mines of South Africa became the focus particularly of British interests. It was only from the 1880s, however, that European investment in Africa became focused on the production of goods for European consumption. In many parts of Africa, foreign capital was used to encourage or establish commercial agriculture for export. Thus cotton and coffee production were stimulated in Uganda; cotton and tobacco in East Africa; cocoa in the Gold Coast; groundnuts and palm oil in Nigeria; and vegetable oil in the Belgian Congo. European capital also helped railway construction in Africa, but no real network resulted. A map of African railways illustrates clearly that lines were constructed between areas of primary production and the coast, for the benefit of the Europeans rather than the Africans. Generally, the process by which the Africans were encouraged to perceive agriculture as an industry of cash crops rather than as subsistence changed the structure of the economy (mainly for the benefit of Europeans) and brought the African continent clearly within the orbit of the European world economy (Munro 1976; Latham 1978; Wolf 1982; Freund 1984).

European investments were therefore of two different types. In the areas of white settlement to which large quantities of capital were transferred late in the nineteenth century, loans were of the non-controllable portfolio variety – that is, Europeans had virtually no control over the funds they committed. In the non-white regions, by contrast, foreign investments were closely directed and typically designed to promote manufactured imports from the lending country and to discourage local industry. Thus between 70 and 80 per cent of European capital exports in 1914 was 'neutral' and for the most part beneficial for the borrower. The remaining portion had complex political implications, and here there was at least some benefit for the lender and, very likely, lasting damage to the borrower. Either way European capital built transport systems and infrastructure and so physically helped to open up the world. For good or ill, most of the economies of the world were drawn even closer together in a complicated network of relationships built upon the movement of commodities, people and capital.

The Expansion of Trade

The impact of trade on European industry came largely from two growth sources before the nineteenth century; the provision of colonial staples and the development of internal demand. While European trade with Asia, Africa and the Americas grew enormously from the seventeenth century, only the Americas constituted an important industrial export market. The African market for European manufactured products was restricted to firearms and linen, while the Asian market remained largely impenetrable to European manufactures (Davies 1957; Richards 1980).

Colonial products not only provided the lynch-pin in Europe's economic relationship with Africa but also stimulated intra-European commerce, especially that between western Europe and northern and eastern Europe. The stimulus colonial products gave to industrial development was also not insignificant.

The most important colonial products to be imported into Europe, until the beginning of the nineteenth century, were tobacco and sugar. Both products required processing before consumption, and, typically, the processing was done in Europe, mainly in port cities. The European economy thus benefited in several ways from the import of colonial staples. In the case of sugar, the Europeans controlled production (as well as the preparatory processing stages) on the slave plantations, and then organized the refining of sugar in Europe.

During the first half of the seventeenth century, Amsterdam became the most important centre for sugar refining in Europe, and handled sugar from Brazil, the Guianas, the English and French colonies, as well as the sugar imported from the east by the VOC (Deerr 1949–50). In 1661, there were reported to be 60 refineries at work in the city. Towards the end of the century, however, Amsterdam lost its monopoly of sugar refining, and the industry began to locate in France, England and Germany, as well as in other European countries.

In France, most of the refining was carried out at or near the ports of Nantes, La Rochelle, Rouen, Bordeaux and Marseilles while in England, refining was concentrated in London, though some sugar was refined in Bristol and Liverpool. In Germany, Hamburg was the chief centre of sugar refining, and by the end of the eighteenth century contained probably the single largest concentration of refineries in Europe (Deerr 1949–50).

Sugar refining in Europe spread as production increased in the New World

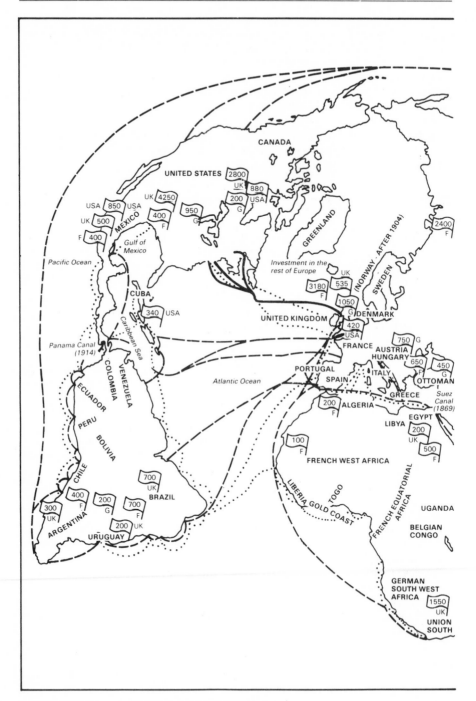

3 The world economy before the First World War

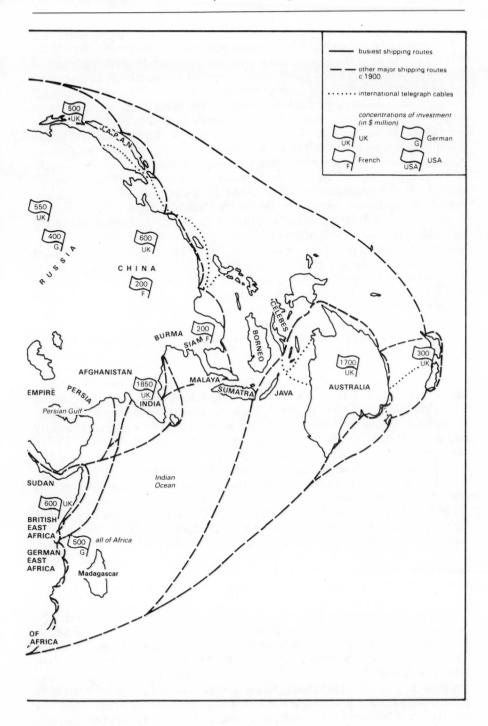

busiest shipping routes

other major shipping routes
c.1900

······ international telegraph cables

*concentrations of investment
(in $ million)*

UK | UK
F | French
G | German
USA | USA

500 UK

550 UK

400 G

600 UK

RUSSIA

CHINA

200 F

JAPAN

BURMA

SIAM

200 F

MALAYA

BORNEO

CELEBES

AFGHANISTAN

EMPIRE

PERSIA

1850 UK

INDIA

Persian Gulf

SUMATRA

JAVA

AUSTRALIA

1700 UK

300 UK

SUDAN

*Indian
Ocean*

600 UK

BRITISH
EAST
AFRICA

GERMAN
EAST
AFRICA

500 G

all of Africa

Madagascar

OF
AFRICA

and as successive colonial possessions were brought under sugar cultivation. The seventeenth and eighteenth centuries witnessed an important shift in the relative positions of the various producing regions. Until 1650, Brazil's annual average production of *c.* 28,000 tons accounted for nearly all of the sugar produced in the New World (Deerr 1949–50). From 1650 to the beginning of the eighteenth century, the English colonies in the West Indies turned increasingly to sugar cultivation and by 1710 had clearly overtaken Brazil as the main supplier of raw sugar in the New World. In that year, the English West Indian colonies accounted for 41 per cent of total supplies; Brazilian production accounted for 37 per cent while French colonial production accounted for the remainder. For most of the eighteenth century, the French and British colonies were the leading producers of sugar in the Americas, followed by Brazil and then, in much smaller amounts, by the Dutch, Danish and Spanish colonies.

Sugar from the French colonies was rapidly re-exported from the main ports of Bordeaux, Nantes and Marseilles. During the eighteenth century, France re-exported an average of 80 per cent of its total sugar imports most of which went to Amsterdam and Hamburg for refining. Sugar refined in France was predominantly for home consumption (Stein 1980). Sugar from Britain's colonies, by contrast, was largely consumed at home; and during the eighteenth century, when sugar consumption in Britain increased five-fold, the proportion of imports retained rose steadily (Mintz 1985).

Tobacco had a similar division of labour between the colonies and Europe. From the seventeenth century, England and Scotland were the main importers of leaf tobacco in Europe, and, while processing was carried out in many parts of Europe, England, Scotland and France were the main beneficiaries (for detailed description of the industry in these countries see Price 1954, 1964, 1973; Devine 1976; McCusker and Menard 1985). Tobacco imports into Britain soared from 1.5 million pounds in 1637 to 38 million at the turn of the eighteenth century and up to 100 million by the outbreak of the American Revolution. Unlike sugar, however, retained imports remained fairly constant over the long run while the volume of re-exports grew considerably (Schumpeter 1960). The main markets for British tobacco were Holland, Germany and, in the eighteenth century especially, France.

For both England and France, sugar and tobacco were the dominant commodites of the re-export trade, a sector of intra-European trade which grew particularly rapidly during the eighteenth century (Davis 1969a, 1969b; Léon 1974). Both products helped to develop trade links with eastern and northern Europe, as the bulk products from this region could now be exchanged for semi-manufactured goods, instead of bullion as had been the case earlier in our period (Johansen 1986).

Not only did Europe benefit from the processing, exchange and re-exchange of colonial products, it also enjoyed the advantages of demographic and ancillary economic development which were stimulated by colonial trade. In the period from 1600 to the end of the eighteenth century, the most dynamic urban centres in Europe were those which engaged in some aspect of colonial trade; and those in which both processing and exchange occurred (in addition to direct participation in the Atlantic slave trade) benefited the most (de Vries 1976). The population of Nantes, for example, rose from 25,000 to 74,000 between 1600 and 1800; that of Marseilles nearly doubled from 40,000 to 78,000 while the population of Bordeaux more than doubled from 40,000 to 88,000. Glasgow's population multiplied from 2000 in 1600 to 77,000 in 1800, while during the same period, the population of Bristol rose from 11,000 to 64,000. Liverpool's population between 1700 and 1750 increased from 6000 to 30,000 inhabitants largely on account of the growing involvement in the colonial and slave trade (de Vries 1984; Clemens 1976; Hohenberg and Lees 1985).

The impact on European industry of the growth in the imports of colonial staples was both specific and wide-reaching. Not only was there a direct benefit to the processing industries, but also to a wide range of ancillary industries of which shipbuilding was most important. Colonial staples were also important by indirectly providing the means by which the major European colonial powers were able to purchase industrial raw materials in the Baltic and thus involve this area in the wider industrial system. During the eighteenth century, shipments of colonial products to the Baltic increased by more than ten-fold. Imports from the Baltic increased by at least this much – in the case of France, imports grew more than fifteen-fold over the course of the century. The goods imported, potash, tallow, iron and wood, were vital to industrial development and at the time there was no other region which could supply industrial Europe with such quantities. Without the colonial staples, a far greater proportion of the payments to the Baltic regions would have had to have been made in bullion, putting additional strain on the bullion supply (Johansen 1986; Davis 1969a, 1969b; Léon 1974; Kriedte 1983).

In relative terms, the eighteenth century was the heyday of colonial staple trade for Europe as a whole. While imports of staple food crops from Asia, Africa, Latin America and the West Indies increased absolutely during the nineteenth century, they were overshadowed by other goods with a direct input to industry. While the output of both sugar and tobacco increased enormously during the nineteenth century, the dismantling of the old colonial system ensured that neither product would remain a monopoly of any particular group of colonial powers. The cultivation of sugar cane and tobacco soon developed in many other parts of the world, leaving the old colonial staples with falling market shares. Nevertheless, processing industries continued to develop during the nineteenth century and in the sugar industry in particular, significant innovations were made in continuous processing.

It is impossible to be precise about the growth of European trade over the entire period from 1600 to 1914. Such scattered evidence as exists from a few European trading nations points to a significant increase between 1600 to 1750 (Wilson and Parker 1977). After 1750, when more evidence is available, it is clear that trading opportunities increased enormously, although it is highly likely that the acceleration in growth probably preceded the middle of the century. Between 1750 and 1913, when the major growth periods were between 1840–80 and 1900–13, European foreign trade grew by a factor of 40 (Woodruff 1966).

Throughout the period 1600–1914, the bulk of European foreign trade was intra-European. With the exception of Britain, the share of European exports and imports in the total for each economy was remarkably constant. In the case of France, for example, Europe accounted for 75 per cent of the imports and 89 per cent of the exports at the beginning of the eighteenth century. Nearly 70 years later the figures were not significantly different standing at 62 and 78 per cent respectively (Léon 1974). The British case was altogether different, and although in 1700, for example, continental Europe accounted for 61 per cent of imports, 74 per cent of re-exports and 81 per cent of exports, by 1785 a distinct change had taken place in Europe's role as a trading region. Its import and export share had fallen to 39 per cent while re-exports had decreased less profoundly to 52 per cent (Davis 1969b, 1979).

During the nineteenth century, important quantitative and qualitative changes took place in the nature and impact of European trade. The value of European exports grew dramatically; between 1830 and 1914, for example, exports rose 16-fold in value and 138-fold in volume, compared to the more modest growth of three or four-fold in the eighteenth century. In the same period, the per capita value of European exports rose seven-fold. The annual rate of growth of exports, while not consistent, remained at an unprecedentedly high level throughout the century. On average, the annual rate of growth of exports in both value and volume terms was between 3 and 4 per cent. Rates of growth of 5 per cent per annum were achieved during the free-trade era of 1846–75; and between 1900 and 1910, when Europe was recovering from a period of depression (1875–95), when the annual rate of growth of exports had stood at only 2 per cent (Bairoch 1973; Milward and Saul 1977; Foreman-Peck 1983; Lewis 1981).

The picture of remarkable and sustained growth of European trade should, however, be qualified in two ways. Firstly, expansionism was not confined to Europe, and, between 1800 and 1913, the European share of total world trade fell from 70 to 57 per cent. This decline was primarily due to expansion in the exports of those few countries outside Europe that were experiencing substantial industrial development, particularly the United States, Japan and Australia. Secondly, the expansion of European trade was not evenly spread, and depended heavily on the contribution of three major nations – Britain, France and Germany. In 1860, for example, the exports of Britain, France and Germany accounted for 70 per cent of the European total, and by 1910, the contribution of the three nations stood at just under 60 per cent. Britain was the single most important trading nation, contributing between 25 and 30 per cent of the European total. Structurally, Britain's trading position was quite distinct from the rest of Europe, as was the relationship between the commercial sector and the economy generally. The fastest growing trading nation in Europe, in relative terms at least was Belgium, whose share of the European total grew from 4 to 7 per cent between 1830 and 1913 and in per capita terms, Belgium had, by 1913, become the most substantial trading nation in Europe.

In broad terms, the geographical structure of European exports did not change significantly during the nineteenth century. The overwhelming majority of exports were destined for other parts of Europe; and between 1830 and 1910, the proportion varied between 68 and 72 per cent. North America was the second most important recipient of European exports – 12 per cent in 1830 and down to 8 per cent in 1910. South America formed the market for 8 per cent of European exports throughout the century. Less developed regions of the world became proportionately more important destinations of exports during the nineteenth century. Asia's share of the European export trade rose from 4 to 10 per cent over the period while Africa's share increased especially after 1880 from 2 to 5 per cent. These figures, however, which present the overall European average, disguise the significant differences in export destination between Britain and the continent of Europe, though even the latter was not a homogeneous bloc. As Table 2.4 below indicates, Britain's distinctive trading structure was very much geared towards extra-European areas.

Table 2.4: *Destination of European exports (% of total exports by value)*

	Europe	North America	South America	Asia	Africa
1830					
Europe	72	12	8	6	2
Britain	47	26	12	13	3
Continent	82	7	6	4	1
1860					
Europe	68	9	8	10	3
Britain	34	17	12	26	3
Continent	82	6	6	3	3
1910					
Europe	68	8	8	10	5
Britain	35	12	13	25	7
Continent	78	6	6	5	4

Source: P. Bairoch, 'Geographical Structure and Trade Balance of European Foreign Trade from 1800 to 1970' *Journal of European Economic History* 3 (1974), 572.

Generally speaking, the markets for European goods became more diverse and widespread during the nineteenth century, especially before 1860 and after 1880, and this trend was particularly marked within the more highly industrialized European regions. The period between 1860 and 1880 saw a liberalization in European commercial policy and a relative strengthening of intra-European trade.

The geographical structure of European imports followed a pattern similar to that of exports. In other words, as Table 2.5 shows, the majority of imports of individual European countries came from other parts of Europe with the exception of Britain, which drew a far larger proportion of its imports from elsewhere, especially North America and Asia. Britain's import trade was more in line with the continental experience by 1910, but its distinctiveness was nevertheless still apparent.

Little has been said so far about the composition of European trade in the nineteenth and early twentieth century. Most of what follows will make reference only to broad categories of goods. Most European trade during this period was characterized by the export of manufactured goods – initially textiles and later metal and machinery products – and the import of primary goods – food and industrial raw materials. While other patterns of exchange clearly existed, those economies that made the largest contribution to total European trade were those with the highest absolute and proportionate manufacturing

Table 2.5: *Origins of European imports (% of total imports by value)*

	Europe	North America	South America	Asia	Africa
1860					
Europe	61	14	7	12	3
Britain	31	27	10	23	5
Continent	78	7	6	6	3
1910					
Europe	60	14	8	10	5
Britain	45	24	9	10	5
Continent	65	10	8	10	4

Source: P. Bairoch, 'Geographical Structure and Trade Balance of European Foreign Trade from 1800 to 1970' *Journal of European Economic History* 3 (1974), 582.

output: that is, the most advanced economies, whose exports, naturally, were composed predominantly of manufactured goods; and whose relatively small agricultural sectors necessitated the import of food as well as raw material inputs (Woodruff 1966; Bairoch 1982).

There is no doubt that the process of industrialization in Europe was enhanced by the expansion of overseas trade, and, as the nineteenth century progressed, the requirements of industrial regions to enlarge export markets and consolidate sources of raw materials became more important (Hanson 1980). The impact on the trading partners of the most heavily industrialized countries, however, is less clear cut. Many nineteeth-century commentators believed that the expansion of trade (especially in an unrestrained form) was beneficial to all participants. Despite the prevalence of this view, even today, there is an alternative belief that foreign trade becomes the means by which backward nations are exploited and subordinated. While it is unlikely that this particular debate will ever be satisfactorily resolved, politically loaded as it is, it is nevertheless worthwhile considering the economic impact of European trade – both within and outside Europe.

Quantitatively, intra-European trade overshadowed any other type during the nineteenth century; and clearly this took the characteristically complementary form – the major industrial powers swapped manufactures for the primary products of the less industrialized European nations (Woodruff 1966; Bairoch 1974). The needs of the developed industrial countries stimulated an export orientation in the typically self-sufficient, consumption-oriented economies of the European periphery, who substantially increased their export of agricultural goods and raw materials. Indeed, the growth in exports of most of these economies (except Spain and Portugal) was faster than the European average. It is assumed by many historians that the industrial nations benefited more from this relationship than the peripheral regions, and that the latter became trapped in the role of primary exporters. Certainly, the economies of southeastern Europe exported widely to industrial Europe, but little industrial development was apparently stimulated by this growth in trade. Insufficient income was generated by trade to modernize the economy; on the contrary, some de-industrialization occurred as local crafts and industries, especially textiles, were often ruined as imported manufactures came to dominate the market for consumer goods (Milward and Saul 1977). For the Italian economy and the economies of Hungary and Russia, however, the trading relationship carried some benefits. Their foreign trade, and the investment that followed, together with internal forces encouraging development, permitted a degree of industrial development. The growth of Hungary's exports amounted to 3 per cent per annum between 1850 and 1913, the chief component of which, grain, was enjoying substantial expansion of demand from the nearby industrial nations. By the late 1860s Hungary began to exploit the industrial potential of its major export by developing the milling and processing of grain. This meant that while a complete economic transformation was not achieved, a degree of industrial development was enjoyed. Russia also had a large grain export sector which grew at an average rate of 3.8 per cent per annum between 1860 and 1910; 30 per cent of the world's total import of wheat was provided by Russia, which also exported ores and other industrial raw materials. Some processing and other manufacturing developments were achieved with the help of foreign loans and earnings from foreign trade, but, by 1914, industrial transformation was far from complete (Berend and Ranki 1980; Hanson 1980).

While the nineteenth century witnessed considerable quantitative and qualitative changes in the structure of European trade, there is a degree of continuity with an earlier period which should not be overlooked. One of the important characteristics of the long-term pattern was the remarkable constancy, Britain apart, of the role of intra-European trade. Regardless of the extent of Europe's commercial involvement in the economies of non-European regions, the main beneficiary, in terms of extending or deepening the structure of trade was Europe itself.

In terms of the composition of foreign trade by goods, one of the most important changes which occurred over the period was in the structure of Europe's imports. In the eighteenth century, these had been largely manufactures, mainly from Asia, but in the nineteenth century, industrial raw materials and food predominated. Between 1831 and 1913, cotton and wool together accounted for between 12 and 26 per cent of Britain's imports and for between 14 and 18 per cent of France's total imports. In 1913, these two industrial raw materials accounted for an average of 12 per cent of the imports of Germany, Belgium and Sweden. There is little doubt that as far as imports were concerned, the prime mover in Europe was the demand of its industries for material and of its population for food (Woodruff 1966).

It would be misleading, however, to argue that raw-material imports before the nineteenth century were unimportant. The massive and increasing imports of cotton from overseas during the nineteenth century has the effect of obscuring an important trade in industrial raw materials before the nineteenth century. In the case of France, industrial raw materials accounted for more than one-third of total imports in the early eighteenth century, rising to 49 per cent by the end of the century. Textile raw materials were the most important item, accounting for no less than 70 per cent of total raw material imports in the early eighteenth century (Léon 1974). In England, at the turn of the eighteenth century, raw materials accounted for 35 per cent of total imports – textile raw materials were 50 per cent of total raw materials (Davis 1969b). Thus, well before the import of cotton, Europe enjoyed a substantial trade in textile raw materials, most of them home-grown.

Although there were vast quantity changes in European trade between 1600 and 1914, trade within Europe changed little in terms of geographical structure and composition. What did change profoundly was Europe's trading relationship with the rest of the world, caused as much by Europe's changing industrial system as by its political influence and power in the non-European world.

Commerce and Industry

The relationship between industrial production and commerce was complex and dynamic. The conventional interpretation argues that before 1800 commerce dominated the industrial system, and from 1800, there were distinct signs that commerce was becoming a handmaiden rather than an engine of growth (Kravis 1970). Changes internal to industry, largely through organizational and technological changes, created the potential for vast increases in output together with a commitment to continuous production. The risk of entrusting substantial investment in plant, machinery and finished goods to the vagaries of a commercial community interested solely in simple financial gains was overwhelming. Industrial concerns therefore sought to redefine their relationship with the commercial sector. Their strategy consisted of establishing their own marketing and commercial facilities, and thereby by-passing the merchant altogether, or, alternatively, contracting with merchants for the distribution of their goods. (Examples of this process are provided throughout Part III). Until the beginning of the nineteenth century, therefore, the expansion in industrial production has been interpreted as a response of manufacturers to the increased demand created by opening new trading opportunities. After 1800, the growth of trade has been interpreted as a response by the commercial sector to the growing demand for raw materials by European industry and the growing market for finished products caused by declining costs of production (Rosenberg and Birdzell 1986).

As a generalization, there is some truth in this interpretation. Before the nineteenth century, commerce expanded largely as a result of improvements in exchange facilities and transport as well as innovations in market research. The substantial increase in the bulk carrying trade in the Baltic–North Sea region, for example, as well as the increase in transatlantic shipping has been sufficiently explained in terms of the falling costs of transport through ship design and production as well as through organizational improvements in handling, sorting and warehousing (North 1968). In the Baltic, shipping improvements led to an increase in the production of grain; while in Holland, it resulted in substantial growth of industrial activities allied to cheese and butter making, and to commerce. The decline in costs of transatlantic shipping caused an increase in the demand for colonial staples in Europe, and for European manufactures in the Americas (Shepherd and Walton 1972). There are, however, other cases where there was little connection between improvements in the means of commerce and its expansion. European demand for Indian cotton cloths and Chinese porcelain, for example, could not be satisfied even while the costs of production and distribution were rising (Chauduri 1978).

The substantial growth in the trade in raw materials in Europe during the eighteenth century, moreover, owed little to changes in the costs of transacting. Despite the undoubted improvements in road, canal and sea transport, commercial improvements until the late eighteenth century were sporadic and slow whereas the growth in the volume of raw materials exchanged was rapid and continuous. The bulk of the raw materials exchanged was textile raw materials, and demand for these did not require the stimulation of commercial improvements. Not only were the determinants of demand for these raw materials generated within the industry itself, but for wool and silk in particular, transport costs accounted for only a very small proportion of the overall costs of production and any improvement in this would hardly show up in the final price.

Not all industrial concerns relied on the commercial system, and Wedgwood in the ceramics industry and Boulton and Watt in steam-engine contruction, for example, developed their own specialized marketing arrangements (McKendrick 1960; Tann 1978). In the case of Wedgwood, the decision to develop independent commercial relationships stemmed partly from his ability to create demand while maintaining relatively high prices, a combination of elements not conducive to general trading. Wedgwood's innovation lay in selling and advertising his own products by establishing warehouses and showrooms in the main centres of demand, and by using agents in foreign markets, rather than relying upon commission merchants. Boulton and Watt, with a very different product, employed a similar tactic and dispensed with commercial merchants to handle the sale of steam engines. Other cases of industrial independence can be cited but it was probably more common to find manufacturers and merchants in partnership in a wide range of industries.

The view of trade as an engine of growth before 1800 incorrectly assumes that European industry either did not or could not lower its costs of production before 1800, and that demand could only be stimulated by rapidly falling prices. The argument that trade was a handmaiden of growth in the nineteenth century and that the real dynamic lay in the industrial sector's ability to decrease its costs of production at the same time as increasing the volume of its output is only partly correct (Lee 1986). Not all industries, for example, grew in scale in the nineteenth century. As a general rule, increasing returns to scale were uncommon in European industry before 1870 and, in many cases, long after that date (Nye 1987). A very large proportion of total industrial output was provided by small-scale units of production where wholesale merchants and middlemen continued to provide the means of exchange and therefore the potential market opportunities (Nicholas 1984). Furthermore, the demand for raw materials, while providing the driving force for Europe's import trade in the nineteenth century, was not an entirely new phenomenon. For much of the nineteenth century, the relationship between commerce and industry fluctuated; in certain periods, trade grew faster than did industrial production; in other periods, the reverse was true.

It is of only limited use to perceive the relationship between industry and the commercial system in terms of engine or handmaiden of growth. The process by which industry disengaged itself from the commercial system was clearly influenced by the developing ability of industry to market its own products. By 1913, for example, large industrial units were, as far as the sales and distribution of their products is concerned, independent of the commercial system. They acted to stimulate and to satisfy demand themselves. While this was an important development, the commercial system was not passive in the nineteenth century; indeed, it continued to develop the process of the integration of world commodity and factor markets. Without this, it is inconceivable that industrial Europe would have developed substantially.

Economic Integration in Europe

By the beginning of the seventeenth century, the European economy had become integrated to an extent which would have been unimaginable in an earlier period (Braudel 1982, 1984). Over the following two centuries, the process of integration continued unabated against a background of general economic stability. The stimulus for integration came from a number of key developments, the most important of which were in commercial organization and shipping technology. technology.

Until the sixteenth century, there was little direct maritime contact between the economies of the Mediterranean and the North Sea–Baltic Sea region. While Italian ships were to be found in English and Flemish ports in earlier centuries loading valuable raw materials, this was not a typical feature of Mediterranean commercial life. For the most part, European shipping was regionally concentrated, and within each region, the technology of shipping – the design of the hull, the design of the sails and rigging and the ratio of crew size to cargo space – developed independently and specifically to meet the precise requirements of climate, degree of piracy and, most important of all, the nature of goods carried. In general, Mediterranean shipping carried goods of greater value and lower bulk than its counterpart in northern waters, and the development of ship design took account of this important difference. By the end of the fifteenth century, however, the distinguishing characteristics of northern and Mediterranean ship design were beginning to erode as new rigging designs incorporating a combination of the two – that is, the simultaneous use of square and lateen sails – proved successful. The Portuguese, in particular, benefited from this development, and their early mastery of navigation in the Atlantic reflected this fact as well as their superior knowledge of ocean sailing (Parry 1963, 1981; Cipolla 1965; Crosby 1986).

While the innovations in rigging made it possible to sail effectively in the Atlantic and indeed to circumnavigate the world, the basic relation between crew size and cargo space remained unchanged (see Chapter 8). This feature, coupled with the fact that, for obvious reasons, the ships were heavily armed, constrained the effectiveness of this type of ship in commercial activities. In particular, only goods of high value relative to weight could be profitably carried in this manner.

To the Portuguese, of course, this was not a major problem, since the cargo they brought to Europe consisted almost exclusively of highly expensive spices; but to the rest of Europe, and in particular to the northern European exporter of goods of low value relative to weight, these innovations in ship design were inappropriate. The Dutch, in particular required an innovation in ship design specifically for this kind of carrying trade. Dutch merchants and shipowners had long specialized in bulk shipping and as the European demand for Baltic grain, timber and naval stores grew rapidly, and as the Dutch Republic began to engage in the Asian trade, the need to ship goods at low prices became pressing. Towards the end of the century, a radical new ship design had emerged which introduced a longer and shallower hull than was usual in ships of the period. It allowed a substantial reduction in the ratio of crew size to cargo space, which reduced operating costs; and it was simple and inexpensive to construct. This new ship, known as the Fluyt (or fluit, flute or fly-boat) easily undercut competition in the bulk carrying trade (de Vries 1976).

The fluyt ship was the first specialized merchant vessel produced and used extensively in Europe (de Vries 1976). Because it was not armed, its use was most effective in waters free of piracy; but even in areas which were not so fortunate, the fluyt proved to be very successful. In the Mediterranean and in the Caribbean, where piracy was rife for much of the early modern period, the fluyts were sent in convoy protected by armed vessels and were thus cheaper to employ than a convoy of individually armed merchant ships. Though the fluyt was designed primarily for bulk cargo, it nevertheless proved adaptable for shipping any kind of good.

Without doubt, the fluyt broadened the scope for long-distance shipping in the early modern period and confirmed the predominant role of the Dutch in European trade; but its role was mainly as an agent of the profound changes which were occurring in the nature of Europe's commercial life. In the first place, as the Portuguese and the Spanish pursued an active overseas trade, they were increasingly drawn into the commercial orbit of northern Europe, first centred on Antwerp and then on Amsterdam. There the products of the east and the silver from the New World were exchanged for Baltic grain and bulk goods, central European metal products and manufactured goods and raw materials from western and northern Europe. So efficient was the Amsterdam market particularly in exchange and distribution, that it quickly came to dominate Europe's commercial system. Financial institutions proliferated as merchants from all over Europe chose to settle accounts in the city; the Amsterdam price lists became the most valued source of market information, and before long, speculative markets in commodities and shares developed (Aymard 1982; Smith 1984). As for the Mediterranean, the Dutch were instrumental in opening the region to regular northern shipping. Beginning with the shipment of Baltic grain to Leghorn in the 1590s to alleviate the agricultural crisis on the Italian mainland, by the early seventeenth century, the Dutch were sending annually hundreds of ships of all kinds, including fluyts to the Mediterranean. The English were not far behind, and before too long, northern ships were common in Mediterranean waters (Rapp 1975).

Certainly by the middle of the seventeenth century, no significant part of western Europe developed in isolation from the rest. Trade routes, offering low rates of carriage, connected one region to another, whether by sea or by land (de Vries 1978). Apart from the changes in shipping technology which allowed direct and regular maritime contact around European shores, the development of international commercial centres linking various regional and international economies played a crucial role in integrating the European economy. Although commercial centres of this kind had appeared before – Venice, Antwerp and Genoa have typically been assigned this role for the period before the seventeenth century – at the beginning of the seventeenth century, Amsterdam assumed dominance over international commerce and finance (Braudel 1984). As one recent study has shown, Amsterdam's critical role in the development of European capitalism was the result of its ability to provide market information accurately, efficiently and cheaply (Smith 1984). The city buzzed with information – any merchant wishing to find the best market and likely prices for goods could do no better than avail himself of Amsterdam's facilities. Even the English East India Company, despite having excellent souces of information itself, used Amsterdam's information networks. Amsterdam's position lasted until well into the eighteenth century. While there is no doubt that London became the dominant commercial centre in the nineteenth century, it would be misleading to single London out and dismiss other important centres. London functioned as an international commercial centre of the kind earlier exemplified by Amsterdam, but the enormous commercial and industrial region which had developed in the heartland of western Europe during the nineteenth century (an area bounded by Paris, Hamburg and Milan) required the operation of several centres to fulfil many of the functions carried out by London (Wrigley 1967; Crouzet 1964; Braudel 1984; Hohenberg and Lees 1985; de Vries 1984).

Market integration means, above all, that prices of both traded and non-traded goods move in unison. While we know little about the latter, it is clear that for a wide range of goods, the move towards market integration was a feature of the period under discussion. Not only had this been achieved by the staples of intercontinental trade before the nineteenth century, namely sugar and tobacco, but also by a wide range of goods traded within Europe. Available price data show quite clearly the high positive correlation between changes in prices in different centres of production. The point has already been made in Chapter 1 for the grain market, but the same applied to manufactured goods (Braudel and Spooner 1967).

If markets became integrated, the same was true for the financial system. Within Europe, by the beginning of the seventeenth century, there was little recourse to payment with bullion. The instruments for multilateral payments, namely, the bill of exchange, deposit banks and credit schemes, were well advanced, with several centres of exchange in Europe (for more details on financial techniques see Sperling 1962; Parker 1974; Riley 1980). With the emergence of Amsterdam, the process was centralized. By 1700, multilateral payments were extensive throughout Europe. Bullion hardly flowed within Europe except on its way to the Baltic, the Levant and Asia. By 1850, even that flow had been checked and international payments for all goods from most of the globe were handled by the instruments of modern finance.

During the nineteenth century, the process of integration continued though it was now on a wholly different scale (Foreman-Peck 1983; McInnis 1986). In the first place, integration was furthered by improvements in transport, especially the building and extension of the railways system throughout Europe as well as in other continents. Maritime transport was also improved, particularly by the introduction of steam-shipping for both ocean as well as river navigation. Ocean steam-shipping resulted in a vast decrease in the time and cost of travel whereas river steam-boating allowed many previously impenetrable areas to be opened up, especially to European exploitation. In addition, after 1870, the opening of the Suez canal – which radically reduced shipping distances from west to east – together with the introduction of the telegraph brought about a revolution in communication (Headrick 1981).

Secondly, and partly because of the improvements in transport and communications, markets in a range of commodities previously regionally bound became integrated. This was especially true of the great raw materials of the nineteenth century – cotton, wool and iron – but was no less true for food products – wheat and rice – and other industrial raw materials such as wood and rubber (Wright 1971; Latham and Neal 1983; Latham 1986; Lindblad 1986).

Finally, the vast migration of European labour and capital to North and South America, to Australia, New Zealand and to the European colonies stimulated the process of integration. It is no coincidence that an international market in raw wool developed only after Australia, South Africa and Argentina received massive in-migration in the nineteenth century (Denoon 1983).

It is necessary, therefore, to understand the development of industrial Europe in the long term not only in its international context, but also in its functional relationship with the commercial system. After all, industrial Europe progressed within the emergence of a world economy which over time became increasingly dominated by Europe's industrial prowess. The next section of the book will concentrate on those changes internal to industry which made it possible for European industry to reap the greatest benefit from the commercial and financial changes around it.

Further Reading

Braudel, F. 1981–84: *Civilisation and capitalism 15th–18th century*. 3 volumes. London: Collins.

Crosby, A. W. 1986: *Ecological imperialism*. Cambridge: Cambridge University Press.

Curtin, P. D. 1985: *Cross-cultural trade in world history*. Cambridge: Cambridge University Press.

Emmer, P. C. (ed.) 1986: *Colonialism and migration*. Dordrecht: Martinus Nijhoff.

Jones, E. L. 1987: *The European miracle*, 2nd edition. Cambridge: Cambridge University Press.

Parker, W. N. 1984: *Europe, America and the wider world. Volume I. Europe and the world economy*. Cambridge: Cambridge University Press.

Rowling, N. 1987: *Commodities*. London: Free Association Books.

Stavrianos, L. S. 1981: *Global rift: the third world comes of age*. New York: Morrow.

Wolf, T. E. 1982: *Europe and the people without history*. Berkeley: University of California Press.

Part II
Internal Dynamics

Introduction

Between the seventeenth and early twentieth century, the economic contexts within which European industry developed were profoundly transformed. Throughout the world, many economies and societies were drawn into a progressively European-centred economic system. Mass migration of people, crops, animals and capital reinforced European dominance. At the same time, within Europe itself, fundamental social and political changes gave rise to economic interests dominated by an urban-industrial complex which could command the resources of Europe as well as those in other distant economies.

During this same period, the nature of European industry, in all of its various facets, also experienced profound changes. In industrial organization, for example, small-scale, home-based and dispersed production, typical of the early seventeenth century gave way, by 1914, to large-scale factory based and highly concentrated forms of production. The technology of industrial production was similarly transformed. At the beginning of the seventeenth century, the majority of production techniques were relatively simple and inexpensive; by 1914, the technology of most industrial production was highly complex and well beyond the resources of individuals. Invention and innovation had, by then, become, an industrial activity in its own right and many of the leading firms especially in the science-based industries produced inventions as part of their industrial processes. At the same time, the nature of labour itself was changing profoundly. Not only did workers forfeit their ownership of the means of production, but within the labour force new divisions were emerging, the most important of which was a growing differentiation according to skill and gender.

It is common to understand these critical changes in terms of the transition from one set of dominant industrial organizations, techniques and division of labour to another. It is misleading, however, to view these transitions as unilinear and inevitable or natural processes. The factory was not, for example, the only possible response to problems encountered within the domestic system of production. Some industrial activities adopted factory methods very quickly while others were very slow to change; and for some industries in the nineteenth century, where factory methods were inappropriate, other paths of industrial change were followed. Technological change did not involve a straightforward transition from simple to complex, and the changes themselves were not always related to changes in industrial organization. Some techniques of production were clearly more appropriate in one manufacturing system than another. A similar complex pattern of change is evident in the history of the division of labour.

The chapters that follow emphasize the complex nature of the changes experienced by European industry. The primary objective is to portray the pattern of industrial development as a complicated system encompassing many seemingly contradictory forces of change. Each chapter pursues a different aspect of the internal transformations of European industry. The first highlights the numerous ways in which Europe's industrial production was organized at various times between the seventeenth and early twentieth centuries. The next chapter considers the nature of the technical aspects of production, focusing on the processes of innovation and diffusion. The final chapter in Part II discusses the nature of skill and gender in the transformation of European industrial labour.

3 Organizations of Production and Business

Until recently, a linear view of the development of organizational forms of production in European industry was generally accepted. A progression from the small-scale and dispersed workshop and putting-out system in both urban and rural areas to the large-scale centralized units of production, whereby the latter replaced the former, was believed to have been the case. A more sophisticated level of understanding was reached with the introduction of the concept of protoindustrialization, which provided the means to explain and understand the transition from pre-industrial to modern industrial forms of production. Despite its importance and originality, the protoindustrial model has not deviated from the notion of organizational change as essentially a linear, unidirectional process. It ignores the possibility that development could take several routes (which is most clearly illustrated in Sabel and Zeitlin 1985; Tilly 1983). This chapter will examine the various forms of industrial organization that existed during the period 1600–1914, and will consider particularly the ways in which these forms related to and supported each other.

The question that has taxed the minds of generations of historians, that is, why a fundamental shift took place from the pre-industrial to the factory form of production, will not be evaded, but the focus of it will be less direct. There is no doubt that the factory became a more common form of industrial enterprise from the late eighteenth century, but even where its diffusion had been most rapid, it had not superseded other types of production by the early twentieth century (Sabel and Zeitlin 1985; Sewell 1980). The question, therefore, becomes less why the factory *replaced* earlier forms than why it very gradually assumed greater quantitative importance; and why, in the context of rapid industrial growth and structural change in the European economies, the vitality of the small-scale enterprises persisted. Clearly, the sluggish and incomplete diffusion of the factory indicated the existence of a number of equally valid and viable routes to industrial expansion (Berg 1985).Industrial enterprises throughout the period from 1600–1914 took quite distinct forms in different industries, and even late in the nineteenth century, European industrial growth was rooted in a rich vein of small-scale enterprise. Skill and craft were still crucial to a number of industries. Steam power and hand technology happily coexisted and innovations in power sources and transmission continually breathed new life into struggling forms of industrial organization. Different forms of production reinforced each other and the overall structure was impressively flexible (as illustrated in the work of Aminzade 1984; Samuel 1977; Sabel and Zeitlin 1985).

Early Modern Industry

In 1600, industrial production was closely tied to agricultural production and commercial and trading activity. Economic activity was not always easily categorized. In the towns and cities, mercantile houses influenced the nature and structure of industrial production and in many instances resembled them (Hicks 1969); in the countryside, though the urban merchants often controlled manufacture, production was largely determined by the vagaries of the agricultural sector. Within these constraints, however, rural industrial production was highly flexible as the labour force was neither highly skilled nor subject to any form of regulation. Thus fluctuations in the supply of raw materials and the demand for finished products could be accommodated quite easily (Pounds 1979). In the towns, however, industrial production was more dependent upon a skilled labour force which was often bound to stringent regulations. Nevertheless, events in the early modern period, such as political upheavals causing mass migrations, or demographic disasters, ensured that even in the towns, the range, quality and quantity of industrial output underwent frequent changes.

By 1600, after more than a century of expansion, European industry seemed to be consolidated into a clear pattern (Sella 1974). From Ghent in the north to Florence in the south, Europe's major industrial cities dominated the industrial landscape. These cities had been in the vanguard of Europe's industrial expansion since the early Middle Ages and their position was strengthened particularly during the expansionary sixteenth century, often in concert with Europe's commercial achievements both abroad and at home. These cities also provided the necessary commercial activities to market the output (Tilly 1983). Commerce and industry were deeply intertwined: the important ports of Venice, Genoa, Antwerp, Amsterdam and London, for example, supported considerable industrial activity (Hohenberg and Lees 1985). The close association between commerce and industry was partly the result of specific historical conditions under which both sectors developed in the Middle Ages and partly because of the similarity of the two sectors in economic terms.

With some notable exceptions, industrial activity concentrated on textile production, of which woollen and worsted cloth was by far the most important and was produced almost everywhere. There was, nevertheless, a high level of specialization and the range of woollen and worsted goods produced was enormous. Cities jealously guarded their output, and strictly controlled their monopoly of a particular design, colour or texture (Sella 1974). Silk, linen and cotton cloth, by contrast, tended to be regional specialties: silk and cotton were produced mainly in the south of Europe, while linen was concentrated in the centre and the north (Pounds 1979; Goodman 1977).

In almost all of the major centres of textile production in Europe, the organization of production known as the putting-out system, which was described in the Introduction, predominated. What needs to be emphasized here is that in this system the ownership of the factors of production and some of the risks involved in production for the market were shared between the putter-out and the worker. The merchant-entrepreneur provided organizational and marketing skills and usually owned the raw materials, the finished goods and the warehousing facilities. The worker owned the means of production, that is, the tools, such as spinning wheels, looms and combs and ancillary items concerned with production, and, of course, provided the labour. The putting-out system was not simple, however, either in its organization or in its operation, and it could become very complicated as the size of the enterprise increased. Some putting-out firms organized several hundred workers, in which case the merchant-entrepreneur might employ assistants to manage the internal affairs of the concern – such as buying, selling, paying wages, stockkeeping, bookkeeping, as well as distributing the raw materials and goods in progress, and collecting the final manufactured items (de Roover 1974; Parker 1974; Supple 1977). It is clear that while putting-out might be a simple system, the complexity of the organizational structure should not be underrated, nor should the sophistication of business organization be unrecognized (de Roover 1974; Goodman 1977). Two examples from Florence, the wool and silk industries, illustrate the complex structure typical of large urban putting-out enterprises in seventeenth-century Europe. Production in the woollen industry, which had been organized for some time on the basis of putting-out, was broken down into roughly five major processes, incorporating a total of 26 distinct stages. Each step was organized in a slightly different way. The initial washing procedure, for instance, was generally subcontracted by factors, who hired the labourers, distributed and supervised work and paid the workers wages from their own remuneration (de Roover 1974). The spinning stage of production was a time-consuming process which required a considerable degree of skill, and was usually undertaken by country women as a by-occupation. The factors were again responsible for organizing the work. They travelled through the villages around Florence to deliver combed or carded wool to the spinners and to collect the yarn after it was spun. The factors were paid per pound of wool to be spun and they, in turn, paid the spinners. The important weaving stage of production was usually supervised by the cloth manufacturer. The weavers typically worked in their own homes and were paid piece-rates which varied according to the type and quality of the cloth. The finishing process required a large number of steps including fulling, which was done by small masters, and stretching and tentering, which was carried out in large units. Most of the other finishers were skilled artisans who worked at home or in small establishments, and who were typically employed by manufacturers and remunerated on a piece-rate basis. In this system, the woollen manufacturer was not simply a producer, nor simply in charge of the production process, but also performed a wide range of commercial functions, such as buying, selling and marketing (de Roover 1974).

 The pivot of the Florentine silk industry was a highly centralized business unit, which differed from the putting-out system in other activities, where individual merchants put out work and made production decisions. The central unit was a shop and warehouse and a managerial centre; in other words, it was a firm, which was headed by a silk manufacturer who was an owner or part owner, and who was ultimately responsible for the liabilities of the firm which could not be covered by its assets (Goodman 1977).

The next rung of the organizational structure consisted of the managers, who directed the production process and decided on the purchases of raw materials and the output mix. Sometimes managers acted as cashiers and bookkeepers, but generally such tasks were undertaken by others. Next came the managerial assistants, whose task it was to police the putting-out of work, checking that no loss occurred, and overseeing the stockkeeping. As in the woollen industry, the intermediate link between the firm and the silk workers was formed by the factors. The factors were responsible for putting out work to the winders, throwsters, weavers and other labourers who were located in and around the town. As with wool, the silk firm took charge of the commercial as well as the production side of the industry. It purchased raw materials and sold finished cloths and was therefore responsible for locating sources of raw materials and for finding final markets (Goodman 1977).

These two Florentine examples reflect a sophisticated business organization which, while not typical of European manufacturing as a whole, nevertheless indicated a structure not unusual in the textile industries of large urban centres in Europe from around the seventeenth century.

Above the productive system in the town stood the guild, an institution originating in the urban revival of the Middle Ages and still evident during this period (MacKenney 1987). The power as well as the functions of the guilds varied considerably across Europe, but in general, contrary to some exaggerated claims, the guild as an economic institution was, in the seventeenth century, a shadow of its former self. The guild no longer determined the quantity of the industry's annual output. Production levels in the early modern period were tied directly to the requirements of the market, rather than to the arbitrary rule of guild officials bent upon restricting output in order to maintain high prices (Deyon and Lottin 1967; Goodman 1977; MacKenney 1987).

Furthermore, while the guild continued to enforce an apprenticeship system which not only restricted entry into the trade but also perpetuated a rigid hierarchical system, the possibilities for evading this dictat changed dramatically (Cipolla 1976). Because guilds did not normally consider women as eligible for apprenticeship, nor had jurisdiction beyond the city walls, merchant-entrepreneurs could avoid any labour-suppy bottleneck created by the guilds by employing women or workers in the countryside (Brown and Goodman 1980; Poni 1985). Finally, the control of the guilds weakened as membership became removed from the main decision-making group as merchants, rather than artisan masters, took charge of the important parts of the productive system (Kriedte, Medick and Schlumbohm 1981).

The extent to which the guild could or did influence the nature of the work process in the seventeenth century is not entirely clear. Transgressions by the work force, such as embezzlement, theft or fraud were, in principle, open to action by the guild authorities, but, in practice, the role of the guild was ambiguous. Clearly, in an organization in which manufacturing was dispersed and over which there was no direct supervision by the owners, the possibilities of influencing the work process both by owners and guild authorities were restricted. If institutional means of control were limited, there were nevertheless, indirect yet effective ways in which the merchant-entrepreneur could guarantee the quality if not the quantity of their output (Goodman 1981).

Recent research has clearly demonstrated the precarious nature of the early modern demographic experience. In particular, cities were crucially dependent upon in-migration to maintain and increase population levels (de Vries 1984; Sharlin 1978; Hohenberg and Lees 1985). Employment opportunities were limited in the urban centres and because of the pool of immigrants from the rural areas, the potential labour supply regularly exceeded the demand for labour. There was, therefore, constant pressure on the work force to accede to the demands placed upon them by their employers. In the industrial cities, where most of the working population was employed in textile manufacturing, bad workmanship or failure to meet the quality requirements of the employer bore huge penalties. Not only was employment terminated, with little chance of locating similar work elsewhere, but also the worker could be forced to dispose of the tools of the trade at very low prices (Goodman 1981).

While the merchant-entrepreneur could exert considerable control over the work force, neither he nor the urban authorities wished to shed labour especially if it would lead to migration from the city. Labour not only owned the means of production but also possessed the skill required to use this in production. The latter was much more significant as the tools themselves were relatively cheap. A loom, for example, could be purchased for the equivalent of six months' wages of the average weaver; spinning wheels were even cheaper. The migration of skilled labour, therefore, was discouraged, except in cases of serious misdemeanours (Hohenberg and Lees 1985).

Demographic conditions, therefore, ensured that the relationship between labour and employer was often very delicately balanced. The merchant-entrepreneur was able to impose sanctions, and where in-migration from rural areas was plentiful, would do so if necessary: but at the same time, skilled labour was a valuable resource to be retained if at all possible. Throughout the seventeenth century, however, conditions for both labour and employer were unusually unstable; and because of the inevitable loss of some skilled workers caused by plague and other epidemic diseases, shifts in the quality and quantity of output were unavoidable. From the point of view of the long-term industrial development of Europe, the migration of skilled labour aided the even distribution of skill throughout the continent and Britain; and the striking examples of mass migrations (of which there were several during the period) transferred the entire skill embodied in one city or region to another (Scoville 1951). The English cloth industry, for example, benefited from the emigration of Flemish weavers; and many parts of Europe, notably Holland, England and Prussia, were quick to offer refuge to the Huguenots and to assimilate their skills in silk production and in clock and precision instrument making (Cipolla 1972; Scoville 1951; Coleman 1969).

The problems inherent in the workings of the urban labour market were only partially overcome in the early modern period. The guild system in particular which had served the useful functions of preserving standards of skill and quality and organizing the training of apprentices, was increasingly accused of hindering progress (MacKenney 1987; Quataert 1985). There is no doubt that the guilds were resistant to change and, particularly, they inhibited the adoption of new techniques and commodities. The guild's loss of power to the merchant capitalist was a protracted process, spanning much of the seventeenth and eighteenth centuries (de Vries 1976). Before the guilds were legally abolished, some attempts were made to amalgamate several crafts and to reduce the supervision of production while retaining the enforcement of apprenticeship, but it was too late to prevent the inevitable growth of manufacturing activity in the countryside (Kellenbenz 1977). In some specialized industries, vestiges of guild influence remained even after abolition of guild privileges in the late eighteenth century (Sewell 1980). Entry to urban industries which embodied high levels of craft or artistry and which required scrupulously trained labour remained strictly controlled with rigid apprenticeship requirements (Cipolla 1976; DuPlessis and Howell 1982; Sonenscher 1987). For the rest, however, especially the basic textile and metal trades, town merchants increasingly sought out cheap country labour. Rural industries flourished as former guild workers found their jobs disappearing (Clarkson 1985).

Industry in the Countryside

Probably the most dynamic form of industrial organization in seventeenth and eighteenth-century Europe was the rural putting-out system, variously referred to as the domestic system, cottage industry and, more recently, protoindustry. Although the systems of production so described are not identical, the terms are effectively employed interchangeably. Protoindustry or protoindustrialization are novel terms used more as conceptual tools than as simple description. While the structure of industrial organization which forms the basis of the proto-industrial viewpoint may also be described as rural putting-out industry, it is the dynamism of the system that is used to understand or analyse the route to factory industry and/or full-blown industrial capitalism (Aminzade 1984). The protoindustrial model, therefore, correctly emphasizes the dynamism of rural industrial production from 1600, but wrongly perceives a linear progression, in terms of industrial organization, from pre-industrial to industrial forms via protoindustry, and a virtually complete replacement of one system by another (Clarkson 1985). In fact, the expansion of industrial output between 1600 and 1914 was achieved by a continuous complexity of industrial forms that interacted and gave rise to an intricate industrial structure (Tilly 1983). This is not to say that all systems were equally efficient or possessed similar long-term potential. Some were clearly more dynamic than others, but each satisfied the requirements of different industries.

Just as urban industry frequently fulfilled the needs of commerce and trade, so rural industry interacted with agriculture and responded to seasonal limitations imposed by it. Urban industrial activity was longer established than rural industry but was relatively static in size. Urban industry concentrated on the production of high-quality luxury items, while rural industry mainly produced basic consumer goods, especially textile products and metal goods for which internal and external demand was substantial (Kriedte, Medick and Schlumbohm 1981; Clarkson 1985; Poni 1985; Goodman 1977). While many of the urban handicraft centres of Europe remained or re-established themselves as important locations of industry through the nineteenth century and into the twentieth century because of the coexistence of skills and the tradition of industrial work, it was rural industry that provided the locus of expansionary industrial forces combining market opportunities abroad with cheap rural labour (Kriedte, Medick and Schlumbohm 1981).

Rural manufacture was organized in a variety of ways, but the putting-out system was typical. The labour force often comprised entire families, working at home and organizing their industrial work around the requirements of their agricultural occupations. A clear sexual division of labour existed within the household for both agricultural and industrial occupations. The male family members were typically more fully employed in farming than the women, who performed the bulk of the industrial work (and helped with the harvest) and specialized in specific kinds of tasks, such as spinning in textile manufacture (Gullickson 1986). The workers performed various processing procedures on the material using rudimentary technology that they themselves owned. Because the preparatory and finishing stages of textile production were generally completed in the town under the supervision of the merchant, the rural workers concentrated on spinning and weaving. The merchant putter-out was very often, but not necessarily, urban-based and had access to substantial markets both locally and overseas (Kriedte, Medick and Schlumbohm 1981).

Concentrations of rural industry were to be found throughout Europe, but especially in the north and west and around large cities. Rural industry has also been associated with poor agricultural land, and while the extent of this has been exaggerated, manufacturing was frequently located in hilly areas with sparse vegetation. Rural industry was spread across Europe, but only a small number of regions contained substantial concentrations; and these foremost producing areas commonly combined textile and metal manufacturing (Pollard 1981). The Sambre-Meuse region in Belgium, for instance, combined woollen production, especially around Verviers, with nail-making in the Liège environs (Gutmann and Leboutte 1984). Silesia produced both linen and coal, and the Nord region of France combined the manufacture of cotton, linen and wool with coal production (Pounds 1979). Other significant rural industrial regions included the Saxon uplands and Lusatia, whose economy grew on the basis of textile and mineral production, and the Siegerland (metals) and the Wupper valley which contained diverse textile manufacturing industries (Pollard 1981); Brittany, Picardy and the Lyonnais in France where textiles of all kinds were made; Catalonia and Lombardy where similar specialization in textile manufacture prevailed (Pounds 1979, 1985).

While industry was attracted to these regions by the availability of resources and good communications, other factors played an important part. Sometimes rural industry revitalized areas of large populations existing on the product of poor or indifferent land. A non-farming activity was needed to offset the cost of the importation of food and other primary produce and manufacturing activity evolved. It has been argued that it was the agriculturally disadvantaged regions that became the major locations of rural industry (Clarkson 1985). This was not necessarily the case, however, and the common feature was, rather a large landless or land-poor population, which could exist even in very fertile regions if, for instance, land was rented out in large plots. The need for supplementary income, therefore, was particularly acute in areas with underemployed or seasonally unemployed labour, which might result from population growth, partible inheritance, subdivision of leaseholds or the concentration of land in a few hands. It was this inability of inhabitants to earn sufficient income that was critical to the emergence of rural industry; and this was caused by inadequate employment, which could exist equally in marginal agricultural regions and in fertile pastoral regions (Gullickson 1983).

Some industrial regions emerged to satisfy the requirements of urban merchants; and there is substantial evidence to illustrate the interaction of town and country and the complementarity of urban and rural needs (Gullickson 1986; Hohenberg and Lees 1985). In the Caux region of Normandy, for example, manufacturing developed because it was close to Rouen, and because the town merchants did not have sufficient workers. In the surrounding countryside there were plenty of female peasants seeking non-harvest employment, but who were depended upon by the farmers at harvest time. The establishment of manufacturing in the Caux was thus to the mutual benefit of all concerned: the Rouen merchants gained access to a cheap source of labour; the peasant women were able to increase their income through full-time employment; and the farmers retained their harvest workers without fear that they might migrate to full-time urban industrial employment. The nature of the gender division of labour in agricultural and textile manufacturing emphasized the compatibility of the two production systems. Weaving, a male trade, was performed by the skilled urban workers. The spinning process, which required 10 times as many workers, was a female specialism and the large pool of women labourers necessary for the Rouen weavers was located in the countryside. In the rural areas, therefore, the vast majority of husbands and wives worked at completely unrelated tasks except at harvest time. This system continued to operate until the mid-nineteenth century, except that early in the nineteenth century women also took over the weaving from the urban workers (Gullickson 1986).

Other regions of dense rural industry, in the north of England, Flanders and South Germany, for example, emerged because of growing problems in agriculture. For example, underemployment and inadequate agricultural income, together with an expansion in national and international demand commonly led to an intense increase in the demand for cheap industrial labour. In these regions, the merchant capitalist chose to expand industrial production by increasingly utilizing underexploited rural resources, especially labour (Kriedte, Medick and Schlumbohm 1981; Berg, Hudson and Sonenscher 1983; Clarkson 1985).

In almost every region of rural industry in seventeenth and eighteenth-century Europe, manufacturing provided a lasting solution to problems in both town and countryside and in both industry and agriculture. Its ability to fit into existing systems of production and to permit the widespread expansion of industrial output was a reflection of its dynamism and durability. The development of rural industry further stimulated regional specialization; and during the seventeenth and eighteenth centuries, the expansion of rural industrial activities in some areas required importation of food and industrial raw materials from specialist agricultural regions. East of the Elbe, for example, cereal monoculture dominated the fertile plains and restricted rural industrial production to the remote mountain zones of east-central Europe (Kriedte, Medick and Schlumbohm 1981).

Thus, as we have shown, industrial expansion in Europe, especially between 1600 and 1800 was located primarily in agricultural regions with easy access to local urban or international markets. Rural industry was not simply a pale anticipation of modern industry and not just a supplement to agriculture. It was a powerful and enduring system with its own logic. In most regions it did not disappear with the emergence of large-scale manufacturing, but coexisted and effectively competed with it (Pounds 1985; Sabel and Zeitlin 1985).

Manufacturing production in the countryside played a crucial role in the long-term development of European industry, and there is no doubt that for 200 years after 1650, industrial output expanded rapidly through the multiplication of small producing units and a modest accumulation of capital. As networks of producers and merchants proliferated, the structure of trade altered and large industrial regions came to life (Tilly 1983). Europe had industrialized significantly before 1800, mainly through the employment of underutilized rural labour, as well as female urban labour. The bulk of the industrial labour force was located near the sources of relatively cheap food. This labour was naturally cheaper than that of urban craftsmen who were forced to buy more expensive food from the market. It was nevertheless the urban merchants who played a fundamental part in creating and sustaining the system; and such capital-intensive branches of production that did exist remained in the cities (Tilly 1983).

Large-Scale Production before the Factory

Large-scale units of manufacturing production were not unheard of before the late eighteenth or early nineteenth century; and when special knowledge and technical ability were required an entrepreneur might concentrate the various processes of production under one roof and thereby create a factory. The production of some textile commodities was, from early on, well suited to factory organization. Calico printing, for example, developed in concentrated units at the end of the seventeenth century in England and Holland and then spread to Switzerland, Augsburg and Saxony. Woollen and silk mills, likewise, developed early and diffused widely. For some commodities where technical requirements were great, in metal production, for example, there was a tendency to centralization where labour was attracted to the physical means of production (Kellenbenz 1977). Some other industries, particularly ships, printing presses, carpets and glass had a very specialized form of centralized manufacture and the majority of them were distinguished from later developments by their dependence on state support. European governments were particularly supportive of industries producing arms and munitions and luxury consumption items. Few examples exist of large-scale centralized industrial enterprises succeeding on their own. The presence of exceptional factors was required to circumvent failure; either a very large guaranteed market, as costly marketing was a principal limitation to scale; or propitious geographical conditions; or most commonly, government support (Supple 1977).

The structure of large industrial enterprises in Europe before the advent of the steam-powered factory varied considerably, the different types fitting into three broad categories. Large urban workshops, sometimes referred to as manufactories, form the first category. These were typically to be found in the textile industry and were organized by the commercial capitalist for the purpose of preparing or finishing the work of rural domestic labourers (Kellenbenz 1977). From the seventeenth century, the merchants increasingly employed direct-wage urban labour in their own premises in order to achieve control over the quality of the product. These centralized workshops frequently housed the operation of several small units, but in fact contained nothing that was technically nor organizationally novel. Exceptionally, these central workshops reached extensive proportions: the Linz woollen manufactory, for instance, housed 102 dyers and finishers in 1786; and in Berlin, the Lagerhaus employed, in 1782, about 400 assorted workers including scribblers, dyers, pressers, fullers and washers (Pollard 1981).

In the second category, large-scale operations were determined or influenced by the technical and/or economic needs of particular industries. Shipyards, most notably the Chatham docks, the Dutch shipyards and the Venetian Arsenal were found in this category as were refineries, iron works, sugar and tobacco processing and ceramics (Pollard 1981). Because these industries frequently depended upon government or Crown support, they are also located in the third category, which comprises industries maintained and often initiated by the State. The majority of large-scale enterprises in Europe before the nineteenth century experienced very large state subsidies as well as heavy state control, and were typically referred to as Royal Factories or Royal Manufactories (Kellenbenz 1977; Supple 1977; Pollard 1981).

Most European states in the seventeenth and eighteenth centuries were guided by a mercantilist impetus and, for a variety of reasons – notably the desire for conspicuous consumption or strong defences, or to respond to the demands of growth and competition – they supported industrial enterprises with tax relief, loans, subsidies and bounties. In France, the strongest influence came from Colbert, who systematically encouraged and coordinated industry and stimulated entrepreneurship. Sometimes the State took over an existing company, as was the case with the Gobelins; but most often Royal Manufactories were private concerns which were judged important for the prosperity of the Kingdom and which received financial support and exclusive privileges prohibiting any competition in the production or sale of goods. Between 1683 and 1753, 1000 new ordinances were granted in France (Deyon and Guignet 1980); and although the new Royal Manufactories remained overwhelmingly concerned with textiles – especially wool – tapestry, glass, mirrors and crystal became increasingly important as did the arsenals of Brest, Toulon and Rochefort (Kellenbenz 1977). After 1753, the French lead in the production of luxury fabrics, notably lace, silk and tapestries was thought to be well established. As a result, private enterprises in these areas was encouraged to proceed independently of royal benefaction. At the same time, greater assistance was given to cotton spinning mills and to the non-textile commodities in order to imitate trends in English manufacturing. In France, therefore, State-directed industrial intervention can be interpreted as an attempt to respond to the demands of growth and competition. There is no doubt that government action helped to reverse the retarding influences of the guilds, stimulated private investment and encouraged individual enterprise and technical innovation. By the early nineteenth century, thanks partly to the State, French industry was virtually self-supporting (Deyon and Guignet 1980).

The aim of the Royal Factories in Spain was explicitly to stimulate economic growth in an attempt to reverse Spain's declining international position by encouraging the diffusion of technique and skill. This was to be achieved by reducing dependence on foreign suppliers by producing the kind of superior textile item that had previously been purchased from abroad. In fact, success was very limited, and more commonly, the Royal textile factories of Spain acted as barriers more than as aids to private enterprise. The management of the factories was placed in the hands of foreign artisans, and skilled labour was imported to make up for domestic deficiency. Thus imported factors of production replaced imported products; and despite being provided with the finest skills, the latest technology, and ample funds, the Royal mills were in continual deficit. The protection that these enterprises received from the Kings was such that management had little incentive to attempt change or become flexible and innovative; and when support for the mills and factories eventually disappeared, no private enterprise emerged to take its place (Clayburn La Force 1964a, b).

The Prussian Royal enterprises emerged in the eighteenth century. Frederick the Great was largely responsible for establishing royal iron works in upper Silesia, gold and silver works, and support to the silk industry (Pollard 1981). In Saxony, mining and metallurgy developed under the active patronage of Duke George; and in southern Germany, Duke Frederick of Württemberg encouraged the linen production of Vrach and the Calw cloth-printing factory (Kellenbenz 1977).

The extent and effectiveness of State factories varied, as did the degree to which private enterprise subsequently took over. Nevertheless, for much of the seventeenth and eighteenth centuries, the majority of large-scale centralized production units, and large trading companies also, required State financial support if they were to exist at all. Private individuals were as yet unwilling and unable to invest because costly concerns often involved partnerships with varying degrees of liability and enterprises producing commodities in the national interest or which required large-scale centralized production units were not, in the short-term at least, profit-making concerns.

The Factory Take-Over Bid?

Beginning in the mid-eighteenth century, factory production became more common and was typically controlled by private enterprise, independent of the State. The process of centralization of production had a number of characteristics which altered the shape of some European industries. Capital became concentrated; fixed capital, in the form of buildings and machinery, assumed a large proportion of total capital needs; the whole productive process came under the control of the capitalist; labour was centralized and subjected to greater discipline than previously; and this, together with a greater reliance on machines and motive power achieved a greater return on labour. To some extent, the concentrations of capital, labour and sources of power altered the location of industrial production, reduced the possibilities for by-employment and thus sometimes precipitated de-industrialization in Europe (Tilly 1983). Where the factory was adopted, specialization of production occurred, and industry, in the long term, both became confined to towns and cities and became radically separated from its rural origins. It should be emphasized, however, that while the factory became a viable and profitable form of organization for the production of some commodities, it was neither rapidly adopted, nor did it replace other types of production processes. Indeed, some of the earlier forms of industrial organization retained and strengthened their position during the nineteenth century under entirely different industrial conditions and dominant systems of production (Berg 1985; Samuel 1977; Sabel and Zeitlin 1985).

While technical innovations are frequently associated with industrial progress and the acceleration of the diffusion of factory production, this was only partially true. On the one hand, it was many years before the majority of industrial processes had been mechanized, and, on the other, it was perfectly possible for firms to exploit new technologies without becoming larger or changing their organizational structure in any significant way. This is not really surprising because, although it has been widely assumed that the factory was more efficient than the putting-out system, recent empirical research shows that, given an identical technology, putting-out was able to compete with the factory and, in many instances, was more economically efficient (Jones 1982). This section will illustrate the diversity of ways in which goods continued to be produced in Europe from the late eighteenth century. The traditional view that mechanization inevitably resulted in large-scale production (and the failure to become large-scale evidence of some structural weakness in the industrial system) is now seen to be untenable. It is essential to understand and appreciate the 'historical alternatives to mass production' (Sabel and Zeitlin 1985).

Within each of the textile industries, the spectrum of organizational forms that prevailed throughout the seventeenth and eighteenth centuries continued, albeit in a changed way, into the nineteenth century. Only some stages of a few of the textile industries relied on factory organization and mechanized power technologies by the middle of the nineteenth century; and many of the new technologies developed from the late eighteenth century could have been adopted, and to some extent were adopted across several systems of work organization. From the late eighteenth century, therefore, some textile manufactures moved into factory production, others remained little changed or found valid alternatives, while yet others experienced decline (Berg 1985; Pounds 1985).

The worsted industry, for example, moved from putting-out to factory production, while in its counterpart, wool, many transitional forms of organization, and not the factory, replaced artisanal methods in the first instance (Hudson 1981; Honeyman and Goodman 1986a). In the silk industry, a variety of organizations persisted. The transition to the factory system was slow, protracted and never encompassed all units of production (Pounds 1985). Sweated workshop conditions emerged particularly in London and several other large cities. In silk weaving, artisan traditions remained even though the technology of production was radically altered (Jones 1987). In linen, putting-out, artisan and factory production coexisted throughout the period (Berg 1985; Pounds 1985; Mendels 1972). While the cotton industry apparently gave rise to new forms of organization, the break with older forms was not as marked as might be assumed. Indeed the expansion of factory production was accompanied by an intensification of several pre-existing methods. The domestic system in the English cotton industry, for example, easily accommodated the small mule and jenny factories which appeared from the 1770s and 1780s. Even the substantial Arkwright-type mills closely interacted with small jenny and mule shops; and domestic weaving organized on the putting-out system remained an important adjunct until the 1840s (Berg 1985). What seemed to be happening in the European textile industries from the late eighteenth century, therefore, was a continuation of existing differences in manufacturing structures. There was very little evidence of a trend towards any single structure or organizational form.

The metal and hardware trades also continued to operate within a variety of business forms and changes in technique. Many metal industries remained organized on a workshop or family production principle throughout the nineteenth century, and adapted steam power and factory premises to the dictates of small-scale production. There developed a distinctive form of specialization and artisan skill within elaborate networks of small-scale production alongside large-scale works (Sabel and Zeitlin 1985; Berg 1985). In many hardware industries a workshop culture persisted with a high level of skill, a preponderance of urban manufacture and the endurance of small units of production. As had been the case since the seventeenth century, the higher-skilled activities continued to be concentrated in the towns with the lower-skilled tasks put out to rural labourers (Sabel and Zeitlin 1985; Berg 1985).

A recurring theme in the recent literature is that not only did a variety of organizational forms continue to be accommodated within the context of factory production, but further, that many earlier or alternative structures were enhanced by the requirements of centralized production. Mechanization in one department of production, for instance, was often complemented by an increase of sweating in others. The growth of the large firms often gave rise to a proliferation of small producing units. The concentration of production in factories was also associated with the spread of outwork, and the increase, at least in the short term, of the number of artisans (Samuel 1977). Rarely were any of these in direct competition. Machine construction, for example, stimulated a new category of prosperous artisans; the demands of factory building and transport could only be met by artisanal labour; and further, because the factories sometimes reduced the cost of raw materials of the artisans, the price of their finished product fell, which raised demand for their work (Sewell 1980, 1986).

The factory was thus a possible response to mechanization, but machines could also make handicraft labour more productive without impairing the skill; and indeed, many trades in the nineteenth century remained divided between machine and handicraft sections. Craft everywhere remained important; industry was dependent on the strength, skill, quickness and sureness of touch of the individual worker more than on the simultaneous and repetitive operations of the machine. The action of machinery was often crude, it was rarely self-acting; it was inflexible and could only be profitable in the context of large-scale production (Samuel 1977; Sabel and Zeitlin 1985). Although mechanization influenced many branches of European industry, there were very few areas where it ruled unchallenged. Many important trades remained labour intensive – notably, engineering, metalwork, clothing and furniture making – and industrial growth in Europe was clearly rooted in small-scale enterprises and remained so, throughout the nineteenth century (Sabel and Zeitlin 1985).

Urban Industrial Production in the Workshop

Perhaps the most striking feature of nineteenth-century European industrial development was the persistence and vitality of work organizations based on artisanal and craft workshop principles. This should not be surprising, because for many industries, a high level of artistry and craftsmanship was vital and could not be replicated by machine. Recent research has confirmed the importance of artisanal workshops in the process of industrialization, finding them to be efficient, dynamic and the most appropriate organizational form for the industries concerned.

Artisanal forms of production were reinforced or at least retained in European industry after 1800 in a variety of ways. Nineteenth-century industrial growth created a range of new trades, many of which – notably engineering, electrics and some chemicals – were best suited to small workshop production, or autonomous workshops within larger units of production using highly skilled artisanal labour. Within the luxury trades, such as jewellery, change was minimal: the market was too restricted to merit investment in new forms of production and labour was too skilled to be replicated by machine. Some potential for deskilling existed in those industries supplying the basic demands of the domestic population such as shoemaking, tailoring and furniture making, but where this did take place, it was typically achieved through a more complex division of labour than by the introduction of new machinery (Breuilly 1985). Most artisanal trades grew or adapted to the changing requirements of nineteenth-century industry; only in a few instances – hand-loom weaving is a case in point – were trades destroyed, though even here the process was protracted (Pounds 1985).

Throughout Europe, at least until the 1870s, and not unusually to 1900, workshop employment expanded. In Germany, for instance, growth was absolute during most of the nineteenth century, though workshop production did begin to decline as a proportion of total manufacturing after 1860. Significantly, the relative contraction was greatest in the least industrialized regions of Germany, with small workshops growing most substantially absolutely and relatively in the areas of major industrial development. In France, the rapid economic growth of the major cities of Paris, Lyons and others was marked by a rapid expansion of small workshops. Similar situations prevailed in England,

Russia and elsewhere (Breuilly 1985).

Although the urban workshop coexisted throughout the nineteenth century with larger-scale centralized units, it was in France that the prevalence of craft activity was most marked. It has been estimated that as late as 1850, 60 per cent of French industrial output came from small-scale household and handicraft production which, in turn employed three-quarters of the industrial labour force (Markovitch 1967). The strength and quality of artisan industry in France, which was influenced by the structure of domestic demand, was reflected in and subsequently reinforced by the French performance at the Great Exhibition of 1851. Most of the French exhibits were of crafted goods, receiving consistently high praise and winning many prizes. In textiles, the small-scale domestic operations of the French proved to be competitive with the more centralized British production techniques. In machine-building, likewise, although there were fewer exhibits to compare, the French product was as viable as the British. The experience of the Great Exhibition serves to emphasize that there were different but equally valid routes to industrial growth; and that cultural and social values influenced the broad structure of industrial organization. While the range of organizational forms in French and British industry was similar, there is little doubt that artisanal workshop production remained more pervasive in France. This was at least partly because manufacturers and consumers in France laid greater emphasis on high quality craftsmanship and within French exports luxury goods predominated. In Britain, the structure of exports was dominated by low-value, lower-quality basic commodities (Walton 1983).

The flexibility and dynamism of French handicraft production is illustrated by the changes that took place in the size of the handicraft industry and within the workshops as they adapted themselves to a different economic context. The growth of St Etienne in the nineteenth century, for example, was founded upon the proliferation of small units of handicraft metal and arms manufacture and especially of household silk-ribbon production (Aminzade 1984; Hanagan 1980; Schnetzler 1975). In 1872, silk workers remained by far the largest segment of the region's working class. The silk-ribbon weavers engaged in urban household production, with family labour sometimes supplemented by several journeymen and/or apprentices, and generally the trade was organized on the putting-out system. Merchant capitalists gradually increased the control over the work process by taking over the initial stages of the ribbon production process and by introducing new techniques. The new technology, such as the Jacquard loom, was still worked by hand and therefore did not transform the household organization of production, but the high cost of machinery increased the financial dependence of the household producers on merchant capitalists (Aminzade 1984; Gordon 1982).

In Toulouse in 1872 most of the industrial labour force (38 per cent of the total) were handicraft artisans employed mainly in the production of food, clothing and housing and remained predominantly based on small-scale units of handicraft production. The master artisan commonly possessed very small amounts of capital, the workshops were small and the tools were cheap and elementary. Factory production did develop later in the nineteenth century, but such factories were small and handicraft-based and within them, artisans continued to work much as before using the tools they owned. Both household and artisanal production retained their hold on Toulousian industry. This was achieved by enlarging the scale and pace of their operations and by inducing productivity gains through more extensive division of labour than by the growing use of machinery (Aminzade 1984).

The adaptation of artisanal trades to requirements of nineteenth-century industrial society was not always without loss. Sometimes artistic standards were compromised, and artisans generally perceived the factory as enforcing a separation of art and industry. Concern with artistry and fine craftsmanship was particularly marked along the Parisian cabinetmakers who, during the course of the nineteenth century, increasingly found themselves supplanted by semi-skilled furniture makers. From the ensuing artisanal struggle against proletarianization emerged the *trôleurs*, cabinetmakers who worked at home and then hawked the furniture they produced. Ironically, although designed to uphold artistic standards, the work of the *trôleurs* had become shoddy by the late nineteenth century (Weissbach 1982). Generally, the artistic decline was only gradual, and artisans in other luxury handicraft industries such as goldsmithing and ceramics believed that cultural values as well as social and economic considerations perpetuated the handicraft production of such items in France, and ensured that the introduction of new methods to produce cheaper imitations of crafted goods was a very protracted process. The producers of luxury items could generally meet the challenge of modern industry confident in the value of their products in the traditional handicraft work organization (Walton 1983).

Industries and processes that developed in the late nineteenth century both ensured the continuance of artisanal industry and forced further adaptations. Some revival of workshop production occurred because of the electrification and the growing demand for consumer goods. Several sectors of the chemical and automobile industries relied upon a skilled workforce in small-scale production. In metalworking, particularly, but in other industries too, artisans adapted to the perceived pressure of large-scale production by operating their workshops within factory premises. In these circumstances, metalworking artisans continued to behave as if in their own small shops with little effective discipline (Hanagan 1980). By 1914, however, pressure was building up in other areas for the replacement of artisans by less skilled workers, through novel worker–management relationships as well as novel technology largely imported from America.

The Sweating System

The threat to the artisan's position was also reflected in the growth of mechanized outwork which may be characterized by the sweating system. In all the major European cities, but especially in Paris, London, Berlin, Vienna and Hamburg, the organization of tailoring, dressmaking, shoemaking, furniture making and chain making was increasingly concentrated into a type of putting-out system, dominated by women and immigrants (Breuilly 1985; Boxer and Quataert 1987). Sweating meant long and tedious hours of labour, very low wages, and degrading and unhealthy surroundings. Work typically took place in unregulated premises, such as the worker's home, a basement or garret shop or a jerry-built workroom. No restrictions existed, which resulted in miserable and squalid conditions for the workers. Almost all sweated workers were outworkers, who collected their work from the employer's shop or factory and returned to the unregulated premises to complete their tasks. In many ways, this outwork or sweated production seems similar to the old putting-out system and this has been seen either as a remnant of the traditional system, or as an appendage of the new factory system. Like most other organizational forms, sweating expanded and adapted to the needs of the larger-scale centralized production (Schmiechen 1984; Dasey 1981).

In some areas of sweated work, in the London clothing industry for example, a symbiosis developed between the sweatshop and the factory. Employers might shift production back and forth between the factory and the home or small outwork shop (Schmiechen 1984). In the London and Parisian clothing trades, the growth of tailoring and dressmaking was the result of an insatiable demand for ready-wear, mass-produced clothing (Scott 1984). Technical innovations, particularly the sewing machine, facilitated this, but also compounded the pressure on the jobs of artisans. Machinery in this case caused an increase in sweating; and for employers who lacked capital and space, mechanized outwork allowed them to expand production without expanding facilities (Schmiechen 1984; Franzoi 1987). The sweated labour force was overwhelmingly female for a number of reasons. Firstly, sweated work was not immediately conspicuous and could be home-based, and, therefore, was not overtly inconsistent with prevailing social values that placed a premium on women's domestic duties. Furthermore, the seasonality and casual character of the work suited the irregularity of many women's lives and, anyway, incomes could be supplemented with harvest work in the nearby rural areas, as in the case of earlier industrial structures (Alexander 1983). The Paris flowermaking trade also illustrates a continuation of domestic industry or industrial homework as well as continuity in the pattern of women's lives, as through this occupation women were able to combine their productive work while fulfilling their roles in reproduction. The making of artificial flowers was an important segment of the ladies' garment trade. Large-scale production never emerged and most work was carried out in the homes of individual workers or in small workshops. There existed a very clear sexual division of labour whereby the men were responsible for the dyeing and cutting while women specialized in the shaping and branching that required more skill and dexterity (Boxer 1982).

The history of outwork and sweating, like that of artisanal trades, shows the generally accepted perception of discontinuity between the factory and the pre-factory stages of industrial growth to be an exaggeration. Indeed, the industrial transformation of the great European cities was characteristically expressed in the shop and sweated trades that resisted the factory throughout the nineteenth century. These trades were of central importance in the economy: they have been unjustly neglected by economic history because they represent neither dramatic growth nor decline.

Conclusion

This chapter has illustrated the variety of work organizations that persisted throughout the period 1600–1914. It has thus challenged the traditional view of industrial transformation in Europe which focuses upon a narrow view of organizational change with little consideration given to alternative paths. A number of directions were equally possible: within the field of technology, for instance, innovation did not necessarily imply complete mechanization; progress could be made in hand or intermediate techniques. In terms of work organization, new forms developed which emphasized decentralization, such as workshops and sweating – alongside the larger-scale and more striking factory forms. There was no necessary progression from any one form to another: there was choice and the final decision rested on a number of factors including the requirements of the individual industry as well as the economic, social and cultural context.

Further Reading

Berg, M., Hudson, P. and Sonenscher, M. (eds.) 1983: *Manufacture in town and country before the factory*. Cambridge: Cambridge University Press.

Clarkson, L. A. 1985: *Proto-industrialization: The first phase of industrialization?* London: Macmillan.

Hicks, J. 1969: *A theory of economic history*. Oxford: Oxford University Press.

Kriedte, P., Medick, H. and Schlumbohm, J. 1981: *Industrialization before industrialization. Rural industry in the genesis of capitalism*. Translated by Beate Schempp. Cambridge: Cambridge University Press. Paris: Editions de la Maison des Sciences de l'Homme.

MacKenney, R. 1987: *Tradesmen and traders: The world of the guilds in Venice and Europe c. 1250–c. 1650*. London: Croom Helm.

Pollard, S. 1981: *Peaceful Conquest. The industrialization of Europe 1760–1970*. Oxford: Oxford University Press.

Rich, E. E. and Wilson, C. H. (eds.) 1977: *The Cambridge economic history of Europe. Volume V. The economic organization of early modern Europe*. Cambridge: Cambridge University Press.

Samuel, R. 1977: Workshop of the world: Steam power and hand technology in mid-Victorian Britain. *History Workshop* 3, 6–72.

Schmiechen, J. A. 1984: *Sweated industries and sweated labour. The London clothing trades 1860–1914*. London: Croom Helm.

Tilley, C. 1983: Flows of capital and forms of industry in Europe, 1500–1900. *Theory and Society* 12, 123–42.

4 Technology and Knowledge

The preceding chapter has argued against a unilinear view of the development of industrial organization and business enterprise. One of the main arguments was that throughout the period from 1600 to 1914 different forms of industrial production not only coexisted but reinforced each other in the making of the industrial economy. Moreover, it was shown that important innovations in industrial organizations, such as the factory, were generally slow to diffuse and, in some key industries, remained entirely inappropriate. Even by 1914, there was little sign that the range of types of industrial organizations was diminishing and the new industrial activities of the late nineteenth and early twentieth centuries, such as chemicals, electricity, and automobiles, adopted the most appropriate and not necessarily the most 'progressive' organization of production.

Another and perhaps more important argument was that the history of industrial organization cannot be reduced simply to issues of relative efficiencies or changes in relative production and transaction costs. The organization of industrial production is essentially the organization of the labour process and is therefore as much a social construction as an economic and technical arrangement. The types and distribution of industrial organizations in the nineteenth century, for example, reflected the distribution of power in production – between capital and labour, between men and women and between the skilled and the unskilled. Any historical analysis of industrial organization must be based on these dialectical relationships and must be placed in the context of the social relations that bind the labour process.

Technology must also be seen in these terms. There are a multitude of approaches to the history of technology but essentially they fall into one of two groups: the first which views technology as an external force that impinges on society, determining events to which people and work must respond; and the second which views technology as part of the process of social and economic change (for a survey of approaches to the history of technology see Hughes 1979; MacKenzie 1984; Smith 1985a).

The most familiar approach to the history of technology is concerned overwhelmingly with cataloguing and explaining technical achievements. This approach is concerned not only with describing the details of technical artefacts, but also examing the processes of invention, innovation and the diffusion of technology. In most cases, technical change is conceived of in economic terms focusing on supply and demand and cost factors. Most accounts of the decisive inventions leading to the mechanization of handicraft production adopt the logic of economic reasoning. Whether seen in comparative perspective or over the long term, this approach to the history of technology assumes that specific economic challenges give rise to technical solutions (Landes 1969; Rosenberg 1976d).

The history of technology in this form is essentially progressive; that is, each new technical achievement is perceived as superior to previous achievements. Technologies which are adopted are successful because they are more efficient or productive than competing ones; and technologies which are not adopted, either at the drawing or prototype stage, are failures because they do not meet the criterion of commercial feasibility or efficiency. This approach also concedes that there is an inherent deterministic logic to the development of technology. Once set in motion, the onward progress of technology is self-determining (for critical assessments see MacKenzie and Wajcman 1985; Noble 1984). To take one historical example: the mechanization of cotton spinning in the latter part of the eighteenth century led inexorably to the mechanization of weaving as well as other preliminary processes of cotton production. The technical breakthroughs in the cotton industry stimulated similar developments in all other branches of textile production. The enormous increase in textile output that accompanied these breakthroughs also led to severe bottlenecks in ancillary industrial activities especially in the inorganic chemical industry. These pressures led to decisive technical achievements in producing bleaching agents and acids in vast quantities. In time, the pressures spilled over to the dyeing industry where towards the last quarter of the nineteenth century, remarkable advances were made in synthesizing the organic basis of specific dyes so that they could be produced commercially under industrial conditions.

In contrast to this external view of technology, the second generalized approach attempts to understand technology as an essential part of the process of social and economic change, as well as a product of it (for examples see MacKenzie and Wajcman 1985). In this analysis, technical achievements are considered within the context in which they operate, with particular emphasis on the workplace environment and the social relations within that environment. Technical change is also viewed in relation to the goals of those who have the power to choose particular technologies from an evolving range of possible techniques (MacKenzie 1984).

Most of the historians of technology who adopt the view that changes in the technology of industrial production are part of a larger social and economic process conclude that the history of technology cannot be isolated from the struggle which characterizes the social relations in production; and that technical change is the result of a complex and continual process of conflict, compromise and cooperation in the workplace and in the community. The capitalists' desire to minimize costs of production is seen as only one element in explaining technical change. Studies of this type have also broadened the institutional reference point for the development of technology to include, above all, the influence of the military and the state in sponsoring specific technologies which satisfy particular goals. The military, in particular, has been shown to foster technical innovation on criteria other than efficiency and commercial viability with the result that the economists' simple notion of choice of technique has had to be significantly modified (MacKenzie and Wajcman 1985; Smith 1985b; Noble 1984; McNeill 1983).

While the general contours of the development of European technology between 1600 and 1914 are fairly clear, there is little consensus about its general interpretation nor about its explanation. The purpose of this chapter is to present an outline of the general features of technical change, emphasizing points of continuity and discontinuity; and to offer insights into this process, by highlighting the relationship between technology, the labour process and the institutional environment.

The Direction of Technical Change

There is a strong tendency in most general accounts of the history of technology to provide a typology of the direction of technical change. The most familiar of these typologies maintains that the general drift of technical change between 1600 and 1914 was from the mechanical industries, particularly textiles and machine making, to the process industries, notably chemicals, metals and electricity. In order to contrast the kinds of technical changes, historians have typically referred to mechanical technology as constituting the First Industrial Revolution and electrochemical technology as constituting the Second Industrial Revolution (for the use of such terms see Landes 1969; Parker 1979; Chandler 1977; Rosenberg and Birdzell 1986).

A fundamental weakness of this typology is that it fails to distinguish invention from innovation and diffusion. There was clearly a greater preponderance of inventions in the mechanical arts in the period before the beginning of the nineteenth century, and a preponderance of inventions in electrochemical technology after the beginning of the nineteenth century (Woodruff 1966). With few exceptions, the fundamental breakthroughs in the technology of textiles production, power transmission, machine tooling and mechanical motion in general did occur before 1850. In textile production, the chronology of the decisive inventions was as follows. In spinning, the jenny, the water-frame and the mule, all of which helped transform spinning from a handicraft to a mechanized process, were invented between 1764 and 1779; the self-acting mule was invented in 1825 and the ring spindle in 1828–29. In weaving, the most significant inventions consisted of the power loom, invented in 1785 and the Jacquard loom in 1802. Few new inventions for textile production appeared after the 1830s with the exception of the machine comb in the worsted industry and several improvements to earlier designs in spinning, weaving and knitting. To substantiate the claim about the typology of inventions, it should be noted that the most important advances in textile technology towards the end of the nineteenth century, were made in the discovery of synthetic fibres; and this owed more to the chemical than to the textile industry.

As far as power transmissions are concerned, a similar picture emerges. The

Newcomen engine, generally accepted as the first steam engine, was invented at the beginning of the eighteenth century and was followed by the Watt engine in the late 1760s. Improvements continued over the following 80 years culminating in the hydraulic turbines and the compound and more sophisticated expansion engines of the 1840s and 1850s. Inventions which were designed to decentralize power sources characterized developments in the second half of the nineteenth century. The crucial inventions in this category were the high-speed petrol engine invented by Daimler in 1886 (following earlier developments in the technology of the internal combustion engine beginning around 1860); and the electrical generators and motors of the last quarter of the century. In clockmaking, the advances followed a similar route; and most of the important inventions in gearing and motion had been made by 1850. Between 1600 and 1850, for example, the precision of clocks and watches increased enormously from an average error of about 500 seconds per day to less than 0.5 seconds per day (Cipolla 1967). The most significant changes in clock and watch making in the second half of the nineteenth century consisted of improvements in manufacturing methods leading to a greater degree of uniformity in parts manufacture (Landes 1983).

In the major fields of mechanical engineering, therefore, inventions before the mid-nineteenth century concentrated on improving the action of the machine or tool beginning with replacing manual operations before leading to integrated production. In the chemical industry, on the other hand, the period before the middle of the nineteenth century witnessed few decisive inventions. Those which were prominent included the discovery of chlorine and its use as a bleach in 1774 and 1785, the Leblanc soda-ash process of 1787 and the absorption and contact processes for the production of sulphuric acid in 1827 and 1831 respectively. While these inventions in the heavy chemical industry were important, they were overshadowed by the discovery of aniline dyes and the foundation of the organic chemical industry towards 1860 which revolutionized many chemical processes. Materials engineering also experienced its major burst of inventive activity after 1850. Significant inventions in this field included the Bessemer converter and the basic process for the production of steel which were developed in the 1860s and 1870s respectively; alloy steel and stainless steel between 1870 and 1914; and the electrolytic method of producing aluminium invented in 1886 (Woodruff 1966).

As far as inventions are concerned, therefore, the typology is reasonably accurate; but it is not as appropriate with respect to the process of the implementation of technology. The development of steam power provides a clear example of the difference between invention and implementation. Though workable steam engines were invented in the eighteenth century, the diffusion of this technology was remarkably slow and limited in extent. Until well into the nineteenth century, for example, most of the steam power was used for non-industrial uses, specifically for pumping water in mining and in the provision of civic amenities (Greenberg 1982). Boulton and Watt, despite an aggressive marketing campaign, found few industrial customers for their engines; only by 1870, in Britain, for example, did steam power account for more than 50 per cent of industrial motive power and in many parts of Europe the percentage was even less. As far as the actual implementation of steam technology is concerned, it would be more accurate to consider it as a feature of the mid-nineteenth century than of the late eighteenth-century. This is also true of the power loom which, while invented at the same time as many other inventions in textile machinery towards the end of the eighteenth century, did not figure prominently until after 1830.

It is well recognized that there are lags between the date of the actual invention of a particular technology, the date of its innovation – that is when it was first used and produced – and the date of its general or at least successful adoption and diffusion. Recent studies have also confirmed that the length of the lags between invention, innovation and diffusion varied greatly (Rosenberg 1976c). Some technologies were transformed rapidly from invention to commercial use; Crompton's spinning mule, Watt's steam engine and the Bessemer converter, for example, each experienced a delay of less than 10 years. Other technologies could take much longer; in the case of the fluorescent lamp there was a lag of 79 years, and the cotton picker took 53 years to be employed commercially.

The timing of inventions, therefore, provides an ambiguous and highly misleading understanding of the nature of technical change. Nevertheless it does provide a reasonable guide to the general direction of technical change. At the turn of the seventeenth century, European industry had already enjoyed centuries of considerable technical achievements. As far as technology is concerned, no industrial activity remained static. The pace of technical change in early modern Europe was certainly slower than that to which we have become accustomed, but the forces at work and the inducement for technical change were not greatly different.

Production technology was a matter of primary concern and it was in the cities of Europe, primarily in those where industrial activity predominated, that technical change was most rapid. There is little doubt that what most appealed to the practitioners of early modern technology was machinery. Moving objects, their manufacture, their understanding and, most importantly, the challenge to make them operate automatically, were central to the direction of technical change during this period (Cipolla 1976; White 1972; Kellenbenz 1974; Mayr 1986). The most important innovations, which consisted of small improvements in gearing and in transmission, were made in the clockmaking industries, but similar changes occurred in most industries using complementary technology. In the silk industry, for example, such advances were crucial in the improvements to and widespread diffusion of water-powered spinning machinery (Poni 1976, 1982). The large concentrated industrial activities in shipbuilding in Amsterdam and Venice as well as in other European ports, illustrate the developments made in the mechanization of production (Unger 1978; Lane 1973; Rapp 1976; LeGoff and Meyer 1971).

Chemical technology was also important at this stage. In the dyeing process in textile manufacture, for example, continuous experiments were made to locate alternative means of producing selected colours. Success normally emerged from the discovery of a new and cheaper source of organic matter, such as cochineal and logwood from Central America, but not infrequently dyers experimented with the possibility of substituting vegetable matter for the more expensive animal sources of dyes (Ponting 1973; Coleman 1973; Rapp 1976). The procedures were highly empirical without doubt, but the need to release the dyeing industry from the constraints of organic sources of dyes was strongly felt. The complete solution to this problem was not, however, realized until the discovery of aniline dyes in the latter part of the nineteenth century. Chemical technology was applied to several industrial activities, particularly to the manufacture of soap, gunpowder, glass, sugar, paper and leather. This technical complementarity was not unusual in the process of European industrialization, and enhanced the advantages of the locational concentration of industrial activities.

Historians have traditionally undervalued the role of technical change in early modern industry, emphasizing, rather, the advances made in navigational instruments, ship design and armaments. There was, in fact, considerable technical advance for industrial purposes, but changes in technology appeared to have lacked momentum because the process of diffusion was relatively protracted and the effects were generally muted by economic conditions.

The history of the water-powered silk-throwing mill is a case in point (for useful analyses see Cipolla 1972; Poni 1972, 1976; 1982; 1983). It was a complicated piece of machinery, resembling some of the late eighteenth-century cotton-spinning techniques and was designed to be operated by a centralized power source, in this case water power. At the same time, its operation required relatively little skill and its labour force consisted largely of women and children. The silk mill was generally sited in the countryside, outside the jurisdiction of the urban guild authorities and was widely held to be responsible for the decline of urban silk spinning. Until the latter part of the sixteenth century, the silk mill was not widely used except in the area around Bologna where, for centuries, its construction and operating characteristics were kept secret. During the seventeenth century, however, this technology began to diffuse more widely, initially at least in northern Italy. By the end of the seventeenth century, the silk mill had been adopted in France and by the second decade of the eighteenth century it had made its appearance in England. The main impulse behind the widespread adoption of this technology lay most certainly in its ability to reduce labour costs as well as to shift from an urban to rural labour force, to the decided advantage of the owner of the silk mill as well as the urban silk manufacturers. By all accounts, the technology not only helped reduce the price of silk cloth but it did not compromise on quality – quite the reverse. Silk thread produced in a silk mill was finer, stronger and of higher quality than anything produced by hand.

There is evidence, however, that the technology embodied in the water-powered silk mill was not the only path taken in order to reduce labour costs. In Venice, and possibly in other Italian cities, there was a simultaneous interest shown in improving the technology of hand-operated silk throwing machines. This particular technology seems to have been superseded by the water-powered mill, though the reasons for its demise are not particularly clear.

By the end of the seventeenth century and also in the first half of the eighteenth century, the silk mill represented a unique form of industrial concentration. In northern Italy, there were many silk mills that employed up to 200 workers working in factory conditions on a waged basis. Despite its significance in the history of European technology, the silk mill had only limited ramifications in European industry generally. It was, for example, unable to generate technological momentum either to complementary industries or within itself, and there were, for example, no spin-offs to the metal industry, which might have been able to furnish the silk mill with metal parts capable of withstanding greater speeds of rotation and stress and thereby increasing the productivity of the mill. Moreover, despite its ability to reduce the cost of silk thread, the silk mill had little effect on the weaving of silk cloth. No important changes in this occurred until near the end of the eighteenth century with the invention of the Jacquard loom. This absence of technological momentum, so characteristic of early modern industrial invention, was largely the result of demand constraints; the market for silk cloth had no real potential for significant expansion.

Throughout the seventeenth and well into the eighteenth century, the technology of textile production dominated industrial and technical developments. In the first half of the eighteenth century, substantial progress was made in advancing the technology of printing cotton textiles both in the making of the pattern-face as well as in the ability to produce cloths with several colours (Chapman and Chassagne 1981). The implications of this for dyeing, and for chemical technology as well as for printing techniques were important. The printing of cotton, for example, required large quantities of sulphuric acid, and the manufacture of heavy chemicals was transformed by significant advances in the methods used to produce the raw materials as well as the finished products. In the second half of the eighteenth century, technical interest focused on the preliminary processes of cotton manufacture culminating in the spinning jenny, the water frame and the mule, which were all in commercial use before 1790. In the nineteenth century, the technology of other stages in the manufacture of all textiles changed substantially.

By the late eighteenth century, the pace of technical change as reflected in innovation and the rate of diffusion had accelerated. This was the result partly of technical complementarity, which continued to underlie the dynamic of technical change until the second half of the nineteenth century. When Arkwright invented the water frame, for example, he drew upon the significant achievements previously made in the production of metal parts for the spinning machinery as well as for the water wheel (Tann 1973). Cotton spinning, in general, could benefit from the innovations made in steam power, though it was many years before this form of power superseded water power.

Until 1850, technical change in European industry occurred along lines which had already been laid down in the seventeenth century and in areas where market penetration was greatest. This accounts for the significant focus on textiles, machinery and power sources. At the same time, the continuity of the direction of technical change was paralleled by a continuity in the means, if not the speed, of diffusing technology. In the mid-nineteenth century as in the seventeenth century, technology diffused generally through the agency of the skilled worker or technician, despite attempts by some governments, especially the British, to curtail the movement of these individuals (Henderson 1972; Jeremy 1977).

The situation altered after 1850 and the forces promoting technical change became more complex (Rosenberg 1976b; Saul 1972; Honeyman and Goodman 1986b). Some traditional relationships continued, however, and the machine-tool industry, the bicycle, car and shipbuilding industries, for example, were fundamentally transformed during the second half of the nineteenth and early twentieth centuries by technical changes that followed a well-trodden path. The skilled craftsman or technician using a practical approach to problem-solving continued to dominate technical advances in this industrial area. At the same time, new paths of technical change appeared in which technical complementarity seemed to matter little. In the production of synthetic dyes, for example, technical change originated from translating scientific understanding into practical manufacture (Landes 1969; Haber 1958). While the technical changes in the heavy chemical industry in the late eighteenth and nineteenth centuries were largely the result of increasing demands placed upon it from the textile industries, the production of synthetic dyes created its own technological momentum independent of other industrial activities. The organic chemical industry soon developed beyond the production of dyestuffs although this remained an essential part of overall production. The dynamic of the industry lay in the application of the scientific principles embodied in synthetic dyes to a wider range of goods (Landes 1980). In time, this included the derivatives of cellulose, giving rise to explosives, paints, celluloid film, synthetic fibres and plastics, all of which were produced before 1914. Thus a general shift occurred after 1850 from technical to knowledge complementarities and this in turn involved a change in the nature of the diffusion of technology, which became based on inter-firm transfer within the constraints of an international patent system (Saul 1972; Noble 1977).

Thus by 1914 a complex system of technical change had emerged in European industry operating at different levels of the industrial economy. The traditional path continued to be followed by those industries which on the one hand were complementary as far as their mechanical technology was concerned and which continued to support an artisanal ideology of production. In the process industries as well as the new industries such as electricity and gas, the traditional path was superseded by a new dynamic consisting largely of the generation of technology by applying science to problems related by their intrinsic scientific structure. In these industries, the large integrated firm and corporate firm were more common than in other industrial activities, and the role played by patents in protecting technologies and abetting the process of monopoly production was crucial (Saul 1972; Noble 1977; Chandler and Daems 1980; Kocka 1981).

Technical Change and the Labour Process

Technical change did not proceed in an autonomous fashion, and its impact was not confined to industrial production. The interaction of technology and changes in the labour process provides an important context for understanding this phenomenon. Some historians have argued that it is only since the mechanization of cotton spinning in the late eighteenth century, when hand spinning rapidly disappeared, that technical change can be seen to have had a significant effect on the labour process (Landes 1969). The resistance of labour to mechanization, as illustrated by Luddism, is also seen to have first appeared at this time. Mechanization, first in textiles and then elsewhere, inevitably resulted in the deskilling and the alienation of the working classes. By the end of the nineteenth century, it is argued, the pervasive attack on skill by new technology was compounded by a confrontation between the owners of capital and labour in the shape of scientific management or Taylorism, which attempted to undermine skill more directly (Braverman 1974; Burawoy 1985).

This view has been closely examined, and while the precise mechanisms of the relationship between technology and the labour process are disputed, it is widely accepted that only in recent times has technology been adopted by capitalists as one of the means by which they have sought to increase their power relative to labour. This section of the chapter will argue that the periodization is misleading and that a fuller analysis must include gender as well as class.

It must be emphasized that the interaction of technology and the labour process originated well before the late eighteenth century (MacKenzie and Wajcman 1985). Indeed, in any historical epoch, changes in technology reflected the relationships embodied in the labour process. Before the nineteenth century, as the preceding chapter pointed out, few industrial enterprises were concentrated. Industrial capital and industrial technology were both highly decentralized. As long as workers owned the means of production, they controlled the design of technology as well as the direction of technical change. Decentralized technology did not mean that technology was unimportant, rather it reflected the fact that the risks of industrial production in early modern Europe were shared between manufacturers and workers. In such an industrial system, one would expect that inventions and innovations would be designed by workers to minimize their part of the risk, especially in the face of competition, either by reducing their costs of production or by reducing the time spent on any one task. In the case where such information is available, it appears that there were indeed many attempts by workers to alter the technology of their production. For example, along with the diffusion of the water-powered silk mill around the turn of the seventeenth century, a serious attempt was made to improve the technology of the hand-operated spinning machine (Poni 1982).

The fact that there were two technologies available, one which was clearly designed to enhance the power of the mill owner and the other of the hand worker, attests to the significant role of technology in the labour process. The two technologies also reflected differences in the gender and age of the labour force. While the centralized silk mill employed mainly women and children in a rural setting, it is likely that hand spinning may have been as much a male as a female occupation. The unusual occurence of male spinners was the result of competition between hand technology and mechanized technology. In Venice, for example at the turn of the seventeenth century, although the number of female spinners is unknown, there were over 250 male spinners and in Florence around the middle of the seventeenth century, nearly one-third of those employed in silk spinning were male (Rapp 1976; Brown and Goodman 1980). The attempt to improve the productivity of hand spinning may indeed reflect more than the struggle between workers and owners to control the spinning sector; what was equally important was the struggle by men to retain their position in this occupation.

The existence of competing technologies embodied in different labour processes also applied to the mechanization of cotton spinning in the latter part of the eighteenth century (Hills 1979; Berg 1985). The first of the attempts to increase the productivity of spinning, the invention of the spinning jenny by

Hargreaves in 1769, was designed to be used by the spinner at home. From what we know of the design, it seems to have been operated by an adult spinner. Since the labour process in cotton spinning in Lancashire at this time was based on the putting-out system, it can only be assumed that this technological change would have reinforced the relations of production since it conferred the control over the technology to the spinner and not the manufacturer. Hargreaves himself was a handloom weaver. At about the same time, Richard Arkwright devised a new way of spinning cotton mechanically. Although, in principle, his machine could have been used in the same way as the jenny, Arkwright licensed only a large version of the water frame, which was built in units of a thousand spindles ensuring that it could only be used in centralized units of production. In this way, Arkwright's invention shifted the control over the technology and over the labour process from the worker to the owner of the water-powered spinning mills. Innovations in cotton spinning from then on accepted that the labour process had been radically altered and designs were based on the premise that the machines would be used in centralized production plants.

The speed with which handspinning and spinning by jenny disappeared has often been attributed to the technical supremacy of the water frame and the mule. While there is some truth in this, the gender dimension is also significant (Trescott 1979; Rose 1987; Lazonick 1978; Perrot 1983). In occupations such as cotton spinning where female labour predominated, mechanization was rapidly adopted. In male-dominated trades, however, such as mule spinning, wool combing, handloom weaving (and a whole host of occupations in the engineering and metal industries) mechanization progressed at a slower rate. It is no coincidence that the power loom, which was invented late in the eighteenth century, did not reach technical viability until the 1830s, and a machine to comb wool, which was not perfected technically until the 1850s, had been invented 60 years earlier.

The history of the self-acting mule also highlights the relationships between technology and the labour process (Lazonick 1979; Freifeld 1986). The self-acting mule began to replace the common, hand-operated mule in British cotton spinning in the 1830s and 1840s and soon diffused to other textile regions in Europe. Although the successful introduction of the self-acting mule has often been accepted as another victory by capital over labour, recent research has amended this interpretation. While the technology of production did change, the work organization remained unaltered. Under the technology of the common mule, an artisanal form of work organization predominated in which mule spinners hired and paid wages to their own assistants. When the self-acting mule replaced the common mule, this system remained. The mule spinners, by virtue of their power in industrial relations, were able to maintain their control over the labour process even though they rescinded their control over the technology of production. The choice of technique and the way it was deployed was the result of a complex process of conflict, compromise and cooperation between capital and labour. Once installed, the self-acting mule and its work organization gave way only very slowly to new technologies.

The pace and direction of technical change in industrial production were clearly influenced by the resilience of the artisanal and male workers (Bruland 1982). In the nineteenth century, production technology in certain industries led to a progressive deskilling, whereas in other industries, technological changes actually enhanced the skills of the operatives. In the machine-tool industry and in the machine workshops, technical changes hardly threatened the artisanal system of production (Sabel and Zeitlin 1985; Aminzade 1984). The increasing complexity of machine tools towards the end of the nineteenth century called for even greater skill and conferred the power over production to the skilled operatives. In typesetting and compositing, technical changes intensified both the artisanal qualities of work and its male exclusivity (Cockburn 1983). In other industries, in textiles and the new chemical, electrical and steel works, however, technical changes led to the progressive deskilling of the workforce and, in the last-mentioned case to the absorption of the knowledge involved in production by the management.

In the history of technology, workers and bosses have used technology to retain or possibly increase their relative power (Marglin 1976; Landes 1986; Berg 1984). In this respect the period from the late eighteenth century was in no way different from any previous period. The adoption of a particular technology is only partly explained by its efficiency compared to competing techniques. Specific technologies emerge from specific social and economic conditions in which human choice, motivations and aspirations are the determining factors.

Not all of the changes in industrial technology in the period from 1600 to 1914 emanated from the productive system in which reducing the costs and allocating the control over production were the guiding principles of the search for new techniques. Some of the most important advances in industrial technology occurred under the influence of the military, whose criterion for technical performance differed significantly from that of the industrial economy.

Military Enterprise and Technical Change

Technological innovation is typically perceived as emanating from the private sector of the industrial economy, either from the lone inventor, the firm or the industrial research laboratory. In the history of technology, each one of these agents of technical change is seen to replace the other over time in a unilinear fashion (Reich 1985; Locke 1984).

It would, however, be misleading to concentrate entirely on the private sector in any discussion of the development of European industrial technology. Military enterprise has, in general, had a strong influence on the direction of technical change throughout the period from 1600 to 1914 and at specific times its influence has been of far greater importance than that of the private sector. The primary objective of military technology (cost being of secondary importance) is to maximize the performance capabilities of weaponry by ensuring readiness and tactical superiority (Smith 1985a; Noble 1985). To achieve this, military enterprise has consistently required large and standardized orders for, of equipment which were typically contracted through private manufacturers (McNeill 1983).

One of the most outstanding facts of military history in the early modern period was the consistent increase in the size of armies and navies. Taking army manpower alone as a guide, it has been estimated that the size of the European land army between 1600 and the early part of the eighteenth century increased more than five-fold (Parker 1976). Efficient control over such numbers required various organizational changes including training and drill. At the same time, the growth in numbers not only called for greater procurement but also standardized artillery weapons. This need for standardized production introduced into the artisanal workshops notions of industrial routinization. Alongside the traditional lines of producing single firearms to personal specifications, the growth of the military in early modern Europe introduced the possibility of large-scale repetitive production in the metals industry (McNeill 1983).

The need to standardize artillery weapons also affected the manufacture of cannon, where, in the eighteenth century, fundamental technical changes with wide-ranging influences occurred (McNeill 1983). Until the middle of the eighteenth century, cannons were typically cast from iron which produced weapons that were not only imperfect, but also varied significantly each time one was cast. Gunners needed to learn the specific features of every cannon they might use. Because of the imperfect quality of the bore caused by the casting process, the cannon had to be very large in order for the casing to absorb the tremendous build-up of heat caused by friction. In the first part of the eighteenth century, several engineers and gunfounders in Europe attempted to solve this problem by casting a solid cannon and then boring out the barrel; and by the mid-1770s an efficient boring machine had been perfected which could bore cannon barrels of uniform size. As far as cannonry was concerned the change was revolutionary. It was now possible to produce uniform cannon, alleviating the need for individual gunner training; but more importantly, cannon could now be made lighter and therefore, cheaper and more transportable than before. The art of war was to change radically.

Technical developments designed for military purposes and financed by the military also influenced the technology of non-military industrial production. The invention of the boring machine, patented in Britain by John Wilkinson in 1774, accelerated the perfection of the steam engine which itself had originated under the patronage of the British Royal Office of Ordnance in the late seventeenth century (Trebilcock 1969; Wallace 1982). Before the availability of Wilkinson's machine, both the Newcomen and Watt engine had suffered similar structural problems when cast as had the cannon.

Wilkinson had perfected his cannon lathe while contracted to British Ordnance and similar work by Jean Maritz in France was also accomplished in close relation with French Ordnance (McNeill 1983). Other examples of the military influence on non-military technology include Cort's puddling process of the 1780s, which was used in the process of turning pig iron into bar iron and was stimulated by the need to produce high quality iron for the Navy and Ordnance. The fundamental developments in machine tools used in mass production were first exploited in the early nineteenth century by Henry Maudslay in the making of ship's blocks at the Portsmouth Naval Dockyards (Rolt 1986; Cooper 1984). The Royal Navy ignored the enormous costs involved in establishing and sustaining the new production system. Metalworking and woodworking machine tools were used in a sequence of operations which heralded the mass-production techniques adopted by other industries later in the century. The military was also instrumental in promoting the idea as well as the manufacturing possibilities of interchangeable parts (McNeill 1983; Smith, M. R. 1982). At the end of the eighteenth century in France, Jean Baptiste de Gribeauval promoted a firearms and machine technology, together with an appropriate organization, in which the ideas of uniformity and order, which had initially achieved practical application in the making of standardized artillery, reached a new and radically different level. Although his system diffused slowly in the European arms industry, it was nevertheless rapidly exploited by American arms manufacturers who pioneered interchangeability in small arms.

During the nineteenth century, the influence of the military on the direction of technical change became far more important than ever before. This was partly because most European countries became increasingly concerned with military strength and tactical superiority. The requirement to be at the forefront of developments in this area of industry was therefore pressing (Crouzet 1974a, b; McNeill 1983). Large firms, such as Schneider in France, Krupp in Germany, Ansaldo in Italy and Vickers in Britain innovated on a considerable scale to ensure the dynamism of technical change (Milward and Saul 1977). These companies were responsible for various new metallurgical practices and particularly for the development of special steels and production methods for special alloys. The Navy, both in France and in Britain, pioneered the application of steam power in ships and boats (McNeill 1983).

The military need for precision strongly influenced the design and dissemination of new technologies. In the nineteenth century, the military in Europe as well as in the United States put increasing pressure on armaments contractors to adopt the latest techniques (Fries 1975; Howard 1978; Showalter 1975; McNeill 1983). Often monetary advances or at least the promise of long production runs accompanied this pressure. The result was often that the technology embodied in military enterprise was far in advance of that which was used in civilian work. Advanced technology, to supply military needs, was developed far sooner than would otherwise have been the case. Maudslay's machine tools, Holzer's work on special alloy steel in the 1870s and the range of specialized machinery subsumed under the description 'American System of Manufactures' are examples of this class of industrial technology.

Because military enterprise was less concerned with cost than with performance, a lag typically occurred between the development of the technology exploited by the military and that absorbed by firms for non-military use. Despite the undoubted ability of certain classes of machine tools to produce interchangeable parts for firearms in the 1840s and 1850s, the expense of these techniques meant that it was not until the latter part of the century that they were applied generally to consumer goods (Hounshell 1984). This occurred first in the manufacture of sewing machines and then towards the end of the century extended to clocks and watches, bicycles and automobiles. The idea of uniformity and order which lay at the heart of the military's design of technology came slow to non-military use, but when it did, the effects were considerable. Not only did these techniques make it possible to manufacture and assemble multi-component consumer goods, but they also allowed arms manufacturers to diversify their output range. Many European firms who were heavily dependent on armaments contracts pursued this path of development. In Britain, examples include small-arms manufacturers such as BSA but also large companies such as Armstrong and Vickers; in France, Hotchkiss was one of the largest arms manufacturers to diversify into automobiles, but Schneider of Le Creusot as well as Jacob Holzer, the specialist steel maker in St Etienne, also had interests in this area. Besides firms diversifying along lines of production where technologies were complementary if not identical, the same was true of certain towns in Europe. Birmingham, St Etienne and Liège, for example, were all important centres for the production of small-arms, bicycles and cars by the turn of the twentieth century (Sabel and Zeitlin 1985).

The military's influence in technical change went beyond the phase of technical innovation; they were also instrumental in diffusing new technology by the movement of skilled labour to complementary industries. It is a well-known fact that the system of interchangeable parts manufacture in the United States in the nineteenth century, for example, diffused primarily by the movement of skilled workers and technicians from the armouries to non-military industrial production (Hounshell 1984). The same was true in Europe. In Turin, for example, the presence of four arsenals and the latest techniques provided momentum to the growth of Fiat and the machine-tool industry, of which the firm of Ansaldo was the most important (Saul 1972). In France, for example, the mobility of skill was institutionalized and it was considered best practice for technicians to learn their craft by moving among firms employing complementary technologies. A well-known example of this method of diffusion of skills between the military and the non-military industries is that of the French engineer, Frédéric Kreutzberger (Edmonson 1981). His education in machine-tool technology included an apprenticeship in a leading Alsatian machine-making company, and a prolonged stay in America working for Remington, the leading small-arms manufacturer, before returning to France to direct production at one of the leading armouries in France where he actively promoted the technology of interchangeability.

The emphasis on uniformity and order which can be seen clearly through all of the technical achievements sponsored directly or indirectly by the military, certainly from the time of de Gribeauval onwards, had their counterpart in organizational changes. Strong management was promoted, and attempts were made to undermine artisanal working practices. In the large arms manufactures such as Krupp, Vickers and Schneider, it was possible to disengage artisanal production, but in the smaller firms, and especially in those which diversified into the complementary consumer-goods industries of the late nineteenth century, artisanal methods continued to dominate well into the twentieth century.

In conclusion, the history of technology in the period from 1600 to 1914 consists of a wide range of experience only some of which corresponds to the simple notions of efficiency and costs. As we have seen, not only were there several directions of technical change throughout the period but the agents of technical innovations often had differing objectives. Nevertheless, in the end the technology applied to industrial production reflected the underlying social and economic processes – there was nothing autonomous, inevitable nor predictable in the development of technology.

Further Reading

Daumas, M. 1980: *A history of technology through the ages,* 3 Volumes. London: J. Murray.

Gille, B. 1986: *The history of techniques,* 2 Volumes. New York: Gordon & Breach.

Headrick, D. 1981: *The tools of empire: Technology and European imperialism in the nineteenth century.* New York: Oxford University Press.

MacKenzie, D. and Wajcman, J. (eds.) 1985: *The social shaping of technology.* Milton Keynes: Open University Press.

McNeill, W. H. 1983: *The pursuit of power.* Oxford: Basil Blackwell.

Mayr, O. 1986: *Authority, liberty and automatic machinery in early modern Europe.* Baltimore: Johns Hopkins University Press.

Smith, M. R. (ed.) 1985: *Military enterprise and technological change.* Cambridge, Mass.: MIT Press.

Trescott, M. M. (ed.) 1979: *Dynamos and virgins revisited: Women and technological change in history.* Metuchen, N.J.: Scarecrow Press.

Uselding, P. 1977: Studies of technology in economic history. *Research in Economic History.* Supplement 1,159–219.

5 Labour, Skill and the Gender Division of Labour

Before the period when the separation of agricultural and industrial work was completed, the industrial labour force is difficult to define and to measure. The nature of industrial work and the character of the labour process changed perceptibly between 1600 and 1914, but the extent of the transformation should not be exaggerated. It is widely believed that during the early modern period described in Chapter 3, pp. 76–99 when the size and output of industrial labour expanded throughout Europe, the labour process underwent little change, but that from the mid-eighteenth century, industrial employment became more distinctive and specialized as factory work was introduced. This characterization of industrial labour in Europe in the period from 1600 to 1914 is too simple, and this chapter will illustrate the complexity of industrial activity and will aim to distinguish the broad categories of industrial workers. Paucity of data makes this task difficult, but sufficient evidence remains to permit reasonably confident conclusions. Previous accounts of industrial labour have been typically confined to the descriptions of the experiences of male labour. Such accounts are clearly incomplete; and the nature of the organization of work, the labour process, the concept of skill, the use of technology and the division of labour, should be considered in terms of the positions of both men and women and their interaction. There is no doubt that women played an important role in the making of industrial Europe; and during the period of industrialization, their particular contribution lay in their position in the secondary labour market, in the elasticity of their labour and in the seasonality of their work. Much industrial employment throughout the period was irregular for a variety of reasons and it was the flexibility of women's labour, imposed upon them by their traditional position in the secondary labour market, that permitted the survival of many industrial enterprises.

Size of the Industrial Labour Force

Until the widespread collection of national or governmental statistics in the late nineteenth century, the precise measurement of the industrial labour force in

Europe is impossible. Indeed the absence of reliable data is compounded by the prevalence of by-employment especially in rural areas; and even when official records were compiled, ambiguities remained. It is now well known, for instance, that women were underrepresented in censuses and other official surveys, which neglected particularly domestic service and part-time and casual women's work (Roberts 1988). Although the real number of industrial workers is still uncertain, some estimates can be made. It is believed that at the beginning of the seventeenth century, industrial workers comprised in the region of 25 per cent of the labour force in Europe (Cipolla 1976; Wrigley 1985). The majority of these workers would have been located in the rural areas, but where urban development was greatest, notably in the Low Countries and northern Italy, the size of the urban industrial labour force was more significant. In France and England, at the beginning of the seventeenth century, the percentage of the population living in towns was 8.7 and 8.0 per cent respectively and about half this number would be expected to be engaged in urban industrial occupations (Wrigley 1985; Hohenberg and Lees 1985). The percentage of the population classified as rural non-agricultural in 1600 was 22.3 and 22.0 per cent respectively, and most of these would be wholly or partially occupied in industrial production. By contrast, 29 per cent of the Dutch population lived in urban areas in 1600 and 21 per cent were classed as rural non-agricultural (Wrigley 1985). In all parts of Europe from 1600 to the early nineteenth century, more of the population became urbanized and thus likely to be working in industrial occupations; and, during the same period, a greater proportion of the total rural population became active in industrial employment. In England, for instance, the urbanized population rose to 27 per cent by 1801 and rural industrial workers reached 36 per cent of the total. By 1800, 23 per cent of the Dutch population was classified as rural non-agricultural and 35 per cent as urban. In France, while the growth of industrial activity continued, the contraction of the purely agricultural population was less marked than in England and Holland, though it was probably more consistent with other parts of Europe. The output of rural industry was more significant than that of French urban industrial trades in 1800, and while this was also true of England, the difference was less marked (Cipolla 1976: Wrigley 1985).

Throughout Europe, the labour force employed in industrial activities grew relatively during the nineteenth century as the production of the agricultural labour force dwindled. The speed of this process varied, however, and while the proportion of the labour force employed in industrial activities in most European economies lay in the range 30–50 per cent and agriculture between 30 and 60 per cent, the British economy employed 70 per cent of its labour force in industry and only 8 per cent in agriculture in 1907 (O'Brien and Keyder 1978; Deane and Cole 1967).

The structure of the industrial labour force varied as well as the size; and 'industry' throughout Europe as late as 1914, comprised modern industry, craft industry, rural industry and outwork, workshop and sweatshop industry. The industrial labour force was, naturally, equally heterogeneous, and although large numbers of industrial workers became organized and centralized units of production, they by no means formed the majority. The real difference among European economies was only one of degree, and because the same processes operated throughout Europe, a similar complexity of industrial employment resulted.

The environment within which the European industrial labour force operated cannot easily be described but it certainly exhibited great variation. From 1600, if not earlier, the organizational forms within which industrial workers operated were as numerous as they were in the early twentieth century; only the proportions had changed. In the seventeenth century, urban industrial workers could be found in small centralized manufacturers, in workshops, and in their own houses working for themselves or for others in the putting-out system. In the countryside, industrial labour congregated in village workshops, or worked in their own homes, or, less frequently, in the houses of friends. During the eighteenth century, the expansion of European industrial production occurred mostly along traditional lines, but the most significant area of growth was that of domestic industry in the countryside. Protoindustry proliferated and dense rural manufacturing areas developed which produced increasingly for supra-regional markets (Kriedte, Medick and Schlumbohm 1981). Regions which had previously depended upon agriculture alone were transformed into mixed zones in which agriculture and rural manufacturing existed side by side. Such was the expansion of rural industrial production that in some regions urban manufacturers were unable to withstand the competition. More typically, however, both urban and rural industry grew in harmony, and in regions such as Normandy and northern France, there developed a dynamic alliance between rural and urban manufacture on the basis of a division of labour (Engrand 1979; Tilly 1983; Gullickson 1986). The merchants of Rouen, for instance, were able to satisfy their demand for spinning labour by providing non-harvest employment for female peasants from the surrounding countryside, who would otherwise have been seriously underemployed. In a case such as this, the process of producing a finished article was organized by an individual who provided employment for female and rural-based spinners and for male and urban-based weavers (Gullickson 1982, 1986). In most cases the individual worker owned the means of production and was thus in a position to choose her/his place of work. This was usually the individual's home but women spinners sometimes worked in groups in the home of one of their number. In other cases, the urban–rural division of labour was less marked and rural households were organized as a family economy producing for the market and dependent on the merchant for work. In such households, the gender division of labour was very clear and the woman's role paramount. Sometimes rural industrial labour worked in centralized workshops, but in comparison with protoindustrial households organized on the putting-out system, the number of workers employed in these enterprises was small (Gullickson 1986; Kriedte, Medick and Schlumbohm 1981).

From the late eighteenth century, it became apparent in some areas that the prevailing system of production had reached the limits of its capacity and manageability. Where this was the case, rural factories were established and landless rural producers, small-holders and protoindustrial manufacturers formed the basis of the labour force. To begin with, the gender division of labour continued as before and children performed the preparatory tasks while women formed the basis of the spinning section. Men continued to weave either at home or in workshops. The factory system spread and increasingly during the nine-teenth century became located in urban areas. While female labour remained important in the textile factories in particular, their work was allocated low status and men filled the skilled and supervisory roles (Lazonick 1979; Freifeld 1986; Berg 1985; Gullickson 1986; Boxer and Quataert 1987). Both male and female labour in the urban factories experienced more tightly controlled working and living conditions, and became subject to more exacting time and work discipline. Despite the obvious attractions of the factory form of industrial organization for the industrial capitalist, most manufacturing even in 1914 took place in non-factory locations. This was as true in England as it was in France, Germany and Italy (for more details see Kaelble 1986; Samuel 1977; Marko-vitch 1967; Kocka 1984). Throughout Europe in the late nineteenth century, a significant proportion of industrial production was carried out in the house-holds of part-time peasants, craftsmen and rural workers in domestic industry or in small workshops. It is in France that the dichotomy of industrial capitalist concentration and small-scale artisanal workshops has been most commented upon, but the structure of the French industrial labour force was by no means unusual. In 1876, according to Markovitch, the industrial population employed in artisanal industry in France was twice that employed in large-scale industry: the greater proportion of those worked in industries not producing for the national and international market but for local markets (Markovitch 1967). In Germany, a similar situation existed. Workshop employment expanded to 1870 and again after 1895, and this growth was most marked in the areas of greatest industrial development (Kocka 1984). Evidence of similar processes exists for England. Arisanal trades grew in all cities including factory towns; indeed, factory industry and artisanal industry seem to have been mutually supportive, as evidence suggests that the growth of factories resulted in an increase in the number of artisans. This can be explained by the demands of factory building and transport construction which could only be met by artisans; by the growing demands for specialized machinery and processes produced in small batches by highly skilled artisanal labour; and because factories sometimes reduced the cost of raw materials used in artisanal production, reducing the price and raising demands for the output (Samuel 1977). Despite the growth of factory produc-tion in Europe, industrial labour was less likely to be found in factories than in smaller workshops or homes, where the level of autonomy and independence was significantly greater.

Skill

Industrial development in Europe clearly altered notions of skill as embodied in labour, but perhaps not as much as is traditionally believed. Before the eighteenth century, when technical changes gave rise to additional determinants of skill, skill definitions were rooted in social and gender divisions (Hanagan 1980). Skilled occupations were filled overwhelmingly by men and were typically protected by guilds. Skill can be defined as a scarce ability that takes time and effort to acquire and, from 1600, access to that scarce ability was strictly controlled (Alexander 1983). Because men dominated the guilds and other apprenticeship bodies to the late nineteenth century, the majority of those in a position to acquire a skill and to become skilled labour were men (Howell 1986a, 1986b; Wiesner 1986b) The work that women did or had access to was classified as 'unskilled'. Women might help their husbands in their skilled trade but only in unusual cases were they permitted to become skilled in their own right (Howell 1986b; Roper 1985; Wiesner 1987).

The introduction of machine technology might have been expected to change both the nature and the embodiment of skill. In principle, the replacement of hands by machines in the production of manufactured goods would reduce the extent to which individuals monopolized skill. Indeed the mechanization of industrial production is believed to have been associated with deskilling, as well as the eradication of the gender component of skill. The evidence provided by recent research, however, has indicated not only that the notion of skill and the differentiation of labour were maintained throughout the nineteenth century both within and outside the factory, but also that skill, as an ideological category, reflected even more closely than before a sexual hierarchy within capitalist industrial production (Kaelble 1986; Lazonick 1979; Philips and Taylor 1980).

The assumption that industrial jobs became increasingly undifferentiated and uniformly unskilled from the late eighteenth century, stems from the rapid mechanization of the textile industry at that time (Kaelble 1986). Studies of the textile industries in Europe, however, have shown the opposite to be true. Indeed significant disparities in the workplace among the workers, as well as a structured hierarchy among the unskilled workers persisted long after the introduction of machinery. A study of a Swiss calico printing factory in the period from 1750 to 1850, for example, illustrated how strongly designers, engravers and foremen, who accounted for 10 per cent of the work force, were distinguished by level of income from both unskilled workers and other skilled workers, such as the printers (Caspard 1976). A well-researched French calico printing enterprise likewise showed similar disparities, particularly between skilled and unskilled workers (Chassagne, Dewerpe and Ganlupeau 1976). In coal mining, as in textile production, deskilling was not apparent, and technical progress resulted in greater job differentiation, between underground and aboveground workers and between men and women. Miners in the Massif Central and in the Ruhr Valley are seen to have become sharply divided following periods of technical change: social heirarchies developed among underground workers and disparities were even greater among workers above ground (Kaelble 1986).

In many industries, the mechanization of production gave rise to a new supervisory function. The effect of this was not only to extend job differentiation in the context of technical change, but also to create a new skill and one that was largely reserved for men. Skill differentials were also maintained in the machine and equipment industries because, until the middle of the nineteenth century, machines were not produced in a precisely uniform way, so highly qualified workers remained vital (Burgess 1969; Sabel and Zeitlin 1985). In the various European engineering industries, however, deskilling in machine building became more noticeable after the 1860s. In an Esslingen engineering factory, for example, disparities among workers became less marked after 1860, while in a machine building plant in Bielefeld between 1860 and 1914 deskilling was very clearly the result of a rapid mechanization of machine production. In European iron foundries and other heavy industrial plants skill differentials were similarly maintained to the second half of the nineteenth century and declined thereafter as deskilling and the growth of supervision followed the introduction of new processes such as the Bessemer converter and the open hearth process (Kaelble 1986).

It is clear, therefore, that labour did not form a uniform unstructured mass of workers during the nineteenth century. Not only was the mechanization of production a protracted process, but the impact of technical change on the industrial labour force varied greatly, and the skilled workers retained a strong, if different, position throughout the nineteenth century.

It is now well known that in France, the skilled craftsman remained central to industrial production to 1914 (Sewell 1986; Hanagan 1980). While the position of the artisan was not supplanted, it was nevertheless subjected to new pressures which forced certain changes. Through much of the nineteenth century, however, decentralized and skilled groups of workers flexibly met the challenge of mechanization by operating independently within factory units. In metal-working, for instance, where demand for skilled labour was expanding in line with the growth of machine construction, artisans began to be employed in factories, but behaved as though they were in their own small shops. They continued to be very highly regarded craftsmen and carried out their work with little effective discipline in a free and easy atmosphere (Hanagan 1980).

Because the process of mechanization was seldom sufficiently rapid to enable employers to dispense completely with the artisan's services, the artisan was often in a position to set the terms by which machinery would be introduced into the factories. Furthermore, the metalworking artisan was well organized and remained competitive for a long time. By the late nineteenth century, however, entry into the trade became increasingly difficult, the division of labour became greater and skills became diluted; and where rapid technical change did occur, the skilled workers could do very little to resist it. The French example is typical; skilled trades and artisan labour were not wiped out by the appearance of the first factory or first machine. Conditions changed only gradually during the nineteenth century and despite the erosion of some differentials, long-established skills were retained and held in high esteem. Trades which supplied the basic demands of the domestic population such as shoemaking, tailoring and furniture making, expanded and retained a high quality component, while at the same time they moved into larger-scale production using more complex divisions of labour (Hanagan 1980). The furniture making trade, and especially cabinet making, clearly reflected the artisans' concern not only to safeguard jobs and skill, but also to maintain levels of artistry and fine craftsmanship, which was vital to their self-image as both workers and artists. Skilled workers in the Parisian cabinet making trade, for example, spent much of the nineteenth century involved in intermittent strike action not simply through material or practical concerns, but also because the destruction of the training system threatened artistic standards. The artisans clearly continued to see themselves as the guardians of artistry in their trades, and resented the possible loss of status and control over production (Weissbach 1982).

While many skills survived the pressure of industrial capitalism, at least in the short term, gender distinctions of skill became more clearly defined. Even before the introduction of large-scale machinery skill had been associated with masculine virtues, but technical developments of the nineteenth century encouraged male labour to reinforce traditional perceptions of skill and to strengthen the sexual hierarchy of skills (Berg 1985; Phillips and Taylor 1980; Rose 1985). Attempts by male skilled labour to appropriate aspects of the work process in order to maintain their skilled status are represented by the example of mule spinning, which was defined as a skilled activity from the start and was assumed to require the use of male labour. Requirements like strength, building maintenance and repair skills accounted for the 'maleness' of the occupation; but the application of water power in the 1790s, which eliminated the need for special strength, and the introduction of the self-acting mule made no difference to the sex structure of the work force. Women, whose particular characteristics of nimble fingers, deftness, powers of concentration for tedious, laborious processes, docility and cheapness, were never regarded as skills, despite their undoubted attraction for the industrial capitalist, were confined to labour-intensive and less efficient techniques (Berg 1985; Freifeld 1986; Lazonick 1979). Throughout the nineteenth century, women were excluded from techniques that were defined as male and skilled, such as printing, cabinet making, compositing, and machine making (Cockburn 1983; Gray 1976). Once the definitions were constructed, women were perceived to be unfit to do the work that men desired because they were deemed unable to supervise men or because they were prevented from learning the skills of machine adjustment and repair (Lazonick 1979).

Just as women had been largely confined to unskilled labour by the operation of the guilds' apprenticeship system that restricted entry to men, so they were confined to the more menial tasks in industrial production from the eighteenth century when guilds disappeared and were replaced by other institutions of restrictive practices. Increasingly from the late eighteenth century skill became a social construction more clearly related to gender than previously (Phillips and Taylor 1980). The definition of skill was manipulated by men to protect them from the competitive threat posed by women, unskilled labour and, ironically, industrial capitalists (Cockburn 1983).

While the heightened gender distinction of skill was a response to the potential deskilling of the labour process, the latter was slow to materialize in Europe before 1914. The experience of factory work was complex and varied; conditions of work, wage rates and job security were by no means uniform, nor was there a general tendency to render earlier skills obsolete. The extent to which machine-production simplified jobs has been overstated; manual labour, either simple or machine assisted, remained quite common in many industries, and a complex division of labour was rare. Continuity of skill was typical; disparities in pre-industrial qualifications and job prestige continued into the factory. By the late nineteenth century, a perceptible tendency towards a narrowing of the disparity between skilled and unskilled labour occurred and this was largely the result of changes in technology and organization. Technology in coalmining (coal cutting), in printing (linotype and monotype), in glass (tank furnace), in steel (Bessemer and open hearth) all served to reduce skill differentials; labour market conditions were secondary (Kaelble 1986). The preservation of skill as a social construction for the male worker was achieved partly by redefining skill using a more rigid demarcation along sexual lines, but also by introducing new skills, especially supervision, which were compatible with the new technologies in the short run at least.

Gender Division of Labour

Most examinations of the industrial labour force implicitly emphasize the role of the male worker, but the distinct functions performed by men and women and the way in which they interacted in the labour process took on a new significance as industrial production became more specialized. Chapter 3 illustrated the emergence of a variety of organizational forms within which industrial production took place from 1600. Some of these were sustained, some disappeared and a few were strengthened in the years to 1914. During this period, the labour process and particularly the gender division of labour adapted to the changes taking place in industrial organization, and in the location of industrial production. During the nineteenth century, many of these changes involved taking manufacture out of the home, which created a novel division of labour between the sexes and stimulated a new spirit of competitiveness between men and women. This section examines the evolution of the gender division of labour in industrial Europe and analyses the relative contributions of men and women to the industrialization process.

Women's work in the town 1600–1800

When they have given the matter consideration, historians have typically assumed that women enjoyed a greater degree of harmony in life and work before they became down-trodden by the capitalist system. With respect to urban industrial production in Europe, it seems more likely that women's position in the labour force had been consistently undermined from the sixteenth century. Women are understood to have been well represented in a variety of high-status occupations in many medieval cities, especially in the manufacture of high quality woollen cloth, and there is sufficient evidence that after 1500, women found it increasingly difficult to continue to participate in those activities (Howell 1986a, 1986b; Wensky 1982). Adult males soon constituted the majority of workers in small commodity and artisanal production in most places and a new gender division of labour developed in which women were relegated to low-status occupations and activities. The trend towards male exclusivity grew in strength until the mid-eighteenth century (Boxer and Quataert 1987).

This marginalization of women's work in early modern European cities took various forms. Firstly, women became barred from guilds, both as active participants in the organization and for the purpose of gaining access to a particular trade through them. Evidence from various cities in Germany, England, France and Italy suggests that by the sixteenth century the majority of guilds were male preserves, and the few that were not, were in activities where women are thought to have been most important, notably needle work, embroidery and belt making (the evidence for the various cities can be found in Wiesner 1986a, 1986b; Howell 1986a, 1986b; Monter 1980; Davis 1982; Roper 1985; Quataert 1985). Thus women's work became clearly defined and institutionalized.

Secondly, there is evidence that guilds were attempting to regulate the employment of women either by constraining it in specific ways or by prohibiting their labour outright. This action was reinforced by male journeymen who began to usurp the tasks associated with production such as preparing and finishing material, previously carried out by masters' wives and daughters. In this way, because women became confined to the cleaning, cooking and maintenance and selling the products of the workshop, the men's position in the household production system was enhanced (Wiesner 1986b; Roper 1985). During the early modern period, therefore, women's work in the workshop was at best, low-paid and of low status and was frequently unpaid. Even where women were employed in skilled trades, there is growing evidence to suggest that as these trades became prestigious or more important in the economy, women found it harder to get established or were forced into peripheral jobs (examples can be found in Phillips and Taylor 1980; Godelier 1980; Monter 1980).

These two characteristics of the gender division of labour gave rise to a third, more positive feature. As many urban trades became male-dominated, and as the demand for the products of the urban artisanal sector grew vigorously during the seventeenth and eighteenth centuries, women increased their participation in the distributive trades (Wiesner Wood 1981). Not only did the demand for female labour grow in the local distribution of goods and services, and in small-scale retail trades, but women also increased their participation in large-scale putting-out industries, especially in textiles, where women dominated the spinning sector. Because between 10 and 20 spinners were required for each weaver, expansion of demand resulted in a progressively greater expansion of women's employment (Reddy 1977; Gullickson 1981, 1986 Wiesner 1986b).

There are a small number of instances of women becoming employed in occupations that had been previously exclusively male, notably in the Florentine wool and silk industries, and in the silk industry in Bologna. Male labour in these cities was concentrated in the expanding high-status artisanal trades, while the woman workers moved into the lower-skill and -status occupations in the textile sector which concentrated on the production of simple cloths (Brown and Goodman 1980). In other cities, where women's work featured little, output more typically consisted of rich, complicated cloths, requiring not only greater skill but also more capital (Goodman 1977; Rapp 1976).

In the urban labour market, in the artisan workshop system, in the putting-out system as well as in the commercial system all described in Chapter 3, women were marginalized. They were, however, important: indeed, because their work required little training, and because they had a weak work identity, women provided the urban economy with its flexibility in response to fluctuating demands. Women effectively formed a secondary labour market which was characterized in the early modern period by low earnings, poor working conditions and uncertain irregular employment (Wiesner 1987; Howell 1986a, 1986b).

Womens work in the countryside 1600–1800:

In the rural labour market, the growth of industrial production in the country-side after 1600 gave rise to broadly similar characteristics with respect to the gender division of labour. The high-status jobs such as weaving, combing and carding for example, were occupied by men, while women were concentrated in lower-status spinning, or in lace making, stocking making or calico printing, or as farm or household servants. It also appears to have been the case that men occupied increasingly specialized and full-time jobs in agriculture, but when they did engage in industrial activities these were likely to require skill and training. Women's work was more protean and irregular than men's, as it was in the urban economy; and their farm work was confined to menial tasks at harvest time, and their industrial contribution was restricted to piecemeal unskilled wage labour, or to the production of items for household use. Women as a group were even more important to the rural industrial economy than to the urban economy, yet it seems that they were equally undervalued.

Some historians of the rural industrial economy of the seventeenth and eighteenth centuries have emphasized the cooperative relationship that existed between men and women in the rural household (Kriedte, Medick and Schlumbohm 1981). It is argued specifically that during this period, the family in the European rural economy was constituted as a unit of labour, in which family labour was distributed without apparent regard for sex and age. Thus there was a strong degree of assimilation between the production functions of men and women. Women's increasing involvement in production frequently reduced their contribution to household duties, as men assumed traditional women's roles. Thus, it is argued, all family members worked at complementary tasks of equal necessity to the functioning of the household. In this situation, men and women seemed to cooperate in their work, and the survival of the family economy depended on the capital and working power of both partners.

The extent of cooperation between men and women has probably been exaggerated; and although it is clear that sometimes interchangeability of tasks did exist within the rural industrial family unit, a gender division of labour was a crucial element in the rural industrial system. In Rouen and the Caux, for example, the gender division of labour which was established in agriculture and textiles and in town and countryside, complemented each other perfectly. In this case, the non-harvest agricultural labour was provided by men, which freed women during the winter months to provide spinning labour for the Rouen merchants. Many more women than men were employed in the textile industry. The organization of industry and agriculture in this region as in many others meant that the majority of husbands and wives worked at completely unrelated tasks. The two production systems operated without conflict for many decades, although by the early nineteenth century, the gender division of labour seemed to be breaking down as more women moved into weaving or worked in the fields throughout the year (Gullickson 1986). The movement of women into tradi-tional areas of men's work at this time did not, however, signify any great change in the definition of men's work and women's work, but rather reflected a shift in labour market requirements. During the seventeenth and eighteenth centuries, the jobs that men and women undertook seemed to be comple-mentary, but it was women's work that was flexible and varied according to a family's need for workers at a particular task. Moreover men's and women's work were by no means equal, and a wage differential further illustrated the persistence of a male/female hierarchy.

Clearly the nature of women's work and the gender division of labour in the rural industrial context remains the subject of debate. The notion that men's work and women's work were effectively interchangeable, and that, within the household, husband and wife worked at complementary tasks creating a family economy, is probably overstated. Although each member of the rural industrial family made a contribution to the household economy, individuals worked independently, and only rarely shared tasks. Men's work and women's work remained distinct. While it is true that much early modern rural manufacture made special use of a female labour force, and that expansion of production was achieved by extending the input of cheap female and child labour, women's work in the country as in the town was undervalued. Indeed, the rural industrial system operated on the basis of low wages and flexibility of labour; and while the employment of women expanded substantially between the seventeenth and eighteenth centuries, it retained many of the characteristics of women's work in the urban economy. Despite the fact that the involvement of women in textile manufacture and particularly in spinning during this period formed the primary link between the villages, the region and the national economy, women had few job options, and none of them paid well. Men's jobs were more specific, better paid and had the advantage of being less dependent on external employers and markets. Male work was almost always valued more highly than female (Gull-ickson 1982, 1986; Tilly and Scott 1978).

Women's work in the context of industrial capitalism:

Whether the gender division of labour during the eighteenth century was more equable than previously is still a matter of debate, but the introduction of new technology from the late eighteenth and throughout the nineteenth century rearoused gender conflict and certainly emphasized the subordinate position of female labour (Rose 1985; John 1986). The cheapness of female labour, however, permitted a high degree of continuity of women's work in the context of technical change. Until recently, it was believed that the emergent forces of industrial capitalism forced a separation of home and work, for both women and men; but it is now known that there were great variations in the trans-formation of the processes of production and, therefore, there was no uniform effect either on the location of waged labour nor on the timing of women's various contributions to their families. Under some conditions, industrial capi-talism precipitated physical separation of home and work; but, much more typically, women continued to be employed within their own homes (Rose

1985; Boxer and Quataert 1987). Women also continued to work in the homes of others, as domestic and farm servants, and in sweat-shop conditions (Hufton 1975; Rendall 1985). Female labour continued to be elastic and it was partly the cheapness and flexibility of the female labour force that permitted the longevity of hand and intermediate techniques of production as an alternative to mechanization and factory production (Berg 1985). In a number of instances, therefore, cheap female labour was used more intensively; and new rural and urban trades emerged on the basis of this cheap supply of labour. From the late eighteenth century, a gender division of labour between trades and within branches of trades complemented a specific division of labour within work processes and technologies. Women were confined to the use of more labour-intensive and less efficient techniques where skilled workers were able to restrict entry.

Detailed research in the complex structure of women's work in nineteenth-century Europe is at an early stage and what follows indicates the current state of knowledge. Changes in techniques and in organizations of production in the nineteenth century seemed to have heightened the complexity not simply of the nature and location of work and of opportunities for waged industrial employment, but also of the relationships between the classes and between the sexes. Just as men and women had performed specific functions within the manufacturing sector before the age of the machine and the factory, this continued to be the case in the nineteenth century but in a much more complicated way. Change gave rise to new opportunities, but in practice, the choices open to women were restricted and certainly more limited than those of men.

The early, rural factories, for example, permitted continuity of employment for women and children, who formed the bulk of the labour force in the spinning mills. Women had traditionally specialized in the spinning process in textile production and initially there was no reason for this to change. For a while, men continued in the traditional rural functions, in farming and domestic weaving, but very quickly they began to create for themselves new and skilled functions within the factory. Mule spinning, for instance, became a skilled occupation and required supervisory functions suitable only for males (Freifeld 1986). Technical change was, in this case, employed as a means for redefining skill and on it was based a gender-segregated workforce. Women were in a position to improve their status, and indeed, the capitalists expressed a clear preference for 'docile' female labour. Men, however, because they saw a threat to their employment, defined the operation of the mule as skilled and prevented women gaining access to it (Berg 1985; Lazonick 1979). A segmented labour market based on gender differences where workers were played off against each other, became more apparent from the late eighteenth century, and had the effect of reinforcing women's position as low-status, badly paid workers. In other words, women moved from a position that was already unequal into categories of unskilled or semi-skilled workers. During the nineteenth century, new skills emerged and men carefully defined most of them for themselves (Berg 1985; Hartmann 1976; Rose 1985).

The marital status of women to a greater extent than previously determined the choice of occupation. In urban industrial centres, for example, the vast majority of female workers were young and single. Mill girls, domestic servants and garment workers in the towns of England, France and Italy (and probably elsewhere) were overwhelmingly of this category (Scott and Tilly 1975). At the peak of female factory employment in England in 1833, for example, only 16 per cent of the work force was married and some of these would soon cease work (Richards 1974). This reflected not that married women found other occupations, although to some extent they did, but that the proportion of married women in urban industrial activity of any kind was very small. In the mill towns of northern France, in Roubaix, for example, and in northern England less than 20 per cent of married women were officially recorded to be in employment in the mid-nineteenth century, of which more than half worked in the textile factories (Tilly and Scott 1978; Hall 1982). While the kinds of jobs women did depended on the particular economic structure of a town or city, it is also the case that many women workers, and particularly those that were married, did not enter the official statistics precisely because of their particular characteristics as irregular and casual workers (Tilly and Scott 1978; Alexander 1983). It is believed that most married women workers in nineteenth-century Europe were clustered in areas of traditional employment, particularly in retail occupations as petty traders and small shopkeepers or as dressmakers, and there is no doubt that they formed an important part of the sweated labour force. In London, for instance, but also in other major European cities, married women were found mostly in the least industrialized sectors of the economy. They worked in the clothing trades, in tailoring, and hat making, sometimes in their own homes, sometimes in overcrowded workshops, but nearly always where the separation between home and workplace was minimal, and where they could control the rhythm of their work (Alexander 1983; Scott 1984; Boxer 1982). The flexibility of their employment, however, was less likely to be determined by themselves than by the vagaries of the trade; but it was the willingness and ability of married women to engage in this type of work that made them attractive employees and indeed permitted the continuation of this informal organizational form (Alexander 1983). While single women were likely to require steady work and therefore to remain at work longer and more consistently, married women clustered in those jobs that were temporary and episodic and low-paying. All of this indicated the employer's exploitation of both married women's need for cash and their lack of skill and organizational support that might otherwise permit higher wages.

The gender division of labour and the notion of distinctive women's work was further emphasized by a new morality portraying women as the 'Angel' of the home with primary responsibility for housework and childcare, which formalized women's domestic and reproductive roles. The separation of home and work, which was believed to have been forced upon women by the spread of the factory system, attracted the attention and concern of contemporaries who feared the breakdown of the family structure. Protective legislation aimed at women, as well as children, effectively prevented the widespread employment of married women in the degrading conditions of spinning mills and coalmines (Boxer 1986; John 1978; Humphries 1981; Rendall 1985). Outwork and industrial home-work provided legitimate employment opportunities for married women as it gave the flexibility also to fulfil their socially determined domestic obligations. Young, single women were less constrained by legal and social roles in their choice of occupation than were those who were married, but they were still subject to parental and other pressures. Many young rural women who were unable to find employment locally were encouraged by their parents to seek positions as urban domestic servants, where their welfare would be supervised and where they might acquire desirable skills for subsequent married life. Urban factories, especially in France and Italy, where dormitory accommodation and supervision was provided by many capitalists to attract a malleable, docile workforce were also considered suitable (Tilly and Scott 1978; Perrot 1983). Later in the nineteenth century, retailing, especially in the new department stores provided an alternative occupation which was consistent with prevailing conceptions of appropriate women's work. The new department stores provided employment on a grand scale; the Bon Marché employed 2500 sales assistants in the 1880s, for example, and the Louvre 3500–4000 in 1900, and while both men and women were employed, women were preferred because of their docility, their cheapness, and because they were polite and sober. While the nature of the work had changed, retailing was a traditional area of women's employment. The work was unskilled and low paid, the women employees were typically young and single, and employment generally ceased upon marriage. To conform to society's requirement for the supervision of young females away from home, daily life was strictly regulated and the majority of shop girls lived in the premises in attic dormitories, with little privacy and freedom (McBride 1978).

By the late nineteenth century, new employment opportunities for both men and women appeared, some, but not all, of which were consistent with the old structure. Shop work, described above, was an example of a new type of occupation operating within the old structure, while new occupations, such as typists, emerged in areas that were traditional male strongholds. As the nature of clerical work changed, therefore, and as some of it was mechanized by the typewriter, women were allocated low-status secretarial jobs in which their apparently caring and subservient natures played an important role, while the men moved into high-status office jobs in banks and insurance companies (Davies 1978; Zimmeck 1986).

Conclusion

The gender division of labour was established early in the evolution of industrial Europe and was typically reinforced by guilds, apprenticeship systems and male notions of skill. While mechanization raised the possibility of creating new opportunities for women, men continued to hold tenure over technique and skill, redefining their positions as required (Berg 1985). Urban and industrial development seem to have generated employment opportunities in a few traditional sectors such as domestic service, dressmaking and laundressing, and the expansion of production of consumer goods involved the growth of a large piecework garment industry in which women worked at home (Scott and Tilly 1975; Dasey 1981; Alexander 1983). Jobs available to women were limited in kind and number and were typically segregated. Most married women worked in non-factory occupations. The nineteenth-century towns, therefore, exhibited an essential continuity and consistency with the early modern period and while aspects of work changed and became more complex, old values very often continued to operate in a new context (Scott and Tilly 1975). Whether they worked outside the home or not, married women defined their role within the framework of the family economy and continued to find jobs consistent with this role.

Both male and female labour operated within contexts that underwent a variety of changes within the period 1600 to 1914. For many people, the nature of work and the circumstances within which they worked changed little. For others, factory employment exemplified the separation of home and work, but this accounted for a small proportion of the total: most people worked in locations and organizations distinct from but often in conjunction with the factory. The new technology threatened to reduce the level of skill, but recent research has shown that while definitions of skill may have changed, actual deskilling did not generally occur until very late in the nineteenth century. Concepts of skill and their redefinition also seemed to emphasize the relative economic strength of male labour and the low status of women's work.

Further Reading

Berg, M. 1985: *The age of manufactures 1700–1820*. London: Fontana.

Boxer, M. J. and Quataert, J. H. (eds.) 1987: *Connecting spheres: Women in the western world, 1500 to the present*. New York: Oxford University Press.

Gullickson, G. L. 1986: *Spinners and weavers of Auffay*. Cambridge: Cambridge University Press.

Hanagan, M. 1980: *The logic of solidarity. Artisans and industrial workers in three French towns 1871–1914*. Urbana, Ill.: University of Illinois Press.

Hohenberg, P. M. and Lees, L. H. 1985: *The making of urban Europe 1000–1950*. Cambridge, Mass.: Harvard University Press.

Hufton, O. 1983: Women in history, I, early modern Europe. *Past and Present*, 101, 125–41.

John, A. V. (ed.) 1986: *Unequal opportunities. Women's employment in England 1800–1918*. Oxford: Basil Blackwell.

Kaelble, H. 1986: *Industrialisation and social inequality in 19th century Europe*. Translated by Bruce Little. Leamington Spa/Heidelberg: Berg.

Scott, J. W. 1983: Women in history, II, the modern period. *Past and Present*, 101, 141–57.

Sewell, W. H. Jnr. 1980: *Work and revolution in France. The language of labor from the old regime to 1848*. Cambridge: Cambridge University Press.

Thane, P., Crossick, G. and Floud, R. (eds.) 1984: *The power of the past. Essays for Eric Hobsbawm*. Cambridge: Cambridge University Press.

Tilly, L. A. and Scott, J. W. 1978: *Women, work and family*. New York: Holt, Rinehart & Winston.

Part III
Industrial Studies

Introduction

Part II was concerned mainly with the general features of the development of European industry. Here, many of the issues raised there will be discussed in greater detail with reference to specific industries.

By 1914, consumer industries still dominated European manufacturing despite the significant advances and importance of capital goods. In terms of labour employed, the traditional industrial concerns were still foremost. Food and drink, textiles, clothing, leather and furniture making, in general, occupied at least 40 per cent and possibly as much as 60 per cent of Europe's industrial workers. The capital-goods industries, by contrast, were still in their infancy, and even in the most advanced industrial economies, they employed barely one-quarter of the industrial working population. Despite their relatively small size, the capital-goods industries had a considerable impact on European industry in terms of the scientific and technical resources which they commanded and which, in time, would provide a potent force of industrial change.

The consumer goods industries, of which textiles and clothing were the most important, were traditional activities, yet they witnessed some of the most profound organizational and technical changes. Textile production was, by 1914, almost totally transformed. All stages of production had been mechanized and some had moved over to an automatic system of manufacture. The hand spinner, the handcomber, even the handloom weaver were largely relics of an earlier age. On the other hand, the clothing industry remained organizationally similar while the techniques of production were considerably altered. The sewing machine, for example, displaced hand sewing but, at the same time, reinforced the dispersed nature of production.

During the nineteenth century, several new industries emerged in Europe. Some, like the bicycle and automobile industries, had antecedents in an earlier period; others, like the steel industry, had existed for a long time, but only became important after 1850, specifically because technical changes profoundly transformed the economics of production; and the origins of activities such as the organic chemical industry and artificial fibres lay in areas unconnected with their position in the industrial system. The interplay of organization of production, of technology and division of labour was just as complex in these industries as it was in the more traditional concerns.

The industries in Part III were chosen not only because they were most appropriate for exploring the themes raised in Part II but, more importantly, because they represent a cross-section of the types of industrial activities prevalent in Europe throughout the period. The consumer-goods industry is represented by textiles and by consumer durables; and the capital-goods industry by iron, steel and chemicals. In addition, because of the considerable impact they had on other industrial activities, the power generating and shipbuilding industries receive separate treatment.

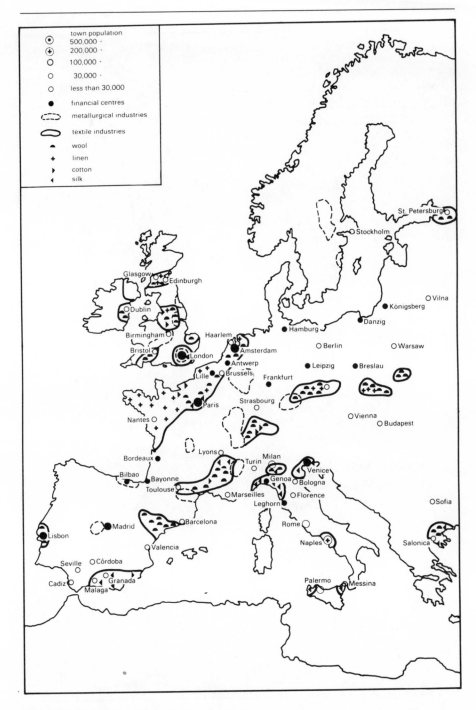

4 Trade and industry in the eighteenth century

5 The industrialization of Europe to 1850

6 The Textile Industry

Throughout the period 1600–1914, the production of textiles constituted an essential component of Europe's industrial base. Until the mid-nineteenth century, whether measured in terms of the proportion of the labour force employed, proportion of total industrial value-added or proportion of total industrial output, textile production in Europe completely overshadowed any other industrial activity. By the early twentieth century, while some of its dynamism had been lost, and other industries strengthened their relative positions, textile activity remained quantitatively important. In 1900, textiles accounted for about 20 per cent of industrial output in both France and Germany and about 15 per cent of the working population in Britain, Belgium and Russia (Deane and Cole 1967; Milward and Saul 1977; Borchardt 1973). In some smaller economies or the less industrialized countries, the relative weight of textiles was even greater – in Switzerland, for example, 56 per cent of the industrial labour force was engaged in textiles and clothing before World War I (Seigenthaler 1976).

The importance of textile production in Europe's industrial economy is difficult to over-emphasize. Europe's industrial strength and wealth was built on textiles; its commerce and industrialization was based on textiles; and its domination of the world's economy was greatly aided by the manufacture of the trade in textiles. Throughout the period, textiles were produced almost everywhere in Europe, in both urban and rural locations. Textile production was, however, far from homogeneous at any time during this period. The technology of production of textiles, for example, varied enormously, from the extremely simple and inexpensive to the highly complex and expensive. The organizational systems within and between each branch of the textile industry were also diverse and the complexity of forms remained throughout the period. The skill necessary to manufacture textiles was widespread and the potential pool of textile labour, for most of the period, was far greater than that used at any one time. Four main textiles – wool, silk, linen and cotton – were produced in Europe, though between 1600 and 1914, the relative performances and importance of these fluctuated. By the end of the period, a significant new concept in textile production emerged in the form of artificial fibres, which had at its root in the burgeoning developments in industrial chemistry of the late nineteenth century.

The Production of Wool and Worsted Goods

The production of wool textiles was ubiquitous. Climatic conditions did not exclude sheep rearing from any but the most remote parts of Europe. Particular types of wool grew better in some regions than others, and, therefore, specialization and exchange in raw wool evolved. Thus, the general availability of raw wool of many varieties and qualities meant that wool textiles formed the basis of non-marketable as well as marketable production. The manufacture of wool textiles was certainly the most important branch of the European textile industry in 1600 (Pounds 1979). While the range of types of cloth produced from wool was enormous, there were two broad categories – woollen cloth and worsted cloth. The essential difference between the two lay in the methods of manufacture. In the production of woollens, the raw material was carded before spinning and the cloth fulled, that is, successively shrunken, beaten and pressed to increase its weight after weaving. This produced a heavy, luxurious yet plain cloth that was relatively expensive. Worsted cloth, by contrast, was manufactured using wool that was combed before spinning and required no further treatment after weaving. This resulted in a lighter and generally less expensive cloth.

Wool products were manufactured in rural areas as well as in towns, and, in the seventeenth century, the former began to assume a more important position. The enormous wealth of many of Europe's cities had been founded on the manufacture of woollen cloth, which had expanded substantially during the sixteenth century. Markets had proliferated and the uses to which woollen cloth were put had multiplied. This success was, however, short-lived and generally, by the 1620s and 30s, output in the urban centres started to decline and continued to do so until well into the eighteenth century (Sella 1974; Cipolla 1976; de Vries 1976). In particularly hard-hit towns, collapse was severe and rapid; in Venice, for example, output and labour force employed fell by 90 per cent during the seventeenth century (Sella 1968; Rapp 1976). In the least affected cities, where output did not decline absolutely, pressure on production was nevertheless intense until the early eighteenth century.

Such problems of decline were not new to European industry; indeed the woollen textile industry itself had experienced difficulties before and had generally managed to overcome them. The seventeenth-century experience, however, was altogether different. Not only was the decline progressive and irreversible, it was also widespread. The towns affected were both traditional centres of production such as Florence, Venice and other southern European cities, and more recent producing areas such as Leiden in the Dutch Republic. The generality of the experience indicates that urban production of woollen cloth was facing a profound structural crisis (de Vries 1976). The precise nature of this crisis has become the focus of some debate among historians.

One group of historians (Verlinden 1972; Davis 1973; de Vries 1976; Wallerstein 1974, 1980) has argued that the decline of urban woollen production was simply a reflection of a deeper change in Europe's economy whereby the traditional and conservative centres of economic power – Mediterranean Europe and southern Germany – were replaced by new, dynamic and innovatory regions located in the north and northwestern parts of Europe. This argument is attractive, yet fundamentally flawed. In the first place, there is no evidence to sustain the view that the decline of urban woollen cloth production was part of a deeper crisis in the urban economy or of the entire region. Though the traditional industrial cities of Europe did not grow significantly during the seventeenth and early eighteenth centuries, their demographic and industrial growth accelerated generally after 1750. The types of cities which did grow in this period were predominantly capital and port cities, not necessarily situated in the favoured northern regions (de Vries 1984). Secondly, many southern regions of Europe did make significant industrial progress between 1600 and 1750 under conditions which might be described as traditional. The silk industry developed considerably, as did many artisanal, handicraft trades. There is little sign, therefore, that industrial decline was generalized (Sella 1969, 1974; Kamen 1980; Phillips 1987).

Other historians have concentrated specifically on the urban component of the debate, arguing that the decline of urban woollen cloth production was indicative of the growing inability of cities to withstand competition from the burgeoning industries in the countryside (de Vries 1976; Sella 1979; Kriedte, Medick and Schlumbohm 1981; Clarkson 1985). Rural industrial production possessed several advantages. In the first place, the absence of guild jurisdiction in the countryside permitted greater flexibility in the use of labour. Because there were no regulations concerning apprenticeship, nor, indeed, entry into the labour market, in general, the supply of labour was relatively elastic. Furthermore, because there were no stringent controls over quality of production in the countryside, rural industry could, given the right market conditions, produce any grade of textiles. Thirdly costs of production were lower in the countryside. In particular, wages tended to be closer to subsistence levels than they were in the towns – at least partly because rural industrial workers had access to supplementary agricultural employment, or land on which to grow food. Finally, the industrial labour supply in the countryside was highly responsive to changing economic and social conditions, largely because of the absence of the social controls over fertility which in towns and in agricultural villages tended to discourage the formation of new families (de Vries 1976; Clarkson 1985).

The relative decline of urban woollen cloth production was clearly related to the expansion of rural woollen cloth manufacture. It is difficult to measure the intensity of rural industry, and only in a few cases do reliable quantitative data exist. It is, however, clear that aggregate output was rising. In France, for instance, where the evidence is particularly striking, the country's total output of woollen cloth production more than doubled between 1650 and 1800, most of the increase being accounted for by rural production (Morineau 1977). During the eighteenth century, the pattern is unmistakable. With the exception of eastern France – from Metz to the Mediterranean – every part of the country experienced an increase in woollen cloth production. The size of the increase varied throughout the regions, but rural areas clearly gained relative to the urban areas. Languedoc and central France registered the greatest gains, more than doubling their output during the eighteenth century (Markovitch 1976). Similar evidence of an expansion of rural woollen cloth production appears in other parts of Europe. In Yorkshire, in England, it is reputed that output may have increased by as much as nine times, and in Tuscany and the Veneto, in Italy, and in the area around Aachen in Germany, there was sustained growth in output (Deane 1957; Wilson 1973; Sella 1969; Kisch 1964).

The growth of woollen cloth production in the countryside was facilitated by the existence of a labour force already skilled in manufacturing. Rather than producing for themselves, as had previously been the case, peasant families began to produce woollen cloths for the market and availed themselves of the benefits (and costs) which involvement with the market brought (de Vries 1976). Although production of wool textiles in the countryside was gaining relative to that in the urban centres, it is clear that the cities, especially those that had once had a thriving woollen cloth industry, remained the financial, commercial and managerial locus of the expanding rural activity. There is thus ample evidence that the seventeenth and eighteenth centuries were a period of marked intensity both in output and in the market involvement of an increasing number of rural inhabitants (Kriedte, Medick and Schlumbohm 1981; Tilly 1983).

The decline of urban woollen cloth production in the seventeenth century was further related to the nature of the product, as the demand for traditional woollen textiles began to fall. This was a direct response to the rigid cost structure of woollen cloth production in the cities where the guilds exercised some economic power. Traditional producers were unable or unwilling to reduce their unit costs of production, while other producers, often operating outside guild control, made cloths of lower quality for sale at lower prices. These distinctive, lighter and cheaper worsted cloths, known as the 'New Draperies' in England, were naturally attractive to poorer consumers, but also to better-off consumers who would be able to pursue fashion trends more closely, by replacing their wardrobe with less expense (de Vries 1976; Coleman 1973).

The output of worsted cloth increased during the seventeenth and eighteenth centuries, and in several regions of Europe, notably East Anglia, Holland and the Champagne region of France, worsted cloth replaced the manufacture of woollen cloths. Generally, however, the manufacture of worsted cloth did not overtake that of woollen cloth until the nineteenth century.

The transformations evident in the manufacture of wool products in the seventeenth and eighteenth centuries, were thus complex and rooted in the changing locus of economic power, protoindustrialization, and changes in fashion. The manufacture of wool products was therefore not only of central importance to Europe's industrial economy in these centuries but was also particularly sensitive to wider economic changes.

During the nineteenth century, the woollen and worsted industries continued to grow, and remained very important within Europe's industrial system. In Germany and France, in particular, woollen and worsted production dominated the textile industry for most of the period for 1800 to 1914 (Landes 1969; Honeyman and Goodman 1986a). In France, raw wool consumption rose dramatically between the early 1820s and 1913 from 54,000 tonnes to 254,000 tonnes; in Germany wool consumption rose from about 30,000 tonnes to over 200,000 tonnes during the same period. British consumption grew from around 60,000 tonnes in the 1820s to around 250,000 tonnes on the eve of the First World War. This pattern of growth was repeated in most of Europe during the nineteenth and early twentieth centuries. Scattered figures for Italy, Austria and Russia point to an expansion of production of the order of three or four times over the period (Mulhall 1892; Mitchell 1973; Markovitch 1966).

Until about 1850, Europe produced most of its own raw wool requirement. One estimate places Europe's share of the world production in 1820 at 94 per cent (Mulhall 1892, 599). Europe's self-sufficiency clearly reflects the historical importance of wool production, but also the high level of intra-European trade in raw wool. In Germany, for example, there was little sign of any sustained movement in cloth production before the middle of the nineteenth century, and considerable quantities of wool were exported primarily to Britain and France. Spain, Russia and Portugal were also net exporters of raw wool during the first half of the nineteenth century (Mulhall 1892). After 1850, however, and especially after the successful mechanization of the combing stage of worsted production during the 1850s, the demand for raw wool increased dramatically, from both established and new producers (Honeyman and Goodman 1986b). Europe's ability to provide its own supply was thus quickly eroded and by the 1860s, Europe became dependent on overseas supplies. South Africa, Argentina and Australia, where European settlers had begun to exploit the vast sparsely populated land, became the main exporting areas. Between 1850 and 1914, wool exports from these three regions grew from 38,000 tonnes to over 500,000 tonnes (figures derived from Barnard 1958; Mitchell 1982, 1983; Denoon 1983).

The expansion of European worsted production accounted for the bulk of the increase in the demand for wool. In France, for example, the capacity of worsted spinning grew 10-fold between 1830 and 1913, most of the growth being registered before the 1870s (Honeyman and Goodman 1986a, 1986b). In Germany worsted production also increased considerably and, most probably, at the expense of woollen production. Raw wool consumption in Germany increased four-fold between 1834 and 1870, but worsted spinning increased more than five-fold and weaving nearly ten-fold – the expansion of woollen spinning and weaving, by contrast, was far less impressive. From 1850 to 1910, the worsted industry continued to grow strongly though, after 1870, growth was less than that registered in cotton, as well as other industries. Nevertheless, between these dates, Germany increased its worsted spinning capacity nearly eight-fold from 300,000 to nearly 2,400,000 spindles (Landes 1969; Milward and Saul 1977, 1979; Pounds 1985). At the outbreak of the First World War, Europe could boast an enormous woollen and worsted industry, and the latter with nearly 11 million spindles was clearly the more important (Honeyman and Goodman 1986b).

The Silk Industry

While the production of woollen cloth had ceased to be an urban monopoly during the seventeenth and eighteenth centuries, the manufacture of silk cloth reaffirmed its place as an essential urban industrial activity, indeed, its expansion played a crucial role in cushioning the effect on Europe's urban economies of the relocation of woollen cloth manufacture to the countryside. Though the organization of silk manufacture resembled that of woollen cloth, the economics of production were vastly different. Raw silk was extremely expensive and represented as much as 80 per cent of the cost of producing silk cloth (Goodman 1977; Sivori 1972). As cost considerations forced woollen production out of the cities, the same forces ensured that silk cloth production remained within city walls.

Before the sixteenth century, silk supply and silk cloth production were concentrated in the main industrial cities of northern Italy – Florence, Bologna, Venice, Genoa and Milan. During the sixteenth and seventeenth centuries, production became established in many other parts of Europe. In France, Tours and Lyons were especially prominent as were Zurich and Geneva in Switzerland. In Spain, Granada and Valencia accounted for the bulk of the country's output, while in England, the industry became concentrated in London. Amsterdam, Antwerp and Krefeld, in the Rhineland, were also important centres of production (Sella 1974; Pounds 1979; Kamen 1980; Ringrose 1983; Phillips 1987; Kisch 1968).

In terms of aggregate growth, the performance of the silk industry was less impressive than wool, but there is little doubt that the European silk industry expanded considerably during this period. Precise data do not exist, but indirect evidence indicates growth. In the first place, the zone of manufacture widened and found a location in most economies (Pounds 1979). Secondly, there is clear evidence that centres of production were importing increasing quantities of raw and worked silk. In England, for example, silk was the most important imported commodity and silk imports from southern Europe tripled in value between the 1660s and the 1770s (Davis 1969 a, 1969 b). Imports of raw and worked silk into France also increased substantially in the seventeenth and eighteenth centuries, despite strenuous efforts to make the country self-sufficient in this valuable and expensive commodity. Both Henri IV and Colbert saw the need to avoid dependence on costly Italian silk yarns, but cultivation was generally a failure except in southern France where the climate was most suitable. Nevertheless, production increased in France, encouraged by royal support (Ciriacono 1981). Elsewhere, information on output, number of looms employed and labour -force size, all indicate a steady growth in silk manufacturing throughout the seventeenth and eighteenth centuries (Ciriacono 1981; Kriedte 1986; Jones 1987).

Despite some concentration of silk production in northern Italy and in southern France, the industry was relatively dispersed, and in some regions, such as Lombardy and around Lyons, silk production coexisted with woollen cloth (Sella 1979; Ciriacono 1981). Demand for silk within Europe was rising along with the expansionary activity of the industry; and wealthy consumers were being joined by those of more modest means to support its growth. Both rising real incomes and an interest in fashion encouraged European consumers to purchase more silk products (Goodman 1983). In the eighteenth century, particularly, design became crucial to the success of silk production, and the increasing use of professional artists in silk cloth production reflected this change. Silk cloth was extremely heterogeneous, not only in appearance and construction, but also in the technology applied to it. Not only were different types of cloths produced – including taffetas, satins, damasks and velvets – but there were also important distinctions in the degree and type of design which the cloth carried.

The intricacy of the design would reflect the complexity of the loom on which the cloth was woven. Unlike woollen and worsted cloth production, in which the loom was of a basic design and the skill was clearly embodied in the weaver and not the machine, the skill in producing elaborate silk cloths lay at least as much in the loom itself as in the artistry of the operator. Thus specialization in silk production involved a long-term commitment or investment in both fixed and human capital (Ciriacono 1981).

Most centres of silk manufacture specialized, and at the end of the seventeenth century, Florence concentrated on taffetas and satins; Genoa on damask and velvet; Venice on cloths inlaid with gold and silver; and Lyons in brocades (Goodman 1983; Sivori 1972; Rapp 1976; Ciriacono 1981). Silk ribbons, which were woven on special ribbon looms, became the speciality of St Etienne, Amsterdam, Geneva, London and Coventry. These specialisms were not static, however, and the cities producing silk cloths frequently altered the structure of their output to suit market conditions, which might involve the upgrading or downgrading of the quality of the output. The Genoese, for example, responded to the increasing superiority of Lyons velvets by shifting their production towards cheap, plain velvets. The Venetians, meanwhile, moved up-market, and began to specialize in rich cloths, abandoning the production of cheaper varieties. Equivalent responses to the market and to competition occurred in other centres of production. The history of the European silk industry, therefore, is one of continuous flux, not only in terms of the volume of output and the relative positions of production centres, but also in the kinds of goods they produced. In some cities, where the woollen and silk industries coexisted, woollen cloth producers were forced to seek labour outside the city walls because the silk producers had successfully bid labour to themselves; and, indeed, the relocation of the woollen cloth industry to the countryside may reflect increasing competition for the city's labour force, not just for silk cloth production, but also sometimes for a wide range of goods in which cities increasingly specialized (Brown and Goodman 1980; Goodman 1983; Hohenberg and Lee 1985; Rapp 1976).

The European silk industry exhibited a remarkable ability not only to adapt to changing circumstances, to respond to changes in demand and competition, but also to provide a positive environment for technical change. Indeed, before the mid-eighteenth century, the silk industry was the locus of most attempts to change the technological basis and the organization of textile production. Because of the growth in demand for new and increasingly complex designs on silk cloths dating from around 1650, there was a great incentive to improve the mechanism as well as the productivity of looms, in particular. Many developments were achieved in this area, and most originated in the Lyonnais region. The success in the eighteenth century of the Dangon loom and subsequently, the Jacquard loom which successfully mechanized the weaving of figured cloths, enabled the French industry first to compete and then to gain a decisive lead over the Italian textile towns. At the same time, much interest was shown in nearly every centre of production in finding new ways of imparting lustre to the cloths; in discovering new colours; and in developing entirely new cloths made by mixing silk with some other fibre (Ciriacono 1981; Hafter 1979).

Technological change in the silk industry was not confined to the final stages of production; in fact, the most important advances probably occurred in the spinning or throwing stage, where technical change was associated with organizational developments (Poni 1972, 1976, 1983). The water-powered silk-throwing mills that were diffused throughout northern Italy, the Rhone valley and subsequently to England, in the seventeenth and early eighteenth centuries, are sometimes referred to as proto-factories; indeed, they were certainly the first significant example of centralized production units, representing a substantial fixed investment. It is ironic that technical and organizational innovations in the silk industry which preceded equivalent developments in other industries, should have been associated with rather limited success, particularly in terms of longevity and output growth. There is no doubt that throughout the seventeenth and eighteenth centuries, the silk industry underwent considerable development and became established in many parts of Europe. Through its dynamism and its flexibility, it sustained great wealth; but, despite improvements in output and productivity, silk remained a luxury, and although real incomes and effective demand rose steadily, the growth of the industry was constrained by this fact.

Silk remained an important branch of textile production through the nineteenth and early twentieth centuries, though its manufacture was confined to a small number of locations, the most notable of which were Lyons, London and Coventry and northern Italy (for analysis of the silk industry in these locations see Pounds 1985; Jones 1987; Lequin 1977; Cayez 1978, 1981; Sheridan 1984; Dewerpe 1984). The nineteenth-century experience of the industry in these cities and regions reflects its continued complexity, vitality and flexibility. Technical and organizational changes continued to be achieved, but they never affected all processes. The adoption of the factory was slow and protracted and, in many stages of production, the workshop form predominated (Sheridan 1979). The performance of the silk industry in Lyons in the nineteenth century exhibited similar innovatory characteristics that had enhanced its success in the seventeenth and eighteenth centuries. When French sericulture was almost destroyed by silkworm disease in the 1850s and early 1860s which led to a rapid increase in the price of raw silk, the Lyonese responded by developing new dyeing techniques that increased the weight of the precious raw silk and allowed the creation of new styles based on vivid colours rather than intricate weaves. When the demand for these bright but expensive cloths was replaced in the 1870s and 1880s by demand for less formal fabrics made of silk wastes and cotton manufactured by the Swiss and the Germans, the Lyonese responded by adding Asiatic silk to mixed fabrics of their own and developing new forms of printing and dyeing which, in turn, gave rise to new, more competitive styles. Factory production in Lyons was very limited – although the sturdier silks and steam-powered looms did encourage some movement towards mass production. Rapid shifts in demand required a flexible response and this was most effectively achieved by a workshop production and by handloom weavers in the surrounding countryside (Pounds 1985; Milward and Saul 1977, 1979; Cayez 1981).

The English silk industry exhibited similar tendencies of dynamism combined with a reluctance to move wholeheartedly into large-scale production (Berg 1985; Jones 1987). Although silk throwing was typically a factory activity, weaving was organized in domestic loom shops or, in the case of ribbon weaving, on the putting-out system. Power looms were strongly opposed and factories provided a less troublesome way of reducing labour costs. The general increase in the demand for silk in the 1850s and subsequently was met by the expansion of cottage factories; this was the means by which silk ribbon weaving was conducted in Coventry, for example. Broad silks, the staple of the nineteenth-century Spitalfields silk weavers, were difficult to adapt to power looms. The delicate and intricate work was best done by artisans and the inferior work was more suitable for factory production.

Between 1600 and 1914, therefore, the silk industry underwent many changes. During the seventeenth and eighteenth centuries, centres of production multiplied and output grew steadily, but as a luxury good, its market was limited and growth was curtailed in the nineteenth century. Unlike most other textiles, the product of the silk industry was not simply heterogeneous, but was constantly changing; new techniques and organizational forms were experimented upon but no consistent pattern emerged. By 1914, although the industry continued to exist in a few exceptional places, and was, as in the case of France, contributing considerably to export earnings, it had become effectively overshadowed by other textiles, especially cotton.

The Linen Industry

For the first half of this period, Europe itself was the most important market for European-produced woollen, worsted and silk cloths. Some attempts were made to locate overseas markets; and although these were unsuccessful in the East, some expansion of overseas trade was achieved with the Americas. The eastern market proved particularly inhospitable to European textiles, partly because it was self-sufficient in textiles and partly because it remained unimpressed by woollen and worsted textiles in particular. The colonial markets in the Americas were altogether different. No substantial indigenous textile industry emerged during this colonial period and therefore a captive market for European textile manufactures existed to satisfy the demands of the slave population and the plantation economies. Colonial demands directly stimulated the European linen industry in particular (de Vries 1976; Kriedte 1983). Linen cloth was used to clothe the slaves, to make into sacks for colonial goods and to make into mattress covers. Throughout the seventeenth and eighteenth centuries, growing quantities of linen cloth from all parts of Europe were channelled through the main colonial ports, and for some parts of Europe, this trade absorbed most of the output.

Like woollen and silk textiles, linen production had a long history as an industrial activity, but before the seventeenth century, its products were rarely marketed. It was deeply rooted in peasant economies, because flax growing was well suited to small-scale production and its transformation into linen cloth required little skill and capital. Thus, wherever flax was grown, there tended to exist linen production and consumption on the spot. There were some important exceptions to this tendency, however. Linen production in southern Germany, for instance, which centred on Munich, Augsburg and Ulm, used flax imported from the Baltic region (Glamann 1977; Kellenbenz 1977). The manufactured cloths were subsequently exported throughout Europe, but principally to Italy. The major cities of Ghent, Bruges and Lille provide further examples of this phenomenon (Kriedte, Medick and Schlumbohm 1981).

Linen production began to spread within many rural regions across Europe in the seventeenth and, more particularly, in the eighteenth century. To some extent, this movement and the associated fall in urban production corresponded to that experienced by the wool textile industry; but in the case of linen, the main source of the increase in output emanated from the growing commercialization of production in the peasant household. In rural Flanders, for example, linen production became widespread and, in some localities, as many as 90 per cent of the households possessed either spinning wheels or looms (Kriedte 1983; Tilly 1983). Similar expansion occurred in northern France and in Britanny and Maine where production increased considerably, especially in the mid-eighteenth century (Kriedte 1983; Engrand 1979; Dornic 1955; Tanguy 1966). Further east, linen production grew in Saxony, Silesia and further east in eastern Europe (Kellenbenz 1977). Output grew dramatically in Scotland and Ireland where, during the eighteenth century, joint production rose from 3 million to 90 million yards (de Vries 1976; Harte 1973).

Linen cloth ranged in quality from the very coarse to the very fine, the latter often competing with better worsted and simple silk. Coarse linens, which formed the bulk of production, found a growing market overseas and many centres of production, regardless of distance to final markets, responded positively to the stimulus. Spain and Portugal, the main colonial powers in the Americas, were the gateway to trade with that part of the world; and many European countries traded directly with Spain (and Portugal) for the primary purpose of tapping that market. French exports to Spain in 1776, for example, ranked first in French trade, accounting for 18 per cent of total French exports (Léon 1974). Breton and Maine linens were foremost in the trade until the end of the eighteenth century (Dornic 1955; Tanguy 1966; Chassagne 1981). Flemish linens found their way to the colonies by the same route. For the British colonies, especially those in the Caribbean, linen producers relied on English merchants; and an analysis of the English re-export trade in the eighteenth century confirms the relative importance of linen re-exports especially to the Americas (Davis 1969b, 1979). Producers from Britanny, Normandy, Flanders, Saxony, Silesia, Russia, Ireland and Scotland competed vigorously for the colonial market. Thus, colonial demand for coarse linen cloth, together with the established networks of both colonial and intra-European commerce and shipping provided a powerful mechanism for integrating many rural industrial areas in a completely new way.

Fine linens, which in contrast to the coarse linens were typically produced in towns, were destined for an altogether different market and were transacted through the established regional networks of Europe. These linens were primarily used for the main household textiles of bedsheets, pillow cases, tablecloths and shirts, and ownership of linen goods was a matter of pride in rural communities (de Vries 1975). Internal European demand for the products of the linen industry, especially fine linens, rose considerably during the seventeenth and eighteenth centuries as real incomes rose.

In the Middle Ages, North Italian textile producers manufactured large quantities of cloth, known as fustians, which combined linen with cotton (Mazzaoui 1981). Fustians were made by both cotton and linen producers. By the fifteenth century, the production of fustians became established in southern Germany where linen producers combined flax with cotton imported from the eastern Mediterranean through Venice. Among the Swabian towns where fustian production was concentrated, the cities of Ulm and Augsburg predominated. In the sixteenth century, these two cities, together with lesser towns in the region were the single largest producers of fustian in Europe, and their products were in great demand throughout Europe. By this time, fustian manufacture had also spread to the Rhineland, Bavaria, Austria, Silesia and further east.

Fustian manufacture represented an important step in the development of the European textile industry. Not only was it the first new type of cloth manufactured in Europe destined for the middle and lower parts of the market, but it depended on a supply of imported cotton, and in some cases of flax or linen yarn. From the outset, therefore, fustian manufacture could be located almost anywhere in Europe, though it was dependent on foreign supplies and therefore closely subjected to the vagaries of an international market. During the seventeenth century, fustian manufacture declined precipitously in the traditional urban centres in southern Germany; and in both Augsburg and Ulm production had virtually collapsed by the end of the century. To some extent, the contraction in urban output was counteracted by the growth of rural production, but evidence suggests that aggregate fustian production was contracting while the more specialized manufacture of pure linen and pure cotton cloth was growing. It is also the case that fustian production was becoming concentrated in other areas of Europe, predominantly in France, the Low Countries and in England (Wadsworth and Mann 1931; Mazzaoui 1981).

French fustian manufacture was located principally in Lyons, Troyes, the Beaujolais, and, to a lesser extent, in Montpellier, Nîmes and Rouen. Lyons was probably the foremost production centre in France, particularly in the seventeenth century, but lost this position in the eighteenth century, partly because of competition from the silk industry and partly because of changes in the source of supply of cotton. Although Troyes continued to manufacture fustians until well into the eighteenth century, French development in the industry at this time was overtaken by expansion in the Low Countries. Amsterdam became an important centre for the import of cotton from the eastern Mediterranean and the West Indies, and from there, cotton found its way to Flanders, to rural areas around Ghent and Bruges as well as to the province of Overijssel and to Westphalia. In England, fustians were manufactured in the sixteenth century in East Anglia, but during the seventeenth and especially the eighteenth century, the industry developed mostly in Lancashire. Fustians, like linens, found a growing market in the colonies of North and South America, but, unlike linens, which were primarily destined for the slave population, the market for fustian was essentially among white settlers (de Vries 1976; Mazzaoui 1981; Wadsworth and Mann 1931).

Historians have typically neglected the history of fustian manufacture in Europe, partly because fustian was a hybrid cloth, as much a part of the linen industry as of the cotton industry, and, therefore, its transitional role in the history of the European textile industry has remained unspecified. Despite this neglect, it is possible to specify several general features of fustian production which are important in the history of the European textile industry. First, fustian production straddled two episodes in European textile production, the one represented by the manufacture of woollens, worsteds, silks and linens, incorporating almost exclusively indigenous raw materials; and the other, represented by the manufacture of cotton, incorporating a wholly non-European raw material. Ironically, cotton enriched the manufacture of linen cloths in the Middle Ages and the early modern period only to destroy it as well as fustian manufacture in the eighteenth and nineteenth centuries. Secondly, fustian manufacture encouraged the spread of textile production generally into the countryside, and increased the dependence of rural workers on merchants and the world market. It also provided textile workers with valuable experience in handling cotton. Finally, it gave rise to the fustian manufacturer whose skills in linking overseas sources of cotton supply to overseas markets were to be crucial in the development of cotton manufacture. Despite its undoubted importance, fustian production itself turned out to be a dead end. In the eighteenth and nineteenth century, it was overtaken by the manufacture of pure cotton cloth which, in terms of the volume of output, of extent of the market and of the organization and technology of production proved to be a considerable force (Mazzaoui 1981).

The Cotton Industry

It is important to put into perspective those features of cotton production which are given pride of place in almost every account of its rise to prominence – the factory and the new technology. At the beginning of the seventeenth century, a kind of cotton cloth was manufactured in many parts of Europe, but the bulk of the raw cotton consumed in Europe was used in the making of fustians. Outside Europe, however, pure cotton cloth was not only common but, in some cases, constituted the most important industrial activity and the most valuable export. Cotton was a truly international commodity and was manufactured wherever it was grown. Thus in the seventeenth century, cotton cloth was manufactured for the market in North and West Africa, throughout the Middle and Near East, and almost everywhere in Asia. India was by far the largest single producer of cotton textiles in the world at this time (Chauduri 1978, 1985).

   The Portuguese were the first to import significant quantities of Indian cotton textiles into Europe, though for them, spices remained more important in the trading relationship (Magalhães-Godinho 1969; Steensgaard 1974). Both the VOC and the East India Company were quick to realize that Indian cotton textiles played a crucial role in intra-Asian trade, which they could tap profitably; and that there was a strong demand for this textile in Africa, in the colonies of North and South America, and in Europe itself. The companies began to make regular shipments of Indian cotton textiles (known collectively as calicoes) in 1613, and it rapidly became clear to both companies that there was enormous demand in Europe for these cloths. In 1625, exports of calicoes from Indian to London reached nearly 250,000 pieces, and, by the mid-1660s had increased to 750,000 pieces. By that date, calicoes accounted for almost 75 per cent of the East India Company's total exports from India. The surge in European demand continued until the 1680s when more than 1.5 million pieces (or 83 per cent of total exports) were handled by the East India Company. Between 1684 and 1689, the VOC sold just under one million pieces of calico in Amsterdam. Exports fell from then to 1700 before rising again to a maximum level of 1.2 million pieces in 1750 (Glamann 1958; Chauduri 1978).

To the VOC and the East India Company, Indian cotton textiles were the most important commodity in their trade with Europe. Between the middle of the seventeenth century and the end of the eighteenth century, cotton textiles regularly accounted for between 30 and 50 per cent of total imports by the VOC in Amsterdam. The East India Company was even more conspicuous in its emphasis on cotton textiles; over the same period, calicoes accounted for as much as 70 per cent and rarely less than 60 per cent of total imports into London. While these two companies were undoubtedly the greatest European purchasers of Indian cotton textiles, they were not alone. The French, the Danes and the Portuguese were also active in the Indian subcontinent and imported significant quantities of cotton textiles into Europe (Glamann 1958; Chauduri 1978; Prakash 1985).

Among the cotton cloths exported from India, an important distinction existed between those produced in Western India and those produced in Madras and Bengal. The former were generally low-cost coarse textiles, while the latter tended to be finer and more expensive. During the seventeenth century, western Indian cotton textiles were clearly preferred, and they were consumed not only by the lower end of the European market but also played a critical role in the West African and West Indian markets. Madras and especially Bengal cloths were clearly destined for the European market, and it was only from the beginning of the eighteenth century that these varieties began to overtake the cheaper cloths in the export trade of India. By the middle of the eighteenth century, Bengal cotton textiles were accounting for as much as 70 per cent of the East India Company's imports of cotton textiles (Chauduri 1978; Prakash 1979).

Madras and Bengal cotton textiles, both printed and plainly dyed, competed directly with finer worsteds and plain silk cloths manufactured in Europe, and the popularity of cottons among European consumers caused anxiety among the producers of these other textiles. In England, opposition to Indian cloths was reflected in the Prohibition Act passed by Parliament in 1700 to stem the consumption of Indian textiles – cottons as well as silks. Indian textile orders fell immediately, but the effectiveness of the Act was short-lived as consumption gradually revived. Twenty years later a second Prohibition Act was passed with equally limited success. Other European countries responded similarly to the competition of Indian textiles. In France, between the 1680s and the 1740s, more than 80 separate pieces of legislation were passed against the import and wearing of Indian printed textiles; in Prussia, calico printing was prohibited in 1721, but since the other German states did not follow suit, the prohibition there was completely ineffective. The legislation in Europe, despite its lack of success, was a public advertisement that the consumption of imported cotton textiles, especially printed ones, had reached worrying levels (Chauduri 1978; Chapman and Chassagne 1981; Leuilliot 1970).

Long before restrictive legislation was enacted, a serious attempt was made by many producers to imitate Indian printed and painted cotton textiles, by printing oriental designs on imported plain white Indian calicoes or on European linens and fustians. Calico printing was found in Europe as early as 1648, but did not become widespread until the last two decades of the seventeenth century. Important concentrations were to be found in Amsterdam, London, Hamburg, Bremen, Frankfurt, Paris and Nantes, but, by far, the greatest producers were in Mulhouse, Neuchâtel and other Swiss towns. Textile printing received an enormous stimulus from Indian cotton textiles, and between 1760 and 1785, the number of calico printers in France, Switzerland and Britain nearly tripled. The spread of calico printing was not confined to this part of western Europe; by the late eighteenth century, central Europe was equally important (Chapman and Chassagne 1981; Caspard 1979).

The expansion of calico printing in Europe during the eighteenth century was crucial in the subsequent development of the European cotton textile industry. In some ways, calico printing provided the first step in the European takeover of world cotton textile production. During the eighteenth century, the production of fustians, on which many of the patterns were printed, was stimulated by calico printing. As late as the 1770s, many prominent printers in Europe were still concentrating their efforts on printing fustians as well as fine linens. In the short term however, the expansion of calico printing also stimulated the import of plain pure cotton textiles from India (Chapman and Chassagne 1981).

Across Europe in the eighteenth century, regional concentrations of cotton production emerged. With few exceptions, cotton production developed in regions associated with calico printing and/or fustian production (Endrei 1963). The reason for this regional correspondence and the nature of the relationship varied. In the case of Lancashire, for example, the cotton industry began to develop when calico printing was introduced into an already well-established fustian producing area – 40 per cent of the cotton spinners in the early stages of the cotton industry in the region had previously been fustian manufacturers or calico printers (Honeyman 1982). In the northern and northeastern region of France, by contrast, cotton production was independent of calico printing and its growth was dependent upon an indigenous linen and fustian industry (Chassagne 1979; Engrand 1979). In Alsace, the cotton industry developed in an altogether different way. Cotton spinning existed in the upland region around Mulhouse, but most of the work seems to have been done for the cotton industry in nearby Basle. Mulhouse, however, developed entirely on the basis of calico printing, which had begun in the city in 1747. Calico printing became increasingly important in Mulhouse and by the end of the eighteenth century, it had the greatest concentration of calico printing works in continental Europe. The local cotton industry itself did not appear to be stimulated by this development. By the end of the Napoleonic Wars, Alsace was, in terms of the output of yarn, one of the smallest cotton producing regions in France, and by the time cotton production did begin to increase, calico printing was in relative decline (Chapman and Chassagne 1981; Milward and Saul 1979; Hau 1985). Cotton production elsewhere in Europe – primarily Switzerland, Normandy, Lombardy and Catalonia – followed variations on these patterns (Milward and Saul 1979; Pollard 1981; Pounds 1985).

The apparently inextinguishable demand for printed (as well as plain) cotton textiles from India (and their European imitations) placed the eighteenth-century European economy, especially its commercial sector, under some pressure. Not only were wool, worsted, and silk manufacturers anxious about the threat to their trade, but governments also were deeply concerned about the enormous trade imbalance which characterized commercial relations between Europe and India. Although the English East India Company, for example, increased its imports into London more than seven-fold between 1660 and 1760, it was generally unable to exchange these imports for European manufactured goods. During this period, precious metals accounted for at least 65 per cent of the Company's exports to India, while cotton cloth manufactured in Europe remained much more expensive than the Indian counterpart. Not only were European wage rates many times greater than the Indian levels, but also Europe depended on relatively inelastic supplies from the eastern Mediterranean, supplemented by those from the West Indies. An increased demand for raw cotton in Europe therefore resulted in raised prices, rather than increased supply (Farnie 1979).

It was clear that the commercial difficulties of eighteenth-century Europe could be largely relieved by productivity growth in the nascent cotton industry. Wherever calico printing or cotton manufacture existed, there was a great need to substitute European manufactured cloths for imported Indian cotton cloth. The fundamental changes in the technology of spinning which were introduced between the late 1760s and 1800 were, of course, directly stimulated by the increased demand for calicoes, but perhaps more importantly by the necessity to reduce dependence on Indian cotton textiles. The mechanization of cotton spinning satisfied the latter requirement because it permitted European producers to undercut significantly the price of Indian cotton yarn. Cotton yarn prices fell so rapidly that by the beginning of the nineteenth century, Indian cotton yarn was estimated to be three times as expensive as English cotton yarn. As one historian has recently remarked; 'Without the cost-reducing function of machinery, it would have been impossible to overcome the comparative advantage possessed by India' (Chauduri 1978, 273). the problem therefore, seemed to be solved, but the increased productivity of cotton spinning could not, by itself, guarantee that the cost advantage would remain, as the problem of inelasticity of raw cotton supply continued. India's advantage in this respect remained, and the increased demand for raw cotton brought about by the mechanization of spinning, raised its price enormously; in the 1790s, for example, the price of raw cotton more than tripled in New York. Because piece rates for weaving also rose, the price of cotton cloth did not fall as much nor as rapidly as that of yarn (Farnie 1979).

Until the end of the eighteenth century, European cotton imports continued to originate from the eastern Mediterranean and the West Indies. Neither the East India Company nor the VOC found it profitable to send consignments of raw cotton from India to Europe, which meant that Europe was dependent on sources of supply which could eventually become exhausted. In the eastern Mediterranean, competition for raw cotton came from indigenous cotton manufacturing industries, while in the West Indies, competition took the form of other crops, such as sugar, in which planters were more inclined to invest their capital and land. The solution to this serious supply constraint came in 1793 with the invention of the cotton gin, which separated the cotton lint from its seeds and allowed profitable cotton cultivation in the southern states of the United States. Raw cotton prices reached their maximum level towards the end of the eighteenth century, but from then on they fell continously (with the exception of the Civil War years) until the end of the nineteenth century (Farnie 1979; North 1966).

This important change finally ended Indian cotton textile imports into Europe. Raw cotton imports grew dramatically. English total imports of raw cotton more than doubled between 1795 and 1805 from 11,000 metric tons to 27,000 metric tons; a doubling of French imports from 4,000 tons to 8,000 tons occurred between 1780 and 1805 despite war and revolution, with a further increase to 19,000 tons by 1820. By the end of the eighteenth century, Europe had already overtaken India as the world's largest producer of cotton goods, and, during the nineteenth century, the trading relationship between England and India was completely overturned as the latter became the main market for English cotton textiles. The massive imports of English cotton goods into India date from 1813 and by the 1830s, the mechanization of spinning had increased productivity in this sector by a factor of 300 to 400 times, effectively ensuring the destruction of the Indian cotton industry. Exports of cotton fabrics from Britain to India grew from 1 million yards in 1814 to 51 million yards in 1830 to 995 million yards in 1870 and 2,050 million yards in 1890 (Farnie 1979).

By the end of the eighteenth century, Europe's predominant position in the world's cotton trade was assured, and it continued to strengthen during the nineteenth century. Tables 6.1 and 6.2 illustrate the phenomenal growth of European cotton production between 1830 and 1914. Continental European consumption of raw cotton rose thirty-fold during this period; and while spindlage grew at a less impressive rate, the quality and efficiency of the spindles improved. The expansion of the industry was such that, by 1914, the total value of cotton products was greater than that of all other textiles combined. The British cotton industry had become by far the largest of the European industries by 1830, and while its rate of growth during the nineteenth century was slower, it retained its lead over the other European economies.

The cotton industry was important for European industrial development in the nineteenth century, both because of the ease with which it was mechanized and because of the large and growing demand for its products. By the early nineteenth century, cotton had become factory-produced in France, Belgium, Germany, Switzerland and the Habsburg Empire; and by 1850, the industry was almost everywhere fully mechanized. Expansion of cotton production took place primarily in areas where textiles had been traditionally manufactured, but because of the reliance on imported raw materials, many cotton areas also developed near ports.

In France, the cotton industry had expanded more rapidly than in any other continental economy by the early nineteenth century. At this early stage, spinning was concentrated in the Nord and neighbouring *départements*, and weaving was mainly located in Normandy. Between 1830 and 1914, the industry's consumption of raw cotton increased four-fold and spindlage rose three-fold. While this represented a slower growth rate than elsewhere, it reflected not only France's earlier achievements in cotton production leading to a higher base in 1830, but

Table 6.1: *Raw cotton consumption in Europe 1835–1914 (000 metric tons)*

	Austria	Belgium	France	Germany	Italy	Russia	Spain	Switz.	UK
1835	8.7	4.8	39	8.9	—	3.6	2.9	—	144
1840	12	9.1	53	8.9	—	6.5	8.4	—	208
1845	24	8.7	60	13	—	12	17	—	275
1850	29	10	59	26	—	20	16	—	267
1855	34	11	76	26	—	25	17	—	381
1860	45	15	115	67	—	47	24	33	492
1865	22	12	61	46	2.8	26	15	24	328
1870	45	16	59	81	15	46	27	38	489
1875	52	18	101	114	19	85	34	22	557
1880	64	23	89	137	47	94	45	22	617
1885	72	17	108	156	79	124	49	23	589
1890	105	32	125	227	102	136	50	27	755
1895	122	22	141	267	108	201	71	26	755
1900	127	35	159	279	123	262	66	24	788
1905	164	48	202	394	165	273	76	26	822
1910	173	63	158	383	175	362	73	24	740
1914	172	140	160	478	191	424	84	24	942

Source: B. Mitchell *European Historical Statistics* (London, 1975), 428–31.

Table 6.2: *Cotton spindles in Europe, 1834–1913 (000 spindles)*

	Austria	Belgium	France	Germany	Italy	Russia	Spain	Switz.	UK
1834	800	200	2,500	626	—	700	—	580	10,000
1861	1,800	612	5,500	2,235	—	1,000	—	1,350	30,387
1877	1,558	800	5,000	4,700	880	3,450[1]	1,865[2]	1,854	44,207
1891	2,400	930	5,040	6,071	1,686	6,000	2,050	1,722	44,509
1904	3,450	880	6,150	8,434	2,435	7,146	2,600	1,600	47,857
1913	4,909	1,492	7,400	11,186	4,600	9,212	2,000	1,398	55,653

Source: B. Mitchell *European Historical Statistics* (London, 1975), 434–5.
[1]average of 1870 and 1882/3.
[2]figure for 1882/3.

also its greater emphasis on high-quality products for which demand grew only modestly. Such growth as did occur from the 1830s was concentrated in Alsace, especially in Mulhouse, where the industry was influenced by Swiss entre-preneurs and technicians. The Alsatian industry adopted larger units of produc-tion and a higher degree of mechanization than other areas, and by the early 1870s, it had overtaken Normandy and rivalled the Nord in both spinning and weaving capacity. The absorption of Alsace into the German Reich in 1871 resulted in a sharp decline in production, but only temporarily, as many cotton workers migrated back to France to establish a rival industry. By 1900, this new sector had become larger in both spinning and weaving than the original Alsatian industry from which it derived. Throughout the nineteenth century, the north of France retained its important position in textile production generally and cotton continued to coexist with wool and linen. There was indeed much transference among these industries, and the production of worsted and linen expanded sharply during the cotton famine of the 1860s. After 1870, the French cotton industry lost some of its dynamism, but it was still the largest employer of labour in 1914 (Landes 1969; Milward and Saul 1977, 1979; Pounds 1985; Heywood 1977).

The cotton industry in Belgium emerged in the late eighteenth century from the traditional industry of the Flanders region. By the 1820s, 70 per cent of Belgium's cotton spindles were located in the Ghent area, where the industry remained concentrated until 1914. During the nineteenth century, the industry expanded in line with the European average (see Tables 6.1 and 6.2), and was determined largely by the growth of the domestic market. In 1832, 87 per cent of Belgian cotton cloth was consumed internally; and by 1840, this proportion had risen to 96 per cent (for more detail on Belgium see Milward and Saul 1977) 1979; Pounds 1985).

Cotton had not developed as a handicraft industry in Germany, but when it did emerge, the industry rapidly adopted large and highly mechanized units of production. Much of the German cotton industry became established in the earlier linen and woollen manufacturing regions of Saxony, southern Germany and the Lower Rhineland, and cotton continued to share the field with these other textiles. As Tables 6.1 and 6.2 show, expansion of German cotton production was remarkable during the nineteenth century; and from the 1890s until 1914, its output was second only to that of Britain.

While the cotton industry of both Alsace and southern Germany had been inspired by Swiss expertise, the industry in Switzerland itself remained small throughout the nineteenth century. By 1827, 106 water-powered mills had been established in the region of Zurich, and during the next 20 years the industry spread a little in the neighbouring valleys. From 1835, the Swiss industry specialized in spinning – indeed, weaving remained unmechanized until the late nineteenth century and concentrated on high-quality cloth for export. Despite its lack of growth, the Swiss cotton industry was highly advanced and by 1850, only Britain had a higher number of spindles per capita output of cotton. The industry, furthermore, remained critical to the performance of the Swiss economy, employing about 50 per cent of the industrial labour force (Milward and Saul 1979).

The expansion of the Austrian cotton industry in the nineteenth century was slightly slower than the European average, and was located in the traditional textile regions around Vienna, Linz and Graz into the Tyrols, Styria and to the mountains of Upper Hungary (Good 1984; Pounds 1985).

In southern Europe a mechanized cotton industry developed relatively late, but in both Spain and Italy, a sizeable industry had been established by 1914 (see Tables 6.1 and 6.2). A modern cotton industry using steam power with imported coal began to develop in the hinterland of Barcelona from 1830. Much of the growth of the Catalan cotton industry in the 1840s and 1850s, however, was based on an enormous number of small, water-powered mills. The industry suffered during the cotton famine of the 1860s, when unsuccessful attempts were made to grow cotton in Spain, but it emerged from the crisis in a more efficient state. The subsequent prosperity of the industry was based on Empire markets before their loss in 1898, and on consistently expanding home demand. The pattern of growth of the Italian cotton industry corresponded to that of the

Spanish industry. Expansion took place using machinery imported from Switzerland, mainly in Lombardy and Piedmont, where water-power was plentiful (Milward and Saul 1977; Pounds 1985).

For most of the nineteenth century, the size of the continental cotton industry was overshadowed by that of Britain; yet in terms of growth rates, its performance outstripped the British. The cotton industry was a significant feature of the process of European industrialization and its momentum was well sustained until 1914. In 1914, two-thirds of the world's cotton spindles were located in Europe (25 per cent in continental Europe and a further 39 per cent in Britain); yet the progress was clouded by the threat of competition from the newly developed synthetic fibres, and by the cotton woven in the Far East.

Conclusion

At first glance, it may seem surprising that the cotton industry rather than some other branch of textile production became the focus of those changes in technique and organization which are often associated with the rise of modern industry. In 1700, the cotton industry, for example, was not as important as the woollen and worsted industries. It produced less, until the end of the eighteenth century, and was less widely distributed. Any problems in output or productivity which might induce changes in production techniques would, in principle, be equally great in each of the industries. Despite the undoubted similarities in many aspects of their production, it was the nature of the market that from the outset distinguished cotton from all other textiles. No other textile in Europe enjoyed the kind of market conditions which prevailed in the cotton industry. Cotton was consumed on a global level; each producing region in the world constituted an enormous potential market for cotton textiles. Cotton, moreover, unlike wool was part of the world trading system, in which Europe was central from the seventeenth century. Therefore, once costs of production in Europe were reduced to below the level in India, cotton manufacturers would be provided with a market so large as to be virtually limitless. Thus the size and extent of the market was the crucial difference between cotton production and other branches of textile production in Europe; and the market to which European cotton manufacturers had access was the same size as that which existed for Indian cotton manufacturers.

The market therefore provided a crucial context within which fundamental changes in production could take place but organizational and technological changes would not necessarily by themselves generate widespread changes in production or output. The factory, for example, was first used for organizing woollen production and potentially revolutionary changes in spinning and weaving technology were first achieved in the silk industry. Each of these changes was limited in its effect. The critical difference in the cotton industry lay in the specific combination of features – the factory, new spinning technology and a world-wide market – and that this combination gave, for the first time in a consumer goods industry, primacy to production over exchange; in other words, to the industrialist over the merchant. The dynamics of European cotton production existed within the producing unit rather than from the commercial system. The traditional relationship between production and exchange was bound to alter once capital became concentrated in the hands of the industrialist; and once factories were designed to operate on continuous rather than batch production, it was necessary for industrial capital to take precedence over merchant capital. Industrialists no longer waited for markets to be opened up by merchants – but rather, they needed to create their own markets not only by producing at lower costs than competitors, but also by undermining the efficacy of indigenous production. The cotton manufacturers in England were particularly successful at this because of the introduction of the new spinning technology, followed by the selective and increasing import duties on Indian textiles from 1797 to 1819 and the abolition of the East India Company's monopoly over trade between India and Europe in 1813. The British cotton industry was able not only to increase its own production and exports but also to expel Indian textiles from third markets and then from India itself.

The cotton industry has been correctly assessed as the locus of industrial capitalism, and it is important to understand that the relationship between cotton production and industrial capitalism was not confined to England, though it was particularly visible there. Factory organization and new production machinery characterized cotton manufacture throughout Europe especially in the spinning sector. Before the mid-eighteenth century, English and continental cotton production responded alike to the same global influences – and both were subsequently transformed with similar results.

Further Reading

Cayez, P. 1978: *Métiers jacquards et hauts fourneaux*, Lyons: Presses Universitaires de Lyon.

Chapman, S. D. and Chassagne, S. 1981: *European textile printers in the eighteenth century: A study of Peel and Oberkampf.* London: Heinemann.

Gullickson, G. L. 1986: *Spinners and weavers of Auffay.* Cambridge: Cambridge University Press.

Kriedte, P. 1983: *Peasants, landlords and merchant capitalists.* Leamington Spa: Berg.

Kriedte, P., Medick, H. and Schlumbohm, J. 1981: *Industrialization before industrialization.* Cambridge: Cambridge University Press.

Mazzaoui, M. 1981: *The Italian cotton industry in the later Middle Ages, 1100–1600.* Cambridge: Cambridge University Press.

Pounds, N. J. G. 1979: *An historical geography of Europe, 1500–1840.* Cambridge; Cambridge University Press.

— 1985: *An historical geography of Europe, 1800–1914.* Cambridge: Cambridge University Press.

Revue du Nord 1981: *Numéro spécial: Aux . origines de la révolution industrielle.* Vol 63, no. 248.

7 The Development of Consumer Durables

It is hard for those living in advanced industrial societies to imagine a world without gadgets. Nearly all households contain a significant array of such items including domestic appliances, electrical and electronic appliances, photographic equipment, watches, clocks, cars, and bicycles. Though performing different tasks, powered by different sources and manufactured from different materials, the consumer gadgets have three important features in common. In the first place, they are all assembled from parts, most of which have little or no utility on their own; they require servicing to a greater or lesser extent; and they can all be repaired usually by simply replacing the defective parts. Secondly, they share certain manufacturing principles – especially that of interchangeability, that is, all equivalent parts are identical – and have many production methods and technologies in common. Finally, they are all items of mass production and consumption.

As industrial processes, the manufacture of these gadgets – or consumer durables – bears significantly on several aspects of the modern industrial economy. Because production is based on parts assembly, there is enormous scope for specialization as well as diversification. In the car, electrical and electronic industries, for example, the production of components is a highly specialized and significant industrial activity in its own right. At the same time, the components industries produce a large range of products which while being manufactured in similar ways are destined for very different final uses. The ability to manufacture a range of items using similar production methods and technologies also ensures that skills are easily transferred among industrial activities, leading to both enhanced competition and mobility. The fact that they are items of mass consumption also provides for generally similar techniques of marketing.

There is little doubt that as far as the twentieth century is concerned, the enormous growth of the consumer-durable industry has had a marked impact on the structure of the industrial economy on an international scale. Multinational enterprises, for example, are most commonly found in this industry. Trade amongst the more advanced industrial economies typically consists of the products of this industry either in their finished form or as components. An explanation for the vast increase in consumer-durable production in this century is certainly not difficult to construct. Real incomes, for example, have grown enormously allowing consumers to release an increasing proportion of their incomes for these goods. But this alone provides only a necessary condition for expansion, for the extra purchasing power could quite easily be expended on other kinds of goods such as clothing, housing and food and drink. Of even greater importance is the dynamism inherent in the production methods and the industrial system itself. In order to understand this particular feature of the twentieth century industrial economy it is necessary to turn to its origins in the nineteenth century and before.

Besides providing an understanding of the modern industrial economy, an examination of the development of the consumer-durables industry in Europe before 1914 also allows us to treat various themes in the making of industrial Europe alluded to in earlier chapters. Before 1914, the range of consumer-durable goods in Europe was narrow. The most important production consisted of clocks, watches, bicycles, sewing machines, typewriters and small arms. With the exception of clocks, watches and small arms, they were entirely new industries, but they emerged from a traditional industrial system where craft skill and artisanship reigned supreme. These consumer-durable industries did not begin life, in Europe at least, in factories nor in large concerns, even though these were typical in many other industrial activities, but rather in small workshops. These workshops were highly innovative in the development of technology and were not an obstacle to the emergence of modern production methods (for a critical appraisal of the centrality of workshop production, see Sabel and Zeitlin 1985). At the same time, these industries were the exclusive locus of male labour. Yet even in these new strongholds of skill and exclusivity, contradictions existed which eventually led not only to the imposition of factory discipline, but also to the coming of the assembly line, scientific management and violent workers' opposition. The stimulus for these changes may not have been the supposed superiority of the factory over the workshop form of organization. The production methods and technologies in fact originated in military establishments where artisan methods were strongly resisted.

An analysis of the development of the consumer durables of the nineteenth century also sheds light on the relationship between production and distribution which was central to the emergence of a strong and thoroughly independent industrial system. In each of the consumer-durable industries, marketing became critical to industrial performance, indeed it was often more important than the methods and technology of production. While the roots of this may be traced back to similar efforts at achieving high-profile marketing by Wedgwood in the ceramics industry in the late eighteenth century, the marketing of consumer durables became, in the nineteenth century, a highly specialized activity. The most visible examples were in the bicycle and car industries, but direct marketing also lay behind the phenomenal success of the sewing machine as a domestic product (Hounshell 1984). The emergence of specialized marketing was not however smooth and the interests of those with commercial expertise and those with engineering interests often collided, especially in the car industry (Church 1982).

The focus of this chapter is the experiences of a variety of industrial activities, some of which like the car, bicycle and sewing machine were entirely new to the nineteenth and early twentieth centuries and others, such as clocks and watches, whose history is of a far longer duration. This chapter will also mention two other industries, the machine tool industry and the arms industry which were critical in the emergence of a viable mass consumer-durable industry. In the machine tool industry, for example, changes in production methods and technology made it technically possible to produce uniform, if not entirely interchangeable parts, which were at the heart of the novelty of consumer durables, and the arms industry in Europe was intimately involved in the development and structure of other branches of consumer-durable production specifically through the exploitation of techniques of machine tooling. Because it provides so much insight into the workings of the industrial system especially in the late nineteenth and early twentieth centuries, the chapter will begin with a discussion of the automobile industry.

The Automobile Industry

The automobile was a European invention of the 1860s and 1870s even though its commercially viable manufacture did not begin until the late 1880s. It is an outstanding example of the convergence of many sources of technical innovation and diffusion, industrial enterprise, and popular culture in a single product (Barker 1987).

By the second half of the nineteenth century, Europeans had become accustomed to public land-transport using an inanimate power source. By 1860, for example, more than 50,000 kilometres of railway line were in operation connecting most of Europe's large and middle-sized cities (Mitchell 1973). The idea of independent travel also became a reality during this time as bicycle production moved steadily from a curiosity to an important item of mass consumption (Barker 1987). Moreover, Europe had already enjoyed almost a century of experimentation in the application of steam power to primitive carriages. Most of these attempts had ended in failure because of the excess weight and instability of the vehicles. Coachbuilders were nevertheless encouraged to produce carriages with better suspension in response to the growth of railway transport and because of the consistent increase in the demand for carriages (Bardou *et al.* 1982).

In the 1860s, the first successful internal combustion engine was developed almost simultaneously in France, Germany and the United States. The Belgian-born Parisian inventor, Etienne Lenoir, however, is usually credited with providing the first practical machine burning gas as its fuel. Initially, the engine was used to provide stationary power in Paris, but was soon used to provide motive power, and was able to substitute petrol for gas (Laux 1976). Lenoir's engine was, however, not suitable for traction but by 1876, the German inventor Nicholas Otto and his engineer partner Gottlieb Daimler had developed and perfected a petrol-burning internal combustion engine operating on a four-stroke cycle (Nübel 1987). While this engine was possibly the first capable of providing traction to a road vehicle, the first motorized vehicle (developed in Mannheim in 1886) was the work of Karl Benz (Nübel 1987; Bardou *et al.* 1982). More than two decades thus elapsed for the power source of the automobile to be developed to the point where it could be used to provide traction.

Meanwhile, because of developments in other industries, specifically in the metalworking industries, in bicycle production and in carriage building, much of the technology necessary for a petrol-burning road vehicle existed by the late 1880s. Gearing, transmission and suspension, for example, as well as important advances in precision metal-working machinery capable of producing interchangeable parts and the pneumatic tyre had all been developed; and, in the late 1890s, manufacturers began to vigorously exploit the idea of using a four-wheeled carriage, instead of the tricycle which had until then been the preferred carriage design (Bardou *et al.* 1982; Caunter 1970).

The first automobiles which were reliable enough to be purchased by the public did not come out of the workshops until the early years of the 1890s. In 1895, after more than 30 years of research and development, production had reached 144 units in France and 135 units in Germany; and fewer than 500 cars were in use throughout Europe (Bardou *et al.* 1982).

Most manufacturers of automobiles before 1900 had experience of other industrial activities. In France, Germany and Britain the most common background was bicycle production. In France, this was true of several of the most important firms including Peugeot, Darracq, Clément, Richard and Chenard and Walcker; in Germany, both Opel and Adler began in this way and in Britain, most of the early firms, Humber, Rover, Riley, Sunbeam and Singer, for example, also began as bicycle manufacturers (Laux 1976; Milward and Saul 1977; Saul 1962). Metalworking was another activity from which automobile manufacturers emerged. This was the case with the famous French company of Panhard and Levassor as it was in Germany with Stoewer and Dürkopp (Flageolet-Lardenois 1972; Bardou *et al.* 1982). Other manufacturers such as Hotchkiss in France and Wolseley, which was owned by Vickers, in England were also involved in armaments production and Mors had a background in electrical equipment (Laux 1976; Saul 1962). Only a minority of firms, of which Renault in France is an example, lacked previous industrial experience. Large engineering and metalworking firms, such as Schneider and SACM in France, Krupp and Borsig in Germany and Platt Bros. in Britain, however, showed little or no interest in car production.

Wherever a sizeable concentration of metalworking establishments and/or bicycle making establishments existed, at least one of the firms would enter into some form of automobile manufacturing. This was true of most large European cities. In France, automobile manufacturers clustered in Paris, where there were many small firms involved in metalworking, and in Lyons and in some other provincial centres (Laux 1976). Stuttgart and Mannheim were the most important centres of manufacturing in Germany as were Coventry, Birmingham, London and Glasgow in Britain. Manufacturers could also be found in Turin, Milan, Genoa, Barcelona, Geneva, Zurich, Vienna, Prague, Amsterdam and Copenhagen (Bardou *et al.* 1982). The capital and labour requirements of automobile production were relatively low and in the early period of the industry's development at least, when small-scale production was usual, no special organizational form or selling methods were required. In the early stages manufacturers simply sold direct to their customers from the workshop on order. When demand rose, however, direct selling ceased to be appropriate; and marketing techniques from the bicycle industry, such as a system of agents and such promotional aids as specialized magazines, were transferred to the selling of cars (Fridenson 1981; Church 1982).

Making cars was not a simple process, however. Automobile workshops utilized the most advanced machine practices available since the complexity of the product required delicate work and high levels of precision. As long as the demand for the product remained small, manufacturers could make do with a small number of general-purpose machine tools operated by highly skilled craftsmen who, if necessary, could use hand tools to put the finishing touches to the individual parts as they came off the machines. As soon as demand rose to the level at which it was no longer possible to craft each automobile individually and to provide an efficient after-sales service, the old artisanal system could no longer operate. The craft system, nevertheless, dominated European automobile production until the inter-war period (Fridenson 1978; Bardou et al. 1982).

The European automobile industry experienced its first boom between 1898 and 1908, when production in the pioneer centres in France and Germany soared. In 1907, total French output reached more than 25,000 units, of which a significant proportion was exported; while in Germany, output stood at just over 5,000 units. During this period of expansion, volume production began elsewhere in Europe, especially in Britain and Italy where, in 1907, output reached 12,000 and 2500 units respectively (Foreman-Peck 1982; Bardou et al. 1982).

After 1908, growth slowed in France while it accelerated elsewhere in Europe, and at the outbreak of the First World War, the total output of the European automobile industry approached 120,000 units, of which French production accounted for 40 per cent (Foreman-Peck 1982). The rapid growth of the industry from the late 1890s, was achieved by the proliferation of small-scale, low-volume producers. The largest European concern, Peugeot, produced 5000 units in 1913, while no other maker in Europe produced more than 2000 units (Laux 1976).

The size and structure of the European automobile industry was quite different from that of the United States until the inter-war period, although it clearly became influenced by its American counterpart. In 1914, even the largest of the European manufacturers maintained a high level of skilled labour and craft-based operations. In the United States industry, however, where the output of the Model T Ford reached 190,000 units in 1913, specialized machine tools had largely replaced skilled craft workers by 1905 (Hounshell 1984). The expansion of the European automobile industry before 1914 had placed some pressure on manufacturers to shift their production technologies from general-purpose to specialized machine tools, but, although a few manufacturers such as Panhard and Levassor were quick to absorb the new American technology, the march of technical progress in Europe was far more gradual than in the United States (Laux 1976).

As far as the organization of production is concerned, there is little doubt that by the outbreak of the First World War, automobile manufacturing employed a significant proportion of the labour of the engineering and metalworking industries. More than 60,000 workers were employed in the French automobile industry and more than 100,000 in the British automobile industry (Laux 1976; Saul 1962). Some of the firms, moreover, were exceptionally large, indeed they were in many cases some of the largest firms in the country. Daimler in Britain and Renault in France employed 5000 and 4000 workers respectively (Saul 1962; Fridenson 1979). Yet, despite their size, their complicated management and manufacturing operations, and the advent of American machine-tool technology, most automobile manufacturing plants in Europe remained the domain of artisanal production. In the Renault plants, for example, skilled workers accounted for more than 70 per cent of the workforce in 1914 (Fridenson 1979; Laux 1976). The European automobile industry before the First World War remained the domain of the mechanic and the skilled worker rather than the production engineer and the unskilled worker. The industry was also male dominated. In one survey of the Paris suburb of Puteaux in 1914, where six automobile manufacturers operated, women constituted no more than 0.45 per cent of the workforce; in Renault's plant in Boulogne-Billancourt, women workers represented about 6 per cent of the total work force. These low figures are hardly surprising. As long as the industry recruited its workers from the metalworking industries at large, men would continue to dominate the workforce (Fridenson 1979). It is interesting to note that on the only occasion when an American observer of the machine-tool industry in 1908 found women workers operating machinery in a French automobile manufacturing plant, they were tending specialized American milling machines (Carden 1909).

By 1914, the European automobile industry showed little sign of concentration. Of a total output of 140,000 automobiles in 1913, 40 per cent were manufactured in the top 20 firms (Laux 1976). No company had a decided advantage in the field in terms of its market share and despite the existence of some very large companies, production generally resembled more the output of large workshops than that of factories. Until World War I and possibly until the coming of the assembly line, the production of automobiles in Europe did not represent a wholehearted transfer to mass production techniques which, more likely, were already in place in the manufacture of bicycles, as well as sewing machines, clocks and watches and office machinery (Fridenson 1978).

The Bicycle and Sewing Machine Industries

The automobile owed a great deal to the bicycle, and wherever bicycles were made, automobiles soon followed. While the debt of the automobile to the bicycle is rightly emphasized in the literature, it is easy to overlook the bicycle industry as an activity in its own right. Not only was the bicycle the precursor of the automobile, but it continued to develop and sustained its momentum alongside the automobile (Trescott 1976).

Bicycle production can be said to have begun in the 1860s when pedals and a crank were fitted to a *draisienne*, a simple two-wheeled machine which was propelled directly by the rider (Laux 1976; Ritchie 1975; Woodforde 1970). The velocipede, penny–farthing or ordinary bicycle, as the new machine with independent power was variously called, went into commercial production in the 1860s in France, Germany and England and in the 1870s in the United States (Harrison 1985). Despite enormous publicity and promotional devices extolling the virtues of cycling, production remained small in the 1870s and 1880s. In England, for example, where cycling was apparently quite popular, the main centres of bicycle manufacturing contained only a handful of complete cycle makers. In the mid-1870s no more than three manufacturers existed in Coventry, six each in Birmingham and Nottingham and a few in London, making 20 cycle makers in the country as a whole (Harrison 1969). At this early stage in its development, the bicycle was largely impractical and served the purpose of a rather expensive toy or an amateurish pastime. Not only was the ordinary bicycle unreliable for long journeys, it was also difficult to mount and dismount and required an immense physical effort to operate since the wheel turned only once for each turn of the pedals.

It was not until the mid-1880s that a design emerged which overcame some of these disadvantages. The new machine, called a 'safety' bicycle, incorporated wheels of equal size and a chain drive to the rear wheels leaving the front wheel free for direct steering. The pneumatic tyre, invented in 1888, completed the transformation of the clumsy ordinary bicycle into a machine of considerable practicality (Ritchie 1975).

The safety bicyle was an immediate success and gave rise to an extensive bicycle industry not only in Europe but also in the United States. In England, where the safety bicycle was first perfected and introduced, the expansion of the industry took the form of the multiplication of manufacturers of completed bicycles and component makers.

In Birmingham, for example, the number of manufacturers of completed bicycles increased from 43 firms in 1880 to 114 in 1891. A similar growth occurred in both Coventry and Nottingham, where the number of firms more than tripled over the same decade. Bicycle production is estimated to have increased from 200,000 in 1882 to 500,000 in 1893. At its peak, in 1895/7 there were probably more than 800 firms in England making completed bicycles (Harrison 1969, 1985). In France, where cycling was initially less popular than in England, the bicycle industry was slower to develop. The first safety bicycles were imported from England and as popularity grew, especially in Paris, many new as well as established firms began to exploit the new technology. One of the leaders in this field was Peugeot, which first produced the safety bicycle in 1886 (Laux 1976). By 1893, there were 150,000 registered users of bicycles in France (Holt 1985). In Germany the production of bicycles reached 250,000 per year by the mid-1890s, while production in the United States outstripped European output (Milward and Saul 1977). In 1897, the 300 American companies produced between 1.5 and 2 million bicycles (Trescott 1976).

The rapid growth of the bicycle industry faltered in 1895/7. Many firms collapsed or entered other activities: but while demand was not as great as it had been, bicycle production continued to grow until the outbreak of the First World War. By then the number of bicycle owners had reached between three and four million in France and Britain, while in the United States, the likely figure exceeded five million (Holt 1985; Trescott 1976). Clearly the bicycle had become a pre-eminent mass-produced consumer durable.

Little is known about the early makers of bicycles, though many entered the industry from the metalworking sector. Some of the leading European bicycle manufacturers, moreover, made a range of products which typically consisted of a combination of any or all of the following – sewing machines, small arms, cars and typewriters. Seidel and Naumann, Germany's largest bicycle makers at the end of the nineteenth century, for example, made both bicycles and sewing machines, employing more than 1,300 workers in their plant (Harrison 1969). Opel combined bicycle and sewing machine production with that of cars. Cars and bicycles were both produced by English firms such as Rover and Singer; sewing machines and bicycles was the combination for several Coventry and Birmingham firms; whilst small arms and bicycles was the preferred combination for firms such as the Birmingham Small Arms Company (Harrison 1985). In Belgium the national armoury in Liège undertook the production of arms, bicycles and cars (Milward and Saul 1977; Harrison 1969). In France, Peugeot, Darracq and Clément, leading automobile manufacturers, were also heavily engaged in bicycle manufacture. Peugeot, for example, produced 80,000 bicycles in 1914; in the same year the output of cars stood at 5,000 units (Laux 1976; Milward and Saul 1977).

From the 1880s, the expansion of output of the European bicycle industry required significant changes in production techniques. Interchangeability became more widely applied; specialized component makers and assembly plants emerged; and most important of all, machined component parts were gradually replaced by pressed and stamped components from sheet metal. These changes together with improvements in the production of tyres and inner tubes were responsible not only for the falling cost of bicycle manufacturing, but also for the introduction of mass-manufacturing techniques into mass-production goods. In the case of Britain, the techniques and machine tools necessary for interchangeable manufacturer were first applied in bicycle production although in both Germany and France such techniques already existed in the technologically associated industries (Harrison 1969; 1985; Saul 1970; Harley 1974). Regardless of the precise channel of innovation, the bicycle industry was clearly instrumental in furthering the mechanization of metalwork, and influencing the techniques adopted by the automobile industry. There is some evidence to suggest that the assembly line was also first used in bicycle manufacture, as was the case in the Peugeot plants on the eve of the First World War (Milward and Saul 1977).

The close relationship that existed between the production of automobiles and bicycles found parallels in a range of consumer-durable goods which European industry was producing towards the end of the century. In the bicycle craze of the 1890s, many new firms entered the field from the armaments, and sewing machine industries, but generally, they did not abandon the one in favour of the other. The techniques learned in any one of these activities could easily be transferred to another.

An industrial culture had been created where techniques of production and methods of distribution and marketing were common over a range of products. In the United States, it has been shown convincingly that the machine-tool industry in New England was primarily responsible for diffusing the techniques of mass production; and that not only was there a flow of technical information among machine-tool makers and industrial manufacturers, but there was a substantial movement of skilled mechanics, inventors, machinists, etc. from the one to the other (Rosenberg 1963). In the case of the sewing machine, the relationship was even more direct. One of the foremost manufacturers of sewing machines in the United States, Willcox and Gibbs, chose to have their sewing machine made by a small general-purpose metal shop of Brown and Sharpe. In order to produce the sewing machines at reasonable cost, Brown and Sharpe built special machine tools, guages and fixtures designed specifically for this purpose, and it was through this process that Brown and Sharpe became one of the leading machine-tool builders in the country and certainly the most innovative (Hounshell 1984).

In Europe, however, there is little sign that the sewing machine provided a direct stimulus to machine-tool production. Indeed, the reverse seems to be true. In Britain, for example, the Singer sewing machine plant in Scotland began to manufacture sewing machines as early as 1870, and by 1900, output had reached 13,000 machines per week employing 7,000 workers. The plant had installed more than 12,000 machine tools in the period from 1870 to 1914, 80 per cent of which had been made by the company itself. Other manufacturers apparently followed a similar course (Saul 1970). In France, sewing machine production was relatively unimportant. In 1896, there were only 900 people employed in the manufacture of sewing machines in all of the country and only four firms employed more than 50 workers (Mill 1985). Germany, however, was a major producer of sewing machines and employed techniques in both production and marketing similar to those of the American producers (Kirchner 1981). Several leading firms of automobiles and bicycles made sewing machines and at least one leading sewing machine maker, Frister and Rossmann, made automobiles. One of the country's most important machine tool makers, Ludwig Loewe of Berlin, began as a sewing machine manufacturer (Carden 1909). The German sewing machine industry was a major employer of labour; in 1907, it employed 20,000 workers compared with the 14,500 employed in automobile manufacture (Milward and Saul 1977).

The Clock and Watch Industry

The sewing machine, bicycle and automobile industries were all characteristic of new engineering industries created in the second half of the nineteenth century. They were inspired and maintained by craft traditions and located in major cities, where such skills and approaches to production were most readily available. In addition, they were products designed for the consumption of an urban market which, by the end of the century, comprised nearly half of Europe's population. The clock and watch industry, by contrast, had a history stretching far into the past, and as such was Europe's earliest consumer-durable industry.

The watch industry had its beginnings in the sixteenth century as an offshoot of the clock industry and other technically similar assembly industries such as locks and small-arms manufacture (Landes 1979; 1983). In common with many other industries in the seventeenth century, watch and clock manufacture took root in the countryside in many parts of Europe, especially in Britain. Switzerland was a particularly important area for watchmaking and the manufacture of rough movements spread into the countryside from Geneva in the eighteenth century. Finishing, as well as marketing, remained the responsibility of Geneva which, in the seventeenth century, had experienced a rapid development in this industrial activity, especially in the making of elegant and complicated time-pieces. At about the same time, an independent development occurred in the Jura district of Switzerland centred on the town of Neuchâtel, There were other centres of watchmaking in Europe, but none rivalled the concentration in Britain and Switzerland. In the last quarter of the eighteenth century, it has been estimated that the total European output of watches was between 300,000 and 400,000 pieces per annum of which 50 per cent originated in Britain; the Genevan industry (that is, including the rural manufacture under its control) accounted for a further 100,000 pieces or roughly 20 per cent of the total (Landes 1983).

Since it was a product assembled from component parts, it is not surprising that as the market for watches expanded in the eighteenth and early nineteenth centuries, the major technical interest centred on the possibility of producing uniform parts and reducing the number of component parts. The decisive innovation in mechanizing stages of the watchmaking process was made before 1780 when Frédéric Japy, a maker of rough watch movements for the Neuchâtel industry, whose works were located in Beaucourt near Montbéliard in eastern France, succeeded in producing uniform parts by machine. In 1780, he reputedly produced 20,000 pieces, rising to 40,000 per year in 1795 and to 100,000 in 1805. As production increased prices fell dramatically from 6.50 francs at the end of the eighteenth century to 1.5–2 francs in 1815. Japy's success inevitably led to the diffusion of mechanized production. By 1843 there were already two factories in Neuchâtel producing 500,000 pieces of rough watch movements. At around the same time, watchmakers in the Swiss Jura dispensed with some component parts of the watch, which allowed a thinner and cheaper product. By the 1840s watches of between 6 and 12 millimetres in thickness were being made in Switzerland (Landes 1983).

The immediate effect of both initial mechanization and redesign of the watch was to increase output substantially. In the eighteenth century, for example, most enterprises could make no more than several hundred watches per year. Using machine-made rough watch movements, the Swiss industry, in particular, produced several thousand pieces per year and in the second half of the century, that figure had risen to tens of thousands per year. Total European output grew from 300,000 – 400,000 watches at the end of the eighteenth century to 2 million pieces in the late nineteenth century, of which the Swiss accounted for as much as three-quarters of the total. By 1914, the Swiss alone manufactured almost 17 million watches annually (Landes 1983).

As with the other consumer-durable industries of the nineteenth century, significant advances were made in achieving interchangeability. In Europe, besides Japy's work, there were various attempts to machine-make parts of the watch to achieve true interchangeability. Several famous names in the history of watchmaking such as Pierre Ingold, Vacheron and Constantin and Georges-Auguste Lescot were concerned with this problem, but before the mid-nineteenth century, the machines devised were either too imperfect or too costly to work with hard metals. Although they were capable of achieving uniform results, the finishing touches still required skilled fitters (Landes 1983). American companies attempted to perfect the machining of watches, but even the United States watch industry did not achieve true interchangeability until the turn of the century, and then only in the very cheapest watches (Landes 1983; Hounshell 1984; Hoke 1987). The exceedingly fine tolerances needed for watch movements obviously stretched the capabilities of the most advanced machine tools to their limit. As far as the most expensive watches are concerned, there is some evidence that true interchangeability was not achieved until the 1930s (Landes 1983).

Whereas the American watch industry attempted interchangeability in all stages of manufacture, the Swiss industry progressed on a piecemeal basis, reflecting the relative dispersal of production. In 1870, 35,000 out of a total of 40,000 watchmakers worked from their homes but, by 1905, the domestic component of the workforce had been reduced to 24 per cent. By then, the Swiss had successfully mechanized some of the other stages of production, though they continued to rely on skilled labour to run the machines (Landes 1983).

The European watch industry in the nineteenth century was concentrated on Switzerland. The British industry in particular played little part in the advancement of watchmaking techniques in this period as their interest foll- owed a different path, sticking more to quality than to quantity output. Conse- quently, the techniques of mass production never used this avenue in Britain as they did in Switzerland (Church 1975). Besides providing an important channel for the diffusion of new techniques of production, the Swiss watch industry provides an excellent example of the various paths taken by industrial activities in achieving high rates of growth. In Switzerland, watchmaking had ceased to be a craft enterprise long before any of its stages of manufacture had been mechan- ized. Geneva stuck more rigidly to the craft basis with the result that output there remained substantially below that of the Neuchâtel and Bern countryside in the nineteenth century. Yet even when mechanization began, the structure of the industry based on domestic production remained largely unaltered. In 1905, the largest watch company in Switzerland employed just under 1100 people in its factory premises, but 161 also worked at home (Landes 1983).

Conclusion

The automobile, bicycle, sewing machine and clock and watch industries were significantly transformed during the second half of the nineteenth and the early decades of the twentieth centuries. Though attention has been focused on them, their experiences were shared by other consumer-durables production. Indeed, the influence of the American system of manufacture and the critical importance of marketing was widespread in all manufacturing characterized by component production and assembly but especially in the sewing-machine industry where Singer's marketing techniques became a model for others to follow (Hounshell 1984; Davies 1969; Church 1982; Fridenson 1981). The possibilities and potentialities of mass production and marketing were recognized even in highly unlikely areas which, until the middle of the nineteenth century, had little consumer appeal. The manufacture of pianos was one such area. It was not until the Steinway brothers in the United States first applied mass manufacturing and marketing techniques to piano manufacture, that the piano started to become an object of consumer interest. The new-found prosperity of the European urban populations together with the falling costs of production of the upright piano gave rise to an enormous increase in piano production. World output, which stood at 43,000 pianos in 1850, reached 600,000 in 1910, of which 60 per cent were manufactured in the United States (Ehrlich 1976; Good 1982).

The consumer-durable revolution had hardly begun by the outbreak of the First World War. Nevertheless, the potential for the European industrial system was already clearly visible. In addition, it was also clear that the most significant exponent of the trend was the United States backed by an enormous domestic market and a considerable ability to substitute machinery for skill. In Europe, Germany was America's most thorough ally and it was there that American-style industrial capitalism made its greatest stride.

Further Reading

Bardou, J. P., Chanaron, J. J., Fridenson, P. and Laux, J. 1982: *The automobile revolution*. Chapel Hill, N. C.: University of North Carolina Press.

Berlanstein, L. R. 1984: *The working people of Paris, 1871–1914*. Baltimore: Johns Hopkins University Press.

Hounshell, D. 1984: *From the American system to mass production 1800–1932*. Baltimore: Johns Hopkins University Press.

Krohn, W., Layton, E. T. Jnr. and Weingart, P. (eds.) 1978: *The dynamics of science and technology*. Dordrecht: Reidel.

Landes, D. S. 1983: *Revolution in time: Clocks and the making of the modern world*. Cambridge, Mass.: Harvard University Press.

Ritchie, A. 1975: *King of the road*. London: Wildwood House.

Rolt, L. T. C. 1986: *Tools for the job*. Revised edition. London: HMSO.

Sabel, C. and Zeitlin J. 1985: Historical alternatives to mass production: Politics, markets and technology in nineteenth century industrialization. *Past and Present*, 108, 133–76.

8 Shipbuilding in Europe 1600–1914

There is little doubt that the shipbuilding industry contributed to the economic strength of the European nations both internally and on a world-wide basis. Europe's industrial expansion between 1600 and 1914 was clearly stimulated by its increasing participation in overseas trade, and its economic dominance was reinforced by sustained imperialist and colonialist activities. It was Europe's shipping prowess that permitted these important features of global development. It was during the sixteenth century that the expanding European economy began to extend its commercial influence. The world economy, with Venice at its centre, operated primarily in the Mediterranean and western Europe; and by way of intermediaries, the network reached the Baltic, Norway and, through the Levant ports, the Indian Ocean. During the seventeenth and eighteenth centuries, the 'octopus grip' of European trade had extended to cover the whole world; and by the end of the eighteenth century the most significant trading networks were those of the English, the Dutch, the Spanish, the Portuguese and the French, all of which possessed, at different times, extensive and innovative shipbuilding industries (Braudel 1984).

The shipbuilding industry itself was influenced by technical and scientific changes elsewhere in the economy, and can be seen as a reflection of industrial development generally. Improvements to shipping design and changes in specialization of function were the most significant features of the industry at the beginning of this period. Until the end of the sixteenth century ships used for commerce were usually also required to be equipped for combat, except in the Mediterranean where there was a long-standing differentiation between ships for fighting and ships for cargo-carrying (Lane 1966; Unger 1980, 1981). In some areas this dual purpose continued well into the seventeenth century, and the foundation of the English East India trade after 1600, for example, strengthened the need for heavily armed ships (Davis 1972). Generally, however, the development of two quite different vessel types – one for fighting and one for carrying goods – meant that each was specialized and interchangeability was impossible. Once the shipbuilders had made the distinction, the two types were subject to separate development. One of the earliest, and certainly the most influential example of this specialization was the Dutch-produced Fluyt (described in Chapter 2, p. 65), a ship designed solely for cargo which ignored defence (Lane 1974; Unger 1981).

During the seventeenth century, the most important shipbuilding developments took place in France, England and the Dutch Provinces. Of these, it was the Dutch who produced the most technically innovative vessels and the greatest variety of ships at this stage. Indeed the framatic growth in the Dutch economy during the seventeenth century was clearly influenced by the wide range of shipping services developed there. It was the volume and extent of shipping and the international connections that set Holland and Zeeland apart from the rest of Europe, as Amsterdam became the most developed capital market in the world. It was, moreover, in shipping and trade that the most significant technical changes took place, as the more efficient use of wind placed Dutch shippers ahead of their European contemporaries (Unger 1978). During the sixteenth century, several towns, of which Edam was the most notable, had gained a reputation for the production of ships of good quality and size. The biggest growth area in the seventeenth century, however, was along the river Zaan. By 1650, more than 25 wharves had been established there; and 20 years later, 60 builders of large ships were in production. The concentration of shipbuilding in this area encouraged the emergence of associated industries which in turn further enhanced the economic position of the Zaan. There was plenty of wood in the vicinity, and the existence of wind-powered sawmills ensured that orders could be met quickly. Sailcloth weaving and cutting, compassmaking, mastmaking and ropemaking were all conducted close at hand. Amsterdam and Rotterdam, which had previously been important shipbuilding towns, responded to the competition provided by the growth of activity on the Zaan, and re-established their superior position following the decline of the Zaan industry at the beginning of the eighteenth century (Unger 1978).

The technical excellence of Dutch ship design had been securely established during the two centuries after 1400, and probably peaked in the 1590s with the development of the Fluyt, which itself ended a period of rapid technical change in the design of seagoing cargo ships (Lane 1974). The Fluyt brought the growth in the size of cargo ships to a stop well below the technically feasible maximum. Fluyts of 800 tons and more could be and were built, but the optimum tonnage for intra-European and for many extra-European trades was in the range of 300–500 tons (Unger 1978). Technical advance in Dutch shipbuilding continued until the 1630s, but was confined essentially to vessels based on the Fluyt model. The Dutch generated ships of special design in smaller cargo craft; and this specialization lowered costs and created opportunities for an increasing volume of commerce. By the beginning of the seventeenth century, the Dutch owned more than 10,000 merchant vessels of different sorts, the most important of which was the Fluyt, with a total of 100,000 crew members. The Dutch ships were very easy to handle, which permitted a low crew-to-tonnage ratio, and corresponding cost reductions. This feature was the envy of the other European sea-faring nations; as early as 1603, Walter Raleigh complained that where a Dutch ship of 100 tons could function with a crew of 10, an equivalent English ship required 30 crew members (Landström 1961).

Typically, the Dutch designed and built smaller and lighter vessels than the other Europeans, and this applied equally to warships and to merchant ships.

The fact that the Dutch devoted little effort to warship design or to the larger commercial vessels was clearly a reflection of the nature of Dutch trade. From the sixteenth century, the Dutch had monopolized the north European trade of mainly cheap and bulky goods. It was therefore pointless to build fast and expensive defensible ships. The cheaply operating Fluyts with their unusually high volume of accessible cargo space were entirely appropriate (Davis 1972; Unger 1978). In terms of warships, while England and France built many three-decked ships during the seventeenth century, the Dutch satisfied themselves with only a few. The most common Dutch men-of-war had two gun-decks, and these ships were also higher built in proportion to the English. Although the Dutch ships were faster and more easily manoeuvred, the light construction proved to be disastrous in exchanges of gunfire (Landström 1961). During the seventeenth century, the Dutch navy survived with its smaller ships, through better seamanship and greater numbers, but subsequently these proved inadequate and the Dutch position as a naval power deteriorated (Unger 1978).

Dutch shipbuilding and design reached its peak early in the seventeenth century and the industry was able to maintain its advantageous position until at least 1700. Although Dutch ship design stagnated relative to progress in other countries after 1630, the benefits of standardization of design – one of the vital components of Dutch shipping success and of lower capital and operating costs – were to be reaped for another hundred years (Unger 1978). Furthermore, the creation of the Fluyt gave Dutch merchant shipping the basis for its grip on much of the carrying trade of Europe in the seventeenth century, and this in turn made it easier to build and operate ships economically (Davis 1972). During the eighteenth century, the Dutch no longer led the way; indeed, overall stagnation in shipbuilding was primarily the result of the failure of Dutch shippers to expand their total volume of trade in the eighteenth century while other countries did. While the Dutch failed to keep pace after 1700, the French and the English became predominant shipbuilding powers (for further information about the activities of the major shipbuilding nations see Cipolla 1965; Davis 1972; Landström 1961; Unger 1978).

French shipbuilding and the French naval fleet were clearly less impressive than those of the Dutch or even the English in the first half of the seventeenth century; and despite the efforts of Richelieu, the modern French navy was still not superior in the 1660s and 1670s when Colbert took over (Pritchard 1987). While Colbert set about the restructuring of the French shipyards for the production of high-quality warships for his new navy, ships for the French fleet were purchased from Holland and elsewhere. Colbert's efforts apparently paid off and during his lifetime French shipbuilding became the foremost in the world (Landström 1961). Emphasis was placed on the design and construction of fighting vessels, and by the beginning of the eighteenth century and for some time afterwards French warships were generally acknowledged to be the finest in the world. The ships were admired for their speed and firepower; the innovative design using larger length-to-breadth ratios, and smaller breadth-to-depth ratios than was common elsewhere, permitted the light ships to carry more and bigger guns (Pritchard 1987).

There is no doubt that the technical superiority of French shipbuilding from the late seventeenth century owed much to the encouragement of Colbert. He sponsored scientific research into shipbuilding problems and established formal education for shipbuilders, which reflected the government's desire to provide a theoretical foundation for ship construction. These governmental initiatives, however, did not immediately give rise to perceptible practical success. The construction of warships continued to be carried out in traditional ways by shipwrights whose training was by apprenticeship, although improvement was initially achieved by the introduction of foreign shipwrights. The theoretical approach, so much favoured by Colbert and the French government agencies, was probably more significant in raising the status of shipwrights and others involved in the construction of ships, than in directly raising the standard of French shipbuilding itself, although the two things were clearly related. There were a number of reasons for the emergence of superior-quality French warships from the late seventeenth century, but the most important was probably the administrative and social changes instigated by the government, which raised the social standing of those who worked in the shipbuilding industry. The long-term impact of this change in social values and attitudes was to be felt not only in shipbuilding but in other industries too (Lane 1974; Pritchard 1987).

While the French placed their shipbuilding industry on a sure footing, the English had also become aware of the deficiencies of their own fleet. Between 1600 and 1660, the English shipwrights who built ships of any size, were committed to substantial, heavily-masted and well-gunned ships for mercantile purposes as well as for privateering and for the navy (Davis 1972). Early in the seventeenth century, the unsuitability of English-built ships for some trades was becoming apparent. The export trade in coal, for example, was nearly all conducted in foreigners' ships. Later in the seventeenth century, the clear superiority of the Dutch Fluyt for many purposes was acknowledged by merchants and shipowners, who were no longer satisfied by the supply of expensive, defensible ships being produced by the English shipwrights (Landström 1961). Sustained criticism of English shipbuilding methods from the 1660s to the 1680s prompted a fundamental shift in design and building practice. By the end of the seventeenth century, the English had learned how to construct cheap vessels, using the Fluyt as a model; and just as the Dutch had led the way in operating with ships that needed small crews in relation to the cargo they carried, the English eventually followed suit. During the 1680s and 1690s, the foreign-built component of the English merchant fleet diminished steadily (Davis 1972).

Although English mercantile shipbuilding was not highly regarded in the early seventeenth century, the naval dockyards were admired by foreign commentators throughout the seventeenth and the eighteenth centuries, especially for their size. Portsmouth and Plymouth rose to importance alongside the existing yards at Chatham, Deptford and Woolwich. While it was the growth of the English navy that led to the establishment of such large industrial plants as these, it was generally commerce rather than war that set the pace in the progress of shipbuilding. The naval ships and naval shipyards were very much larger than their civilian counterparts of the seventeenth and eighteenth centuries, and only the naval shipyards had the capacity to build the large naval ships. All naval vessels built in this period exceeded 1000 tons, while most English ships used for intra-European as well as longer distance trade ranged from 60 to 400 tons (Coleman 1953). State expenditure on the naval dockyards, and their impact on the local economy in terms of demand for labour and a wide range of goods and services, reflect their economic significance, but their influence on commercial shipbuilding was slight. Specialization in shipping function from the seventeenth century also meant that technical developments in commercial vessels and fighting ships were quite distinct (David 1972).

During the eighteenth century, English merchant shipbuilders made their own way to operational efficiency, and gradually reduced the ratio of crew to tonnage. Probably the main technical development in English shipbuilding was the adoption of the hull forms used earlier by the Dutch especially in the Fluyt, which made possible a high carrying capacity in relation to the ship's main measurements. By the mid-eighteenth century, ships of many sizes were being built which could be operated with a much smaller crew than earlier designs of a similar scale (Lane 1974; Walton 1970). The cost implications of this were enormous, given that in the days of sail, the cost of sea transport was overwhelmingly that of paying and feeding a crew. The size of ships was not constrained by technical obstacles, but for some time growth was held back by market possibilities, and the larger the ship, the greater the risks of delay in filling up the ship. Until the 1740s, economies of scale were quite small, and a larger ship operated at hardly less per ton than a smaller one; but from the 1760s, the margin of efficiency of the large ship over the smaller one began to increase rapidly, and the risks of underutilization had to be large to outweigh such economies. The maximum size of merchant ship in use certainly increased significantly after 1750. The East Indiamen, for example, which had typically been between 500 and 700 tons during the first half of the eighteenth century, rose to a tonnage approaching 900 by 1769. In the Baltic trade, the 300–350 ton trader of the previous half century was replaced in the 1760s by ships of 400–500 tons; and a few giants of 600 or even 700 tons were appearing in the North Russian timber trade (Davis 1972).

During the eighteenth century, such technical improvements in ship design and construction as there were, emanated from England in the case of merchantmen, and from France where warships were concerned. The English system of rounded stern was developed and taken up by other powers, although most merchant-ship designs were directly or indirectly connected to the original Fluyt. The eighteenth century also saw the emergence of the cutter and the schooner (Landström 1961). Apart from small changes in hull design and in ratio of length to breadth, the basis of the improved functioning of ships was in sail design and rigging. Rigs generally became more efficient, and there was particularly a steady growth in the complexity of the three-mast rig. The gain from this gradual multiplication of sails was an improved capacity for sailing close to the wind (Davis 1972).

By the end of the eighteenth century, European shipbuilding had reached the stage where it could satisfy the requirements of both merchants and shipowners. Intra-European trade and commercial links between Europe and the rest of the world had grown in complexity as well as in quantity; and this had been achieved with the help of the increased capacity and reliability of European ships. Ships were more commonly designed for specific purposes, and the significant reduction in costs that the Fluyt, for example, permitted, enabled trade in cheap and bulky goods to be extended (North 1958). Furthermore, as it became less necessary for merchant ships to carry guns in case of attack – and indeed the carriage of cheap commodities reduced the likelihood of armed confrontation – more cargo space would be available, and less expensive ships could be designed and built. Although great strides were made between 1600 and 1800, it was probably in the nineteenth century that the links between shipbuilding and other industries became particularly pronounced, especially in terms of technical innovations. It was during the nineteenth century also that the impact of European shipping on the structure of the world economy was most striking.

The most fundamental changes in shipbuilding technique that were introduced during the nineteenth century involved the substitution of iron and later steel for wood in the construction of the hull, and the replacement of sail by steam power (described in Harley 1971, 1973). Neither of these major breakthroughs had been completely adopted by the end of the nineteenth century, when the economic advantages of the sailing ship were still apparent on some trading routes. The idea of the steamship seems to have originated in 1685 when it was presented by the French physician, Denis Papin. Many designs followed during the eighteenth century, including several for paddle-wheel steamers. In 1785, Joseph Bramah obtained a patent for a propeller, to be used in place of a paddle wheel. The first viable steamship did not materialize until the early nineteenth century, when, in 1812, the Comet – the first merchant steamship – was launched on the Clyde (Landström 1961).

The early steamships, those of the 1820s and 1830s, however, were so unprofitable to operate that their use was limited to governments, and then only when there was a pressing political need. Ordinary freight and passengers continued for many years to depend on sailing ships. Before sea-going steamships could compete effectively with sailing ships, particularly on long voyages, several improvements were required. The iron hull had to be adopted; the propeller had to be introduced; and the high-pressure engine had to be perfected. Iron possessed great advantages over wood as a shipbuilding material. Iron was much stronger, particularly in the face of collision or grounding, so less of it was needed to build a ship, resulting in a lighter ship than a wooden one of comparable strength. The iron ship would provide more cargo space, and this, together with the weight saving, meant that 65 per cent of the weight of a fully loaded iron ship could be cargo, compared with only 50 per cent of a wooden ship. Iron ships had fewer structural limitations, and could be constructed to almost any size; they could be much thinner than wooden ships, and therefore faster; they were safer, more cost-effective and more durable (Headrick 1981).

Despite these apparently overwhelming advantages, the introduction of iron into shipbuilding on a regular, commercial basis was delayed until experimental efforts had proved conclusive, and until economic forces became irresistible. Improvements to iron ships continued to be made throughout the 1830s and 1840s. In 1838, the Great Western and the Sirius crossed the Atlantic, the first iron steamships to do so; and in the same year the screw propeller was applied for the first time (Headrick 1981). In 1843, Brunel's Great Britain was launched; it combined all the latest features of shipbuilding and was the largest iron ship using a propeller (Landström 1961). By 1850, the use of iron and steam together in shipbuilding had ceased to be a novelty and had become accepted as the standard shipbuilding technology. The transition from wooden to iron ships was also stimulated by economic factors, notably the relative prices of wood and iron, and this in turn eventually secured for Britain an advantageous position in world shipbuilding (Harley 1973).

From the late seventeenth century, the cost of British wood increased consistently; and by the late eighteenth century, wood alone accounted for 60 per cent of the cost of constructing a ship. British shipbuilders began to purchase cheaper foreign timber, mainly from Scandinavia and North America. At this point, the United States, with its strong maritime tradition and its access to cheap and abundant timber, was clearly competing with British shipbuilding. From the early nineteenth century, however, pig iron became significantly cheaper as its production climbed, and this, because of its advanced iron industry, benefited Britain's shipbuilding trade. In 1810, pig iron was produced at £6.30 per ton; by 1840 the cost of a ton of pig iron had fallen to £2.60 (Headrick 1981). By the mid-1850s, British shipbuilders had developed the construction of iron ships to a routine process, but wooden shipbuilding remained important in North America until the 1880s, which effectively explains the decline of the industry there. The building of iron ships and the introduction of steam-powered shipping were clearly related; and technical factors, relating to hull fineness, water flow and local stress early dictated that steamers be built of metal. Iron was also used in the construction of sailing ships and developments within the British iron industry greatly influenced the price of sailing ships after the 1850s (Harley 1973). Iron ships displaced wooden sailing ships because of technical change and the falling price of British iron. The persistence of wooden shipbuilding in the United States, which had a detrimental effect on the industry, stemmed from the immobility of labour and other factors employed in shipbuilding (Harley 1973; Headrick 1981).

Although iron-hulled steamships were generally preferred from the late 1840s, which gave British shipbuilding a boost, the engines themselves were still relatively rudimentary. Since the early nineteenth century, engineers had known how to make engines more efficient by raising the pressure of the steam, but because marine engines used sea water, salt deposits remained in their boilers, which, in high-pressure engines, were very dangerous. Until the late 1850s, when an improved surface condenser was incorporated into sea-going steamers, therefore, marine engines operated under limited pressure. The development of the compound engine was a further improvement which utilized more effectively the higher pressure permitted by the surface condensers. The compound engine, introduced as early as 1854 but not widely adopted until the 1860s, used two cylinders, one of which fed high-pressure steam from the boiler into a larger one which was filled with the low-pressure steam exhausted from the smaller one (Headrick 1981). The compound engine had many advantages including enhanced fuel efficiency, which was a particularly significant feature on the longer-haul voyages (Harley 1971; Knauerhase 1968).

Developments in various branches of engineering in the second half of the nineteenth century further transformed shipbuilding technology, and in the short term at least, served to emphasize the supremacy of Britain's shipbuilding industry. Steel replaced iron for hull construction in the late 1870s when the price of steel had become competitive with that of wrought iron. By 1885, 48 per cent of all new steamers were built of steel, and by 1900, the proportion had risen to 95 per cent. As a shipbuilding material, steel had the advantage of strength; and a steel ship could be built 15 per cent lighter than an iron ship of equal strength and dimensions, which permitted higher speeds and lower fuel consumption. The other improvements in shipbuilding focused on engine development. The triple expansion engine progressed naturally from the compound engine. Steel was used in the boilers and other engine parts, and this permitted yet higher steam pressure, allowing extra energy to pass through a third cylinder. As a result, ships were able to run faster and more smoothly on less fuel than a compound engine would achieve. By 1914, the development of the steam turbine and the diesel engine enabled ships to run even more efficiently (Headrick 1981).

The major nineteenth-century technical changes in shipbuilding were particularly applicable to ocean shipping. Greater speeds were achieved and freight rates were reduced, thus encouraging a significant expansion of world trade. Although the advantages of iron, steel and steam were quickly appreciated, the displacement of sail by steam occurred only gradually between 1850 and the early twentieth century; and indeed, the greatest age of the sailing ship coincided with the early years of the ocean liners (Graham 1956). The most important technical change specific to steamships was the improvement in the fuel consumption of the marine engine, which took place gradually, but continuously, over the second half of the nineteenth century (Harley 1971). For much of this period, the persistently high costs of steam transportation meant that for many purposes the sailing ship effectively competed with steam (North 1958). Steam could provide lower-cost carriage than sail only on the shorter routes; and for transporting bulky cargoes on the longer routes, the sailing ship was generally to be preferred, particularly because the speed of shipment was of very little significance for shippers of bulk commodities. Steamships, however, were often preferred for passenger trade on the longer journeys (Harley 1971).

The lengthy coexistence of the sailing ship and the steamship clearly reflected the fact that the two types did not directly compete, but were, rather, complementary in their uses. Steam, for instance, offered speed and reliability, which permitted a saving on inventory costs on expensive, non-seasonal goods. Speed was not an advantage for the transportation of bulky and non-perishable seasonal agricultural products, so the cheaper sailing ship continued to be employed for this purpose. Indeed, because the sailing ship effectively provided cheap warehousing for these goods, the faster steamship would have been a real disadvantage. It was on the short routes, where passenger traffic was important and where the cargo was relatively valuable, that the benefits of steam were undeniable, and where steam initially replaced sail. By 1855, 30 per cent of European trade with the Mediterranean was conducted in steamships; the new type of vessel was particularly suitable for transporting the typically perishable commodities in the region of light winds. By 1865, steamships were extending into trade routes of up to 3000 miles distance; and certainly the North Atlantic trades were commonly served by steam transportation during the 1870s and subsequently (Harley 1971; North 1958).

In the European and Atlantic trades steam gradually displaced sail on increasingly longer journeys. This displacement was accelerated both by the opening of the Suez canal, which effectively reduced journey length, particularly in the China trade; and by the constant improvements made to the marine engines, which reduced coal consumption. This increased fuel efficiency meant that not only could longer distances be covered and more cheaply, but also that the reduced amount of ship space and crew devoted to the transportation of bunker coal, increased the quantity of saleable cargo carried. By the late nineteenth century, the popularity of the sailing ship was clearly waning. In 1900, while 60 per cent of all ships were of the sailing variety, this represented only 25 per cent of the world's total shipping tonnage (Headrick 1981). The persistence of sail after this date was confined to the round-the-world trades and to those to the west coast of the United States. It also reflected the natural disjunction that occurred as shipowners made adjustments to their fleets. The replacement of sail by steam was thus a lengthy process; sail remained a lower-cost alternative on long voyages as inputs per ton-mile for sailing ships were largely unaffected by voyage length, which was not the case with steam. By 1914, however, the improvements in marine engineering made steam competitive on even the longest voyages (Harley 1971).

The technical changes of the nineteenth century clearly enhanced the position of Britain as a shipbuilding and as a maritime power; and there is no doubt that Britain's trading advantage and its shipbuilding superiority interacted to the benefit of both to 1914. Between 1800 and 1850, the United States was probably the world's foremost shipbuilding nation; but Europe remained competitive (Harley 1973), and throughout the first half of the nineteenth century, ships were built in typically small yards on the coastline of the European continent. Although Britain and the United States were rivals technically until the late 1840s, the introduction of commercially viable iron ships in Britain halted North America's competitive bid. From early in the nineteenth century, Britain had little to fear from other shipbuilding nations in Europe. Although the quality of continental ships remained high, the output fell much below that of Britain. The output of French merchant ships, for example, which was in any case never as large as that of warships, was at a low level throughout the nineteenth century. In the 1860s, any one of the large Thames shipbuilding establishments had a capacity as large as all the French yards combined (Pollard and Robertson 1979). The German shipbuilding industry, which was effectively established in the 1830s, did not pose a serious threat to the British industry until the last quarter of the nineteenth century (Henderson 1975).

Although many of the metallurgical and engineering developments applicable to ship construction originated outside of Britain, particularly in France, the United States and Germany, it was the British industry that gained most from them. It was from the late 1860s that Britain's lead became most striking. In 1870, when steel-hulled steamships were changing the shape of trans-world transportation, 50 per cent of the world's shipping capacity was British (Pollard and Robertson 1979); and by the 1890s, as Table 8.1 indicates, Britain was producing almost 80 per cent of world output. The very great increase in international trade from 1870 onwards, in which Britain played a major part, gave a further impetus to British shipbuilding.

The size of British shipbuilding capacity enabled it to survive better than others the periods of fluctuating demand, to which shipbuilding was particularly prone in the last quarter of the nineteenth century. There was a pronounced depression during the 1880s, and this hit the German, French and American shipyards heavily. Because of the severity of the fluctuations of the late nineteenth century, it was essential that shipbuilders minimize total overhead expenses while maintaining the ability to build large and complex ships at prices that were competitive on the world market. The British shipyard owners were successful at this, as they employed highly skilled workers and invested only in equipment that was absolutely necessary to manipulate the large and heavy components of modern ships. The German and the American shipbuilders, by contrast, were involved in heavy capital expenditure (Pollard and Robertson 1979). The Germans had the most modern equipment, but even in good years they were unable to meet the prices of their British competitors, because, despite their superior machinery, the German workers were less productive than British workers (Knauerhase 1968; Lorenz 1984). In the United States, the vast overheads of the shipbuilders crippled all but the best yards (Pollard and Robertson 1979).

For a number of reasons the shipbuilding industry in Britain not only suffered less than shipbuilding elsewhere in the late nineteenth century, but it was also less affected by depression and foreign competition than other British industries. British shipbuilders clearly had the advantage of a large and secure domestic market, in addition to a large overseas demand for second-hand as well as new British ships; and this continuity of demand permitted a degree of specialization impossible in competing maritime nations. Even in Britain, however, instability was a potential problem and chronic swings between overcapacity and shortage of ship space did result in marked fluctuations in demand for new construction. Ship production was, in principle, very risky, and most builders therefore built only to order. The implication of the bespoke nature of demand was to limit the scope for standardizing ship production. So while the extent of Britain's market for ships was sufficiently large to suggest the possibility of specialization, and indeed yards did tend to specialize by class of vessel, in fact the variations in specifications remained wide, thus reducing some of the benefits of economies of scale (Lorenz and Wilkinson 1986).

Specialization in British shipbuilding essentially meant specialization of individual yards in a particular class of vessel – cargo ship, passenger liner, or warship –, or locational specialization, that is specialization between shipbuilding districts. Shipbuilders in Britain became expert in the construction of certain types of vessels, and in the needs of certain types of owners. The frequent association between shipbuilders and shipowning firms ensured for the yard repeat orders and appreciable savings on overheads, through the use of standard designs and templates (Pollard 1957). Yards specializing in the production of passenger liners were able to secure a degree of market protection by forming close links with the owners. Harland and Wolff of Belfast, for example, enjoyed a long-term relationship with White Star Line; and from the large and stable demand that developed, the shipbuilders were able to expand their yard and reap some of the benefits of economies of scale. Warship builders could similarly reduce the level of risk incurred, by establishing connections with the Admiralty, though only a small number of firms were so favoured. British shipbuilders also gained orders for the novel specialist ships which originated from 1875, such as oil tankers and refrigerated ships (Lorenz and Wilkinson 1986).

Regional specialization also encouraged stability; and the bunching together of many yards on rivers like the Clyde, the Tyne, the Wear and the Tees, provided the shipbuilders with a large pool of skilled labour, and gave rise to local independent marine engineering firms and other component suppliers for the shipbuilding industry (Lorenz 1984). The concentration of the building of transatlantic liners on the Clyde and in Belfast; of cargo tramps and colliers in the northeast of England; of fishing vessels in Hull, Aberdeen and Dundee; and of warships in Barrow, Birkenhead and on the Clyde, not only reflected easy access to the market, and the shipowners' desire to have, wherever possible, the yards close at hand, but also permitted greater efficiency and productivity (Lorenz 1984; Pollard and Robertson 1979).

The structure of the British shipbuilding industry was ideal for reducing the risks involved in production. Most firms, for instance, retained small-scale, labour-intensive production techniques, in order to avoid high overhead costs during recessionary periods (Lorenz and Wilkinson 1986). The emphasis which British shipbuilders placed on skilled labour was entirely appropriate and further strengthened its comparative position. Its shipbuilding tradition and policy of on-the-job training provided the industry with a labour force more able to adapt to late nineteenth-century technical developments than labour in other maritime nations. The reputation of British shipbuilding was to a large extent based on the skill of its artisans, boilermakers and shipwrights (Pollard 1957). Late nineteenth-century ship production was lengthy and required a wide range of skills involving design and preparation, hull construction and fitting out. Although the hand tools of the early nineteenth century were replaced by increasingly specialized machine tools, these new devices were not single-purpose instruments for the mass production of identical components. Indeed the inherent lack of standardization in ship production ensured that shipyard machine tools remained sufficiently versatile to produce a variety of components of differing dimensions; and most of the operations continued to require a skilled hand (Lorenz and Wilkinson 1986).

Throughout the period to 1914, shipbuilding technology placed a premium on a highly skilled and versatile workforce, so British builders were able to benefit from their favoured labour-supply position. In many ways, the experience of British shipbuilders in the years between 1870 and 1914 was typical of other British industries. In other words, craft-based and small-scale production methods were retained in the face of the trend towards large-scale organization and capital-intensiveness in other industrializing nations; but whereas in other industries this frequently resulted in a relatively poor performance, in shipbuilding, Britain retained its competitive advantage (Lorenz and Wilkinson 1986).

Table 8.1 illustrates the extent of Britain's superiority in shipbuilding in the two decades before the First World War despite the growth in capacity particularly in Germany. Many of the ships built outside Britain received subsidies or the benefit of protective legislation, without which Britain's position would have been even less assailable. It has been estimated that in 1914, Britain retained 80 per cent of the unprotected market (Lorenz and Wilkinson 1986). In Germany, the development of the shipbuilding industry in the mid-nineteenth century was

Table 8.1: *Shipbuilding in leading nations 1892–1914. Average annual launchings in thousand gross tons*

	Mercantile vessels			Warships
	1892–96	1901–05	1910–14	1892–1914
UK	1021	1394	1660	112
Germany	87	217	328	49
USA	85	347	253	39
France	26	123	105	39
Holland	10	52	97	—
Norway	17	44	45	—
Italy	9	50	32	17
Russia				29
World (incl. others)	1299	2354	2739	340
UK as % of world	78.6	59.2	60.6	33

Source: A. Pollard, 'British and World shipbuilding, 1890–1914: A study in comparative costs' *Journal of Economic History*, 1957, p. 427.

slow, despite progress in the engineering and iron-making sectors; but after 1870, capacity expanded rapidly as the German state took an active interest in it (Pollard and Robertson 1979). Even in the late 1880s, German production was still dependent on official encouragement. The Reich established state naval dockyards; ordered warships; subsidized certain shipping lines (notably the Hamburg Amerika line and the North German Lloyd) on condition that their new ships were built in German shipyards; and until 1898, it allowed shipbuilders to import their raw materials free of duty (Henderson 1975; Lorenz 1984). After 1890, the German shipbuilding industry progressed more or less on its own merits, but although German shipowners were placing more of their contracts with German shipyards, Germany was still one of the leading markets for British vessels at the close of the nineteenth century (Henderson 1975; Pollard 1957).

The German shipbuilding industry had so many apparent advantages that it is surprising that it did not become a greater threat to Britain. Because the growth of the industry began in earnest in the 1880s, most shipbuilders were able to concentrate immediately on the construction of iron and steel steamships, leaving the older and smaller yards to continue building sailing ships. There was therefore no painful transition from sail to steam or from wood to metal (Henderson 1975). The new shipbuilding companies received substantial bank support and were thus able to invest heavily in docks and engineering workshops in which they installed the most modern equipment. This included electrically driven machines and pneumatic power stations, using the most up-to-date means of power transmission and mechanical rivetting. Their engineers, managers, designers and other technicians benefited from training at special technical colleges established by the state. Raw materials, particularly iron and steel, were readily available; and close links were forged between steel, engineering and shipbuilding firms (Henderson 1975). Despite all this, but probably because of the emphasis on capital-intensive equipment, the costs of German ships were simply too high for world markets, and certainly they failed to obtain sufficient foreign orders to effectively compete with Britain. By 1900, however, when German output, comprising high quality large and fast ships, had reached 15 per cent of the British level, Germany was perceived to be the potential threat that it had become in other industries. By 1903, the threat had passed; the period of German expansion had ended as the German merchant fleet had found its level and only replacement orders were required (Pollard and Robertson 1979).

The shipbuilding industry in France during the nineteenth century continued in its eighteenth-century tradition and produced some fine warships and other vessels, but was hopelessly uncompetitive and way out of line with world prices. The industry relied heavily on the protective policies of the government, but the impact of protection was almost wholly negative. The laws failed to shift the demand of the French owner decisively towards the French builders and many French-owned ships continued to be British-built. Protectionist policies even resulted in the expansion of the production of obsolete sailing vessels, because these happened to be favoured by the Subsidy Act of 1891 (Pollard 1957). French producers suffered irregular and insufficient demand during the late nineteenth century, and the domestic market grew at a slower rate than that of Britain. Because they lacked continuity of demand, French builders were forced to produce a wide range of vessel types. The Penhoet Yard, for example, was particularly suitable for producing a large class of sophisticated vessel, especially trans-Atlantic liners, naval cruisers and battleships; but because of inadequate demand for these types, the yard was forced to construct tug boats, cargo vessels, torpedo boats and trawlers as well, which meant that it could not reach the productivity and efficiency levels achieved in British yards (Lorenz 1984).

The cyclical fluctuations in French shipbuilding output between 1880 and 1900 were three times as severe as in Britain, and exacerbated the structural difficulties of the French labour market (Lorenz 1984). During the late nineteenth century, the labour requirements of French shipbuilders varied enormously, and this worsened the problems of recruiting and training an adequate supply of labour for periods of peak demand. Employers could not hold onto a reasonable workforce, and many labourers would seek alternative employment. A temporary improvement in the condition of French shipbuilding was enjoyed between 1896 and 1902, as is reflected in Table 8.1; and during the boom of 1901–2, 80 per cent of the additions to the French fleet were built in France. After 1903, however, output declined and the proportion of French additions purchased abroad rose to almost 40 per cent (Lorenz 1984).

Throughout the period between 1600 and 1914, the expansion of shipping and shipbuilding was part of an even larger change in world economic relations, which was examined in Chapter 2. This chapter has shown that until the early nineteenth century, the European maritime nations produced more or less their individual requirements of ships; the fluctuating output of the different economies, and their relative strengths, reflecting the changing positions in trading activity and in colonial and imperialist expansion. During the seventeenth and eighteenth centuries, several economies, notably France, England and the Dutch

Provinces, vied for the position of supreme shipbuilding nation; and several more, including Spain and Portugal, produced a significant quantity of ships. From early in the nineteenth century, however, the situation began to change. The expansion of world trade and the changing nature of imperialism required a significant increase in the European-owned fleet. At the same time and not by coincidence, important developments were introduced into shipbuilding technology. The replacement of wood by metal in hull construction, and the use of steam power to replace sail, improved enormously the speed and efficiency of ships.

For a number of reasons, it was British shipbuilding that benefited most from these innovations. In the early nineteenth century, Britain's maritime supremacy had been threatened by an American shipbuilding boom, based on limitless supplies of cheap timber, but the shift to iron ships rescued Britain's dominance. Britain's lead in the steam-engine and metal-hull industries was reinforced by its possession of the richest deposits of the world's best steamer coal. Further large quantities of coal were later discovered near the Indian Ocean in Natal, Bengal and Borneo, all of which were in British colonies, as were the most convenient coaling stations on the Far Eastern shipping routes (Headrick 1981).

The majority of Britain's large home and overseas markets for ships was secured between 1850 and 1880, when Britain was the best-equipped European nation to supply the shipyards with sufficient iron and steel and engineering capacity. Although this was no longer true during the last quarter of the nineteenth century, once the markets had been captured, the reputation of British shipbuilding and the scale of the industry ensured the perpetuation of its predominance. No other economy, however suitably equipped, was able thereafter to achieve a sufficiently high degree of specialization either to replicate the quality of British ships, or to undercut its prices on the world market. By the end of the nineteenth century, German prices were the most competitive, but were still 10 per cent above British prices; and the price of United States ships was 30 per cent higher (Pollard and Robertson 1979).

There was little sign of Britain's dominance ending before the outbreak of the First World War, at which point many other of its industries were dependent on Empire markets for their survival. The continued strength of the shipbuilding industry was the result of its continued access to large markets, to a reasonable degree of specialization and mass production, to external economies, to a stable and cheap supply of the industry's raw materials and components, and to the skill and experience of the workforce. No other economy in Europe was able to acquire these advantages in the years before 1914.

Further Reading

Cipolla, C. M. 1965: *Guns, sails and empires: Technological innovation and the early phases of European expansion, 1400–1700.* New York: Minerva Press.

Davis, R. 1972: *The rise of the English shipping industry.* Newton Abbot: David & Charles.

Headrick, D. R. 1981: *The tools of empire. Technology and European imperialism in the nineteenth century.* Oxford: Oxford University Press.

Landström, B. 1961: *The ship*. London: Allen & Unwin.

Parry, J. H. 1973: *The age of reconnaissance. Discovery, exploration and settlement, 1450–1650*. London: Sphere.

Pollard, S. 1957: British and world shipbuilding, 1890–1914: A study in comparative costs. *Journal of Economic History*, 17, 426–44.

Pollard, S. and Robertson, P. L. 1979: *The British shipbuilding industry 1870–1914*. Cambridge, Mass.: Harvard University Press.

Unger, R. W. 1978: *Dutch shipbuilding before 1800: Ships and guilds*. Assen: Van Gorcum.

Unger, R. W. 1980: *The ship in the medieval economy, 600–1600*. London: Croom Helm.

Walton, G. M. 1970: Obstacles to technical diffusion in ocean shipping, 1675–1775. *Explorations in Economic History*, 8, 123–40.

9 The Basic Industries: Iron, Steel and Chemicals

The analysis of industries in the preceding chapters has shown that important changes in industrial production occurred throughout the period 1600 to 1914. In some cases, the changes were organizational; sometimes they were technical; and at other times the observed changes were a mixture of both. Certainly, it is misleading to impose artificial divisions in this period according to what historians often perceive to have been the prevailing force of change. European industry did not develop along discrete stages of development moving, for example, from an age of organizational change to an age of technical change and through to an age of scientific change. The reality was far more complex.

This complexity is evident in the history of the basic industries of iron, steel and chemicals. Each of these products has been linked to the nineteenth century, but it is important to view their progress in a longer perspective. Most discussions of these industries have also focused on their technical aspects and, because the inventions and innovations were often spectacular, it is difficult to avoid this bias. Emphasis on technology, however, can impair historical understanding. The real success of the Singer sewing machine, for example, lay not in its production technology, as commonly believed, but in the marketing activities of the company. Similarly in the organic chemical industry: while it has been considered to be the first important example of the wholesale integration of science and technology in the creation of an industrial product, in fact, as the section on the organic chemical industry will show (below), the success of the firms who dominated this industry, principally in Germany and Switzerland, can be accounted for by sales techniques as much as, if not more than, scientific input.

The history of the chemical industry, and to a lesser extent, that of iron and steel, highlighted European industry's need and ability to reduce its dependence on imported natural raw materials, especially vegetable matter. Between the seventeenth and twentieth centuries, this strategy consisted mainly of attempts to manufacture a product identical to the natural one by chemical means using indigenous and plentiful and thus relatively cheap raw materials. This was successfully achieved in the manufacture of alkalis and acids in the eighteenth century; in the manufacture of dyes in the second half of the nineteenth century;

and in the manufacture of ammonia and textiles at the beginning of the twentieth century. Some attempts failed, however, such as the manufacture of synthetic rubber in the nineteenth century and synthetic petrol in the twentieth century. Experience such as this cannot be separated from the fact that major European as well as American tyre manufacturers owned extensive rubber plantations in Asia and Africa while the burgeoning petroleum companies owned lucrative oil concessions in the Middle East.

The Iron and Steel Industries

Iron can be produced in three basic forms; as pig or cast iron, wrought or bar iron, and as steel. What distinguishes one from the other is the amount of carbon present which the iron absorbs chemically as it is liberated from the iron ore. Wrought iron has virtually no carbon; steel is iron containing from 0.1 to 1.7 per cent carbon; while cast iron contains from 1.7 to 4.5 per cent carbon.

At the turn of the seventeenth century, the most useful iron product was wrought iron. The absence of carbon made the iron both easy to work and resistant to corrosion. There were at the time two basic ways of producing wrought iron; the direct method or the indirect method. In the former, iron ore was smelted with some combustible material, usually charcoal, which produced a lump of iron in a semi-molten state. Because the temperature in the furnace was not great enough for the iron to absorb carbon from the fuel, the resulting mass of iron was virtually carbon free. The first stage of the indirect method was to produce pig iron. The iron ore was smelted with a combustible material in a blast furnace, where the temperature was great enough to melt the iron as well as allow it to absorb carbon from the fuel. The resulting liquid was either cast directly into some required form or into some standard shape called a pig. In order to produce wrought iron, this pig iron (or cast iron) was alternately heated and hammered in a forge until the carbon content had been virtually eliminated.

Cast iron or pig iron was very brittle and could not be easily cut or shaped in any way and was principally used for vats and other large vessels, domestic utensils, pipework and munitions. Wrought iron, by contrast, was soft and highly malleable and was used mainly for decorative work such as lamps, candle holders, common items such as horseshoes and keys and for more intricate devices such as locks. Where neither brittleness nor softness was desired, however, the choice was steel.

Because the carbon content of steel lay between that of cast and wrought iron, it was hard without being brittle and yet malleable enough to be shaped. In the seventeenth century, steel was commonly made by a process which sought to reintroduce carbon into wrought iron by what was called cementation: that is, the wrought iron was surrounded by charcoal, and heated to a temperature great enough for the iron to absorb some of the carbon from the fuel. For various reasons, the steel thus produced was not uniform in quality as the carbon was not evenly distributed. Despite its poor quality, steel had a wide demand for making tools, knives, cutlery, swords, saws and watch springs.

Iron and steel production was intensive in its use of raw materials and plant; and although labour requirements at the point of production were relatively low, demand for labour extended well beyond the confines of the furnace or forge, for iron-ore miners, charcoal burners and carters (Woronoff 1976). The location of a furnace or a forge was determined less by labour supply considerations than by proximity to ore, charcoal and water. While many possible sites existed, there was already in the seventeenth century a tendency towards some geographical concentration. In England, for example, towards the end of the sixteenth century, roughly two-thirds of the furnaces and possibly a similar proportion of forges were located in the Weald in the counties of Sussex, Kent, Surrey and Hampshire, but by the end of the seventeenth century, a new concentration was to be found in South Wales, the West Midlands and Yorkshire (Hammersley 1973; Aström 1982). Iron works were more scattered in France, but important concentrations were to be found in the eastern Pyrenees, in Lorraine, Champagne and Burgundy. In Belgium, the area around Liège was most important but smelting and refining was also carried on in the adjoining provinces of Brabant, Hainaut and Namur. German production was located on both sides of the Rhine – to the east in Siegerland and Hesse and to the west in the Eifel. Spain had its major production in the Basque region while in Italy, Elba and parts of Tuscany were especially important (Pounds 1979; Pounds and Parker 1957).

Geographical concentrations notwithstanding, the European iron and steel industry at the turn of the seventeenth century consisted of a relatively small number of furnaces and refineries with relatively small production. The available evidence suggests that furnaces produced on average 200 tons of pig iron each annually and forges produced on average 100 tons of wrought iron annually. The estimated total output of pig iron in Europe in 1600 was 130,000 tons, suggesting that there were probably 650 furnaces and probably twice as many forges in operation (Pounds and Parker 1957). By 1910, there were probably as many as 2000 blast furnaces in operation in Europe each producing on average 35,000 tons of pig iron annually (Allen 1979).

Iron making was thus a characteristic rural industry, typically employing family labour (Woronoff 1976). Not only was the scale of operation small but the rhythm of work was dictated by the demands of the agrarian system as well as by climate. There was a season for everything, from the mining of the ore to the production of pig and wrought iron. It was customary for the furnaces and forges to remain idle for long periods during the summer, not only because of the relative shortage of labour, as workers left for the harvest, but also because of the scarcity of charcoal and water (Pounds and Parker 1957).

Evidence suggests that the European output of pig iron increased significantly throughout the seventeenth and especially in the eighteenth century. From a level of 130,000 tons around 1600, output reached close to 170,000 tons by the early eighteenth century and over 400,000 tons by 1800 (Pounds and Parker 1957; Braudel 1981; de Vries 1976; Hansotte 1980). During the seventeenth century, Germany and Sweden became the leading European pig-iron producers, but were replaced in the eighteenth century by France and Britain (Kellenbenz 1977). Data indicate that pig-iron output in the eighteenth century grew most rapidly in France where it increased from 25,000 tons to 140,000 tons (Kriedte 1983; Markovitch 1966; Woronoff 1984). In Britain, where growth was also impressive, output increased from 24,000 tons in the early eighteenth century to just over 100,000 tons by the early 1790s (Riden 1977). Belgian output also grew considerably especially during the second half of the century (Hansotte 1980).

In the intervening years, both the smelting and refining processes were transformed, especially in the type of fuel used. The substitution of coke for charcoal is considered by historians to have been one of the most fundamental breakthroughs in the history of iron and steel production, but the protracted nature of the substitution process is typically overlooked.

Charcoal was used exclusively in the European iron and steel industry until the beginning of the eighteenth century, despite earlier attempts to use coal, coke and peat in the smelting process (Pounds and Parker 1957). The most promising of these alternatives was coke, that is, coal processed in such a way as to eliminate most of the impurities while raising the carbon content. Until recently, it was assumed that the charcoal iron industry, particularly in Britain faced problems towards the end of the seventeenth century because of rising charcoal prices caused by the insatiable demand of blast furnaces for woodland. It now appears, however, that this interpretation is largely unwarranted; and not only did charcoal remain readily available, but charcoal smelting was the preferred method for some time. The results of coke smelting were generally unsatisfactory; and certainly, wrought iron refined from coke-smelted pig iron was more expensive than that refined from charcoal-smelted pig iron (Hyde 1977).

Abraham Darby successfully smelted iron with coke at Coalbrookdale in Shropshire in 1709, yet despite the superb quality of the product, it was not until the end of the century before coke smelting had become the dominant technique in England. Indeed, between 1720 and 1755, for example, 22 new charcoal blast furnaces were erected, making a total of 68, while in 1750, there were only 4 coke smelting furnaces in operation in Britain. From 1750, however, the balance began to change and by the late 1780s, 72 coke furnaces had begun production, together accounting for 70,000 tons of pig iron. At the same time, the remaining 24 charcoal furnaces produced 10,000 tons of pig iron. In 1805, 11 charcoal furnaces were still in operation, producing 7800 tons of pig iron (Hyde 1977).

Despite the tenacity of charcoal-produced iron, the advantages of coke smelting became increasing apparent from mid-century. After 1750, for example, the differential cost of coke and charcoal pig iron began to decrease, raising the demand for coke pig iron. Secondly, there was an increased demand for quality cast-iron products – for urban construction, sewers and piping, for use in steam-engine cylinders employed in the provision of urban amenities; the supply of domestic utensils especially pots, vats and pans; as well as for the increased demand for military ordnance, for cannon, muskets and ammunition – which only coke furnaces could achieve. Cast-iron output as a share of total blast furnace output grew considerably over the period. At the beginning of the eighteenth century only 5 per cent of the output of blast furnaces was used for cast iron; around 1750, the figure stood at 20 per cent rising to 40 per cent in 1815, by which time foundries had become a significant part of the industry (Hyde 1977).

On the continent of Europe, the diffusion of coke smelting was an even lengthier process. Even in Belgium, where coke smelting was adopted on a large scale before either France or Germany, charcoal smelting predominated until the early 1830s (Fremdling 1982). In the early nineteenth century, the charcoal iron industry was located in the Ardennes region which spilled over into France, Luxembourg and Germany. The first important coke blast furnace was built in Seraing outside Liège in 1823, and seven years later, there were still only four coke furnaces in the country producing just over 10 per cent of total pig-iron output (Pounds 1985; Milward and Saul 1979). Thereafter, the progress of coke smelting was extremely rapid, and by 1836, 70 per cent of the country's pig iron came from coke smelters (Fremdling 1982). Charcoal smelting was virtually eliminated by the 1860s. In France, only 15 per cent of pig-iron output came from coke smelters in 1836 rising to 41 per cent by 1850. By the 1860s the corresponding figure stood at 85 per cent at which time charcoal pig-iron production reached its maximum level of 314,000 tons. It was only in the 1870s that charcoal pig-iron production contracted absolutely falling to 94,000 tons in 1870 and to no more than 20,000 tons in 1890 (Fremdling 1982; Pounds and Parker 1957). The German iron industry was the most tenacious in its production of charcoal pig iron (Brose 1985). As late as 1853 charcoal pig iron still accounted for as much as 70 per cent of the country's pig-iron output, and between 1834 and 1856 charcoal pig-iron production increased considerably from 100,000 tons to 275,000 tons. From that maximum output began to decline both relatively and absolutely. In 1880, there were still 27 furnaces producing 50,000 tons of charcoal pig iron, but by then this represented no more than 2 per cent of total output. Charcoal iron in Germany did not die without a struggle and in 1914, there were still three furnaces making charcoal iron (Fremdling 1982; Brose 1985). Italy was also late in switching to coke smelting, and evidence suggests that charcoal smelting did not disappear until the 1890s (Wertime 1961; Milward and Saul 1977). In Sweden, charcoal pig iron continued to account for the bulk of iron output; in 1913, for example, 86 per cent of total pig-iron output was charcoal smelted and it was not until 1941 that coke smelting surpassed that of charcoal. The growth of the charcoal iron industry continued despite the fact that charcoal pig iron was at least 50 per cent more expensive than coke pig iron. The determining factor in the survival of this technique in Sweden seems to have been that the Swedish iron industry found a particular niche in the market which it was able to exploit successfully (Söderlund 1958).

Throughout Europe, therefore, coke was only slowly substituted for charcoal in the smelting of iron, despite the apparent superiority of coke. Indeed, both techniques of producing pig iron coexisted for a long time, and the output of both types increased until the late nineteenth century (Fremdling 1982, 1983). Traditionally, historians have attributed the persistence of charcoal smelting to the poor quality of coke, the high cost of transporting coke, and abundant supplies of wood, as well as to inertia on the part of European ironmasters. Recent research, however, has suggested that the market strongly influenced the choice of technique. The best information concerns the German charcoal iron industry, where it appears that charcoal and coke-smelted iron served different markets, which from the 1830s to the last decades of the nineteenth century grew in parallel (Brose 1985). Until the 1830s, the quality and versatility of charcoal iron satisfied the main demands of the market for iron and was particularly well suited to the structure of the refining sector. The wrought iron produced from charcoal pig iron was used largely in making wires and nails, tools and other utensils, and there was little demand for the cast iron produced by the coke smelters. In the 1830s, coke smelting grew very rapidly in response to the demand for rails, construction and machinery, all of which tolerated the particular metallurgical characteristics of coke pig iron. The charcoal iron industry retained its traditional markets for a while but as coke smelting expanded, the quality of the output increased to the point where it was able to invade the markets of the charcoal iron industry. The high quality range of charcoal iron also faced considerable competition from the Swedish iron industry, but the most serious attack came from steel making (Brose 1985).

The case of the German charcoal iron industry provides convincing evidence that ironmasters were neither irrational nor prejudiced in their adherence to charcoal smelting. Not only did they increase their output, but there is also some evidence that in the face of competition, they achieved considerable productivity gains giving them a new lease of life.

If continental Europe was slow in adopting coke smelting technology, the same was definitely not true for the other great invention of the late eighteenth century, the puddling process for the production of wrought iron. By the end of the eighteenth century, the majority of producers had shifted from the direct method, whereby wrought iron was produced from iron ore, to the indirect method which processed pig iron. Improvements to blast furnaces in the seventeenth and eighteenth centuries, which improved the quality of pig iron and thus of wrought iron, accounted for a large part of the change.

For most of the period, however, the refining of pig iron to produce wrought iron remained a tedious and complicated process (Pounds and Parker 1957). Pig iron was heated and reheated in charcoal fires and hammered until the carbon was driven out. Coal or coke could not be used in this method because the iron would absorb sulphur from the fuel causing it to be brittle and difficult to hammer. Many attempts were made, however, to use coal in the reheating process when the temperature of the hot iron was not high enough to cause any chemical disturbance. Recent research suggests that in England, at least, coal was widely used in the reheating stage of refining pig iron by the 1760s (Hyde 1977). The solution to the problem of using coal in the first stage of processing came in the 1760s and 1770s in what was called the potting process. In the new process coal was used in the initial heating, and the iron, which as a result became contaminated with sulphur, was subsequently heated in special pots where a chemical reaction removed the sulphur. The resultant mass was then hammered as in the earlier processes. Although potting lengthened the overall production process, the use of coal produced greater heat and thus a superior end-product. Potting was rapidly diffused, and by 1788, was used in the manufacture of 50 per cent of England's wrought iron (Hyde 1977). Before then, however, another method for refining iron had emerged. The puddling process, patented by Henry Cort in 1783 and 1784 (though there were earlier patents by others), contained a technology which not only totally removed the necessity of using charcoal in refining but also simplified the entire refining process. Pig iron was melted and thereby decarburized in a coal-fire furnace using reflected rather than direct heat from the fire. In the process of melting, the mass or 'puddle' of iron was stirred in order to speed up the process. Because the iron and the fuel were never in direct contact, there was no need to heat, reheat and hammer the iron. Instead, the metal from the furnace was rolled to remove further impurities and to form it into standardized bars (Hyde 1977).

In Britain the puddling technology was not adopted on a large scale until the late 1790s and did not entirely replace other methods of refining iron until 1815. In the meantime, the production of wrought iron had increased considerably from 32,000 tons in 1788, to 150,000 tons in 1815, and by its peak in the early 1870s, the figure ranged between 3 and 3.5 million tons (Hyde 1977). No technological breakthrough of the kind exemplified by Cort's invention occurred in wrought-iron production during the nineteenth century, though many minor improvements as well as significantly lower raw material prices accounted for the increased output (Hyde 1977).

On the continent, where there are scattered references to the use of coal in the eighteenth century, the puddling process, if not earlier coal-using technologies, spread rapidly (Wertime 1961; Fremdling 1983). In France, for example, puddling appeared at the ironworks at Le Creusot around 1785 and diffused rapidly to other regions (Woronoff 1984). By the late 1820s, the 150 puddling furnaces in France accounted for 30 per cent of total wrought iron output of 136,000 tons, though at the same time, there were more than 1000 refineries dotted around the countryside producing wrought iron with charcoal as a fuel (Pounds and Parker 1957; Gille 1968). In relative and absolute terms, puddling grew very rapidly and accounted for 47 per cent of output in 1836, over 70 per cent around mid-century and over 90 per cent in the 1860s. Unlike charcoal smelting, which grew absolutely in the nineteenth century, the output of charcoal refining remained remarkably constant at around 100,000 tons until the 1860s, after which total output began to fall rapidly (Fremdling 1982). Overall the wrought-iron sector developed considerably during the nineteenth century reaching peak output between the 1860s and the early 1890s of around 800,000 tons annually (Fremdling 1982; Gille 1966; Mill 1985).

Germany's experience in the wrought-iron industry was somewhat different from that of France and the diffusion of puddling technology began later and was generally faster. While French output of wrought iron probably surpassed that of Germany during the first half of the nineteenth century, by the peak of output, German wrought-iron production was possibly twice that of France at her maximum (Fremdling 1982).

Clearly, the puddling process was responsible for an enormous increase in the output of wrought iron in Europe and together with the coke blast furnaces accounted for an awesome increase in the consumption of iron. Precisely how great an increase is largely a matter of guesswork but some figures give a rough guide. At the beginning of the eighteenth century, per capita consumption of iron in Europe was probably no more than two kilos annually; by the beginning of the nineteenth century, the figure was close to nine kilos, and by 1870, the consumption of iron had reached a figure of more than 70 kilos of iron per capita (Mitchell 1975).

In continental Europe, unlike in Britain, it was the puddling process and not the smelting process that brought about an integration of iron and coal in the nineteenth century and was certainly responsible for dramatically altering the structure and geography of the industry (Pounds 1985). While smelting remained tied to traditional sources of supply, especially of charcoal, the coal-based technology of refining encouraged a relocation of wrought-iron production to the coal fields of Europe. In France, for example, refining became concentrated on the coalfields in the northeast quadrant of the country as well as in the centre of the country, which were not traditional centres of ironmaking. In 1872, refining was carried on in only 15 departments whereas smelting was scattered over 45 departments (Pounds and Parker 1957). At the same time, production became highly concentrated in a small number of very large and growing firms. The seven largest producers of wrought iron in France in 1812 accounted for 21 per cent of the country's output, but twenty years later, their combined output accounted for almost 38 per cent rising to 53 per cent by 1860 (Gille 1968). In Germany, where a similar process of geographical concentration occurred as in France, many new firms became established in the Ruhr, where local coal and pig iron imported from Siegerland were used. Blast furnaces were not erected until 20 years after the puddling process was introduced into the local refining industry (Pounds and Parker 1957).

In the long term, whatever the type of fuel used in smelting and refining, whichever of the various techniques were employed, whatever the structure and geography of production, the demand for wrought iron was consistently high from 1600 to the 1860s. Cast iron enjoyed some growth in England in the late eighteenth century, and on the continent before the middle of the nineteenth century, but even at its height, it ranked poorly to wrought iron, which consumed 70–80 per cent of pig iron output (Hyde 1977; Pounds and Parker 1957). Only for armaments production did cast iron experience significant demand; and it was only during times of war that demand for cast iron approached that for wrought iron.

There was apparently no limit to the uses of wrought iron. Yet it could not compete with steel where strength or a resilient cutting edge was required. As an iron product, steel stands midway between pig iron and wrought iron; indeed, steel was a transient product, both created and destroyed in the process of making wrought iron. Nevertheless, steel was a mysterious product, the making of which few ironmasters understood. Most processes to make steel involved the addition or extraction of carbon, but it was not until the middle of the nineteenth century that it was generally agreed that the critical chemical was indeed carbon (Smith 1964). Even then, the function of other chemicals such as phosphorus, silicon, and manganese, was not firmly established (Wertime 1961).

Because of the complexity of the product and because ironmasters could not easily interrupt the forging process, so that steel and not wrought iron would emerge, steelmaking became a highly specialized occupation. Unlike smelting and to a lesser extent refining, steelmaking was, from the outset, an urban industry. Many towns throughout Europe had steelmakers, and some of these, such as Solingen, Brescia, and Liège had already become quite famous by the beginning of the seventeenth century.

In the seventeenth century, there were several methods of making steel, including direct methods (variants of the one previously described for wrought iron) and indirect methods comprising both decarburizing pig iron and carburizing wrought iron. During the century, one particular method, cementation, grew in popularity and, by the end of the century, became the standard method of producing medium-quality steel. The basis of the technique lay in heating in a furnace bars of wrought iron which had been interlaced with layers of charcoal. During the baking, the surface of the bars of iron would absorb carbon leading to a process of hardening. The depth to which the hardening penetrated depended on several factors including the amount of heat used, the time of processing and other unknown (at the time) but obviously crucial elements (Wertime 1961; Barraclough 1984). In the eighteenth century, for example, Swedish wrought iron was considered to be superior to other irons but the precise reason remained a mystery. It was not until well into the nineteenth century that it was discovered that phosphorus (which, for instance, was present in sizeable proportions in French iron) inhibited the absorption of carbon, while manganese (which was found in Swedish iron) encouraged the absorption of carbon in the cementation process (Wertime 1961).

Cemented steel, besides having a constituency which was little understood, also suffered from uneven quality. One particularly successful solution to this problem came in the early 1740s when Benjamin Huntsman, a Yorkshire clockmaker, invented a technique whereby he melted cemented steel in a tightly closed crucible until its quality was even. The result was crucible steel which was very hard and greatly superior, in quality, to cemented steel; but it could only be produced on a small scale. The crucible technique was therefore employed to produce excellent quality steel where hardness was desired and limited output was not important (Barraclough 1984; Wertime 1961; Tweedale 1986).

In the early part of the nineteenth century, there were three main methods of producing steel; the partial decarburizing of pig iron producing natural steel; the cementation and crucible technique; and, a relative newcomer, partial puddling, where the puddling process was interrupted at a crucial moment before all the carbon had been eliminated. The technique of puddled steel was introduced into Germany in 1835 and into France in 1855 (Pounds and Parker 1957; Gille 1968). Before 1850, despite the emergence of giant firms like Krupp in Essen and Schneider in Le Creusot, the scale of steelmaking enterprises was typically small.

The growth in the productivity of steelmaking remained marginal and until the second half of the nineteenth century there was no satisfactory method of producing steel on a large scale. The economic conditions for mass production of steel were certainly present. The increase in the demand for iron throughout the eighteenth and first half of the nineteenth centuries had led not only to a rapid increase in pig-iron and wrought-iron production, but also to significant innovations in blast furnace and refining technologies. Neither this nor the heightened demand for wrought iron from railway construction in the 1840s and 1850s, however, gave rise to mass-produced steel (Fremdling 1977). Steel was clearly a substance which could only be understood with considerable chemical and metallurgical insight, which at this stage was incomplete. Nevertheless, many industrial processes in the nineteenth century were commonly employed long before their scientific bases were discovered, and many of the subsequent leading innovators in the mass production of steel had little or no theoretical metallurgical insight.

Progress towards large-scale steel production accelerated in the 1850s and 1860s and, like Cort's puddling process in the eighteenth century and Krupp's puddling process for steel in the early nineteenth century, clearly received important impetus from the military (McNeill 1983; Trebilcock 1969; Manchester 1968). During the 1850s, as a result of the Crimean War, there was concern in the European armaments business and the military that the techniques of artillery and small-arms manufacturing were hopelessly inadequate (McNeill 1983). Henry Bessemer's revolutionary techniques for producing steel was a response to this concern and to the particular need to find a new gun metal to support the explosive charge of the artillery shell that he himself had devised (Bessemer 1905). His technique to produce bulk steel was perfected in the late 1850s and early 1860s, and consisted of blasting molten pig iron with cold air which oxidized the required proportion of carbon in the process, giving steel as the end product. This technique was simple and very quick. One estimate suggests that four tons of molten iron could be converted into steel in 15 minutes whereas an equivalent amount required 24 hours in the puddling furnace (Landes 1969). Furthermore, Bessemer's process stimulated the development of large-scale steelmaking firms, whose size was limited only by that of the converter; and, by dispensing with the services of the puddler, it required little skilled labour, a feature of great consequence (Landes 1969; Courtheoux 1959).

There were however, problems with the Bessemer converter which were only partially solved by the open-hearth technique of steel production introduced by William Siemens and improved by Emile and Pierre Martin in the 1860s. The main disadvantage was that neither Bessemer's converter nor the open-hearth process could expel phosphorus from the metal, thus the steel produced was particularly brittle. Both techniques, therefore, required the use of iron ore which yielded low-phosphorus pig iron. Ores of this character were in short supply in Europe, and were located only in northwest England, the Basque region of Spain, in the Rhineland, southern Sweden and central France (Landes 1969; Pounds 1985). The vast iron-ore deposits elsewhere in Europe were largely unsuitable for these techniques. In 1879, Sidney Gilchrist Thomas suggested that the problem caused by the presence of phosphorus could be solved by changing the lining of the converter from one which was essentially acid to one which was essentially basic in chemical composition. In this way, the phosphorus would be chemically attracted away from the metal, absorbed in the slag and discarded. Because of the immediate success of this modification, the entire landscape of steel production in Europe was changed. The iron-ore deposits in Lorraine and Luxembourg, in the Midlands, in Normandy and above all, in the Ruhr became usable. Gilchrist Thomas's basic process applied either to the Bessemer converter or to the open-hearth method transformed European steel production, and output surged ahead. No other innovation in iron and steel production diffused as rapidly as the basic process. Within no more than one year of its public pronouncement, the basic process was being used in the Ruhr, in Lorraine, in Austria and in Luxembourg (Wertime 1961; Landes 1969; Pounds and Parker 1957).

Taken together, the new techniques of steel manufacture adopted in Europe between the 1850s and 1880 resulted not only in a boom in steel output, but also, as the cost of steel fell, in the relative contraction of wrought iron as the basic constituent of iron demand. The transition from wrought iron to steel in Europe was quick. In 1861, before the adoption of the Bessemer converter, approximately 125,000 tons of steel were produced in Europe (Landes 1969). In the same year, the output of wrought iron reached 4.3 million tons (Hyde 1977; Fremdling 1982; Gille 1968; Beck 1903). In 1885, steel output matched that of wrought iron. By 1900, the output of crude steel reached 15.6 million tons and had risen to 38.2 million tons by 1913 (Mitchell 1975). In that year, Europe's production of wrought iron was between 8 and 9 million tons (Pounds and Parker 1957; Mitchell and Deane 1962).

Between 1870 and 1913, steel produced by the Bessemer and open-hearth processes (both acid and basic), gradually replaced wrought iron for many uses. Throughout Europe and in the United States as well, an overwhelming proportion of steel output went into three main large-scale uses; rails, shipbuilding and construction. In France, Germany and Great Britain, as much as 80–90 per cent of crude steel output was absorbed in this way (Mill 1985; Beck 1903; Elbaum 1986). The rail boom began to wane during the 1880s and steel rails were used primarily to replace wrought iron ones. At the same time, shipbuilding became more important and the rise in the production of ship-plate reflected the buoyant demand. In France, in 1890, for example, ship-plate accounted for as much as 20 per cent of the country's steel output; in Britain, shipbuilding absorbed 30 per cent of total steel output and 42 per cent of open-hearth steel by 1910–12 (Mill 1985; Elbaum 1986). From 1900, new demands for steel came from the armaments, automobile, electrical and chemical industries.

Despite the enormous progress made in steel production which put pressure on other parts of the iron and steel industry, the absolute output of wrought and cast iron in France, Germany and Britain remained impressive. Puddled steel, which had been the main form of bulk steel before the 1870s when it reached its peak level of output, continued to find an important niche in the market for speciality steel. Crucible-steel making, however, retained a more important position in the industry than did puddled steel. It became concentrated in specific cities for the purpose of cutlery making in Essen, Solingen, Remscheid, St Etienne and Sheffield, and was generally characterized by a relatively small scale of production (for all these examples see Sabel and Zeitlin 1985; Gras 1904, 1908; Hanagan 1980; Schnetzler 1975; Pounds 1985; Tweedale 1987). Throughout Europe, crucible-steel gained in importance from its inception until 1914. In France, crucible steel output grew from as little as 168 tons in 1831 to over 22,000 tons in 1912, while in Germany, output reached over 100,000 tons in 1914 (Barraclough 1984).

Wide-ranging metallurgical development continued to transform metal making and associated trades until 1914. The most significant of these was the production of alloy steels using manganese, nickel, tungsten and chrome and high-speed steel, a specially treated steel of chromium and tungsten, designed specifically to cut steel in a machine-tool assembly. The considerable improvement in the ability of machine tools to cut metal precisely would not have been possible without the use of alloy steels. This branch of the steel industry, though much smaller than the highly visible Bessemer and open-hearth operations was nevertheless critical to the entire metalworking industry, which included the burgeoning consumer-goods industries described earlier (Tweedale 1987).

It must be emphasized that what distinguished the iron and steel industry in the late nineteenth century from its earlier counterpart was not simply that the quantity of output had increased sharply but that the variety had expanded considerably. This led not only to many new kinds and uses of iron and steel, but also to a wide range of industrial experiences from the giant Bessemer plants to the small firms specializing in special steels where technical vitality, skill and flexibility were consistently encouraged.

The Chemical Industries

The iron and steel industry grew considerably over the entire period from 1600 to 1914, with the help of specific and important technical innovations as well as a series of minor improvements. Both of these main paths of technical change in iron and steel making were, until 1914 at least, generally uninformed by scientific procedures and principles. Even many of the crucial discoveries concerning alloy steel were made by individuals whose theoretical knowledge of metallurgy and chemistry was basic to say the least.

By contrast, the chemical industry has often been portrayed as the first of the so-called science-based industries. It was the production of organic chemicals in Europe in the last quarter of the nineteenth century, according to many sources, which witnessed the first example of the industrial use of routine scientific investigation and the systematic application of science to industrial production. Not only did the industry begin with specific scientific discoveries but it required science as a factor of production to sustain it. The inorganic branch of the industry, which long predated the organic side, is often portrayed as having been unscientific in its development and outlook. This characterization of the chemical industry, however, especially the distinction between the inorganic and organic branches, is not entirely accurate.

Throughout the period from 1600 to 1914, the production of inorganic chemicals, that is, compounds formed without carbon, was central to the European chemical industry. Until the end of the nineteenth century, the most important products of the inorganic branch were heavy chemicals, principally alkalis (specifically soda ash and caustic soda), sulphuric acid and bleaching materials. Although a small quantity of sulphuric acid was used in the making of other chemicals, most of the products of the inorganic branch were used in other industries, especially in textiles, glass, paper and soap-making (Hohenberg 1967; Smith 1979; Warren 1980).

Until the middle of the nineteenth century, soda ash (sodium carbonate) was the principal end-product of the chemical industry. In the seventeenth and eighteenth centuries, natural alkalis in the form of vegetable matter provided the only source of soda. Natural soda was obtained from the ash of a small number of alkali bearing plants, the most important of which was barilla. The best of these plants grew naturally on the Mediterranean shore in Spain, Sicily and the Levant and much of the soda required by France and Britain was imported from these sources (Barker *et al.* 1956; Smith 1979).

The dependence on imported soda intensified, and the vulnerability of supply, especially in wartime, stimulated the search for an alternative source of soda in both France and Britain. Attempts focused on the chemical production of soda, using a plentiful, non-vegetable source. The method by which the idea of producing artificial soda became a reality was lengthy and complicated, but began in 1737 when a renowned French chemist, Henri-Louis Duhamel du Monceau, established a clear chemical relationship between salt and soda by producing soda from salt through a series of chemical reactions. He further revealed that natural alkali was obtained in plants by a similar chemistry using salt in the soil. While de Monceau was not interested in the commercial possibilities of his important discovery, attempts were made by others in both France and Britain from the 1760s to the early 1790s to devise a workable industrial procedure for converting salt into soda. Little success was achieved, however, and before 1790, only a small amount of soda was being produced artificially. The significant breakthrough came in 1789 when Nicolas Leblanc conceived of a relatively straightforward process which produced soda by a commercially viable method. A factory was established in St Denis outside Paris in 1791 and production began (Smith 1979).

The Leblanc method was straightforward and used easily available raw materials. It stimulated the production of sulphuric acid, which was required to decompose salt in the first stage of the Leblanc process, producing hydrochloric acid and chlorine used for bleaching materials, and the intermediate, sodium sulphate, used in the second stage of the process.

In its early years of operation, many of the by-products of the Leblanc process were discarded or, as in the case of hydrogen chloride gas, simply blown into the atmosphere. During much of the nineteenth century, chemists and soda-makers made strenuous efforts to find a way of using these by-products. The problems often seemed insurmountable. The conversion of the waste gas from the Leblanc process, for example, was finally achieved in the 1860s and 1870s. A means of recovering the valuable sulphur which emerged from the process in waste form was discovered in the late 1880s. The Leblanc process also encouraged improvements in the technology of sulphuric acid production. In the early part of the nineteenth century, the price of sulphuric acid was halved by increasing the productivity of the main industrial process. Subsequently, more substantial technical changes were made, the most important of which involved altering the chemical engineering of sulphuric acid production. The work of Joseph-Louis Gay-Lussac and John Glover in the 1840s and 1850s greatly increased the concentration of sulphuric acid, which was to become extremely valuable later in the century (Smith 1979; Haber 1958; Hohenberg 1967).

The importance of the Leblanc process for making soda was two-fold. Firstly, and most significant for contemporaries, it ended the dependence on imports of vegetable matter by substituting an artificially created product. The benefits accrued directly to European manufacturers and workers, not only those directly employed in the soda works, but those indirectly involved in salt mining and panning, in construction, and in transport. The second impact was more enduring, as the production of artificial soda led to the creation of an entirely new industry. The Leblanc process acted, in a technical manner, to integrate the various industrial chemicals produced at the time, and thus the process, rather than the product became the centre of the chemical industry (Hoenberg 1967). In early nineteenth century France, for example, of a total output of sulphuric acid approaching 10 million kilos of sulphuric acid, more than 70 per cent was consumed to make soda (Smith 1979).

Demand for soda increased considerably during the seventeenth and eighteenth centuries from its principal users, the expanding textile, glass and soap industries. Once the Leblanc process was established the growth of output was rapid and the manufacture of soda spread from France to Britain, Switzerland and the Rhineland. In France, where the production of artificial soda successfully ousted natural soda from the marketplace, the process of import substitution was especially rapid. In 1789, for example, France imported around 15,000 tons of soda, but within 20 years of the appearance of the Leblanc process, output of artificial soda had reached 15,000 tons and imports had fallen to 10 per cent of their former level on the eve of the Revolution (Smith 1979). British production of artificial soda was much lower until the 1820s, after which growth was very rapid (Warren 1980). In the middle of the century, France and Britain dominated the alkali industry in Europe and in 1852, output of soda in the two countries was 45,000 tons and 152,000 tons respectively. Twenty years later, output had grown further, and production of alkali in Britain had reached around 350,000 tons and in France 67,000 tons. Germany had now entered the field with total output of 45,000 tons (Haber 1958).

The Leblanc process had permitted an enormous growth in alkali production, yet it had two substantial disadvantages. Firstly, its heavy dependence on sulphuric acid implied the possibility of bottlenecks, and thus it was essential that the technology of the two processes was always in harmony. This was clearly difficult to ensure. Secondly, the Leblanc process produced considerable quantities of expensive waste. Not surprisingly, therefore, an alternative process was developed that dispensed with these disadvantages. At about the same time as Leblanc successfully demonstrated his method for soda manufacture, other chemists and manufacturers were approaching the problem from another direction considering a process which used only easily obtainable materials (Smith 1979). The ammonia soda process, as it was called, required only ammonia and salt to react chemically in several stages to produce soda. Its fundamental advantage lay in the fact that ammonia was both used and produced in the process, yet the problem of how to recover the ammonia industrially remained a stumbling block. In the 1840s and 1850s, there was a rush of interest in this process throughout Europe, but the solution to the ammonia recovery problem did not come until the late 1860s and early 1870s when Ernest Solvay managed to produce soda from ammonia commercially in Belgium (Haber 1958).

Because of its independence from other processes, the Solvay ammonia soda process was destined to be the victor in the competitive field of soda production. Although it was rapidly diffused, producers of soda attempted to forestall the competition by enhancing the Leblanc process. Attention was focused on the recovery of waste products, particularly the hydrogen chloride and sulphur discharge. The ability to produce chlorine from the waste of the Leblanc process was clearly of great importance, but towards the end of the century, other methods, especially those using electrolytic techniques, for making chlorine (as well as other chemicals) eroded whatever advantages the Leblanc process had (Haber 1958; Landes 1969). Between 1870 and 1900, therefore, European chemical manufacturers moved increasingly to the Solvay process. In France and Germany, in the 1880s the two processes were each responsible for 50 per cent of the output of soda. By the turn of the century, however, especially after the discovery of alternative sources of chlorine, the Leblanc process had almost disappeared in France and Germany, where the Solvay process accounted for as much as 95 per cent of soda production in 1900. Only in Britain, which in 1894 produced 75 per cent of the world's output of Leblanc soda, did the Leblanc process continue to dominate the production of alkali (Warren 1980; Landes 1969; Milward and Saul 1977; Richardson 1968).

The success of the Solvay process led to a rapid growth in output of alkali. Between 1880 and 1913, the combined output of France and Germany grew from 170,000 tons to 860,000 tons while British output grew at a slower rate from around 500,000 tons to 700,000 tons (Haber 1958, 1971; Landes 1969; Milward and Saul 1977). The new process also liberated sulphuric acid for wider use. The production of fertilizers became the chief user of sulphuric acid (accounting for between 50 per cent and 75 per cent of total sulphuric acid output in France and Germany in 1913), and dye manufacturers were particularly interested in the concentrated version. Changes in the technology of soda production affected the location of the production of sulphuric acid. In the 1860s, for example, when its total output was 480,000 tons, Britain was the largest producer of sulphuric acid. At the same time, French and German production combined totalled 200,000 tons. By 1913, the positions were reversed, and while British output stood at just over 1 million tons the German and French combined output was over 2.6 million tons (Haber 1958, 1971; Mitchell 1975). In the meantime, other producers had emerged, of which the most important was Italy. The Solvay process was also indirectly responsible for the scientific search for other independent means of obtaining valuable chemicals. The progress made in electrolytic techniques for producing chlorine (and hydrochloric acid), sodium and high-pressure techniques for ammonia, all developed between the 1890s and the First World War, can be attributed in part to the abandonment of process interdependence (Haber 1971).

The inorganic chemical industry produced chemicals whose composition was relatively simple but whose manufacture was often extremely difficult. The chemical reactions necessary to produce a particular chemical were often known far in advance of its successful manufacture. The reactions required to produce soda from ammonia, for example, where known as early as 1822, yet it was not until Solvay's important work in the late 1860s that an industrial solution was available. Similarly, the production of ammonia from its constituent elements of nitrogen and hydrogen took more than 130 years to emerge after its constitution was first described. The Haber–Bosch process for ammonia production which was developed just before the First World War required an enormous scientific and engineering effort which tested the limits of industrial process technology (Haber 1971).

Until the middle of the nineteenth century, the production of these relatively simple chemicals defined the chemical industry. Indeed, the demonstration that artificial equivalents of naturally occuring chemicals could be produced under industrial conditions was the most significant feature of the industry at that time. Artificial soda was probably the best example of this, but there appears to have been a more general interest in synthetic products than this. In the field of medicine, for example, demand grew for a synthetic version of quinine, the malaria-inhibiting drug whose manufacture depended on a natural product grown in Peru and Asia. William Henry Perkin was one of many chemists seeking a synthetic form of the drug in the 1850s, when he discovered a substance which, upon further analysis, yielded a colouring matter. It dyed silk cloth the colour of mauve (Haber 1958).

What Perkin had discovered was a dye derived from aniline, a chemical obtained from benzene through the distillation of coal-tar. It was well known by this time that coal-tar, a by-product of the burning of coal to make gas, was an extremely complex substance, and that it yielded, through the technique of fractional distillation, a whole series of chemicals. Perkin's discovery of aniline dyes was revolutionary, but the highly original colours produced were complementary to, but not substitutes for natural dyes (Beer 1959; Hohenberg 1967).

During the 1860s, more colours were prepared from aniline, and a new class of dyes, known as azo dyes, was developed which obviated the need for a mordant to fix the colour. At the end of the 1860s, an entirely, new class of dyes – alizarin – was discovered which was derived from another product of coal-tar distillation extracted with the aid of sulphuric acid. The significance of alizarin dyes lay in three main areas. Firstly, they effectively replaced natural dyes, the first of the dyes being identical to madder, a reddish-purple natural dye. Secondly, they were perfect for dyeing cotton, whereas aniline dyes worked best with silk. Finally, their discovery was based on the theoretical insights into the structure of organic compounds which made it possible to conceive of synthetic compounds in abstract as well as empirical terms (Haber 1958).

Both Britain and France had profited directly from the discovery of aniline and azo dyes and had entered the market vigorously, but they were completely overtaken by Germany when the alizarin dyes were developed. The patent for alizarin dyes, though hotly contested, went to the German company BASF (Badische Anilin- und Soda-Fabrik) which had previously made soda by the Leblanc process as well as some aniline dyes (Hohenberg 1967; Haber 1958). BASF started producing alizarin dyes in 1870 and by 1902, its annual output was in the range of 2000 tons, making it the largest producer of that class of dyes in the country (Haber 1958, 1971).

The domination of the coal-tar dysestuff industry by Germany was swift and decisive. Only five years after BASF began producing alizarin dyes, there were 12 firms producing alizarin in Germany compared to a combined total for the rest of Europe of five firms. In terms of output, total world production of dyestuffs was valued at £400,000, of which Germany was responsible for a relatively small proportion. By 1878, however, the value of world output had grown to about £4 million, 63 per cent of which was accounted for by Germany. The gain in relative strength continued unabated until by 1913, as much as 85 per cent of the world's dyestuffs were made in Germany. Germany's domination of dyestuffs production was even greater than these figures suggest. While France, for example, produced 8000 tons of synthetic dyestuffs in 1913, most of these dyes were made from imported German intermediates, that is, from substances which were formed during one of the stages of the chemical process eventually producing dyes. The same was true of the United States, which did not have its own dyestuff industry until after the start of the war (Haber 1958, 1971; Meyer-Thurow 1982; Noble 1977).

The German industry underwent a relentless process of concentration of productive activity within a few very large firms. The three firms that gave much impetus to the German dyestuff industry were BASF, Bayer and Hoechst. In 1883, these firms alone accounted for 55 per cent of German output and 33 per cent of the world market; by 1913, they had grown to such an extent that their combined output accounted for 80 per cent of Germany's and 60 per cent of the world's total value of dyestuffs (Haber 1958, 1971; Meyer-Thurow 1982). The major German dyestuff firms received an important boost from the appropriation of alizarin, but their continued success was assured by the addition of increasing numbers and varieties of dyes. A complementarity of interest developed amongst the firms, which enhanced total production. BASF concentrated on alizarin and aniline dyes as well as on the synthesis of indigo, which took as much as 20 years to produce; Hoechst concentrated on alizarin as well as new azo dyes which came on the market in the 1870s and 1880s; and Bayer's production centred on azo dyes. Firms in Switzerland, the second largest producer of dyestuffs in Europe, also participated in this rationalization. The dyestuff industry was established in Basle (with considerable French expertise and capital) where the major firms rapidly found their own place in the market. The largest of these, CIBA, retreated from alizarin and aniline production in the face of German strength in these areas and focused principally on azo dyes. Geigy, the next largest firm, did likewise. The two other main companies settled on the production of intermediates and a special class of dyes respectively (Haber 1958, 1971; Hohenberg 1967).

The distillation of coal-tar, therefore, produced a number of chemicals which themselves yielded other classes of chemicals. Dyestuffs were found along a particular chemical route from the original coal-tar distillation. Another of the various possible chemical paths, whose existence was predicated upon a well-grounded theoretical understanding of the chemical structure of coal-tar, led in the 1880s to pharmaceuticals. Hoechst pioneered pharmaceutical production by preparing the first painkiller in 1888 followed by serums and anaesthetics. Bayer produced its own painkiller later in the same year and sedatives and barbiturates soon followed. Aspirin was first made in 1897 and became the company's pharmaceutical flagship almost immediately. These same firms also carried their interests into photographic film and synthetic rubber. By 1914, most of the top German and Swiss firms were broadly diversified; but even then, their dye business accounted for as much as 70 per cent of total income (Haber 1958, 1971; Meyer-Thurow 1982; Hayes 1987).

The phenomenal success and extremely rapid growth of the German (and Swiss) dyestuff firms in particular, and the organic branch of the chemical industry in general has long attracted the interests of historians, more to marvel than to analyse. One of the recurrent themes which the literature considers is the degree to which the industry and the firms in it institutionalized science for commercial ends – one commentator has referred to this phenomenon as the industrialization of invention (Meyer-Thurow 1982). It was in the dyestuff industry that applied science became the productive driving force and basic research was central to its dynamic. The key to competitive success lay in developing newer, better and cheaper dyestuffs as well as complementary products. That this happened is true enough. As one recent study has shown, Bayer's research laboratories in 1906 synthesized as many as 2600 dyestuffs although only 36 of these were marketed (Meyer-Thurow 1982).

There is little doubt that the German dyestuff firms institutionalized science (Beer 1958). The number of chemists employed at Bayer grew from 11 in 1880 to 262 in 1912, while between these years growth at Hoechst was from 12 to 307 (Meyer-Thurow 1982; Haber 1958). Although this suggests the growth of internal science, in fact many more chemists were employed in production than in research; and the growth of scientific staff was far slower than that of the commercial staff. Indeed, there is strong evidence of the enormous importance of marketing to the overall success of the firms. Hoechst, for example, employed as many chemists as commercial staff in the late 1870s, but by 1912, twice as many people were employed in the commercial branch as in the scientific branch. Bayer also placed great emphasis on marketing; in 1914 it had 44 sales branches and 123 agents worldwide. Marketing strategy was characterized by Bayer's promotion of Aspirin which used inducements to doctors to prescribe the drug. The big German and Swiss dye firms engaged in market and product research; they supported an enormous fund of market information; they advertised heavily; they did their own wholesaling and they tailored their laboratories to the needs of the market (Meyer-Thurow 1982; Beer 1958, 1959; Haber 1958; Milward and Saul 1977).

Recent historical research has tended to downgrade the importance of systematic industrial research in the organic chemical industry before 1914 (Meyer-Thurow 1982; Lundgreen 1984; Shinn 1980; Hoddesdon, 1981). The role of industrial research, while important, was entirely dependent on the previous growth record of the industry. The dominance which German firms enjoyed on the world organic chemical market can best be attributed to aggressive marketing techniques and to the stream of new products with which the sales respresentatives could exercise their prowess. Chemical knowledge was an international commodity over which no nation, industry or firm had a monopoly. Success in the organic chemical industry depended on well-worn factors; the ability to respond to and manipulate the market.

With respect to the appropriation of science as a productive force, the division between the inorganic and organic branches has been overstated. It is now apparent that the inorganic chemical industry, which began with the successful synthesis of soda, had important roots in scientific discovery and, to a lesser extent, in scientific technology. The major innovations in heavy chemical manufacture during the eighteenth and nineteenth centuries were the work of chemists or of individuals instructed in chemistry. The degree of theoretical understanding was probably greater than is commonly supposed and, while heavy chemicals have often been portrayed as the triumph of the salesman and the engineer rather than the chemist, this is certainly an exaggeration (Smith 1979). Similarly, the success of the organic branch of the chemical industry was, contrary to common belief, at least as much the result of commercial activity as scientific research. The two branches were clearly converging.

By 1914, the chemical industry was substantially different from what it had been two centuries earlier. It had succeeded in producing a range of chemicals, the most important of which replaced vital natural products. Interestingly, despite the great propaganda of the novelty of certain aspects of the chemical industry especially in the second half of the nineteenth century, chemical production was still largely a service industry. It is often forgotten that the textile industry which, in 1914 was still the largest employer of labour in Europe, consumed the bulk of the output of the chemical industry, especially the organic branch.

Though the discussion has focused on the heavy chemical and organic sectors of the chemical industry, it should be emphasized that the industry contained at least two other important areas of production. The first consisted of chemical firms, typically small, artisanal and located in industrial cities, that specialized in consumer chemicals, principally inks, paints, lacquers and adhesives (Hohenberg 1967; Laferrère 1972). At the other end of the scale were highly capital and resource-intensive firms which emerged from the 1880s in the electrochemical industry, of which aluminium production was the most important part. Relying heavily on cheap hydroelectric power, aluminium production was pioneered in France and the country dominated the industry until at least 1914, when it accounted for as much as 40 per cent of European production (Shinn 1980; Gignoux 1955; Schmitz 1979; Hall 1976).

Further Reading

Fox, R. and Weisz, G. (eds.) 1980: *The organization of science and technology in France, 1808–1914.* Cambridge: Cambridge University Press.

Haber, L. F. 1958: *The chemical industry during the nineteenth century.* Oxford: Oxford University Press.

— 1971: *The chemical industry 1900–1930.* Oxford: Oxford University Press.

Krohn, W., Layton, E. T. and Weingart, P. (eds.) 1978: *The dynamics of science and technology.* Dordrecht: Reidel.

Landes, D. 1969: *The unbound Prometheus.* Cambridge: Cambridge University Press.

Locke, R. R. 1984: *The end of the practical man.* London: JAI Press.

Mathias, P. (ed.) 1972: *Science and society 1600–1900.* Cambridge: Cambridge University Press.

Russell, C. A. 1983: *Science and social change 1700–1900.* London: Macmillan.

Smith, J. J. 1979: *The origins and early development of the heavy chemical industry in France.* Oxford: Oxford University Press.

Wertime, T. 1961: *The coming of the age of steel.* Leiden: Brill.

10 Power in European Industry 1600–1914

Most industrial production in Europe in the seventeenth century was conducted on the basis of simple technology powered by hand, wind, water or animals. When large units of production were essential for technical or economic reasons, the windmill, the oldest power source, was frequently applied. In the Dutch Republic particularly, the windmill permitted the mechanization of a wide range of industrial processes. A wind-powered timber sawing mill, developed in 1596, replaced hand sawing wherever the guilds did not prevent it (de Vries 1976); and by the late seventeenth century, around 600 industrial windmills existed in the shipbuilding villages of the Zaan alone (Pollard 1981). They were used mainly for timber sawing, paper making, oil pressing, starch making and lead milling, and in sugar refining. Windmills were commonly used for the grinding of corn for flour making throughout Europe, but especially in the flat regions (Pollard 1981).

Water power, easily harnessed from fast flowing streams, was also used in European industry during the seventeenth century, as the siting of early textile factories and metal making concerns on river banks testifies. Although a great many industrial processes required only simple hand tools, machinery was becoming more complex from the early seventeenth century, and was operated increasingly with the help of water power. In the silk industry, for example, throwing and ribbon making became mechanized at this time, and both the hydraulic throwing machine and the so-called Dutch loom or ribbon frame – which spread from northern Italy, to Lyons and then to England – were typically water-powered. In the seventeenth-century metal industry, slitting mills, to convert iron bars to sheets and rods for nail making, were built mainly on the banks of rivers, using water power (de Vries 1976). Animal, especially horse, power, was employed extensively in mines and quarries for drainage purposes, sometimes alone, but frequently to supplement insufficient water power.

The way in which these diverse sources of power were used grew in sophistication before the introduction of the steam engine in the eighteenth century, and continued to progress subsequently. The development of different types of water wheel, for instance, raised the efficiency of water power and increased the number of viable water-mill sites. Between 1700 and 1825, the technology of water power underwent radical transformation and was converted from a traditional craft into a scientific technology. The power sources that had been known for several centuries were perfectly adequate to move the increasingly complex industrial machines of the eighteenth and nineteenth centuries. The significant textile spinning technologies of the 1770s and 1780s were operated for many decades by water power, and the greater part of the power used by the first big factories was provided by water. These mills were not always driven by traditional craft-made wheels, but increasingly accurately designed machines based on new scientific ideas (Cardwell 1965).

Despite the alternative uses to which the perfected steam engine could be put from the late eighteenth century, this new source of power was more important in widening the choice available or in extending the potential location of industrial production, than in sweeping away other existing power systems. Moreover, water and heat-power technology advanced together to some extent, and influenced each other's development through cross-fertilization. The development of the water engine greatly extended the range of water power. The rotative engine, for example, driven by water pressure, ended the restriction of water power to certain falls and to given rates of flow. The water engine could also be used safely in mines where a steam engine might have been inconvenient or dangerous. The advance of high-pressure techniques gave rise to the column-of-water engines which were analogous to the steam engines and continued to develop alongside them. Between 1750 and 1825, the column-of-water engine represented an ingenious and scientifically advanced method of harnessing water power, which preceded the turbine. During the eighteenth century, and well into the nineteenth, water and steam-power technologies were on converging lines of development (Cardwell 1965).

The evolution of the water turbine in the nineteenth century further extended the possibilities of water power. This development, which initially drew its inspiration from water wheels and turbine-like devices, involved the intense interaction of science and technology, and continued to exploit nineteenth-century advances in these. The use of the water turbine in place of water wheels originated in the 1820s, and evolved from a number of earlier water wheel designs, in particular the reaction wheel. The first completely successful water turbine appeared in 1824, and was the work of the Frenchman, Fourneyron. This, and subsequent designs, such as Jonval's axial flow reaction turbine (1841), and Girard's axial flow partial admission impulse design (1850), emphasized experimental research rather than mathematical theory. After the mid 1850s, however, European water-turbine practice became more mathematically oriented, depending upon a basic understanding of hydraulics, and production concentrated on custom design for specific installations (Constant 1983).

The continued improvement of traditional power sources from the late eighteenth century to the early twentieth century and beyond, reflects not simply scientific and technical advance, but also the differing power requirements of the European economies. It has often been argued that the advent of steam power in the eighteenth century was essential for the development of mechanized industry. The first workable engine was Thomas Savery's 1698 combined pump and steam engine. It had no piston, no transmission of power to other machinery and was wasteful of energy. In 1705, Thomas Newcomen developed an engine that both generated and transmitted power. These two engines were used for complentary purposes during the eighteenth century. The Savery engine was used mainly to pump out waterlogged mines; while the Newcomen engine dominated the market for large prime movers, and remained in use even after many of its functions had been superseded by James Watt's steam engine (Landes 1969). Watt's 1769 patent was of critical significance: not only was the machine more economical in its use of fuel than previous inventions, but it formed the basis of subsequent advances in efficiency. Watt's knowledge of the physics of gasses permitted developments in the expansive use of steam, such as the compound engine first produced in 1804 by Arthur Woolf. The compound engine was widely adopted for ships from the 1850s; and its logical successor – the triple expansion engine – was introduced in 1874, and by the end of the nineteenth century had become standard for big plant both on land and at sea (Landes 1969).

While steam power was clearly significant in terms of the scientific progress that it represented, its immediate importance for industrial transformation should not be overestimated. In most scholarly writing, steam is perceived as synonymous with productivity and progress; and the increasing use of steam power in the first half of the nineteenth century has been viewed as responsible for basic alterations in manufacturing techniques. Toynbee identified steam as the catalyst for profound industrial and social transformation (Toynbee 1916); and David Landes, among more recent economic historians, writes that the concentration of mechanized industry in large units of production would have been impossible without the strength of power that steam provided (Landes 1969). Even those modern writers who have accurately perceived the continuity of traditional techniques have often presumed that these processes were marginal to that of steam (History Workshop Editorial 1977). It must be appreciated, however, that for some European economies, particularly those that were deficient in coal, the cost of steam may well have outweighed its potential advantages. For these economies, the continued progress of water-power technology, and the subsequent leap into hydroelectric power, must have represented a viable, and often a preferable alternative. Just as there existed a number of feasible routes to industrial development, so there was a choice between different types of motive power. Steam was not omnipotent (Musson 1976).

Recent work on energy utilization has begun to place steam power in particular, and motive power generally, into perspective. It has now been shown that steam was not nearly as significant as was commonly believed between 1780 and 1850. By 1800 certainly, and even by 1850 there had been relatively little adoption of power-driven machinery in the majority of industries, but even where this had occurred, power typically continued to be derived from humans, horses and water wheels. The limitations and power inadequacies of people and animals, however, became increasingly apparent as advancement in machinery gave rise to demands for uniform and continuous motion, and for greater force than animate power could provide (Greenberg 1982). It was shown in Chapter 3 that handicraft methods continued to characterize much manufacturing until the late nineteenth century, and just as machines themselves did not always prove to be the appropriate technology for production, so problems of power transmission meant that innovations in power technology were slow to be seen as preferable to earlier systems. In the case of steam, for instance, the early engines had such substantial shortcomings that for work requiring smoothness and regularity of motion, the gently turning water wheel was more suitable (Landes 1969).

The unreliability of early steam engines and the high cost of repair restricted their use either to supplementing other sources or as a last resort. Recent empirical research into the use of power in European industry confirms that until well into the nineteenth century, steam power was used only when alternative methods – usually water power – proved inadequate (Greenberg 1982). Furthermore, the employment of steam engines was confined to a very narrow area of activity, overwhelmingly mining, where the engines typically functioned to pump water, but could exceptionally be adapted to wind coal by means of a crank and drum. Steam engines were used to a lesser extent in textile manufacturing and the primary processes of iron production. In Britain, the Newcomen engine remained concentrated outside manufacturing throughout the eighteenth century, and in 1800, by which time about 2100 individual engines had been built (although only about 1500 engines with 15hp were in actual operation), 50 per cent of all engines were used in mining (Kanefsky and Robey 1980). Most of the 21 per cent of steam engines that were employed in the textile industry, functioned as an accessory form of pumping power for water wheels, (Greenberg 1982), although in some cases they might be used to drive machinery directly. At iron works, steam engines were used in conjunction with water wheels to ensure the water supply for the wheels which drove the bellows of the furnace (Kanefsky and Robey 1980).

Even by the middle of the nineteenth century, when the early technical problems had been reduced, steam power in British industry remained a comparative rarity. Although other forms of power predominated, larger quantities of steam were used in Britain than elsewhere in Europe. In 1850, British railway engines utilized 750,000 steam hp, while the whole of manufacturing industry used only 500,000 hp. Steam was still limited in diffusion and in application, and was concentrated, as in the late eighteenth century, in textiles, coal and the primary stages of iron making. Even in textiles, however, steam was only employed in a small number of steps in production (Greenberg 1982). In metal mining, the use of steam power increased substantially; and by 1865, about 650 steam engines, providing in total 40,000 hp, were in operation in 400 metal mines in Cornwall; 200 water wheels were still in use giving some 5000 hp. Most of the other mining areas – the lake district and Wales – remained heavily dependent on water power (Kanefsky 1979).

By 1870, steam supplied 50 per cent of the motive power market (from a level of 1 per cent in the 1780s), and provided 1.1 million hp to British industry. In the same year it has been estimated that 100,000 hp of water power was supplied to industry. In 1870, textiles alone accounted for about 50 per cent of all steam used in British industry; while several major industries, such as chemicals, clothing, building and shipbuilding, as well as small metal works and boots and shoes, made little use of steam (Greenberg 1982). Advanced steam engineering, in fact, had its most immediate and far-reaching impact on transportation, particularly steam shipping and railways. Data collected in 1907 indicate that despite the appearance of electrical power as a source for moving industrial machinery, horse power provided by steam continued to grow absolutely; although the growth rate of steam power was apparently faster before 1870 than subsequently. Steam was producing 9.6 million horse power, of which 2.3 million was consumed by coal mining, 2.4 million by steel and engineering, and about 2 million by the textile industry (Kanefsky 1979).

Despite the significance of the invention of the steam engine in the eighteenth century, therefore, its adoption as a source of motive power for industry was a protracted process in Britain. It was only in the 1840s that steam power began to take hold, and then mainly in areas where water power was unavailable. The rapid expansion of the output of coal, iron, tin and copper depended to a great extent on the availability of steam power; and water power could not have provided the necessary force to drain the northwestern collieries or the metal mines of Cornwall (Kanefsky and Robey 1980). Nevertheless, these were exceptional cases, and steam power did not surpass water power until after 1850. Even where the locational advantages of steam seemed clear, as in urban manufacturing, its adoption was slow. The move to steam-powered machinery came slowly; and even in the largest metropolitan centres, the relative mobility of steam engines did not result in early or extensive application. Most urban industry in fact, remained hand-powered until mid-century, and steam did not act as a positive inducement to industry to move to towns until the problems of cost, capital and technical inefficiencies could be overcome. It was not until the 1870s that the concentration of large-scale, steam-powered manufacturing in cities became significant. For much of the nineteenth century British industry relied on traditional sources of power, although in some cases the earlier techniques had undergone substantial updating (Greenberg 1982).

On the continent of Europe, the steam engine was adopted early in the eighteenth century, but its diffusion was as protracted as in Britain and even more confined both geographically and as to purpose. From 1720, steam-engine construction was carried on in a sustained fashion in two areas, Hainaut, and further east in Liège and Namur, where steam engines were used primarily to drain coal mines of water. Because the mines were low-lying, they could not be pumped by the traditional means of hydraulic engines (Hollister-Short 1976–77). English engineers were sometimes called in to assist at the mines and to train local craftsmen. Very rapidly, therefore, sufficient engineers capable of sustaining the new technology became available. This area of Belgium took very quickly to steam, because coal was plentiful and water power very inadequate and expensive. By 1790, 39 Newcomen engines were in operation in the Mons basin, and another 15 in Liège, where most of the Belgian engines were built, and 9 in Charleroi. Five more were installed in the Bassin du Centre to the east of Mons, and 14 in French Hainaut. Although diffusion of steam power was rapid in the coalfields, industries outside of mining continued to use water power for some time (Hollister-Short 1976–77; Van Neck 1979).

Steam power was exceptional elsewhere on the continent in the eighteenth century. In France, the rotative steam engine was first operated at Le Creusot iron works where, in 1784, one was used to drive the hammers of the forge, and four others to pump the mines and blow the furnaces. These engines were built in France by the Perier brothers at their works at Chaillot, just outside Paris

(Landes 1969). Although industries in Alsace and the Nord moved to steam power quite early on, most of the other industrial areas in France continued to depend on water power (Payen 1984). The availability of cheap water power, especially in Normandy, acted as a deterrent to change. Germany's first steam engine was installed, by a Liège mechanic, in 1751 at a lead mine near Dusseldorf. Thirty-five years later the same person set up a machine at Eschweiler; but in spite of Belgian and British encouragement, German industry made relatively little use of steam power until the mid-nineteenth century (Landes 1969).

On the continent of Europe, even more than in Britain, the steam engine was linked to mining, metallurgy and to shipping (Tann and Breckin 1978); while water power sufficed for textile production for most of the nineteenth century. Technologically, more emphasis was placed on fuel economy than in Britain, which meant that high-pressure engines were more commonly used. From the start the high pressure Woolf compound engine (1803–4) offered a fuel economy over the Watt engine of approximately 50 per cent, and found its largest market in France. Most other continental countries preferred the less expensive simple engines that worked at medium or high pressure (Landes 1969).

During the nineteenth century, the steam engine became quite widely diffused on the continent, although it never reached the levels achieved in Britain. As Table 10.1 indicates, British industry in 1840 used 13 times as much steam power as Belgium and France, 17 times as much as Germany, 35 times as much as Russia, and 127 times as much as Austria. Subsequently, the gap narrowed so that by the early twentieth century, French use of steam power stood at one-third of the British level, and German at two-thirds (Van Neck 1979). Water power remained important, particularly in Italy and Switzerland and in France, where the absence of cheap coal stimulated developments in the technology of water power. In other parts of continental Europe manufacturers also used water power wherever possible, and steam power was used only when water was insufficient (Landes 1969).

In Belgium, where, because of cheap coal and the absence of fast-flowing rivers, conditions were most conducive for steam-powered technology, the concentration of steam power was greater than anywhere else on the continent until about 1860. Table 10.2 shows that while they were never used much in textile production, the adoption of steam engines outside of mining and into metallurgy and food processing was rapid from the late 1820s. Steam engine construction was also relatively more advanced in Belgium, where there were more machine-making workshops than anywhere else, and of all the steam engines installed in Belgium by 1850, 96 per cent had been built there (Van Neck 1979). In France, where, along with Belgium, mechanics were the first continentals to conceive and build their own machines, dependence on foreign sources grew during the nineteenth century; particularly after 1850. In 1860, although most of the builders and creators of French engines were indigenous, the number of foreign names was growing; and in 1913, the input of non-French expertise was much more significant. While British and Belgian makers made a sizeable contribution to the foreign component in both years, German and American machinery was more important in 1913, when the technology had become much more complex. Germany had only begun to enter the independent

Table 10.1: *Steam power in Europe 1825–1914 (horse power)*

	Belgium	Britain	France	Germany	Austria	Russia
1825	8,916	200,000	—	—	—	—
1833	—	—	14,000	—	—	—
1837	25,326	—	—	—	—	—
1840	—	350,000	34,000	20,000	—	10,000
1850	50,439	—	67,000	70,000	9,060	35,000
1860	98,757	—	178,000	365,000	46,387	60,000
1870	175,723	1.5M	336,000	900,000	—	149,000
1880	273,309	2.0M	544,000	1.7M	173,065	—
1890	380,933	3.3M	863,000	2.0M	396,573	300,000
1900	647,378	5.5M	1.8M	2.7M	849,564	1.0M
1907/9	1.1M	9.6M	2.8M	6.7M	—	1.7M

Source: Anne Van Neck, *La révolution industrielle: Les débuts de la machine à vapeur dans l'industrie belge 1800–1850.* Brussels, 1979, 770.

Table 10.2: *Uses of steam engines in France and Belgium 1838/9 and 1845*

1838/9	% machines	% h.p.	1845	% machines	% h.p.
Coal mining					
Belgium	39.9	64.1		39.7	64.6
France	16.2	27.4		11.3	21.7
Metal and machine making					
Belgium	15.6	14.3		15.4	13.9
France	13.5	17.9		15.5	21.4
Textiles					
Belgium	20.9	10.3		17.9	10.2
France	37.2	30.5		33.0	30.3
Food					
Belgium	15.8	8.0		17.0	5.6
France	14.8	13.1		13.7	11.3
Other					
Belgium	7.8	3.3		10.0	3.6
France	18.3	11.1		26.5	15.2

Source: Anne Van Neck, *La révolution industrielle: Les débuts de la machine à vapeur dans l'industrie belge 1800–1850.* Brussels, 1979, 749.

stage of engine construction in the 1850s, but the activity grew very rapidly along with heavy industry (Payen 1984).

The diffusion of steam power in European industry from the late eighteenth century depended on a number of factors, and the uses to which steam engines were put in the different economies varied. The proportion of energy derived from coal naturally differed in each economy principally according to resources. Germany and Britain, both coal-rich economies, came to rely heavily on the steam engine as a prime mover, although water power remained important for a long time. Belgium, a flat land with no high-fall streams, and rich in minerals, was even more dependent on steam. By contrast, France, with a perennial coal deficit, but abundant fast moving water, made proportionately less use of steam engines. Italy and Switzerland came to depend almost entirely on water power, because they had virtually no coal, but many high mountains. In terms of the usage of steam power, there was no consistent pattern, yet a relationship did emerge generally between the steam engine and heavy industry; and this was particularly striking in Belgium and Germany, where power units were generally greater than elsewhere (Hollister-Short 1976–77; Landes 1969).

Mining, metallurgy and later the railway provided the major market for steam engines. The railway was perhaps the most important single user, and it also encouraged significant innovations in the working and handling of heavy forms, particularly the steam hammer. Later in the nineteenth century, new techniques generally gave rise to increased power requirements, which typically led to a growing reliance on the steam engine as a prime mover. On the whole textile production relied relatively less on steam power than the heavy industries; yet in France steam engines were much more numerous in textiles than in any other industrial sector (Van Neck 1979), and in Britain likewise, the cotton industry consumed as much steam power as any of the heavy industries. Clearly this is largely a reflection of the relative size of the sector, but there is no doubt that in most other parts of Europe, including Germany and Belgium, the textile industries operated mainly on the basis of water power. By the late nineteenth century, the rate of growth of steam power had slowed, and the use of the steam engine in industrial production had reached its peak. Sophisticated improvements to water power technology, as well as the invention of the dynamo and the production of an electric current, gave rise to new alternatives in terms of motive power (Layton 1979).

It was in Germany that the possibilities of electrical power generation were initially realized; and under the influence of German and American companies (Brittain 1974), the various strands of the electrical industry spread into other European economies. In 1847, Werner Siemens and his friend Johann Halske established a telegraphic construction business, and became involved in setting up telegraphic networks and underwater cable laying. In the mid 1860s, following a decade of research to remove the problems that constantly cropped up with relays and battery driven current on the long-distance telegraph lines, a series of projects concerned with transport and communications began to bear fruit. The most important of these was the laying of a durable trans-Atlantic cable in 1865. In 1866, after many years of research, Siemens produced a working model that realized the dynamo-electric principle. During the following 12 years essential improvements were made to its construction, and from 1878, it grew from strength to strength and eventually dominated the market (Von Weiher 1980).

Although Siemens (Halske resigned in 1867) concentrated on the building and laying of cables and telegraphic lines throughout the late 1860s and 1870s, his interests soon widened, so that by 1877 he had turned to telephone production; and by 1879 had built the first electric railway, which was displayed at the Berlin Exhibition of that year. In the late 1870s he illuminated the Kaiserpassage in the capital by means of self-regulating differential arc lamps, but he did not attach great importance to electric lighting, believing that gas lighting would remain more popular (Von Weiher 1980). During this period, the expansion of the company and the international character of its activities were such that branches had been established in most European countries. Indeed, by 1872, two-thirds of the firm's workforce was employed outside Germany, and the electrical industries of many European economies were founded upon Siemens external operations (Milward and Saul 1977).

Until the 1880s, Siemens's place in the world electrical industry outside the United States was unassailable, and his consistent commitment to research and invention ensured his future position. Emile Rathenau was his first rival, and his only serious competitor. In 1883 Rathenau established the Deutsche Edison-Gesellschaft (DEG), with several licensing agreements with Siemens (Von Weiher 1980). Four years later Rathenau established the enduring Allgemeine Elektrizitäts-Gesellschaft (AEG), for the purpose of exploiting Edison's lamp patents in Germany. Initially, AEG bought its plant and machinery from Siemens, but from 1894, AEG and Siemens made a new agreement, whereby AEG acquired full freedom to manufacture all plant except cables, which had to be bought from Siemens until 1898 (Byatt 1979; Milward and Saul 1977).

While Siemens had taken the lead in the practical industrial application of electrical energy, it was Rathenau who was quicker to respond to the new trend towards the production and distribution of electricity for industrial and domestic use, and to purchase the relevant patents. In other words Siemens emphasized the invention, engineering and industrial science aspects of electricity, while Rathenau personified the interaction of industrial capital, industrial enterprise and highly organized marketing. The priorities of the two firms were to some extent complementary, and certainly together they made a major contribution, not just to the electrification of industry, but also to experimental work and research (Von Weiher 1980). Not only did AEG and Siemens establish a virtual duopoly in Germany, but they also came to dominate the whole continental electrical manufacturing industry (Byatt 1979). By 1903, AEG employed 17,000 people; and although Siemens had only 4000 employees in 1902, its 1903 merger with Schuckert, whose strength was on the current distribution side of the industry, resulted in a massive expansion of the business, and by 1913, Siemens-Schuckert employed 57,000 people in Germany and a further 24,000 abroad (Milward and Saul 1977).

After 1890, the demand for electric power took off for both industrial and domestic purposes, and electrics became the fastest growing branch of industrial production in Germany. Electric motors were widely adopted, and greatly enhanced the efficiency of factory production. By 1907, 48 per cent of engineering firms in Berlin, for example, used electric power; and although the percentage rate for Germany as a whole was lower than this, electrical power was becoming a permanent replacement for steam power as a motive force for industrial production. Much of the demand for electricity, and much of the stimulus for the development of the electrical industry, came from the rapid growth of cities. In Germany this came particularly from the requirements of municipal lighting and municipal transport, such as electric tramways and electric underground railway systems (Milward and Saul 1977). Berlin was the most striking example, and, motivated by industrial needs and technical opportunities, it developed an exemplary transportation system. Berlin's electric utility supplied the power when much of the city's transport was electrified. Berlin, like other German cities, boasted beautifully lit streets. There is no doubt that AEG and Siemens were the major architects of the electrification of industry and transport in Berlin and other German cities; and AEG particularly not only provided the electric streetcar systems, and made the incandescent lamps, but was also responsible for building and largely financing the requisite power stations. Other major power plants were also held disproportionately by AEG and Siemens (Hughes 1983).

The growth of electrical power generation was associated with several different branches of manufacture. The heavy sector produced generators, accumulators, transformers and equipment for power stations, factories and tramway undertakings; and the light sector was responsible for providing cables, lamps, telephonic and telegraphic equipment and household appliances (Henderson 1975). The production of electricity also gave rise to new industries, such as electro-metallurgy, which originated with an electric furnace invented by Wilhelm Siemens in 1878, and electro-chemistry which began in the late 1880s. Electrical engineering and electrical machine making were natural spinoffs, which were eminently exportable (Milward and Saul 1977). Electrical machinery dominated the industry's exports; and Germany's exports of electrical products, which comprised about 50 per cent of the world's trade in these items, were valued at 220 million DM in 1913 (Henderson 1975). There was little competition between Germany and the USA in each others' home markets, indeed as early as 1903, Rathenau of AEG reached an agreement with General Electric, the biggest US company, to divide their world markets, whereby AEG was to have virtual freedom in the European markets, while General Electric would have control over the United States. Both German and American companies, however, established offices in many European economies, where the indigenous industry remained smaller-scale.

Indeed, the domination of the European electrical industry by German and American companies was so rapid that in most European economies and industry failed to develop autonomously. In Italy, for example, the electrical industry was overpowered by German companies and technology. According to several industrial surveys taken by the Italian government between 1898 and 1908, more than 70 per cent of the country's installations were operated by Siemens and Halske; and the remainder, controlled by Italian companies, were significantly smaller and less technically advanced (Giannetti 1985). Electrical companies in Switzerland, Belgium, France, Britain, Austria, Sweden and Hungary were equally influenced by German companies, and as in Italy, were generally of a smaller capacity.

Electrical power generation in France, while not large by German standards, was nevertheless of particular significance. For much of the nineteenth century, the development of motive power for mechanized industry had been hindered to some extent by the high price of coal. Although water power was perfectly adequate in some areas, and relatively cheap, the absence of choice constrained progress. The appearance of electricity, and particularly the development of hydro-electric power, gave rise to an intensive industrialization in some regions based on entirely new techniques (Morsel 1972). Conventional electrical power generation influenced by foreign companies also existed, and was used primarily for urban lighting and transport (Milward and Saul 1977). Hydro-electricity, however, was of far greater economic importance to France, as it exploited a free natural resource, and lessened the economy's dependence on coal. Hydro-electricity was generated from the 1860s in the valleys of both the Alps and the Pyrennees, where a range of sophisticated processes and industries developed, based on the French-invented electrolytic techniques which consumed huge quantities of power. The products of these electro-metallurgical and electro-chemical industries formed an important part of French exports, and accounted for a large proportion of world output of such items. These advanced electrical industries would not have been viable had they been dependent on the steam-generated electricity on which most other areas, and most other components of the electricity industry depended (Milward and Saul 1977; Morsel 1972).

In the Dauphiné, where natural resources were scarce, and where industrial progress had been negligible, industrialization suddenly became a reality in the 1860s, although it was not until the 1880s that expansion became rapid. Several industries were directly stimulated by the growth of local electricity. The manufacture of barrages, pylons, and dynamos were all required for the generation of hydro-electric power, and once established, this new cheap power was harnessed for the electro-chemical and electro-metallurgical industries, especially aluminium (Morsel 1972). In 1910, 33 per cent of hydro-electricity was used for lighting and power, 44 per cent for the metallurgical works and 13 per cent in the electro-chemical industry. On the basis of development in this area, France became a major exporter of electric arc equipment for steel manufacture, and of the 160 electric arc furnaces installed in the world by 1914, 83 had been constructed in the French Alps (Milward and Saul 1977). Capital for these ventures was largely raised inside France, from the big banks and the railway companies, and in the most significant period of growth there was a preponderance of capital from Switzerland, Lorraine and from around Lyons (Morsel 1972).

Although the French electrical industry developed new techniques between 1860 and 1880, the foreign influence became stronger from the 1880s. Initially, much equipment was made in France under licence to companies such as Edison, Westinghouse, Siemens, AEG or Brown Boveri, and then American firms began to manufacture in France. Until the 1890s the French economy was considered too sluggish for the huge German companies to contemplate investment there (Broder 1984). In 1881, Edison set up three enterprises in France: Edison Industrial, Edison Electric and Edison Continental. Two years later, Thomson Houston installed International Thomson Houston in Paris, and in 1892, the fusion of Edison-Thomson took place. The American groups brought considerable investment to the French electricity industry, particularly the Compagnie Française Thomson Houston, which, by the early twentieth century, directly or indirectly controlled 40 per cent of the French output of electricity, and had produced 60 per cent of the equipment installed in France (Broder 1984).

Before the late 1890s the only German connection was at Belfort, where, in 1888, a branch of the Société Alsacienne de Constructions Mécaniques, in association with Siemens, became a pioneer in the construction of motors and dynamos. From 1898, when the French economy appeared more dynamic, the German interest became more serious. While AEG restricted its investment to the hydro-electric enterprises established by Thomson Houston, Siemens formed an important relationship with Schneider at Le Creusot. Schneider was already a significant constructor of locomotives, and an important metallurgist, but had not yet become successful in electrical operations. Under the agreement with Siemens, the expertise of the two firms was combined, and while Schneider continued to deal with the mechanics of the locomotives and the pylons, Siemens obtained the traction, posts and catenaries. This became a formidable partnership, which was able to withstand all competition in the field (Broder 1984).

Despite the importance of the American and German multinationals in French electricity supply from the late nineteenth century, the French were anxious to reduce the level of dependence on foreign firms. The Compagnie Générale d'Electricité was formed in 1898, and became, with the help of private finance, the largest single enterprise in the sector. Although the French electrical industry achieved its desired growth it was never able to rid itself of its foreign interlopers. By 1914, if not well before, the world market in electro-technical equipment was sewn up by four non-competitive groups, General Electric, AEG, Westinghouse and Siemens, none of which was French. In fact France was little disadvantaged by this control of the market by multinationals; indeed they helped to enliven a sluggish market and to compensate for inadequate internal finance (Broder 1984). In any case nothing could be done to halt the progress of the German companies in particular.

The British electrical industry was largely an offshoot of the more important electrical manufacturers in Germany and the United States, with whom the domestic producers established a cooperative relationship. While the heavy plant side of production was, as elsewhere, dominated by the German and American firms, the light sector had a larger British input. The British electricity supply cable-making industry in particular was a fairly stable oligopoly, dominated by the two major domestic producers: British Insulated Wire, and Callenders. The only important foreign firm in this sector was the London branch of Siemens. Arc lighting dominated domestic manufacture in the early 1880s, when it expanded rapidly. The depression of 1882, however, caused a number of failures and aroused considerable foreign interest. An Edison company was founded in 1882 to build and run the Holborn installation using imported plant. Domestic producers were not completely overcome by foreign enterprise, however, and in 1883, the machine making firm of Mather and Platt acquired the English rights to the Edison dynamo and subsequently redesigned it and improved its capacity and performance considerably (Byatt 1979).

Public lighting failed to become established until much later than in Germany and the United States, and the main British market in the middle 1880s was for isolated installations in country houses. In the late 1880s, a big increase in demand for electrical plant stimulated the expansion of existing firms and the emergence of new ones. The boom of 1896–1903 was characterized by the growth of foreign investment, particularly from Westinghouse (£3 million), General Electric and British Thomson Houston, the expansion of Siemens, and the British companies of GEC, and Dick, Kerr and Co. Between 1903 and 1910, demand grew slowly except for factory electrification plant; and German firms wisely turned their attention from power-station building to industrial work. After 1910, the demand for electrical machinery rose again sharply, and the output of the major firms of Westinghouse, BTH, Siemens and GEC soared (Byatt 1979).

The British electricity industry often appeared out of step with developments in the more advanced electrical manufacturing nations; and throughout the period to 1914, sluggishness and disorder typified the industry's performance. In the first place, English engineers were slow to adopt the polyphase system and the induction motor that were developed in the United States and on the Continent during the 1890s. In 1896, AEG set up a sales agency in Britain, directed primarily towards selling factory electrification plant, but progress in Britain remained slow, and in 1901 the total power of induction motors in Britain was at most 7000hp (Byatt 1979). Secondly, British electrical engineering firms paid little attention to turbine development despite the fact that it was a British invention. Foreign firms stepped in first, and Westinghouse bought the US rights to the Parsons turbine in 1896. Shortly afterwards, Brown Boveri bought some of the continental rights, and General Electric and AEG began to develop their own turbines. The third major area of apparent British incompetence was in electrical supply and traction in the urban areas. While the growth of urban lighting and transportation had boosted all facets of the electrical industry in Germany and elsewhere, in Britain and especially in London, it served simply to highlight the weakness in the system. Electrical supply in London was fragmented and therefore irrational; it was disordered and small-scale at a time when rationalization and mass production were desirable, if not absolutely necessary. While Berlin's centralized light and power system ran from a handful of modern power stations by the late nineteenth century, London had 65 electrical utilities, 70 generating stations, 49 different systems of supply, 10 different frequencies, 32 voltage levels for transmission and 24 for distribution. Different functions and districts used a variety of types of electricity. A complex administrative structure was largely to blame, as 28 local authorities together with the city of London were responsible for integrating the capital's electricity supply (Hughes 1983).

The brilliant electrical engineer, Sebastian Ziani de Ferranti, was appointed by the London Electric Supply company to build a large central power station at Deptford and rectify some of the more obvious problems of London's electricity supply. The project was an expensive failure, suffering from teething troubles before being destroyed by fire in 1890. After 1907, the utilities of London improved their technical performance, but made little progress towards establishing a unified centralized supply system before 1914 (Hughes 1983). Where traction was concerned, Mather and Platt built the electrical equipment for the first London underground, but when tramway and railway electrification began in earnest it was the American firms that led the way. In the 1890s traction was mainly imported from the US, and General Electric sent many engineers to Britain, to work out comprehensive electrification schemes, and the company provided a high proportion of tram motors installed in the late 1890s. Westinghouse also became active in the British electric traction market (Byatt 1979).

Despite the obvious difficulties in coordinating Britain's electrical supply, several important sectors of British industry adopted electrical power. In 1907, although electricity accounted for only 10 per cent of total power used, factory motors used 50 per cent of all electricity produced. The development of electricity also brought power driving within the reach of small workshops that had previously used no power at all. In 1907, of total power used in mining and manufacturing, more than 25 per cent was used in mining, a further 25 per cent in textiles and 20 per cent in iron and steel production. In the first two groups, less than 5 per cent of power used was electricity, while the proportion in iron and steel was 8 per cent. Those industries that used a higher proportion of electricity were engineering and food and drink, but the total power consumed was relatively small. In chemicals, and the non-ferrous metals group, power was used for heating as well as for driving, and much of the electricity was used for electro-chemical purposes. By 1914, 25 per cent of all power used was electric, but the industry differences persisted. The overall percentage of power applied electrically rose as a consequence both of a slow change in industrial structure, and of increased electrification within each industry group. The effect of the changing structure by itself was not great, and the big difference in the degree of electrification between Britain and Germany is largely accounted for by the different industrial structures, although in chemicals and non-ferrous metals, there was relatively much more electric power in Germany (Byatt 1979).

As a power source, electricity had many advantages over earlier forms; and because steam power had reached the limit of its potential by the early twentieth century, the appearance of electricity was well timed to replace it. Electricity was clearly cost-saving in its efficiency. It introduced a flexibility that steam power lacked. Electrical generation was ideal when power was required in several scattered points in a works and in fairly small quantities. Electrical power transmission was relatively more advantageous where connection to a central power supply was difficult. Electricity also gained where several types of power were needed under the same roof. Electricity further gave rise to a new group of industries over time, each one becoming more sophisticated than the last. While steam was simply a source of motive power, for industrial machinery and for traction, both of which were gradually replaced by more modern methods, electricity was a great deal more, both actually and potentially. By the early twentieth century, it had become a vital component, if not a creator of modern industry.

Further Reading

Byatt, I. C. R. 1979: *The British electrical industry 1875–1914: The economic return to a new technology.* Oxford: Oxford University Press.

Greenberg, D. 1982: Reassessing the power patterns of the Industrial Revolution: An Anglo-American comparison. *American Historical Review*, 82, 1237–61.

Hughes, T. P. 1983: *Networks of power: Electrification in western society, 1880–1930.* Baltimore: Johns Hopkins University Press.

Landes, D. S. 1969: *The unbound Prometheus. Technological change and industrial development in western Europe from 1750 to the present.* Cambridge: Cambridge University Press.

Tann, J. and Breckin, M. J. 1978: The international diffusion of the Watt engine, 1775–1825. *Economic History Review*, 31, 541–64.

Von Tunzelmann, G. N. 1978: *Steam power and British industrialization to 1860.* Oxford: Oxford University Press.

Part IV
Conclusions

11 The Process of Industrialization

European industrialization was both a complex and a protracted process. What has been shown in the course of this book is not simply an amalgam of different industrial processes which coalesced, but more that industrial Europe in 1914 was the product of many centuries of interacting forces which together constituted a single process of industrialization. It is hoped that this book has finally obviated the notion of the Industrial Revolution, which in the past has misdirected the thoughts of historians. Ever since the term Industrial Revolution achieved scholarly status, it has been largely associated with technical innovations, particularly those employed in the manufacture of cotton and in the production of power by steam generation, in Britain, during the second half of the eighteenth century.

Criticisms of the usage of the term Industrial Revolution have generally been confined to temporal disagreements, while tacitly accepting the premise that technical developments constituted the focus of change (Tilly 1983). Attempts to re-date the Industrial Revolution either to the beginning of the eighteenth century, or to the sixteenth century, or even to some time in the Middle Ages, therefore, have focused upon the dates of specific inventions or innovations (Coleman 1962; Fores 1981; Nef 1954). Those who locate the origins of the Industrial Revolution in the early eighteenth century, for example, usually cite the critical innovations leading to the introduction of the use of coke in smelting iron in 1709, and the first use of the Newcomen steam pump in 1712. The association of the Industrial Revolution with technical changes stems from the role that machinery has been perceived to have played in the process of industrialization, and from the specific nature of technical changes.

Recent criticism has followed a more profound and a more fruitful tack, while not yet advocating complete abandonment of the notion of Industrial Revolution. One of the more radical critics, Rondo Cameron (1981, 1985), has argued that the term is a misnomer. He rightly concludes that in no sense were the technical events of the late eighteenth century revolutionary; on the contrary, they were rudimentary in character and limited in extent. Not only was industry itself little changed by these events, but, in most of Europe, structural changes in the economy leading to an increasing emphasis on industrial activity were gradual. As late as 1851, traditional sectors of employment still accounted for the greater proportion of the labour force throughout Europe. Few historians would disagree that the term revolution inaccurately describes the changes that took place in European industry in the late eighteenth and early nineteenth centuries, yet they continue to use the term Industrial Revolution arguing that it constitutes a justifiable shorthand. In fact it is seriously misleading.

One of the persistent themes of this book is the protracted nature of innovation, irrespective of the timing of invention. This is, of course, entirely consistent with the view of industrialization as a prolonged process; and while it is not surprising, it is frequently overlooked by historians, who assume that invention and innovation were more or less contemporaneous. The steam engine, for example, has long been perceived as the critical breakthrough of the Industrial Revolution. To many writers, the advent of steam power has meant more than the substitution of inanimate for human and animal power; it has, rather, symbolized mankind's fundamental break with the constraints imposed by nature (Landes 1969). Centralized industrial production, it is argued, no longer depended on the water power provided by fast-moving rivers and streams, so locational decisions could be based on more important economic factors, and industrial production could be released from the vagaries of the weather. In principle all this was true, but the assumption made by most historians that steam power rapidly replaced other forms of motive power as industrialists absorbed the new technology has little empirical foundation. As a previous chapter revealed, the benefits of steam power were not indisputable, and its diffusion was slow in pace and limited in extent from the late eighteenth century and throughout most of the nineteenth century. The use of the steam engine was, from the start, greatest in the non-manufacturing activities; and throughout Europe predominated in mining, transport and in the provision of public amenities. Although steam power did play a role in manufacturing industry, its use was confined to metal working and to small sections of the textile industry, and very often its purpose was to pump water. Industry generally was slow to make use of steam power, and only after 1870 did it account for 50 per cent of industrial motive power in Britain, where the proportion was greater than in any other European economy. For most of the nineteenth century, water power continued to be an important determinant of the location of industry, as well as of the scale of production and the level of output (Greenberg 1982).

The slow and specific diffusion of the steam engine was seemingly mirrored in all other cases of technical development in the process of European industrialization. Many of these have been examined in earlier chapters, but it is worth re-emphasizing the more important instances. In the textile industries, for example, the apparent flood of inventions which occurred during the second half of the eighteenth century, were in fact very limited in scope and quality as well as in diffusion. The mechanization of cotton spinning was certainly rapid, but apart from the memorable inventions of Arkwright and Hargreaves, the adoption of new techniques in textile production was slow. The weaving process, for example, was not widely mechanized until the second half of the nineteenth century, even though the power loom was invented towards the end of the eighteenth century. This slow diffusion partly reflected the inadequacies of the early power looms, and the continued superiority of the hand process.

This inability of the machine to adequately replicate the hand was to be found also in woolcombing, where a satisfactory solution to the problem of mechanizing the process eluded inventors from the first attempt in the late eighteenth century until the 1850s, when workable machines were produced simultaneously in France and in Britain (Honeyman and Goodman 1986b).

The example of the textile industry reflects not only that diffusion of new ideas and techniques was slow and ultimately incomplete, but also that this was hardly surprising. Not only were the inventions of the late eighteenth century therefore rudimentary both in construction and performance, but the process of innovation was complex and diffusion was protracted in time and space. Existing technologies were frequently not inferior, and, in some cases, remained greatly superior to the new technologies. Conventional techniques persisted alongside or in the face of new methods for far longer than is commonly supposed, and generally for very sound reasons. Sometimes new methods replaced the old, as in the case of cotton spinning in some areas; but more often than not, old methods either remained viable, or even preferable, or became adapted to new economic circumstances (Berg 1985). The persistence of water power, for example, was facilitated by (though not dependent upon) continuous improvements to the water turbine during the nineteenth century (Layton 1979).

The recent insights into the history of technology of the eighteenth and nineteenth centuries, which challenge the view of rapid and universal technical change embodied in conventional notions of the Industrial Revolution, find parallels in recent research into the history of mechanization and factory organization. The substitution of machinery for labour, the proletarianization of the workforce and the alienation of the labour process, all of which are essential features of the Industrial Revolution concept, were equally uneven and protracted processes (Berg 1985; Kaelble 1986). These processes, furthermore, originated well before the eighteenth century and continued much beyond it. Mechanization, for example, had proceeded substantially before 1700 in a wide range of industrial activities. Early modern European industrial history, as previous chapters have outlined, is replete with instances of the use of quite sophisticated machinery, such as the water-powered silk spinning mills, mechanical saw mills and hammering and forging mills (de Vries 1976). By the beginning of the eighteenth century, craft traditions in some important industries were already obsolete, while in many others, mechanization progressed only slowly before the early twentieth century (Tilly 1983). Mechanization led the way in the iron industry and cotton textile manufacture, but even in these trades it was incomplete. In other industries, such as small metal-goods manufacture, clocks and armaments, mechanization was strictly limited before 1914.

Correspondingly, the factory was neither the invention of the period of the Industrial Revolution, nor was it synonymous with mechanization. Centralized production was not unknown in Europe before 1700; indeed in some industrial activities it was the norm. During the seventeenth century, centralized production was common in shipbuilding, in sugar and tobacco refining and in many state-run enterprises, such as tapestry, porcelain and glass making (Kellenbenz 1977; Supple 1977). From the late eighteenth century, the diffusion of the factory followed a similar course to that of technology and mechanization, for similar reasons. Just as several alternative, and often equally viable, technologies coexisted, so mass production based on mechanized and centralized manufacture was only one of many possible choices in industrial organization. Not only were less centralized and capitalized forms of industrial production not inferior to those of mass production, but under certain circumstances, they could be economically preferable and entirely consistent with the demands of industrial capitalism (Aminzade 1984; Sabel and Zeitlin 1985; Samuel 1977). This applied to handicraft industries, for example, which became adjuncts to highly centralized production, such as textile weaving and gun manufacturing, as well as to entire industries, such as cars, clocks and machine tools.

There is no clear relationship between technology, mechanization, organization of production and industrial development. A variety of configurations existed over time, over space and among industries, throughout the period covered by this book. There are few, if any, features that distinguished the late eighteenth century from other periods. Recent evidence shows without question that changes at the point of production during the age of the so-called Industrial Revolution were slow, complex and without any clear trend. In terms of technology, mechanization and centralization of production, therefore, there is hardly any justification for the term Industrial Revolution.

The technological view of the Industrial Revolution has traditionally been supported by specific evidence on the quickening pace of industrial change, but recent research has cast serious doubt on the validity of this evidence. Quantitative studies of most European economies in the late eighteenth and nineteenth centuries have provided very little support for the notion of a discontinuity in the pace and pattern of industrial development (recent examples of such work includes Cameron 1985; Crafts 1987; Crouzet 1975; O'Brien 1986).

Clearly, European economic historians of the 1980s are moving towards a position where the performance of individual economies is no longer compared, nor measured against an optimum yardstick, but rather examined in terms of its own particular potential. Characteristic of this tendency is the work of historians of French industrialization (Cameron and Freedman 1983; O'Brien and Keyder 1978; Roehl 1976, 1983). In the past, historians unfavourably compared growth rates for France with those for England in the early nineteenth century, and with those for Germany in the late nineteenth century, and with those for the United States in the twentieth century. Attempts were made constantly to explain the 'retardation' of French industrial performance, particularly its poor showing when compared with Britain (Crafts 1977; Crouzet 1985b). Recently, however, the focus has changed, and the French economy generally and the industrial sector in particular have been perceived as healthy in the eighteenth century and displaying continuity from then until the early twentieth century. While not all facets of French industrialization are seen in a positive light, a more objective attitude has replaced the earlier value judgements. The French performance is no longer seen as a failed effort to imitate the British achievements, but as an entirely appropriate response to the French situation (Crafts 1984; Heywood 1981; Honeyman and Goodman 1986a; Roehl 1983). Just as the French path to a modern industrial economy is accepted as a valid route, and not as an inferior substitute, so the performance of other economies is presented as a viable formula given the circumstances of its development. Historians are no longer seeking uniformity, and have rejected efforts to generalize; and they are increasingly viewing diverse patterns as an integral part of a single process, that of a move towards a European-wide industrialism (Cameron 1985; Pollard 1973).

That a variety of routes to industrial development existed between 1600 and 1914 is generally accepted by historians but these differences have not been perceived as viable alternatives. They have, rather, been ranked according to subjective opinions as to what constituted successful industrialization, and this analysis, in turn, has tended to be focused on the Industrial Revolution. As has already been implied, the Industrial Revolution has created an artificial chronological and organizational division in European economic history which historians have tended to accept, regardless of ideological persuasion. This acceptance has compelled early modern historians to search in their period for the origins and preconditions of modern industrialization, and to treat the years before 1750 as the breeding ground for something altogether different. Typical of many characterizations of early modern economic history is that given by Jan de Vries in the introduction to his textbook. He describes the seventeenth and the first half of the eighteenth century in the following way: 'It begins as the long sixteenth century expansion . . . sputters fitfully to its end. Around the mid-eighteenth century, it is dissolved by a quickening of demographic and economic life that inaugurates a long secular expansion. Fundamentally shaped by the Industrial Revolution, this new expansion altered the most enduring structural characteristics of economic life to usher in the Brave New World that we inhabit today . . . here (in the seventeenth and early eighteenth centuries) one could perhaps find the cause of the exhaustion of the vast empires and early capitalism of the sixteenth century as well as the preconditions of modern industrialization' (de Vries 1976, 1).

The general concern with preconditions among early modern economic historians, which de Vries's work typifies, has served to reinforce the concept of the Industrial Revolution, which in turn emphasizes the differences among European economies in their progress towards industrialization. This concern is beginning to lose favour, however, and some recent research into aspects of early modern economic history have provided the potential for an alternative view which permits the notion of continuity and parallel development that we support. Rather than focus on those aspects of the early modern economy that were fundamentally altered by the new technologies and organizational methods of the late eighteenth century, recent research has concentrated on two related areas. The first deals with aspects of early capitalism which were deemed to have been swept away by the Industrial Revolution; and the second with industrial activities which retained many of their pre-industrial characteristics until well into the nineteenth century.

The social and economic profile of early industrial entrepreneurs is traditionally believed to have been diverse; recent work, however, indicates that these individuals were drawn from exactly the same class as before, and had therefore previously been merchants and landowners (Crouzet 1985a; Honeyman 1982). Continuity rather than discontinuity in this case suggests the possibility of continuity in other areas. Pursuing the theme of economic power from the seventeenth to the mid-nineteenth century, a recent appraisal of the foundations of British imperialism has shown convincingly that similar economic interests dominated imperialist impulses throughout the period (Cain and Hopkins 1986, 1987). The research rejects the conventional separation of commercial and industrial capitalism pivoted on the Industrial Revolution as unhelpful and misleading, and suggests a position in which capitalism provides the essential element of continuity as well as power. Capitalist enterprises, therefore, whether in agriculture, industry or services, were the locus of the drive towards imperialist expansion; and even if there were an Industrial Revolution, it emerged from an already highly successful capitalist system and took place without any fundamental transformation of property ownership.

Recent research has also questioned the previously dominant belief in a linear progression of organizational systems from urban putting-out to urban factory, which regards the survival of pre-industrial economic forms into the era of modern industrialization as exceptional, outmoded and ultimately exhaustible under the rule of industrial capitalism. Attention has recently focused on the transitional form labelled protoindustry and defined as rural industrial activity organized on the putting-out system (Clarkson 1985). It was anticipated that this research would locate a genetic, or at least a conceptual link between protoindustry and the Industrial Revolution; but it is now clear that no such relationship existed. It has become apparent that organizational systems could progress linearly, but that the pattern was complicated and there existed other paths to development. The putting-out system, for example, survived for far longer than is usually appreciated even within the most advanced industrial activities. The system not only contributed significantly to the growth of the industrial economy, but also, in organizational terms, proved to be a vital part of the industrial complex. Far from constituting a relic of the past, putting-out in nineteenth and twentieth-century Europe was a dynamic form which responded actively to the demands of the capitalist system (Aminzade 1984; Sabel and Zeitlin 1985).

Craft industries, likewise, were not swept away in the wake of modern industry, and indeed they continued to predominate in some parts of the economy. Shoemaking, leather, clothing and highly technically advanced trades such as machine tooling were examples of craft industries. In some major industries like steel making, the workshop and the artisan continued to operate within giant enterprises, and craft traditions, especially in the labour process, remained. In cotton spinning also, in much of Europe, many forms of labour contract were more reminiscent of preindustrial guild production than of factory organization and alienated labour processes (Lazonick 1979; Reddy 1979, 1984).

As the positive and dynamic elements of craft production and the putting-out system of manufacture have been recognized, and their role in nineteenth century industry more fully understood, new light has also been thrown on other problems in European economic history. The rise of labour movements in nineteenth century Europe, for example, has been linked to the skilled workers in craft workshops and households engaged in domestic manufacture, rather than to the more recently established factories (Sewell 1980). Although artisans were subjected to new pressures and challenges by the development of industrial capitalism, their responses were inevitably shaped by values, traditions and organizational experiences that predated the modern industrial era. This insight has led historians of labour to re-examine early modern European economic history as part of a long-term historical process, and not, as de Vries and others have seen it, as a short-lived experience (Sonenscher 1983, 1986, 1987).

Recent research, therefore, has emphasized the continuity of important economic structures throughout the period 1600 to 1914. It has also revealed the substantial growth of the early modern economy, and studies of industrial activities have noted the remarkable capacity of various organizational systems to respond to changing economic circumstances. Total output, productivity and the division of labour increased within a relatively unchanging technical context. The supply of labour was far more elastic and more diversified than is generally held. Women and children, for example, occupied a central position in the labour market. Their employment could, at times, create entirely new industrial activities in areas where industry was typically uncommon; in other cases, and usually to reduce overall labour costs, women were recruited to fill occupations previously held by men.

All of this indicates not just continuity in the process of European industrialization, but also highlights the variety of possible ways in which industrial expansion could occur. Previous searches for the origins of modern industrialization have included analyses of the European agrarian system to locate pent-up industrial expansionary forces. Surprisingly little attempt has been made, however, to pursue a long-term view of agrarian development, and this hinders a complete understanding of long-term industrial expansion. Some progress has been made, however, and studies of British agriculture in the eighteenth century, for example, have revealed the unevenness of growth and the poor correlation between the periodicity of agrarian productivity and industrial growth (O'Brien 1985). The steady growth of French agriculture throughout the eighteenth and nineteenth centuries, as well as the positive contribution of peasant agriculture to the process of industrialization have been highlighted by recent research, as has the ambiguous contribution of the agrarian system to industrial growth in the Dutch Republic (de Vries 1974; Heywood 1981). These and other examples show that the agrarian sector was by no means a consistent prerequisite to industrial development, and that the relationship between industry and agriculture was not at all clear-cut.

Developments in the commercial and financial sectors of early modern Europe have traditionally been assessed for their contribution to the Industrial Revolution, but more recently this has been replaced by examination of the long-term significance of the highly sophisticated techniques of commercial capitalism. This research has shown that business organizations and procedures prevalent in the early modern period persisted into the modern industrial economy where they coexisted with other forms and sustained the industrial as well as the service sector in general (Lee 1986; Smith W. D. 1982). Such revelations have resulted in a more general rejection of the thesis which views commercial capitalism as the mode of production within which the capital and demand pressures necessary for industrialization were assembled, and which in turn was dissolved by the weight of industrial capitalism in the modern period.

By searching for preconditions, therefore, historians have not only accepted the notion of the Industrial Revolution, but in doing so have seriously under-estimated the nature and power of the economic structures of the early modern period, and overestimated those which originated in the modern period. They have thus fallen victim both to the view of discontinuity, and to the view which ranks paths of development in terms of their revolutionary potential and their success. Recent work, which tends to adopt a longer and more flexibile perspec-tive, has effectively criticized the approach and the conclusions of earlier his-torians. What we have portrayed in this book is entirely consistent with the trend of recent research. In presenting European industrialization as both a long-term and a general process to which all European economies contributed in different ways, we not only support the notion of continuity but also remove the need for an attempt to place the economies of Europe into hierarchical cate-gories.

Analyses of European industrialization, whether or not they have focused explicitly on the Industrial Revolution, have typically excluded an international dimension, and have particularly neglected the impact of European industriali-zation on the rest of the world, as well as the contribution made by extra-European economies to progress within Europe. This is a significant omission; European industrialization needs to be seen in perspective. During the nine-teenth century, for example, the industrialization of western Europe coincided with the deindustrialization of much of the rest of the world, especially in Africa and Asia. It is likely that these two processes were not unrelated, but the precise nature of the connection remains intuitive. Some recent work, however, has begun to illuminate the relationship, and according to the findings of Paul Bairoch, it was only during the period 1830–60 that the economic division between the future developed world and the future underdeveloped world began to take shape. The proportional contribution of each region to the total output of manufacturing production was almost exactly reversed during these years. In 1830, therefore, 63 per cent of world manufacturing potential was located in what became the Third World, and only 37 per cent in Europe; and by 1860, the proportions had become 39 and 61 per cent respectively. By 1860, Britain alone was producing manufactured goods equal to 35 per cent of the 1750 world total; and the manufacturing product of Europe together with that of the United States, amounted to more than the 1750 world total. Between 1860 and 1914, the rate of growth of manufacturing output accelerated consistently, as the economies that had become primary producers no longer affected world pro-duction levels (Bairoch 1982).

The process by which a world-wide specialization in manufacturing industry or agriculture took place was accelerated if not in fact caused by the trade in European manufactures. In the words of Bairoch, 'there cannot be any question but that the cause of the deindustrialization in the Third World lay in the massive influx of European manufactured products, especially textiles, on the markets of these countries' (Bairoch 1982, 277). The productivity growth achieved by modern industrial methods, particularly in cotton, where spinning became 300 or even 400 times more productive, meant that European manufac-tured goods could be sold more cheaply than local artisanal and craft products; and because of the low wage costs, distant markets remained profitable even allowing for transport costs and the profits of intermediaries. The indigenous craft products were thus unable to compete with manufactured imports, and artisanal producers were forced into specialization in primary production. During the second half of the nineteenth century, therefore, industrial production using traditional methods, in what were soon to become Third-World economies, declined absolutely and relatively, until by 1900, per capita output was only 30 per cent of the 1750 level. Although some re-industrialization began from the 1880s, this took place from a very low level (Bairoch 1982).

There is no doubt that the industrial development of Western Europe and the overseas trade associated with it, had a devastating impact on the economies of Africa and Asia, which had been, until the mid-eighteenth century, respectable industrial producers (Bagchi 1982; Stavrianos 1981). India had probably achieved the highest level of industrialization, and subsequently suffered commensurately. Once exposed to the products of European manufacturers, these regions became transformed largely into primary producers and exporters of food and raw materials for industry. The negative impact of the relationship with Europe on those destined to become and to remain primary producers was enormous but cannot be accurately quantified. The benefits of the same trading connection enjoyed by the European industrial powers were probably not as great. On the whole, it seems that access to the markets of the Third World constituted no more than a subordinate stimulus to the industries of the European economies. Britain was an exception, however, and its export markets, particularly in Asia, but also in parts of Africa and South America, were much more important than those of the rest of Europe.

By the mid-nineteenth century, therefore, trade between industrialized Europe and the non-industrialized world was based upon, and reinforced inequality. While it is unlikely that spinoffs from trade with the periphery promoted the economic growth of western Europe in decisive ways (O'Brien 1982), it nevertheless served to widen continuously the gap in per capita income levels between those economies specializing in manufacturing industry, and those that became specialist primary producers. Table 11.1 indicates the extent of the gap and its growth before 1914. In 1800, the average per capita GNP level in Europe was 20 per cent higher than in the Third World; by 1860 it was 100 per cent higher, and by 1910, 210 per cent higher. In 1913, the gap between the four richest countries in the developed region and that of Africa and Asia, was around 1200 per cent (Bairoch and Lévy-Leboyer 1981). The direct benefits to Europe of its international trade in the nineteenth century may not be quantifiable, but there is no doubt that the speed of its development was enhanced by the absence of significant development in other parts of the world.

The fact that Europe became distinguished economically from the rest of the world has, or at least should have, an important bearing on the way European industrialization is perceived and understood. On the one hand, therefore, the experience of industrial development varied among individual European economies, while on the other hand, the divergence between industrializing Europe and the rest of the world renders these differences insignificant, and in global terms, industrialization in Europe must clearly be seen as a single process (Ashworth 1974; Pollard 1973).

The major strands of the approach to European industrialization that have been adopted in this book have been emphasized in this chapter. The

Table 11.1: *Distribution of World Income in 1860 and 1913*

	1860 Aggregate income ($ millions)*	%	1913 Aggregate income ($ millions)*	%
North America	14,400	14.8	100,300	32.9
Oceania	500	0.5	4,100	1.4
North West Europe	28,500	29.4	84,000	27.5
Soviet Union	7,000	7.0	22,500	7.4
South East Europe	9,500	9.7	26,000	8.5
Latin America	3,700	4.0	12,300	4.1
Japan	1,300	1.6	4,600	1.5
Near East	—	—	—	—
Far East	1,300	1.4	5,700	1.8
Central Africa	—	—	—	—
South East Asia	11,500	11.8	21,000	6.9
China	19,500	19.8	24,300	8.0
Total	95,900	100.0	304,800	100.0

Source: A. J. H. Latham, *The international economy and the undeveloped world 1865–1914* (London, 1978), 123, 124.
* of 1952–54

homogeneity of the process has been a core theme, stressing the integration of the European industrial economy into a single system. This homogeneity is particularly marked when perceived in its international context, which in turn is an important feature of this book's approach. Industrialization occurred in a number of contexts – region, nation, continent and world – simultaneously, though, at different times, certain contexts mattered more than others. In the seventeenth and eighteenth centuries, for example, industrialization was both regionally and globally based; whereas, towards the end of the nineteenth century, the national base increased in relative importance. The degree of international competition in industrial production, the prohibitive influence of protectionism, and the growing power of the central state in the latter part of the nineteenth century, are all reflections of this trend. In understanding the process of industrialization, the role of context is crucial. Finally, this book has attempted to highlight the multiplicity of industrial experiences within Europe between 1600 and 1914. Regardless of period, there was always available a wide range of techniques, organizations of production and markets; and each industrial economy made use of different ones, in different ways and for different purposes. This heterogeneity is an important feature of European industrialization, and should militate against the perception of industrial development as a race, with the implied winners and losers. That both homogeneity and heterogeneity are presented as features of industrialization is apparently contradictory. They are consistent, however, as homogeneity refers to the singularity of the general process and the overall objectives particularly when viewed globally; while the term heterogeneity applies to the means by which individual economies contributed to the process and fulfilled their objectives.

Further Reading

Bairoch, P. and Lévy-Leboyer, M. (eds.) 1981: *Disparities in economic development since the Industrial Revolution.* London: Macmillan.

Bairoch, P. 1982: International industrialization levels from 1750–1980. *Journal of European Economic History,* 11, 269–333.

Cameron, R. 1985: A new view of European industrialization. *Economic History Review,* 38, 1, 1–23.

O'Brien, P. K. 1986: Do we have a typology for the study of European industrialization in the XIXth century? *Journal of European Economic History,* 15, 291–333.

Pollard, S. 1973: Industrialization and the European economy. *Economic History Review,* 26, 636–48.

12 The Problems of Industrial Europe and the International Economy Before 1914

This book has not been about specific European nations and their different experiences of industrialization. It has been intended to make a contribution to the understanding of the process of industrialization, and to the mechanisms by which this process was restricted to a compact geographical area. It has therefore been about the making of industrial Europe, and about the way in which it became both internally convergent and at the same time distinct from the rest of the world. The complexity of the process does not belie the essential similarity of overall experience, which contrasts with the traditional technique of highlighting differences normally achieved by a country by country approach. While differences clearly existed, these are generally confined to the micro level, and do not overwhelm the essential similarity of experience that characterizes the shift to a modern industrial Europe.

By the mid-nineteenth century, the European economic system was characterized by a boundless industrial dynamic. Industry not only began to supersede agriculture in economic importance within the new system, but at the same time became organizationally and locationally distinct. The opportunities for by-employment, and the occupational interaction of the industrial and the agricultural sectors, contracted as specialization in both agriculture and industry became a central feature of the new economic structure (Thirsk 1980). The mercantile sector also adopted an entirely new relationship with industry. The two sectors, which, in the early modern period, were similar in terms of organization and capital structure (Hicks 1969), became entirely distinct, but at the same time became involved in a new form of interaction. Trade was a crucial determinant of the success of European industrial development; rapid increases in productivity and output were maintained with the help of large and growing foreign markets. The tertiary sector of the economy, which included trade, transport and other service activities, grew alongside the manufacturing sector, and contributed to the relative decline of the agricultural sector.

During the early stages of industrial development, the basic techniques of production were associated with the output of consumer goods, which had formed the basis of industrial output for several hundred years. These included a wide range of textiles; leather and small metal goods; household commodities, such as glassware and pottery; and food processing. Technical and other developments subsequently influenced some changes in industrial structure. Once the potential for growth within consumer goods production was reached, more sophisticated technology encouraged, or permitted, a shift into capital-goods production, which ensured for the time being more growth in returns to scale (Hoffman 1958; Roehl 1976). These gains were subsequently further enhanced by the addition of scientifically based manufactures within the industrial structure, which depended on technology that embodied scientific principles.

Associated with these developments in the process of European industrialization emerged the notion of long-term and sustained economic growth. While the industrial system was clearly designed for expansion, self-sustained growth was by no means automatic. It was, however, necessary that growth be maintained so that the changes that were involved with industrialization, such as population growth, urbanization, infrastructural developments and transportation networks, could be supported. Until 1914, European industry was generally successful in sustaining its growth, by exploiting new technology and achieving the reproduction of fixed capital by a high rate of return on capital and high profit levels. Expansion of firms within the consumer goods sector in the early stages of modern industrial development was frequently accelerated by the retention of a large proportion of these profits (Crouzet 1972a; Mathias and Postan 1978). Expansion in the later stages was dependent upon sustained investment in plant and machinery and then in research and development.

Progress was by no means assured, however, and in the decades before 1914, Europe began to face problems caused specifically by industrialization and associated political developments. The most serious of these problems was the depression that characterized European economic experience in the last quarter of the nineteenth century. Indeed, as industrialization progressed, irregularities in production and investment became increasingly influenced by trade, and generally became more regular and predictable. Cyclical fluctuations became international in scope as the convergence and interaction of the European economies grew and their overseas activities extended. As European economies became structurally more similar, therefore, and as intra-European trade took on a more intricate form, each economy became subject to the same cyclical crises. While the process of European industrialization entailed a complex interdependency, this in turn gave rise to increasingly severe crises.

The most serious of these, the period of depression which began in the early 1870s and continued to the mid-1890s, was characterized by a secular decline in prices, initially of primary products, and by pressure on trade and investment opportunities. The expansion of the output of wheat in the prairie lands of the United States caused cheaper grain to be available world-wide; European beet subsidies resulted in a fall in the price of sugar, and petroleum prices dropped as new oil wells were brought into operation. Subsequently the fall in prices became generalized. The impact of this downturn in prices was particularly severe on the primary producing nations, which suffered continuously unfavourable terms of trade (Latham 1978). Industry in Europe was initially able to benefit from cheaper raw materials; and European agriculture withstood the shock to some extent by shifting production into areas where demand was

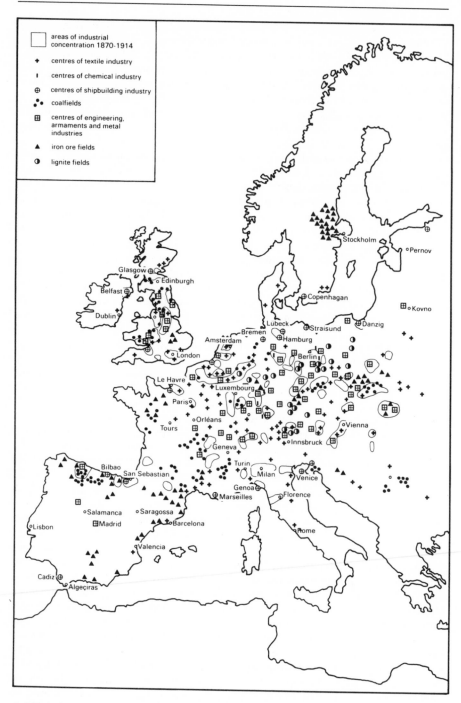

6 The industrialization of Europe 1870–1914

rising, such as meat and dairy products (Kindleberger 1951).

There is no agreement about the cause of the so-called Great Depression, but it was probably the result of a combination of factors, including the growth of production of several major commodities at a time when the growth of world demand was decelerating. The situation was generally compounded by the extension of rail networks, and by technical developments in shipping which meant that all kinds of goods could be carried throughout the world more cheaply. Low-value, high-bulk commodities could, for the first time, be transported over long distances (Harley 1986). The price fall may also have been exacerbated by the failure of the world's money supply to keep pace with the growth of activity (Foreman-Peck 1983).

Economies responded differently to the general price fall, but none avoided the shock of the initial impact (Kindleberger 1951). In Britain, for instance, the agricultural sector felt the effect of the depression particularly strongly, and the position of the farming community was worsened by the government's policy of free trade. The cheap grain from the United States, which entered Britain freely, virtually liquidated its arable sector, because it was unable to compete with the imported product. The successful farms moved into meat and into mixed farming, and these were able to take advantage of the cheaper feedstuffs and the growing demand for their produce. Many farms, however, were forced to close, and thousands of agricultural workers sought employment in the industrial towns, as the agricultural labour force shrank from 15 per cent to 7 per cent of the total employed population (Deane and Cole 1967). The industrial sector in Britain was also depressed in the last quarter of the nineteenth century, as reflected in a deceleration in the rate of growth of per capita industrial output, though the world depression was only part of the reason for this. Structural inflexibility, inefficiency and overcommitment to the staple industries were also to blame (Aldcroft 1968; McCloskey 1981). In general Britain suffered badly from the depression, and its relative position worsened because of the ability of some European economies to respond positively to the changed conditions.

The typical reaction to the threatened influx of cheap primary products by European nations was to adopt a protectionist commercial policy, and the majority of them enjoyed the decisive guidance of the state, in some cases for the first time. Germany, for example, refused to allow imports of grain below a certain price and thereby avoided the major effects of the depression. Neither agriculture nor industry was held back, and during the last quarter of the nineteenth century, the German economy moved ahead relatively and absolutely, in terms of industrial production and trade. The economies of Belgium, France, Italy and the Netherlands were also protected by the commercial policies of their governments. In Denmark, however, government policy was decisive but not protectionist. Its objective was to turn the reduced cost of wheat to the advantage of the economy, by diversifying from grain production into animal production and dairy produce. The agricultural sector thus gained from the cheaper feedstuffs for livestock, which in turn produced a valuable export commodity. Typically, the European economies survived the period of depression and emerged relatively unscathed at the end of the nineteenth century (Kindleberger 1951). The primary producing nations, however, suffered greatly as the value of their exports was reduced which impaired their ability to purchase manufactured goods from the industrial nations. In this respect, the crisis of the late nineteenth century served to heighten the inequity between the European industrial nations and the primary producing economies (Stavrianos 1981).

The period of depression coincided with, and is sometimes confused with, structural problems in the European economy, which became manifested in intra-European rivalry, commercial and economic competition, nationalism and finally hostility. Until 1870 or thereabouts, industrial expansion in Europe proceeded unhindered, and export markets within and outside Europe expanded to absorb the production of the industrial economies. The growth of trade in manufactures was particularly rapid between 1850 and 1870, and was accompanied by a liberalization of commercial policy, most notably in the 1860s (Kindleberger 1975). Competition certainly existed during this period, but because European markets were not yet saturated, and because there were still many untapped markets outside of Europe, the competition was not aggressive. During this period, sometimes referred to as the phase of competitive capitalism (Stavrianos 1981), international interaction generally flourished and served to enhance the relative strength of the industrial nations *vis-à-vis* the primary producers. From 1870, however, while international relationships became institutionalized, giving greater structure to the international economy, forces of nationalism, particularly within Europe, altered the underlying nature of international relationships.

Intra-European rivalry from the 1870s reflected the changing environment within which the industrial powers operated. Some writers have seen this as a shift from the vigorous and competitive phase of industrial development, to the monopolistic phase, which was characterized by economic crises, resulting from overproduction (Stavrianos 1981). The first phase depended largely on the mechanization of the traditional industries, while industrial developments from 1870 depended more on scientific progress of a theoretical kind. In principle, the opportunities brought about by the application of science to products and to the organization of industry were enormous, and much more significant in the long term than the earlier developments. It was, however, precisely the wide-ranging impact of the new technologies and the new processes as well as the new industries associated with these, that changed the external requirements of the European industrial nations. Growth in production and productive capacity, for example, exceeded that of markets from the 1870s, and this overproduction put pressure on prices and profits. The continued spread of industrialization intensified the competition for markets, and changes in the structure of industrial production heightened competition for the raw materials produced outside of the industrial regions. While competition within European economies was reduced by the introduction of cartels and trusts, therefore, competition among industrial nations grew for markets, for capital outlets and for raw material supplies. Governments intervened to safeguard the position of their economies, and economic nationalism and rivalry thus replaced the earlier commercial liberalism and open competitiveness (Buchheim 1981).

As pressure on industrial growth increased, governments sought ways to protect their industries from negative external forces. Initially this was achieved through commercial policy. While the period of competitive capitalism was associated with free trade, the last quarter of the nineteenth century saw the general adoption of protectionist measures. Germany and France, where the governments reacted to the pressure of powerful economic groups, were the most aggressive protectionists. Germany had been a keen advocate of free trade during the 1860s, but during the 1870s, both industrialists and farmers, blaming foreign imports for their problems, actively sought protection which the government granted (Kindleberger 1951, 1975). In France, the transition to protectionism was not rapid; throughout the 1870s and 1880s, pressure from industrialists grew until the government eventually responded by introducing the Méline Tariff in 1892 (Smith 1980). Austria, Italy, Russia and most other European economies raised tariffs during the 1880s (Kindleberger 1975).

Great Britain was the most significant exception to this trend, although both Denmark and Holland remained essentially free trading nations. Britain persisted in its free-trade policy until the inter-war period, partly because of its longer and deeper commitment to it, and partly because Britain's external circumstances meant that it had little direct competition with other industrial nations. Britain, for example, began to export capital earlier and in much larger quantities than other European economies, which enabled Britain to control both export markets and sources of supply (Feis 1930). This was particularly notable in the case of India, where the location of markets and sources of raw materials corresponded (Charlesworth 1982). Britain, therefore avoided much of the competition which, in most other European industrial nations gave rise to aggressive trading policies.

While overseas activity was a crucial part of the process of European industrialization, therefore, it was by no means trouble-free in the years before 1914. The solution to the problems faced by industrial Europe in the late nineteenth century could not be solved completely in the kinds of external activity that had typified the period before 1870. The evidence suggests that the problems of industrial Europe in the late nineteenth century encouraged non-neutral expansionary activities, and many European economies turned to imperialism as a means of economic salvation. Imperialism was an inescapable aspect of Europe's role in the international economy. The territorial expansion of Europe in the world played an integral part of the development of the international economy. Although the outward push was particularly marked after 1870, and was clearly associated with the problems of industrialism at this time, the European control of overseas territories had exceeded the area of Europe itself as early as 1850. Between 1860 and 1900, the Europeans increased their control over non-European land eight or nine-fold (Stavrianos 1981; Woodruff 1966).

The imperialism of the late nineteenth century differed from previous forms. Most of the world was involved in the process of imperialism, either as imperialist powers (such as much of Europe and the United States), as outright colonies (Africa and parts of Asia), or as semi-colonies (Ottoman and Chinese Empires). Before 1870, competitive capitalism was associated with free-trade imperialism, a non-aggressive form which nevertheless resulted in the world-wide division of labour between agriculture and industry. From 1870, however, large-scale capital intensive industrial production, or monopoly capitalism, gave rise to a more aggressive, global colonialism. This ensured that the sharp distinction between agricultural and industrial economies was maintained or even institutionalized. The general pressure of competition, especially during the years of depression, with falling prices and rising tariffs, led policy makers to think of colonies not only as short-term outlets for surplus capital, but also as future markets for manufactured goods and sources of raw materials (Cain and Hopkins 1986, 1987; Stavrianos 1981).

European imperialism of the late nineteenth century as manifested in the Scramble for Africa was also supported by rising incomes and growing consumption needs and wants in the industrial European economies (Freund 1984; Hopkins 1973; Munro 1976). The demand for such commodities as soap, margarine, cocoa and rubber was thus stimulated. The satisfaction of such demand required large-scale imports from tropical regions, which initially entailed the construction of such local infrastructures as harbours, railways, telegraphs and postal systems. Such infrastructures needed security, and the outflow of capital from Europe, in the form of loans or direct investment in these projects, frequently resulted in control over recipient countries.

Although Britain was the most important imperialist when judged quantitatively, most of Europe was involved in imperialist activities. By 1914, industrial European powers not only owned outright vast colonial territories, but they also dominated the economically and militarily weak areas that were not formally annexed. China, Persia and the Ottoman Empire, for instance, were all nominally independent, but in fact were controlled in various direct and indirect ways. Latin America was also an appendage of the great powers (Stavrianos 1981). In many ways it was the trading relationships that developed between Europe and the rest of the world that most clearly reflect the character of late nineteenth-century imperialism. Throughout the nineteenth century Europe became increasingly dependent on areas outside of Europe for a range of primary products and markets. The division of the world into specialist primary exporters and industrial producers was largely achieved by Europe's industrial development before extensive formalized control (Bairoch 1982); but European territorial expansion not only ensured the continuation of this, but ensured Europe's need to maintain it. By the late nineteenth century, food and raw materials were imported relatively cheaply into Europe, and were financed with the products of Europe's rapidly expanding industries. By 1900, Europe was beginning to export the process as well as the produce of industrialization.

European expansion overseas was an indispensable part of European industrialization, and also ensured the absence of industrial development elsewhere (Bairoch 1982). Many extra-European primary producing nations became perilously dependent on the continuation of Europe's system of world trade and specialization, often to the extent of becoming tied to monoculture and to a single European economy (Munro 1976). This naturally constrained development and precluded diversification. Dependence, however, operated in both directions, and late in the nineteenth century, the European powers began to rely increasingly on primary producing countries for industrial raw materials that were simply not available in Europe. Unlike the raw materials for textile production, many of which could, if necessary, be produced in Europe, the essential inputs for the new industries, such as copper for electricity, potash for chemicals, bauxite for aluminium and rubber for tyres and cables, could only be found in sizeable quantities in parts of Africa, Asia and Latin America (Albert 1983; Munro 1976, 1981). The dependency thus produced was emphasized by Europe's growing need to locate markets for the greater levels of output and for surplus capital. As Europe's need for cheap, imported food and raw materials, and for secure export markets became more urgent and complex, so Europe's external activities shifted from a gentle and implicit 'informal' imperialism, to a more aggressive and explicit 'formal' imperialism (Cain and Hopkins 1987; Gallagher and Robinson 1953).

Before 1870, Britain was the major imperial power among European economies in an informal way. Relationships and dependencies developed without the sanction of formal agreement. Within Latin America, for example, the economies of Brazil, Peru and Argentina were bound up with the activities of the British economy (Albert 1983). No force or compulsion was involved, but exports of British capital there, which were directed to the building of railways and other infrastructural developments, encouraged a cementing of the relationship through trade and investment, which appeared to be fully supported by all parties. At this stage Britain's relationship with India, with the Ottoman Empire and China followed a similar course; but parts of Africa were increasingly brought under formal control, either for strategic reasons, or because of uncertain local economic conditions (Bagchi 1982). By the 1870s Britain had assumed control of vast areas of the globe; and the activities of the other European economies was limited to French control over Algeria and Senegal, and the annexation of Angola and Mozambique by Portugal. During the 1870s, however, most of industrial Europe perceived the advantages of imperial and colonial possession, and rivalry among the European powers for overseas territories reached great intensity by the end of the decade, at which point only the African continent remained substantially unannexed (Stavrianos 1981).

The way in which the Europeans took control of Africa illustrates most clearly the transition from free-trade imperialism to global colonialism. The partition process in Africa was triggered by King Leopold of Belgium who hired the explorer Henry Stanley to acquire territory in the rich Congo Basin. In 1879, he gained title to 800,000 square miles (76 times the entire area of Belgium). The French and the Germans soon followed suit, and the race for colonies was underway. To establish ground-rules for future acquisitions of African lands, the European powers met at a conference in Berlin in 1884–85. A distribution of Africa among the European powers was agreed, and by 1914, the entire continent had been partitioned except for Ethiopia and Liberia. The ultimate aim of partition was to integrate Africa fully into the global economy and to enhance the economies of industrial Europe. Many historians have expressed doubt about the economic motivation of the European takeover of Africa, arguing that the poverty of the continent offered little demand for European products, and not much scope for European capital exports. Although there appears to be some truth in this argument, there is much evidence to show that some African countries experienced a distorted development serving the interests of the Europeans. Even the very poorest regions provided cheap and secure sources of raw materials, such as rubber, copper, minerals, cocoa, coffee and palmoil, many of which were essential for European industry. European capital in Africa was invested in infrastructure to permit commerce, or in local mines and plantations where wage rates were very low, and where profits were often substantial (Stavrianos 1981).

Although the extent of Europe's gain and the Empire regions' loss from late nineteenth-century imperialism cannot be precisely quantified, Europe clearly achieved its desire for global hegemony. Furthermore, global considerations of empire building, reduced, in the short term at least, the level of internal European rivalry. No European economy, however, derived such benefits from its possessions as did Britain from its relationship with India. From the early nineteenth century, Britain and India developed an intricate trading link which typified free-trade imperialism (Cain and Hopkins 1986, 1987; Charlesworth 1982; Harnetty 1972). Britain's manufactured goods, especially textiles, were exchanged for India's raw materials. This relationship was later reinforced by investment in infrastructure, to guarantee a steady supply of raw materials and access to markets, before formal ties between Britain and India were established. During the course of this process, the Indian economy became subordinated to the needs of Britain, and experienced deindustrialization (Bagchi 1976). The two economies became inextricably linked, which operated to the advantage of Britain in the short term, and to the detriment of India in the long term. By 1914, however, Britain had become dangerously dependent on its relationship with India. Britain's outmoded industrial structure, and its massive trade deficit with continental Europe and the United States, was only sustained by its ability to trade outside of Europe, most particularly its surplus with India (Saul 1960).

While Britain's domination of India found no parallel elsewhere in Europe, the late nineteenth-century competition for colonies was a European phenomenon. The process was at least partly determined by the search for markets and raw materials, and by the general desire to extend the field of capitalism (Brown 1974). Imperialism also had political determinants, and it has been seen as a manifestation of popular and emotional concern for national prestige and power. Whatever the level of economic gain to be made by imperialism, empire was considered a necessary part of the process of European industrialization, and a reasonable response to the problems faced by industrial Europe in the late nineteenth century. During the period between 1870 and 1914, therefore, the European powers were forced to confront major difficulties within their own economies, which gave rise to intense nationalism and intra-European rivalry (Pollard 1981). Paradoxically, this was a period which, in global terms, the European economy as a whole became more cohesive in its outward thrust through which the primary producing nations became more fully absorbed in a world economy where power was located in the industrial nations of Europe and the United States.

Further Reading

Albert, B. 1983: *South America and the world economy from Independence to 1930*. London: Macmillan.

Brown, M. B. 1974: *The economics of imperialism*. Harmondsworth: Penguin.

Cain, P. J. 1980: *Economic foundations of British overseas expansion, 1815–1914*. London: Macmillan.

Charlesworth, N. 1982: *British rule and the Indian economy 1800–1914*. London: Macmillan.

Kindleberger, C. P. 1978: *Economic response: Comparative studies in trade, finance and growth*. Cambridge, Mass.: Harvard University Press.

Latham, A. J. H. 1978: *The international economy and the undeveloped world, 1865–1914*. London: Croom Helm.

Munro, J. F. 1976: *Africa and the international economy 1800–1960*. London: Dent.

Rodney, W. 1972: *How Europe underdeveloped Africa*. London: Bogle-L'Ouverture Publications.

Stavrianos, L. S. 1981: *Global rift: The third world comes of age*. New York: Morrow.

Woodruff, W. 1966: *The impact of western man*. London: Macmillan.

Bibliography

Abel, W. 1980: *Agricultural fluctuations in Europe*. London: Methuen.

Albert, B. 1983: *South America and the world economy from Independence to 1930*. London: Macmillan.

Albert, B. and Graves, A. (eds.) 1984: *Crisis and change in the international sugar economy, 1860–1914*. Norwich: ISC Press.

Aldcroft, D. H. 1968: *The development of British industry and foreign competition 1875–1914*. London: Allen & Unwin.

Alden, D. 1965: The growth and decline of indigo production in colonial Brazil: A study in comparative economic history. *Journal of Economic History 35*, 35–60.

—— 1987: Late colonial Brazil, 1750–1808. In Bethell, L. (ed.), *Colonial Brazil* (Cambridge: Cambridge University Press), 284–343.

Alexander, S. 1983: *Women's work in nineteenth-century London. A study of the years 1820–50*. London: The Journeyman Press.

Allen, R. C. 1979: International competition in iron and steel, 1850–1913. *Journal of Economic History 39*, 911–37.

Aminzade, R. 1984: Reinterpreting capitalist industrialisation: A study of nineteenth-century France. *Social History 9*, 329–50.

Andrews, K. R. 1978: *The Spanish Caribbean: Trade and plunder 1530–1630*. New Haven: Yale University Press.

Appleby, A. B. 1979: Grain prices and subsistence crises in England and France, 1590–1740. *Journal of Economic History 39*, 865–87.

Ashworth, W. 1974: Industrialization and the economic integration of nineteenth-century Europe. *European Studies Review 4*, 291–315.

Aston, T. H. and Philpin, C. H. E. (eds.) 1985: *The Brenner debate: Agrarian class structure and economic development in pre-industrial Europe*. Cambridge: Cambridge University Press.

Åström, S-E. 1982: Swedish iron and the English iron industry about 1700: Some Neglected Aspects. *Scandinavian Economic History Review 30*, 129–41.

Attman, A. 1973: *The Russian and Polish markets in international trade 1500–1650*. Gothenburg. Institute of Economic History of Gothenburg

University.
—— 1986: Precious metals and the balance of payments in international trade 1500–1800. In Fischer, McInnis and Schneider 1986, vol I, 113–21.

Atwell, W. S. 1982: International bullion flows and the Chinese economy circa 1530–1650. *Past and Present* 95, 68–90.

Aymard, M. (ed.) 1982: *Dutch capitalism and world capitalism*. Cambridge: Cambridge University Press.

Bagchi, A. K. 1976: De-industrialization in India in the nineteenth century: Some theoretical implications. *Journal of Development Studies* 12, 135–64.

—— 1982: *The political economy of underdevelopment*. Cambridge: Cambridge University Press.

Bairoch, P. 1973: European foreign trade in the XIXth century. *Journal of European Economic History* 2, 5–36.

—— 1974: Geographical structure and trade balance of European foreign trade from 1800 to 1970. *Journal of European Economic History* 3, 557–608.

—— 1982: International industrialization levels from 1750 to 1980. *Journal of European Economic History* 11, 269–333.

Bairoch, P. and Lévy-Leboyer, M. (eds.) 1981: *Disparities in economic development since the Industrial Revolution*. London: Macmillan.

Ball, J. N. 1977: *Merchants and merchandise: The expansion of trade in Europe 1500–1630*. London: Croom Helm.

Bardou, J. P., Chanaron, J. J., Fridenson, P., Laux, J. 1982: *The automobile revolution*. Chapel Hill: University of North Carolina Press.

Barker, T. 1987: Introduction. In Barker, T. (ed.), *The economic and social effects of the spread of motor vehicles* (London: Macmillan), 1–54.

Barker, T. C., Dickinson, R., Hardie, D. W. F. 1956: the origins of the synthetic alkali industry in Britain. *Economica* 23, 158–71.

Barnard, A. 1958: *The Australian wool market, 1840–1900*. Melbourne: Melbourne University Press.

Barraclough, K. G. 1984: *Steelmaking before Bessemer*. London: The Metals Society.

Beck, L. 1903: *Die Geschichte des Eisens in technischen und kulturgeschichtlichen Beziehung*. Braunschweig: Vieweg.

Beer, J. J. 1958: Coal tar dye manufacture and the origins of the modern industrial research laboratory. *Isis* 49, 123–31.

—— 1959: *The emergence of the German dye industry*. Urbana: University of Illinois Press.

Berend, L. T., and Ranki, G. 1980: Foreign trade and the industrialization of the European periphery in the XIXth century. *Journal of European Economic History* 9, 539–84.

Berg, M. 1984: The power of knowledge: Comments on Margolis 'Knowledge and power'. In Stephen, F. H. (ed.), *Firms, organization and labour: Approaches to the economics of work organization* (London: Macmillan), 165–75.

—— 1985: *The age of manufactures 1700–1820*. London: Fontana.

Berg, M., Hudson, P. and Sonenscher, M. (eds.) 1983: *Manufacture in town and country before the factory*. Cambridge: Cambridge University Press.

Berlanstein, L. R. 1984: *The working people of Paris, 1871–1914*. Baltimore:

Johns Hopkins University Press.

Bessemer, Sir H. 1905: *An Autobiography*. London: 'Engineering'.

Biraben, J-N. 1968: Certain demographic characteristics of the plague epidemic in France, 1720–1722. *Daedalus* Spring, 536–45.

Blau, F. D. and Jusenius, C. L. 1976: Economists' approaches to sex segregation in the labor market: An appraisal. *Signs* 1, 181–99.

Bogucka, M. 1980: The role of the Baltic trade in European development from the XVIth to the XVIIIth centuries. *Journal of European Economic History* 9, 5–20.

Borchardt, K. 1973: The Industrial Revolution in Germany 1700–1914. In Cipolla, C. M. (ed.), *The Fontana economic history of Europe* (Glasgow: Collins), vol. 4 part 1, 76–160.

Boxer, C. R. 1969: *The Portuguese seaborne empire 1415–1825*. London: Hutchinson.

Boxer, M. J. 1982: Women in industrial homework: The flowermakers of Paris in the Belle Epoque. *French Historical Studies* 12, 401–23.

—— 1986: Protective legislation and home industry: The marginalization of women workers in late nineteenth – early twentieth-century France. *Journal of Social History* 20, 45–65.

Boxer, M. J. and Quataert, J. H. (eds.) 1987: *Connecting spheres: Women in the western world, 1500 to the present*. New York: Oxford University Press.

Braudel, F. 1981: *The structures of everyday life*, vol 1 of *Civilization and capitalism 15th–18th Century*. London: Collins.

—— 1982: *The wheels of commerce*, vol 2 of *Civilization and capitalism 15th–18th Century*. London: Collins.

—— 1984: *The perspective of the world*, vol 3 of *Civilization and capitalism 15th–18th Century*. London: Collins.

Braudel, F. and Spooner, F. 1967: Prices in Europe from 1450 to 1750. In Rich, E. E. and Wilson, C. H. (eds.), *Cambridge Economic History of Europe* (Cambridge: Cambridge University Press), vol IV, 374–486.

Braverman, H. 1974: *Labor and monopoly capital*. London: Monthly Review Press.

Breuilly, J. 1985: Artisan economy, artisan politics, artisan ideology: The artisan contribution to the nineteenth century labour movement. In Emsley, C. and Walvin, J. (eds.), *Artisans peasants and proletarians, 1760–1860* (London: Croom Helm) 187–225.

Brittain, J. 1974: The international diffusion of electrical power technology. *Journal of Economic History* 34, 108–21.

Broder, A. 1984: La Multinationalisation de l'industrie électrique française, 1880–1931: Causes et pratiques d'une dépendence. *Annales: E.S.C.* 39, 1020–43.

Brose, E. D. 1985: Competitiveness and obsolescence in the German charcoal iron industry. *Technology and Culture* 26, 532–59.

Brown, J. C. 1986: 'Woman's place was in the home': Women's work in renaissance Tuscany. In Ferguson, M. W., Quilligan, M. and Vickers, N. J. (eds.), *Rewriting the renaissance* (Chicago: University of Chicago Press), 206–24.

Brown, J. C. and Goodman, J. 1980: Women and industry in Florence. *Journal of Economic History* 40, 73–80.

Brown, M. B. 1974: *The economics of imperialism.* Harmondsworth: Penguin.

Bruland, T. 1982: Industrial conflict as a source of technical innovation: Three cases. *Economy and Society* 11, 91–121.

Buchheim, C. 1981: Aspects of XIXth century Anglo-German trade rivalry reconsidered. *Journal of European Economic History* 10, 273–89.

Burawoy, M. 1985: *The politics of production: Factory regimes under capitalism and socialism.* London: Verso.

Burgess, K. 1969: Technological change and the 1852 lock-out in the British engineering industry. *International Review of Social History* 14, 215–36.

Byatt, I. C. R. 1979: *The British electrical industry 1875–1914: The economic return to a new technology.* Oxford: Oxford University Press.

Cain, P. J. 1980: *Economic foundations of British overseas expansion, 1815–1914.* London: Macmillan.

Cain, P. J. and Hopkins, A. G. 1986: Gentlemanly capitalism and British expansion overseas: I The old colonial system, 1688–1850. *Economic History Review* 39, 501–25.

— 1987: Gentlemanly capitalism and British expansion overseas: II New imperialism, 1850–1945. *Economic History Review* 40, 1–26.

Cameron, R. 1981: The Industrial Revolution: A misnomer. In Schneider J. (ed.), *Wirtschaftskräfte und Wirtschaftwege: Festschrift für Hermann Kellenbenz* (Stuttgart: Klett-Cotta), vol. 5, 367–76.

—— 1985: A new view of European industrialization. *Economic History Review* 38, 1–23.

Cameron, R. and Freedman, C. E. 1983: French economic growth: A radical revision. *Social Science History* 7, 3–30.

Carden, G. L. 1909: *Machine-tool trade in Germany, France, Switzerland, Italy and United Kingdom,* Washington, DC: Special Agents' Series no. 26.

Cardwell, D. S. L. 1965: Power technologies and the advance of science, 1700–1825. *Technology and Culture* 6, 188–207.

Caspard, P. 1976: La Fabrique au village. *Le Movement Social* 97, 15–37.

—— 1979: L'accumulation du capital dans l'indiennage au XVIIIème siècle. *Revue du Nord* 61, 115–24.

Caunter, C. F. 1970: *The light car: a technical history.* London: HMSO.

Cayez, P. 1978: *Métiers jacquards et hauts fourneaux.* Lyons: Presses Universitaires de Lyon.

—— 1981: Une Proto-industrialisation décalée: La Ruralisation de la soierie lyonnaise dans la première moitié du XIXe siècle. *Revue du Nord* 63, 95–104.

Chalmin, P. G. 1984: The important trends in sugar diplomacy before 1914. In Albert and Graves 1984, 9–19.

Chandler, A. D. 1977: *The visible hand.* Cambridge, Mass.: Harvard University Press.

Chandler, A. D. and Daems, H. (eds.) 1980: *Managerial hierarchies: Comparative perspectives on the rise of the modern industrial enterprise.* Cambridge, Mass.: Harvard University Press.

Chapman, S. D. 1974: The textile factory before Arkwright: A typology of factory development. *Business History Review* 48, 451–73.

Chapman, S. D. and Chassagne, S. 1981: *European textile printers in the eighteenth century: A study of Peel and Oberkampf.* London: Heinemann.

Charlesworth, N. 1982: *British rule and the Indian economy 1800–1914.* London: Macmillan.

Chassagne, S. 1979: La Diffusion rurale de l'industrie cotonnière en France, (1750–1850). *Revue du Nord* 61, 97–114.

—— 1981: Industrialisation et desindustrialisation dans les campagnes françaises: quelques réflexions à partir du textile. *Revue du Nord* 63, 35–57.

Chassagne, S., Dewerpe, A. and Ganlupeau, Y. 1976: Les Ouvriers de la manufacture des toiles imprimées d'Oberkampf à Jouy-en-Josas (1760–1860). *Le Mouvement Social* 97, 39–88.

Chauduri, K. N. 1975: The economic and monetary problems of European trade with Asia during the seventeenth and eighteenth centuries. *Journal of European Economic History* 4, 318–48.

—— 1978: *The trading world of Asia and the English East India Company 1660–1760,* Cambridge: Cambridge University Press.

—— 1983: Foreign trade and balance of payments, 1757–1947. In Kumar, D. and Desai, M. (eds.) *Cambridge Economic History of India* (Cambridge: Cambridge University Press), vol. 2, 804–77.

—— 1985: *Trade and civilisation in the Indian Ocean: An economic history from the rise of Islam to 1750.* Cambridge: Cambridge University Press.

—— 1986: World silver flows and monetary factors as a force of international economic integration 1658–1758. In Fischer, McInnis and Schneider, vol. 1, 61–82.

Church, R. A. 1975: Nineteenth-century clock technology in Britain, the United States and Switzerland. *Economic History Review* 28, 616–30.

—— 1982: Markets and marketing in the British motor industry before 1914 with some French comparisons. *The Journal of Transport History* 3, 1–20.

Cipolla, C. M. 1965: *Guns, sails and empires: Technological innovation and the early phases of European expansion, 1400–1700.* New York: Minerva.

—— 1967: *Cocks and culture 1300–1700.* London: Collins.

—— 1972: The diffusion of innovations in early modern Europe. *Comparative Studies in Society and History* 14, 46–52.

—— (ed.) 1973: *The Fontana economic history of Europe* vol. 3 The industrial revolution. Glasgow: Collins.

—— (ed.) 1974: *The Fontana economic history of Europe* vol, 2 The sixteenth and seventeenth centuries. Glasgow: Collins.

—— 1976: *Before the Industrial Revolution,* London: Methuen.

Ciriacono, S. 1981: Silk manufacturing in France and Italy in the XVIIth century: Two models compared. *Journal of European Economic History* 10, 167–99.

Clark, P. (ed.) 1976: *The early modern town.* London: Longman.

—— 1985: *The European crisis of the 1590s: Essays in comparative history.* London: Allen & Unwin.

Clarkson, L. A. 1971: *The pre-industrial economy in England 1500–1750.* London: Batsford.

—— 1985: *Proto-industrialization: The first phase of industrialization?* London: Macmillan.

Clayburn La Force, J. 1964a: Royal textile factories in Spain, 1700–1800. *Journal of Economic History* 36, 337–63.

—— 1964b: Technological diffusion in the 18th century: The Spanish textile industry. *Technology and Culture.* 5, 322–43.

Clemens, P. G. E. 1976: The rise of Liverpool, 1665–1750. *Economic History Review* 29, 211–25.

Coale, A. J. and Watkins, S. C. 1986: *The decline of fertility in Europe.* Princeton: Princeton University Press.

Cockburn, C. 1983: *Brothers: Male dominance and technological change.* London: Pluto Press.

Coleman, D. C. 1953: Naval dockyards under the later Stuarts. *Economic History Review* 6, 134–55.

—— 1962: Industrial growth and industrial revolutions. In Carus-Wilson, E. M. (ed.), *Essays in economic history* (London: Edward Arnold), vol. 3, 334–52.

—— 1969: An innovation and its diffusion: The 'new draperies'. *Economic History Review* 12, 417–29.

—— 1973: Textile growth. In Harte, N. B. and Ponting, K. G. (eds.), *Textile history and economic history* (Manchester: Manchester University Press), 1–21.

—— 1983: Proto-industrialization: 'A concept too many? *Economic History Review* 36, 435–48.

Collins, J. B. 1984: the role of Atlantic France in the Baltic trade: Dutch traders and Polish grain at Nantes, 1625–1675. *Journal of European Economic History* 13, 239–89.

Constant, E. W. 1983: Scientific theory and technological testability: Science, dynamometers and water turbines in the nineteenth century. *Technology and Culture* 24, 183–98.

Cooper, C. C. 1984: The Portsmouth system of manufacture. *Technology and Culture* 25, 182–225.

Coppola, G. 1979: *Il mais nell'economia agricola lombarda.* Bologna: Il Mulino.

Courtheoux, J-P. 1959: Privilèges et misères d'un métier sidérurgique au XIXe siècle: le puddleur. *Revue d'histoire économique et sociale* 37, 161–84.

Crafts, N. F. R. 1977: Industrial revolution in England and France: Some thoughts on the question: 'Why was England first?'. *Economic History Review* 30, 429–41.

—— 1984: Economic growth in Britain and France, 1830–1910: A review of the evidence. *Journal of Economic History* 44, 49–67.

—— 1987: British economic growth: Some difficulties of interpretation. *Explorations in economic history* 24, 245–68.

Crosby, A. W. 1986: *Ecological imperialism.* Cambridge: Cambridge University Press.

Cross, H. E. 1983: South American bullion production and export 1550–1750. In Richards 1983b, 397–423.

Crouzet, F. 1964: Wars, blockade and economic change in Europe, 1792–1815. *Journal of Economic History* 24, 567–88.

—— 1972a: *Capital formation in the Industrial Revolution.* London: Methuen.

—— 1972b: Western Europe and Great Britain: 'Catching-up' in the first half of the nineteenth century. In Youngson, A. J. (ed.) *Economic development in the long run* (London: Allen & Unwin), 98–125.

——1974a: Recherches sur la production d'armements en France (1815–1913). *Revue Historique* 251, 45–84.

—— 1974b: Remarques sur l'industrie des armements en France (du milieu du XIXe siècle à 1914). *Revue Historique* 251, 409–22.

—— 1975: Quelques problèmes de l'historie de l'industrialisation au XIXe siècle. *Revue d'histoire économique et sociale* 53, 526–40.

—— 1985a: *The first industrialists: The problem of origins*. Cambridge: Cambridge University Press.

—— 1985b: *De la superiorité de l'Angleterre sur la France: L'économique et l'imaginaire XVIIe – XXe siècles*. Paris: Librarie Académique Perrin.

Curtin, P. D. 1969: *The Atlantic slave trade: A census*. Madison Wisc,: University of Wisconsin Press.

—— 1984: *Cross-cultural trade in world history*. Cambridge: Cambridge University Press.

Dasey, R. 1981: Women's work and the family: Women garment workers in Berlin and Hamburg before the First World War. In Evans, R. J. and Lee, W. R. (eds.), *The Germany family: Essays on the social history of the family in nineteenth and twentieth century Germany* (London: Croom Helm), 221–55.

Davies, K. G. 1957: *The Royal African Company*. London: Longman.

——1974: *The North Atlantic world in the seventeenth century*. Minneapolis: University of Minnesota Press.

Davies, M. 1978: Women's place is at the typewriter: The feminization of the clerical labour force. In Eisenstein, Z. (ed.), *Capitalism, patriarchy and the case for socialist feminism* (New York: Monthly Review Press), 248–66.

Davies, R. B. 1969: 'Peacefully working to conquer the world: The Singer manufacturing company in foreign markets, 1854–1889. *Business History Review* 43, 299–325.

Davis, N. Z. 1982: Women in the crafts in sixteenth-century Lyon. *Feminist Studies* 8, 46–80.

Davis, R. 1969a: English foreign trade 1660–1700. In Minchinton, W. E. (ed.), *The growth of English overseas trade in the seventeenth and eighteenth centuries* (London: Methuen), 78–98.

—— 1969b: English foreign trade 1700–1774. In Minchinton, W. E. (ed.), *The growth of English overseas trade in the seventeenth and eighteenth centuries* (London: Methuen), 99–120.

——1972: *The rise of the English shipping industry* Newton Abbot: David & Charles – 2nd impression.

—— 1973: *The rise of the Atlantic economies* London: Weidenfeld & Nicolson.

—— 1979: *The Industrial Revolution and British overseas trade*. Leicester: Leicester University Press.

Dean, W. 1987: *Brazil and the struggle for rubber*. Cambridge: Cambridge University Press.

Deane, P. 1957: The output of the British woollen industry in the eighteenth century. *Journal of Economic History* 17, 207–23.

Deane, P. and Cole, W. A. 1967: *British economic growth 1688–1959* 2nd ed. Cambridge: Cambridge University Press.

Deerr, N. 1949: *The history of sugar* vol. 1. London: Chapman & Hall.

—— 1950: *The history of sugar* vol. 2. London: Chapman & Hall.

de Maddalena, A. 1974: Rural Europe, 1500–1750. In Cipolla 1974, 273–353.

Denoon, D. 1983: *Settler capitalism: The dynamics of dependent development in the southern hemisphere.* Oxford: Oxford University Press.

de Roover, R. 1974: A Florentine firm of cloth manufacturers. In Kirshner, J. (ed.) *Business, banking and economic thought* (Chicago: University of Chicago Press), 85–118.

Devine, T. M. 1976: The colonial trades and industrial investment in Scotland c. 1700–1815. *Economic History Review* 29, 1–13.

de Vries, J. 1974: *The Dutch rural economy in the Golden Age.* New Haven: Yale University Press.

—— 1975: Peasant demand patterns and economic development: Friesland, 1550–1750. In Jones, E. L. and Parker, W. N. *European peasants and their markets: Essays in agrarian history* (Princeton: Princeton University Press), 205–68.

—— 1976: *The European economy in an age of crisis.* Cambridge: Cambridge University Press.

—— 1978: Barges and capitalism: Passenger transportation in the Dutch economy, 1632–1839. *AAG Bijdragen* 21, 33–398.

—— 1984: *European urbanization 1500–1800.* London: Methuen.

—— 1985: The population and economy of preindustrial Netherlands. *Journal of Interdisciplinary History* 15, 661–82.

Dewerpe, A. 1984: Genèse protoindustrielle d'une région dévelopée: l'Italie septentrionale (1800–1880). *Annales: E.S.C.* 39, 896–914.

Deyon, P. 1972: La Concurrence internationale des manufactures lainières aux XVIe et XVIIe siècles. *Annales: E. S. C.* 27, 20–32.

Deyon, P. and Guignet, P. 1980: The Royal Manufactures and economic and technological progress in France before the Industrial Revolution. *Journal of European Economic History* 9, 611–32.

Deyon, P. and Lottin, A. 1967: Evolution de la production textile à Lille aux XVIe et XVIIe siècles. *Revue du Nord* 44, 23–33.

Diffie, B. W. and Winius, G. D. 1977: *Foundations of the Portuguese empire, 1415–1580.* Minneapolis: University of Minnesota Press.

Dornic, F. 1955: *L'Industrie textile dans la Maine et ses débouches internationaux (1650–1815).* Le Mans: Editions Pierre-Belon.

Drabble, J. H. 1973: *Rubber in Malaya 1876–1922.* Kuala Lumpur: Oxford University Press.

DuPlessis, R. S. and Howell, M. C. 1982: Reconsidering the early modern urban economy: The cases of Leiden and Lille. *Past and Present* 94, 49–84.

Edmonson, J. M. 1981: From mécanicien to ingenieur: Education and the machine building industry in nineteenth century France. Unpublished PhD dissertation: University of Delaware.

Ehrlich, C. 1976: *The piano: A history,* London: Dent.

Elbaum, B. 1986: The steel industry before World War I. In Elbaum and Lazonick 1986, 51–81.

Elbaum, B. and Lazonick, W. 1986: *The decline of the British economy.* Oxford: Oxford University Press.

Eltis, D. 1983: Free and coerced transatlantic migrations: Some comparisons.

American Historical Review 88, 251–80.

—— 1987: The nineteenth century transatlantic slave trade: An annual time series of imports into the Americas broken down by region. *Hispanic American Historical Review* 67, 109–38.

Endrei, W. 1963: L'Evolution de l'industrie de l'impression sur étoffes en Europe et les obstacles à son progrès (1700–1900). *Cahiers de l'ISEA* Série AD, 2, 209–28.

Engerman, S. 1986: Servants to slaves to servants: Contract labour and European expansion. In Emmer, P. C. (ed.), *Colonialism and migration* (Dordrecht: Martinus Nijhoff), 263–94.

Engrand, C. 1979: Concurrences et complimentarités des villes et campagnes: Les manufactures picardes de 1780 à 1815. *Revue du Nord* 61, 61–81.

Farnie, D. A. 1979: *The English cotton industry and the world market 1815–1896*. Oxford. Oxford University Press.

Feis, H. 1930: *Europe, the world's banker, 1870–1914*. New Haven: Yale University Press.

Felloni, G. 1977: Italy. In Wilson and Parker 1977, 1–36.

Fischer, W., McInnis, R. M. and Schneider, J. 1986: *The emergence of a world economy 1500–1914*. Papers of the IXth International Congress of Economic History. 2 vols. Wiesbaden: Frantz Steiner Verlag.

Fisher, H. E. S. 1969: Anglo-Portuguese trade 1700–1770. In Minchinton, W. E. (ed.) *The growth of English overseas trade in the seventeenth and eighteenth centuries* (London: Methuen), 144–64.

Flageolet-Lardenois, M. 1972: Une Firme pionnière: Panhard et Levassor jusqu'en 1918. *Le Mouvement Social* 81, 27–49.

Flinn, M. W. 1974: The stabilisation of mortality in pre-industrial western Europe. *Journal of European Economic History* 3, 285–318.

——1981: *The European demographic system 1500–1820*. Brighton: Harvester.

Foreman-Peck, J. 1982: Multinational companies and the international transfer of technology in the motor industry to 1939. In Jörberg, L. and Rosenberg N. (eds.) *Technical change, employment and investment*. Contributions to the A3 Theme of the Eighth International Economic History Congress in Budapest. Lund: Department of Economic History, University of Lund.

—— 1983: *A history of the world economy: International economic relations since 1850*. Brighton: Wheatsheaf.

Fores, M. 1981: The myth of a British industrial revolution. *History* 66, 181–98.

Franzoi, B. 1987: '. . . with the wolf always at the door . . .': Women's work in domestic industry in Britain and Germany. In Boxer and Quataert 1987, 146–55.

Freifeld, M. 1986: Technological change and the 'self-acting' mule: A study of skill and sexual division of labour. *Social History* 11, 319–43.

Fremdling, R. 1977: Railroads and German economic growth: A leading sector analysis with a comparison to the United States and Great Britain. *Journal of Economic History* 37, 583–604.

—— 1982: Foreign trade patterns, technical change, cost and productivity in the west European iron industries, 1820–1870. In Fremdling, R. and O'Brien,

P. K. (eds.) *Productivity in the economies of Europe* (Stuttgart: Klett-Cotta), 152–74.

—— 1983: Die Ausbreitung des Puddelverfahrens und des Kokshochofens in Belgien, Frankreich und Deutschland. *Technikgeschichte* 50, 197–212.

Freund, B. 1984: *The making of contemporary Africa*. London: Macmillan.

Freudenberger, H., Mather, F. J. and Nardinelli, C. 1984: A new look at the early factory labour force. *Journal of Economic History* 44, 1085–90.

Fridenson, P. 1978. The coming of the assembly line to Europe. In Krohn, W., Layton, E. T. and Weingart, P. (eds.), *The dynamics of science and technology*. (Sociology of the Sciences Yearbook vol. ii). (Dordrecht: Reidel).

—— 1979: Les Premiers ouvriers français de l'automobile (1890–1914). *Sociologie du Travail*. 21, 297–325.

—— 1981: French automobile marketing, 1890–1979. In Okochi, A. and Shimokawa, K. (eds.), *Development of mass marketing* (Tokyo: Tokyo University Press), 127–54.

Fries, R. I. 1975: British response to the American system: The case of the small-arms industry after 1850. *Technology and Culture* 16, 377–403.

Furber, H. 1976: *Rival empires of trade in the orient, 1600–1800*. Minneapolis: University of Minnesota Press.

Gaastra, F. S. 1983: The exports of precious metal from Europe to Asia by the Dutch East India Company. In Richards 1983b, 447–75.

Gallagher, J. and Robinson, R. 1953: The imperialism of free trade. *Economic History Review* 6, 1–15.

Galloway, J. H. 1977: The Mediterranean sugar industry. *Geographical Review* 67, 177–94.

Giannetti, R. 1985: *La conquista della forza*. Milan: Franco Angeli.

Gignoux, C. J. 1955: *Histoire d'une entreprise française*. Paris: Hachette.

Gille, B. 1966: *Histoire de la métallurgie*. Paris: Presses Universitaires de France.

—— 1968: *La Sidérurgie française au XIXe siècle: Recherches historiques*. Geneva: Droz.

Glamann, K. 1958: *Dutch-Asiatic trade, 1620–1740*. The Hague: Martinus Nijhoff.

—— 1977: The changing patterns of trade. In Rich, E. E. and Wilson, C. H. (eds.) *The Cambridge economic history of Europe* (Cambridge: Cambridge University Press), vol. V, 185–289.

Godelier, M. 1980: Work and its representations: A research proposal. *History Workshop* 10, 164–74.

Goldsmith, J. L. 1984: The agrarian history of pre-industrial France. Where do we go from here? *Journal of European Economic History* 13, 175–99.

Godthwaite, R. A. 1980: *The building of Renaissance Florence*. Baltimore: Johns Hopkins University Press.

Good, D. F. 1984: *The economic rise of the Hapsburg Empire 1750–1914*. Berkeley: University of California Press.

Good, E. M. 1982: *Giraffes, Black Dragons and other pianos*. Stanford: Stanford University Press.

Goodman, J. 1977: The Florentine silk industry in the seventeenth century. Unpublished PhD dissertation: University of London.

—— 1981: Management, organisation and the labour process in the seventeenth century Florentine silk industry. Unpublished paper presented at the Pasold Conference on Textile History, Oxford.

—— 1983: Tuscan commercial relations with Europe, 1550–1620: Florence and the European textile market. In *Firenze e la Toscana dei Medici nell'Europa del'500* (Florence: Olschki), vol. I, 327–41.

Gordon, D. M. 1982: Industrialization and republican politics: The bourgeois of Reims and St Etienne under the Second Empire. In Merriman, J. M. (ed.), *French cities in the nineteenth century* (London: Hutchinson), 117–38.

Gould, J. D. 1979: European inter-continental emigration 1815–1914: Patterns and causes. *Journal of European Economic History* 8, 593–679.

—— 1980a European inter-continental emigration. The road home: Return migration from the USA. *Journal of European Economic History* 9, 41–112.

—— 1980b: European international emigration: The role of 'diffusion' and 'feedback'. *Journal of European Economic History* 9, 267–315.

Graham, G. S. 1956: The ascendancy of the sailing ship 1850–85. *Economic History Review* 9, 74–88.

Gras, L-J. 1904: *Essai sur l'histoire de la quincaillerie et petite métallurgie . . . à Saint-Etienne et dans la région stéphanoise.* St Etienne: Théolier.

—— 1908: *Histoire économique de la métallurgie de la Loire, suivi d'une notice de la construction mécanique et l'industrie des cycles et des automobiles dans le région stéphanoise.* St Etienne: Théolier.

Graves, A. and Richardson, P. 1980: Plantations in the political economy of colonial sugar production: Natal and Queensland, 1860–1914. *Journal of Southern African Studies* 6, 214–29.

Gray, R. Q. 1976: *The labour aristocracy in Victorian Edinburgh.* Oxford: Oxford University Press.

Greenberg, D. 1982: Reassessing the power patterns of Industrial Revolution: An Anglo-American comparison, *American Historical Review* 82, 1237–61.

Greenfield, S. M. 1979: Plantations, sugar cane and slavery. *Historical Reflections* 6, 85–119.

Gullickson, G. L. 1981: The sexual division of labour in cottage industry and agriculture in the Pays de Caux: Auffay 1750–1850. *French Historical Studies* 15, 177–99.

—— 1982: Proto-industrialization, demographic behaviour and the sexual division of labor in Auffay, France, 1750–1850. *Peasant Studies* 9, 106–18.

—— 1983: Agriculture and cottage industry: Redefining the causes of proto-industrialization. *Journal of Economic History* 43, 1983.

—— 1986: *Spinners and weavers of Auffay.* Cambridge: Cambridge University Press.

Gutmann, M. P. and Leboutte, R. 1984: Rethinking proto-industrialization and the family. *Journal of Interdisciplinary History* 14, 587–607.

Haber, L. F. 1958: *The chemical industry during the nineteenth century.* Oxford: Oxford University Press.

—— 1971: *The chemical industry 1900–1930.* Oxford: Oxford University Press.

Hafter, D. M. 1979: The programmed brocade loom and the 'decline of the drawgirl'. In Trescott 1979, 49–66.

Hall, M. B. 1976: The strange case of aluminium. *History of Technology* 1, 143–57.

Hall, C. 1982: The home turned upside down: The working class family in cotton textiles 1780–1850. In Whitelegg, E., (ed.), *The changing experience of Women* (Oxford: Martin Robertson), 17–29.

Hammersley, G. 1973: The charcoal iron industry and its fuel, 1540–1750. *Economic History Review* 26, 593–613.

Hanagan, M. 1980: *The logic of solidarity: Artisans and industrial workers in three French towns 1871–1914*. Urbana: University of Illinois Press.

Hanawalt, B. A. 1986: *Women and work in pre-industrial Europe*. Bloomington: University of Indiana Press.

Hanson, J. R. 1979: World demand for cotton during the nineteenth century: Wright's estimates re-examined. *Journal of Economic History* 39, 1015–21.

——— 1980: *Trade in transition: Exports from the Third World, 1840–1900*. New York: Academic Press.

Hansotte, G. 1980: *La Métallurgie et le commerce international du fer dans les Pays-Bas autrichiens et la Principauté de Liège pendant la seconde moitié du XVIIIe siècle*. vol. 2 part 3 of *Histoire Quantitative et Développement de la Belgique*. Brussels: Académie Royale de Belgique.

Harley, C. K. 1971: The shift from sailing ships to steamships, 1850–1890: A study in technological change and its diffusion. In McCloskey, D. N. (ed.), *Essays on a mature economy: Britain after 1840* (London: Methuen), 215–31.

——— 1973: On the persistence of old techniques: The case of North American wooden shipbuilding. *Journal of Economic History* 33, 372–98.

——— 1974: Skilled labour and the choice of technique in Edwardian industry. *Explorations in Economic History* 11, 391–414.

——— 1986: Late nineteenth century transportation, trade and settlement. In Fischer, McInnis and Schneider 1986, vol. II, 593–617.

Harnetty, P. 1972: *Imperialism and free trade: Lancashire and India in the mid-nineteenth century*. Vancouver: University of British Columbia Press.

Harrison, A. E. 1969: The competitiveness of the British cycle industry 1890–1914. *Economic History Review* 22, 287–303.

——— 1985: The origins and growth of the UK cycle industry to 1900. *Journal of Transport History* 6, 41–70.

Harrison, J. 1978: *An economic history of modern Spain*. Manchester: Manchester University Press.

Harte, N. B. 1973: The rise of protectionism and the English linen trade, 1690–1790. In Harte, N. B. and Ponting, K. G. (eds.), *Textile History and economic history* (Manchester: Manchester University Press), 74–112.

Hartmann, H. 1976: Capitalism, patriarchy and job segregation by sex. *Signs* 3, 137–69.

Hau, M. 1985: *L'Industrialisation de l'Alsace 1803–1939*. Thèse de doctorat d'état: University of Paris X.

Hayes, P. 1987: Carl Bosch and Carl Krauch: Chemistry and the political economy of Germany, 1925–1945. *Journal of Economic History* 47, 353–63.

Headrick, D. R. 1981: *The tools of empire: Technology and European imperialism in the nineteenth century*. New York: Oxford University Press.

Henderson, W. O. 1972: *Britain and industrial Europe, 1750–1870*. 3rd ed. Leicester: Leicester University Press.

—— 1975: *The rise of German industrial power 1834–1914*. London: Temple Smith.

Heywood, C. 1977: *The cotton industry in France, 1750–1850: An interpretative essay*. Loughborough: Department of Economics Loughborough University.

—— 1981: The role of the peasantry in French industrialization. *Economic History Review* 34, 359–76.

Hicks, J. 1969: *A theory of economic history*. Oxford: Oxford University Press.

Hills, R. L. 1979: Hargreaves, Arkwright and Crompton. Why three inventors?. *Textile History* 10, 114–26.

History Workshop Editorial 1977: British economic history and the question of work. *History Workshop* 3, 1–4.

Hoddesdon, L. 1981: The emergence of basic research in the Bell Telephone System, 1875–1915. *Technology and Culture* 22, 512–44.

Hoffmann, W. G. 1958: *The growth of industrial economies*. Manchester: Manchester University Press.

Hohenberg, P. M. 1967: *Chemicals in western Europe 1850–1914*. Chicago: Rand-McNally.

—— 1977: Maize in French agriculture. *Journal of European Economic History* 6, 63–101.

Hohenberg, P. M. and Lees, L. H. 1985: *The making of urban Europe 1000–1950*. Cambridge, Mass.; Harvard University Press.

Hoke, D. 1987: British and American horology: Time to test factor-substitution models. *Journal of Economic History* 47, 321–27.

Hollister-Short, G. J. 1976–77: The introduction of the Newcomen engine into Europe. *Transactions of the Newcomen Society* 48, 11–24.

Holt, R. 1985: The bicycle, the bourgeoisie and the discovery of rural France, 1880–1914. *The British Journal of Sports History* 2, 127–39.

Honeyman, K. 1982: *Origins of enterprise: Business leadership in the Industrial Revolution*. Manchester: Manchester University Press.

Honeyman, K. and Goodman, J. 1986a: Regional integration and specialization in the French worsted industry, 1810–1910: An aspect of industrialization in France. *Textile History* 17, 39–50.

—— 1986b: *Technology and enterprise: Isaac Holden and the mechanisation of woolcombing in France, 1848–1914*. Aldershot: Scolar Press.

Hopkins, A. G. 1973: *An economic history of West Africa*. London: Longman.

Hounshell, D. 1984: *From the American system to mass production 1800–1932*. Baltimore: Johns Hopkins University Press.

Houston, R. and Snell, K. D. M. 1984: Proto-industrialisation? Cottage industry, social change and industrial revolution. *Historical Journal* 27, 473–92.

Howard, R. A. 1978: Interchangeable parts re-examined: The private sector of the American arms industry on the eve of the Civil War. *Technology and Culture* 19, 633–49.

Howell, M. C. 1986a: Women, the family economy and the structures of market production in cities of northern Europe during the late Middle Ages. In

Hanawalt 1986, 198–222.
—— 1986b: *Women, production and patriarchy in late medieval cities.* Chicago: University of Chicago Press.

Hudson, P. 1981: Proto-industrialisation: The case of the West Riding wool textile industry in the late 18th and early 19th centuries. *History Workshop* 12, 34–61.

Hufton, O. 1975: Women and the family economy in eighteenth century France. *French Historical Studies* 9, 1–22.

Hughes, J. R. T. 1970: *Industrialization and economic history.* New York: McGraw Hill.

Hughes, T. P. 1979: Emerging themes in the history of technology, *Technology and Culture* 20, 697–711.

—— 1983: *Networks of power: Electrification in western society 1880–1930.* Baltimore: Johns Hopkins University Press.

Humphries, J. 1981: Protective legislation, the capitalist state and working class men: The case of the 1842 Miners' Regulation Act. *Feminist Review* 7, 1–33.

Hyde, C. K. 1977: *Technological change and the British iron industry, 1700–1870.* Princeton: Princeton University Press.

International Sugar Council 1963: *The world sugar economy: Structure and policies. vol II The world picture.* London: ISC.

Jackson, R. V. 1985: Growth and deceleration in English agriculture, 1660–1790. *Economic History Review* 38, 333–51.

Jeremy, D. 1977: Damming the flood: British government efforts to check the outflow of technicians and machinery, 1780–1843. *Business History Review* 51, 1–34.

Johansen, H-C. 1986: How to pay for Baltic products. In Fischer, McInnis and Schneider 1986, vol. I, 123–42.

Johnson, C. 1975: Economic change and artisan discontent: The tailors' history, 1800–1848. In Price, R. (ed.) *Revolution and reaction* (London: Croom Helm), 87–114.

Jones, S. R. H. 1982: The organization of work: A historical dimension. *Journal of Economic Behavior and Organization* 3, 117–37.

—— 1987: Technology, transaction costs, and the transition to factory production in the British silk industry, 1700–1870. *Journal of Economic History* 47, 71–96.

John, A. V. 1978: Colliery legislation and its consequences: 1842 and the women miners of Lancashire. *Bulletin of the John Rylands Library* 61, 78–114.

—— (ed.) 1986: *Unequal opportunities: Women's employment in England 1800–1918.* Oxford: Basil Blackwell.

Kaelble, H. 1986: *Industrialisation and social inequality in 19th century Europe.* Leamington Spa: Berg.

Kamen, H. 1980: *Spain in the later seventeenth century.* London: Longman.

Kanefsky, J. W. 1979: Motive power in British industry and the accuracy of the 1870 Factory Return. *Economic History Review* 32, 360–75.

Kanefsky, J. W. and Robey, J. 1980: Steam engines in eighteenth century Britain: A quantitative assessment. *Technology and Culture* 21, 161–86.

Katznelson, I. and Zolberg, A. R. (eds.) 1986: *Working-class formation:*

Nineteenth-century patterns in Western Europe and the United States. Princeton: Princeton University Press.

Kawakatsu, H. 1986: International competition in cotton goods in the late nineteenth century: Britain versus India and East Asia. In Fischer, McInnis and Schneider 1986, vol II, 619–43.

Kellenbenz, H. 1974: Technology in the age of the scientific revolution, 1500–1700. In Cipolla 1974, 177–272.

—— 1977: The organization of industrial production. In Rich, E. E. and Wilson, C. H. (eds.), *The Cambridge economic history of Europe.* (Cambridge: Cambridge University Press), vol. V, 462–548.

Kindleberger, C. P. 1951: Group behavior and international trade. *Journal of Political Economy* 59, 30–46.

—— 1975: The rise of free trade in Western Europe, 1820–1875. *Journal of Economic History* 35, 20–55.

—— 1978: *Economic response: Comparative studies in trade, finance and growth.* Cambridge, Mass.: Harvard University Press.

Kirchner, W. 1981: Russian tariffs and foreign industries: The German entrepreneur's perspective. *Journal of Economic History* 41, 361–79.

Kisch, H. 1964: The growth deterrents of a medieval heritage: The Aachen area woollen trades before 1790. *Journal of Economic History* 24, 513–37.

—— 1968: Prussian mercantilism and the rise of the Krefeld silk industry: Variations upon an eighteenth century theme. *Transactions of the American Philosophical Society* 58, part 7.

Klein, H. S. 1986: *African slavery in Latin America and the Caribbean.* New York. Oxford University Press.

Knauerhase, R. 1968: The compound steam engine and productivity changes in the German merchant marine fleet, 1871–1887. *Journal of Economic History* 28, 390–404.

Kobata, A. 1965: The production and uses of gold and silver in sixteenth and seventeenth century Japan. *Economic History Review* 18, 245–66.

Kocka, J. 1981: Capitalism and bureaucracy in German industrialization before 1914. *Economic History Review* 34, 453–68.

—— 1984: Craft traditions and the labour movement in nineteenth-century Germany. In Thane, Crossick and Floud 1984, 95–117.

—— 1986: Problems of working-class formation in Germany: The early years, 1800–1875. In Katznelson and Zolberg 1986, 279–351.

Kravis, I. 1970: Trade as a handmaiden of growth: Similarities between the nineteenth and twentieth centuries. *Economic Journal* 80, 850–72.

Kriedte, P. 1983: *Peasants, landlords and merchant capitalists.* Leamington Spa: Berg.

—— 1986: Demographic and economic rhythms: The rise of the silk industry in Krefeld in the eighteenth century. *Journal of European Economic History* 15, 259–89.

Kriedte, P., Medick, H. and Schlumbohm, J. 1981: *Industrialization before industrialization.* Cambridge: Cambridge University Press.

Kulikoff, A. 1986: *Tobacco and slaves: The development of southern culture in the Chesapeake.* Chapel Hill: University of North Carolina Press.

Kunitz, S. J. 1983: Speculations on the European mortality decline. *Economic*

History Review 36, 349–64.

Laferrère, M. 1972: Le Rôle de la chimie dans l'industrialisation à Lyon au XIXe siècle. In Léon, Crouzet and Gascon 1972, 393–99.

Landström, B. 1961: *The Ship*. London: Allen & Unwin.

Landes, D. S. 1969: *The unbound Prometheus*. Cambridge: Cambridge University Press.

—— 1979: Watchmaking: A case study in enterprise and change. *Business History Review* 53, 1–39.

—— 1980: The creation of knowledge and technique: Today's task and yesterday's experience. *Daedalus,* Winter, 111–20.

——1983: *Revolution in time: Clocks and the making of the modern world.* Cambridge, Mass.: Harvard University Press.

—— 1986: What do bosses do? *Journal of Economic History* 46, 585–623.

Lane, F. C. 1966: *Venice and history*. Baltimore: Johns Hopkins University Press.

—— 1973: *Venice: A maritime republic*. Baltimore: Johns Hopkins University Press.

—— 1974: Progrès technologiques et productivité dans les transports maritimes de la fin du Moyen Age au début des Temps Modernes. *Revue Historique* 251, 277–302.

Langer, W. 1975: American foods and Europe's population growth, 1750–1850. *Journal of Social History* 8, 51–66.

Latham, A. J. H. 1978: *The international economy and the undeveloped world 1865–1914*. London: Croom Helm.

—— 1986: The international trade in rice and wheat since 1868: A study in market integration. In Fischer, McInnis and Schneider 1986, vol. II, 645–63.

Latham, A. J. H. and Neal, L. 1983: The international market in rice and wheat 1868–1914. *Economic History Review* 36, 260–80.

Laux, J. M. 1976: *In first gear: The French automobile industry to 1914*. Liverpool: Liverpool University Press.

Layton, E. T. Jr. 1976: American ideologies of science and engineering. *Technology and Culture* 17, 688–701.

—— 1979: Scientific technology, 1845–1900: The hydraulic turbine and the origins of American industrial research. *Technology and Culture* 20, 64–89.

Lazonick, W. 1978: The subjection of labor to capital: The rise of the capitalist system. *Review of Radical Political Economics* 10, 1–31.

—— 1979: Industrial relations and technical change: The case of the self-acting mule. *Cambridge Journal of Economics* 3, 231–62.

Lee, C. H. 1986: *The British economy since 1700*. Cambridge: Cambridge University Press.

Lee, W. R. (ed.) 1979: *European demography and economic growth*. London: Croom Helm.

LeGoff, T. J. A. and Meyer, J. 1971: Les Constructions navales en France pendant la seconde moitié du XVIIIe siècle. *Annales: E.S.C.* 26, 173–85.

Lenman, B. 1977: Scotland. In Wilson and Parker 1977, 142–51.

Léon, P. 1974: Structure du commerce extérieur et évolution industrielle de la France à la fin du XVIIIe siècle. In *Conjonctures économiques, structures sociales. Hommage à E. Labrousse* (Paris: Mouton), 407–32.

Léon, P., Crouzet, F. and Gascon, R. (eds.) 1972: *L'Industrialisation en Europe au XIXe siècle.* Paris: CNRS.

Lequin, Y. 1977: *Les Ouvriers de la région lyonnaise, 1848–1914.* Lyons: Presses Universitaires de Lyon.

Leuilliot, P. 1970: Influence du commerce oriental sur l'économie occidentale. In Mollat, M. (ed.) *Sociétés et compagnies de commerce en Orient et dans l'Océan Indien* (Paris: SEVPEN), 611–29.

Lewis, W. A. 1981: The rate of growth of world trade, 1830–1973. In Grassman, S. and Lundberg, E. (eds.) *The world economic order, past and prospects* (New York: St Martin's Press), 11–74.

Lindblad, J. T. 1986: International trade and colonial economic growth: The case of Indonesia 1874–1914. In Fischer, McInnis and Schneider 1986, vol. II 665–705.

Locke, R. R. 1984: *The end of the practical man.* London: JAI Press.

Lockhart, J. and Schwartz, S. B. 1983: *Early Latin America: A history of colonial Spanish America and Brazil.* Cambridge: Cambridge University Press.

Lorenz, E. H. 1984: Two patterns of development: The labour process in the British and French shipbuilding industries, 1880–1930. *Journal of European Economic History* 13, 599–634.

Lorenz, E. H. and Wilkinson, F. 1986: The shipbuilding industry, 1880–1965. In Elbaum and Lazonick 1986, 109–34.

Lovejoy, P. E. 1982: The volume of the Atlantic slave trade: A synthesis. *Journal of African History* 23, 473–501.

Lundgreen, P. 1984: Education for the science-based industrial state? The case for nineteenth-century Germany. *History of Education* 13, 59–67.

McBride, T. M. 1978: A woman's world: Department stores and the evolution of women's employment, 1870–1920. *French Historical Studies* 10, 664–83.

McCloskey, D. N. 1971: *Essays on a mature economy: Britain after 1840.* London: Methuen.

—— 1981: *Enterprise and trade in Victorian Britain.* London: Allen & Unwin.

McCusker, J. and Menard, R. R. (eds.) 1985: *The economy of British America 1607–1789.* Chapel Hill: University of North Carolina Press.

McInnis, R. M. 1986: The emergence of a world economy in the latter half of the nineteenth century. In Fischer, McInnis and Schneider 1986, vol. II, 361–69.

MacKenney, R. 1987: *Tradesmen and trades: The world of the guilds in Venice and Europe c. 1250 – c. 1650.* London: Croom Helm.

McKendrick, N. 1960: Josiah Wedgwood: An eighteenth century entrepreneur in salesmanship and marketing techniques. *Economic History Review* 12, 408–33.

Mackenzie, D. 1984: Marx and the machine. *Technology and Culture* 25, 473–502.

Mackenzie, D. and Wajcman, J. 1985: *The social shaping of technology.* Milton Keynes: Open University Press.

McNeill, W. H. 1977: *Plagues and people.* Oxford: Basil Blackwell.

—— 1983: *The pursuit of power.* Oxford: Basil Blackwell.

Magalhães-Godinho, V. 1969: *L'économie de l'empire portugais aux XVe et XVIe siècles.* Paris: SEVPEN.

Manchester, W. 1968: *The arms of Krupp 1587–1968*. Boston, Mass.: Little, Brown & Co.

Marglin, S. 1976: What do bosses do?. In Gorz, A. (ed.) *The division of labour: The labour process and class struggle in modern capitalism*. Brighton: Harvester.

Markovitch, T. J. 1966: L'industrie française de 1789 à 1964. *Cahiers de l'ISEA* ser, AF 6.

—— 1967: Le revenu industriel et artisanal sous la Monarchie de Juillet et le Second Empire. *Economies et Sociétés* ser. AF 8.

—— 1976: *Les industries lainières de Colbert à la Révolution*. Geneva: Droz.

Marks, S. (ed.) 1984: *International labour migration*. London: Maurice Temple Smith.

Mathias, P. and Postan, M. M. (eds.) 1978: *Cambridge economic history of Europe* vol. VII, part 1. Cambridge: Cambridge University Press.

Mauro, F. and Parker, G. 1977: Spain. In Wilson and Parker 1977, 37–62.

Mayr, O. 1986: *Authority, liberty and automatic machinery in early modern Europe*. Baltimore: Johns Hopkins University Press.

Mazzaoui, M. 1981: *The Italian cotton industry in the later Middle Ages 1100–1600*. Cambridge: Cambridge University Press.

Meinig, D. W. 1986: *The shaping of America* vol. I *Atlantic America*. New Haven: Yale University Press.

Mendels, F. 1972: Proto-industrialization: The first phase of the process of industrialization. *Journal of Economic History* 32, 241–61.

Meyer-Thurow, G. 1982: The industrialization of invention: A case study from the German chemical industry. *Isis* 73, 363–81.

Mill, A. W. 1985: French steel and the metal-working industries: A contribution to the debate on economic development in nineteenth-century France. *Social Science History* 9, 307–38.

Milward, A. and Saul, S. B. 1977: *The development of the economies of continental Europe 1850–1914*. London: George Allen & Unwin.

—— 1979: *The economic development of continental Europe 1780–1870*. 2nd ed. London: George Allen & Unwin.

Mintz, S. W. 1985: *Sweetness and power*. New York: Viking.

Mishra, G. 1966: Indigo plantations and agrarian relations in Champaran during the nineteenth century. *Indian Economic and Social History Review* 3, 332–57.

Mitchell, B. R. 1973: Statistical appendix 1700–1914. In Cipolla, C. M. (ed.) *The Fontana economic history of Europe* (Glasgow: Collins), vol. 4 part 2, 738–820.

—— 1975: *European historical statistics, 1750–1970*. London: Macmillan.

—— 1982: *International historical statistics. Africa and Asia*. London: Macmillan.

—— 1983: *International historical statistics. The Americas and Australasia*. London: Macmillan.

Mitchell, B. R. and Deane, P. 1962: *Abstract of British historical statistics*. Cambridge: Cambridge University Press.

Monter, E. W. 1980: Women in Calvinist Geneva (1550–1800). *Signs* 6, 189–209.

Morineau, M. 1970: La pomme de terre au XVIIIe siècle. *Annales: E.S.C.* 25, 1767–84.

—— 1977: France. In Wilson and Parker 1977, 155–89.

—— 1985: *Incroyables gazettes et fabuleux métaux*. Cambridge: Cambridge University Press.

Morsel, H. 1972: Les industries électrotechniques dans les alpes françaises du nord de 1869 à 1921. In Léon, Crouzet and Gascon 1972, 557–83.

Mulhall, M. G. 1892: *The dictionary of statistics*. London: George Routledge & Sons.

Munro, J. F. 1976: *Africa and the international economy 1800–1960*. London: Dent.

—— 1981: Monopolists and speculators: British investment in West African rubber, 1904–14. *Journal of African History* 12, 263–77.

—— 1983, British rubber companies in East Africa before the First World War. *Journal of African History* 24, 369–79.

Musson, A. E. 1976: Industrial motive power in the United Kingdom, 1800–1870. *Economic History Review* 29, 415–39.

Nef, J. U. 1954: The progress of technology and the growth of large-scale industry in Great Britain, 1540–1640. In Carus-Wilson, E. M. (ed.) *Essays in Economic History* (London: Edward Arnold), Vol. 1, 108–34.

Nicholas, S. J. 1984: The overseas marketing performance of British industry 1870–1914. *Economic History Review* 37, 489–506.

Noble, D. F. 1977: *America by design*. New York: Knopf.

—— 1984: *Forces of production*. New York: Knopf.

—— 1985: Command performance: a perspective on the social and economic consequences of military enterprise. In Smith 1985b, 329–46.

North, D. 1958: Ocean freight rates and economic development 1750–1913. *Journal of Economic History* 18, 537–55.

—— 1966: *The economic growth of the United States 1790–1860*. New York: Norton.

—— 1968: Sources of productivity change in ocean shipping 1600–1850. *Journal of Political Economy* 76, 953–70.

Nübel, O. 1987: The beginnings of the automobile in Germany. In Barker, T. (ed.) *The economic and social effects of the spread of motor vehicles* (London: Macmillan), 55–56.

Nye, J. V. 1987: Firm size and economic backwardness: A new look at the French industrialization debate. *Journal of Economic History* 47, 649–69.

O'Brien, P. K. 1982: European economic development: The contribution of the periphery. *Economic History Review* 35, 1–18.

—— 1985: Agriculture and the home market for English industry, 1660–1820. *English Historical Review* 100, 773–800.

—— 1986: Do we have a typology for the study of European industrialization in the XIXth century? *Journal of European Economic History* 15, 291–333.

O'Brien, P. K. and Keyder, C. 1978: *Economic growth in Britain and France, 1780–1914*. London: Allen & Unwin.

Ormord, D. 1975. Dutch commercial and industrial decline and British growth in the late seventeenth and early eighteenth centuries. In Krantz, F. and Hohenberg, P. M. (eds.) *Failed transitions to modern industrial society:*

Renaissance Italy and seventeenth century Holland (Montreal: Interuniversity Centre for European Studies), 36–43.

Overton, M. 1984: Agricultural productivity in eighteenth-century England: Some further speculations. *Economic History Review* 37, 244–51.

Owen, R. 1969: *Cotton and the Egyptian economy 1820–1914*. Oxford: Oxford University Press.

—— 1981: *The Middle East in the world economy 1800–1914*. London: Methuen.

Parker, G. 1974: The emergence of modern finance in Europe 1500–1730. In Cipolla 1974, 527–94.

—— 1976: The 'Military Revolution', 1560–1660 – a myth?. *Journal of Modern History* 48, 195–214.

Parker, W. N. 1979: Industry. In Burke, P. (ed.), *The new Cambridge modern history* (Cambridge: Cambridge University Press) Companion volume to Vol. XIII, 43–79.

Parry, J. H. 1963: *The age of reconaissance*. London: Weidenfeld & Nicolson.

—— 1966: *The Spanish seaborne empire*. London: Hutchinson.

—— 1981: *The discovery of the sea*. Berkeley: University of California Press.

Payen, J. 1984: La position de la France dans l'industrie européenne des machines à vapeur durant la seconde moitié du XIXe siècle. *History and Technology* 1, 175–211.

Perrot, M. 1978: De la nourrice à l'employée . . . travaux des femmes dans la France du XIXe siècle. *Le Mouvement Social* 105, 3–10.

—— 1983: Femmes et machines au XIXe siècle. *Romantisme* 41, 5–17.

Phillips, A. and Taylor, B. 1980: Sex and skill: Notes towards a feminist economics. *Feminist Review*, 6, 79–88.

Phillips, C. R. 1987: Time and duration: A model for the economy of early modern Spain. *American Historical Review* 92, 531–62.

Pollard, S. 1957: British and world shipbuilding 1890–1914: A study in comparative costs. *Journal of Economic History* 17, 426–44.

—— 1973: Industrialization and the European economy, *Economic History Review* 26, 636–48.

—— 1981: *Peaceful conquest: The industrialization of Europe 1760–1970*. Oxford: Oxford University Press.

—— 1985: Capital exports, 1870–1914: Harmful or beneficial?. *Economic History Review* 38, 489–514.

Pollard, S. and Robertson, P. L. 1979: *The British shipbuilding industry, 1870–1914*. Cambridge, Mass.: Harvard University Press.

Poni, C. 1972: Archaéologie de la fabrique: La diffusion des moulins à soie 'alla bolognese' dans les Etats vénitiens du XVIe au XVIIIe siècle. *Annales: E.S.C.* 27, 1475–96.

—— 1976: All'origine del sistema di fabbrica: tecnologie e organizazzione produttiva dei mulini da seta nell'Italia settentrionale (sec. XVII–XVIII). *Rivista storica italiana* 88, 444–97.

—— 1982: Piccole innovazioni e filatoi a mano: Venezia (1550–1600). In *Studi in memoria di Luigi dal Pane* (Bologna: Editrice CLUEB), 371–85.

—— 1983: Innovazione tecnologica e rivoluzione dei prezzi: Il caso della seta. In *Studi in onore di Gino Barbieri* (Milan: Edizioni IPEM), vol 3, 1261–68.

—— 1985: Proto-industrialization, rural and urban. *Review* 9, 305–14.
Ponting, K. G. 1973: Logwood: An interesting dye. *Journal of European Economic History* 2, 109–19.
Post, J. D. 1976: Famine, mortality and epidemic disease in the process of modernization. *Economic History Review* 29, 14–37.
Pounds, N. J. G. 1979: *An historical geography of Europe 1500–1840*. Cambridge: Cambridge University Press.
—— 1985: *An historical geography of Europe 1800–1914*. Cambridge: Cambridge University Press.
Pounds, J. J. G. and Parker, W. N. 1957: *Coal and steel in Western Europe*. London: Faber & Faber.
Prakash, O. 1979: Asian trade and European impact: A study of the trade from Bengal, 1630–1720. In Kling, B. B. and Pearson, M. N., *The age of partnership* (Honolulu: University Press of Hawaii), 43–70.
—— 1985: *The Dutch East India Company and the economy of Bengal 1630–1720*. Princeton: Princeton University Press.
—— 1986: Precious metal flows in Asia and world economic integration in the seventeenth century. In Fischer, McInnis and Schneider 1986, vol. I, 83–96.
Price, J. M. 1954: 'Tobacco trade': The rise of Glasgow in the Chesapeake tobacco trade, 1707–1775. *William and Mary Quarterly* 11, 179–99.
—— 1964: The economic growth of the Chesapeake and the European market, 1697–1775. *Journal of Economic History* 24, 496–511.
—— 1973: *France and the Chesapeake: a history of the French tobacco monopoly, 1674–1791*. Ann Arbor: University of Michigan Press.
Pritchard, J. 1987: From shipwright to naval constructor: the professionalization of 18th century French naval shipbuilders. *Technology and Culture* 28, 1–25.
Pullan, B. (ed.) 1968: *Crisis and change in the Venetian economy in the sixteenth and seventeenth centuries*. London: Methuen.
Quataert, J. H. 1985: The shaping of women's work in manufacturing: Guilds, household and the State in Central Europe, 1648–1870. *American Historical Review* 90, 1122–48.
Rapp, R. T. 1975: The unmaking of the Mediterranean trade hegemony: International trade rivalry and the Commercial Revolution. *Journal of Economic History* 35, 499–525.
—— 1976: *Industry and economic decline in seventeenth-century Venice*. Cambridge, Mass.; Harvard University Press.
Reddy, W. M. 1977: The textile trade and the language of the crowd at Rouen, 1752–1871. *Past and Present* 74, 62–89.
—— 1979: Skeins, scales, discounts, steam and other objects of crowd justice in early French textile mills. *Comparative Studies in Society and History* 21, 204–13.
—— 1984: *The rise of market culture: The textile trade and French society, 1750–1900*. Cambridge: Cambridge University Press.
Reich, L. S. 1985: *The making of American industrial research*. Cambridge: Cambridge University Press.
Rendall, J. 1985: *The origins of modern feminism: Women in Britain, France and the United States, 1780–1860*. London: Macmillan.

Rich, E. E. and Wilson, C. H. (eds.) 1977: *The Cambridge economic history of Europe*. vol. V. Cambridge: Cambridge University Press.

Richards, E. 1974: Women in the British economy since c. 1700: an interpretation. *History* 59, 337–57.

Richards, J. F. 1983a: Introduction. In Richards 1983b, 3–26.

—— (ed.) 1983b: *Precious metals in the medieval and early modern worlds*. Durham, NC: Carolina Academic Press.

Richards, W. A. 1980: The import of firearms into West Africa in the eighteenth century. *Journal of African History* 21, 43–59.

Richardson, H. W. 1968: Chemicals: In Aldcroft 1968, 274–306.

Riden, P. 1977: The output of the British iron industry before 1870. *Economic History Review* 30, 442–59.

Riley, J. C. 1980: *International government finance and the Amsterdam capital market 1740–1815*. Cambridge: Cambridge University Press.

—— 1986: Insects and the European mortality decline. *American Historical Review* 91, 833–58.

Ringrose, D. R. 1983: *Madrid and the Spanish economy 1560–1850*. Berkeley: University of California Press.

Ritchie, A. 1975: *King of the road*. London: Wildwood House.

Roberts, E. 1988: *Women's work 1840–1940*. London: Macmillan.

Roberts, M. 1979: Sickles and scythes: Women's work and men's work at harvest time, *History Workshop* 7, 3–29.

Robinson, E. H. 1974: The early diffusion of steam power. *Journal of Economic History* 34, 91–107.

Roehl, R. 1976: French industrialization: A reconsideration, *Explorations in Economic History* 13, 233–81.

—— 1983: Britain and European industrialization: Pathfinder pursued?, *Review* 6, 455–73.

Rolt, L. T. C. 1986: *Tools for the job*. Revised edition. London: HMSO.

Romano, R. 1968: Economic aspects of the construction of warships in Venice in the sixteenth century. In Pullan 1968, 59–87.

Roper, L. A. 1985: Work, marriage and sexuality: Women in Reformation Augsburg. Unpublished PhD dissertation, University of London.

Rose, S. 1985: 'Gender at work': Sex, class and industrial capitalism. *History Workshop* 11, 113–31.

—— 1987: Gender segregation in the transition to the factory: The English hosiery industry, 1850–1910. *Feminist Studies* 13, 163–84.

Rosenberg, N. 1963: Technological change in the machine tool industry, 1840–1910. *Journal of Economic History* 23, 414–43.

—— 1976a: *Perspectives on technology*. Cambridge: Cambridge University Press.

—— 1976b: The direction of technological change: Inducement mechanism and focusing devices. In Rosenberg 1976a, 108–25.

—— 1976c: Problems in the economist's conceptualization of technological innovation. In Rosenberg 1976a, 61–84.

—— 1976d: Science, invention and economic growth. In Rosenberg, 1976a, 260–79.

Rosenberg, N. and Birdzell, L. E. 1986: *How the west grew rich: The economic transformation of the industrial world.* New York: Basic Books.

Sabel, C. and Zeitlin, J. 1985: Historical alternatives to mass production: Politics, markets and technology in nineteenth century industrialization. *Past and Present* 108, 133–76.

Samuel, R. 1977: Workshop of the world: Steam power and hand technology in mid-Victorian Britain. *History Workshop* 3, 6–72.

Saul, S. B. 1960: *Studies in British overseas trade, 1870–1914.* Liverpool: Liverpool University Press.

—— 1962: The motor industry in Britain to 1914. *Business History* 5, 22–44.

—— 1969: *The myth of the Great Depression, 1873–1896.* London: Macmillan.

—— 1970: The market and the development of the mechanical engineering industries in Britain, 1860–1914. In Saul, S. B. (ed.) *Technological change: the United States and Britain in the nineteenth century* (London: Methuen), 141–70.

—— 1972: The nature and diffusion of technology. In Youngson, A. J. (ed.), *Economic development in the long run* (London: Allen & Unwin), 36–61.

Scammell, G. V. 1981: *The world encompassed: The first European empires c. 800–1650.* London: Methuen.

—— 1982: England, Portugal and the Estado da India c. 1500–1635. *Modern Asian Studies* 16, 177–92.

Schmiechen, J. A. 1984: *Sweated industries and sweated labour. The London clothing trades 1860–1914.* London: Croom Helm.

Schmitz, C. J. 1979: *World non-ferrous metal production and prices, 1700–1976.* London: Frank Cass.

Schnetzler, J. 1975: *Les industries et les hommes dans la région stéphanoise.* St Etienne: Privately published.

Schumpeter, E. B. 1960: *English overseas trade statistics, 1697–1808.* Oxford: Oxford University Press.

Scott, J. W. 1974: *The glassworkers of Carmaux.* Cambridge, Mass.: Harvard University Press.

—— 1984: Men and women in the Parisian garment trades: Discussions of family and work in the 1830s and 1840s. In Thane, Crossick and Floud 1984.

Scott, J. W. and Tilly, L. A. 1975: Women's work and the family in nineteenth-century Europe. *Comparative Studies in Society and History* 17, 36–64.

Scoville, W. C. 1951: Minority migrations and the diffusion of technology. *Journal of Economic History* 11, 347–60.

Sella, D. 1968: The rise and fall of the Venetian woollen industry. In Pullan 1968, 106–26.

—— 1969: Industrial production in seventeenth-century Italy: A reappraisal. *Explorations in Entrepreneurial History* 6, 235–53.

—— 1974: European industries 1500–1700. In Cipolla, 1974, 354–426.

—— 1979: *Crisis and continuity: The economy of Spanish Lombardy in the seventeenth century.* Cambridge, Mass.: Harvard University Press.

Sewell, W. H. 1980: *Work and revolution in France: The language of labour from the Old Régime to 1848.* Cambridge: Cambridge University Press.

—— 1986: Artisans, factory workers and the formation of the French working class, 1789–1848. In Katznelson and Zolberg 1986, 45–70.

Shammas, C. 1984: The eighteenth-century English diet and economic change. *Explorations in Economic History* 21, 254–69.

—— 1986: The world women knew: Women workers in the north of England during the late seventeenth century. In Dunn, R. S. and Dunn, M. M. (eds.), *The world of William Penn* (Philadelphia: University of Pennsylvania Press), 99–115.

Sharlin, A. 1978: Natural decrease in early modern cities: A reconsideration. *Past and Present* 79, 126–38.

Sharrer, G. T. 1971: The indigo bonanza in South Carolina, 1740–90. *Technology and Culture* 12, 447–55.

Shepherd, J. F. and Walton, G. M. 1972: *Shipping, maritime trade and the economic development of colonial North America*. Cambridge: Cambridge University Press.

Sheridan, G. J. 1979: Household crafts in an industrializing economy: The case of the silk weavers of Lyons. In Merriman, J. M. (ed.) *Consciousness and class experience in nineteenth century Europe* (New York: Holmes & Meier), 107–28.

—— 1984: Family and enterprise in the silk shops of Lyon: the place of labor in the domestic weaving economy, 1840–1870. *Research in Economic History* supplement 3, 33–60.

Shinn, T. 1980: The genesis of French industrial research 1880–1940. *Social Science Information* 19, 607–40.

Showalter, D. E. 1975: *Railroads and rifles: Soldiers, technology and the unification of Germany*. Hamden, Conn.: Shoestring Press.

Sicilia, D. B. 1986: Steam power and the progress of industry in the late nineteenth century. *Theory and Society* 15, 287–99.

Siegenthaler, H. 1976: Switzerland 1920–1970. In Cipolla, C. M. (ed.) *The Fontana economic history of Europe* (Glasgow: Collins), vol. 6, part 2, 530–76.

Sivori, G. 1972: Il tramonto dell'industria serica genovese. *Rivista storica italiana* 84, 893–944.

Slicher Van Bath, B. H. 1977: Agriculture in the vital revolution. In Rich and Wilson 1977, 42–132.

Smith, C. S. 1964: The discovery of carbon in steel. *Technology and Culture* 5, 149–75.

Smith, J. G. 1979: *The origins and early development of the heavy chemical industry in France*. Oxford: Oxford University Press.

Smith, M. R. 1982: Military entrepreneurship. In Mayr, O. and Post, R. C. (eds.), *Yankee enterprise: the rise of the American System of Manufactures* (Washington, DC: Smithsonian Institution Press), 63–102.

—— 1985a: Introduction. In Smith 1985b, 1–37.

—— (ed.) 1985b: *Military enterprise and technical change*. Cambridge, Mass.: MIT Press.

Smith, M. S. 1980: *Tariff reform in France 1860–1900: The politics of economic interest*. Ithaca: Cornell University Press.

Smith, W. D. 1982: The European–Asian trade of the seventeenth century and the modernization of commercial capitalism. *Itinerario* 6, 68–90.

—— 1984: The function of commercial centers in the modernization of

European capitalism: Amsterdam as an information exchange in the seventeenth century. *Journal of Economic History* 44, 985–1005.

Söderlund, E. F. 1958: The Swedish iron industry during the First World War and the post-war depression. *Scandinavian Economic History Review* 6, 53–94.

Sonenscher, M. 1983: Work and wages in Paris in the eighteenth century. In Berg, Hudson and Sonenscher 1983, 147–72.

—— 1986: Weavers, wage-rates and the measurement of work in eighteenth-century Rouen. *Textile History* 17, 7–18.

—— 1987: Journeymen, the courts and the French trades, 1781–1791. *Past and Present* 114, 77–109.

Sperling, J. 1962: The international payments mechanism in the seventeenth and eighteenth centuries. *Economic History Review* 14, 446–68.

Stavrianos, L. S. 1981: *Global rift: The Third World comes of age*. New York: Morrow.

Steensgaard, N. 1974: *The Asian trade revolution of the seventeenth century: The East India companies and the decline of the caravan trade*. Chicago: University of Chicago Press.

—— 1981: The companies as a specific institution in the history of European expansion. In Blussé, L. and Gaastra, F., *Companies and trade* (The Hague: Martinus Nijhoff), 245–64.

Stein, R. 1980: The French sugar business in the eighteenth century: A quantitative study. *Business History* 22, 3–17.

Supple, B. 1977: The nature of enterprise. In Rich and Wilson 1977, 393–461.

Tanguy, J. 1966: La production et le commerce des toiles 'bretagnes' du XVIe au XVIIIe siècle: Premiers résultats. In *Actes du 91e Congrès national des Sociétés Savantes* (Paris: Bibliothèque Nationale), 105–41.

Tann, J. 1973: Richard Arkwright and technology. *History* 58, 29–44.

—— 1978: Marketing methods in the international steam engine market: The case of Boulton and Watt. *Journal of Economic History* 38, 363–91.

Tann, J. and Breckin, M. J. 1978: The international diffusion of the Watt engine, 1775–1825. *Economic History Review* 31, 541–64.

Tepaske, J. J. 1983: New World silver, Castile and the Philipines, 1590–1800. In Richards 1983b, 425–45.

Thane, P., Crossick, G. C. and Floud, R. 1984: *The power of the past: Essays for Eric Hobsbawm*. Cambridge: Cambridge University Press.

Thirsk, J. 1980: Policies for retrenchment in seventeenth-century Europe. *Comparative Studies in Society and History* 22, 626–33.

Thomas, B. 1985: Escaping from constraints: The Industrial Revolution in a Malthusian context. *Journal of Interdisciplinary History* 15, 729–53.

Thomson, J. K. J. 1982: *Clermont-de-Lodève 1633–1789*. Cambridge: Cambridge University Press.

Tilly, C. 1983: Flows of capital and forms of industry in Europe, 1500–1900. *Theory and Society* 12, 123–42.

Tilly, L. A. 1971: The food riot as a form of political conflict in France. *Journal of Interdisciplinary History* 2, 23–57.

—— 1981: Paths of proletarianization. *Signs* 7, 400–17.

—— 1982: Three faces of capitalism: Women and work in French cities. In

Merriman, J. (ed.), *French cities in the nineteenth century* (London: Hutchinson, 165–92.

Tilly, L. A. and Scott, J. W. 1978: *Women, work and the family.* New York: Holt, Rinehart & Winston.

Tilly, L. A., Scott, J. W. and Cohen, M. 1976: Women's work and European fertility patterns. *Journal of Interdisciplinary History* 6, 447–76.

Tinker, H. 1974: *A new kind of slavery: The export of Indian labour overseas* Oxford: Oxford University Press.

Todd, J. A. 1923: *The world's cotton crops.* London: A & C Black.

Tomlinson, J. 1981: *Problems of British economic policy, 1870–1945.* London: Methuen.

Toynbee, A. 1916: *Lectures on the industrial revolution of the eighteenth century.* London: Green & Co.

Trebilcock, C. 1969: 'Spin-off' in British economic history: Armaments and industry, 1760–1914. *Economic History Review* 22, 474–90.

Trescott, M. M. 1976: The bicycle: A technical precursor of the automobile. *Business and Economic History* 2nd ser. 5, 51–75.

—— (ed.) 1979: *Dynamos and virgins: Women and technological change in history.* Metuchen, NJ: Scarecrow Press.

Turner, M. 1982: Agricultural productivity in England in the eighteenth century: Evidence from crop yields. *Economic History Review* 35, 489–510.

Tweedale, G. 1986: Metallurgy and technological change: A case study of Sheffield specialty steel and America, 1830–1930. *Technology and Culture* 27, 189–222.

—— 1987 *Sheffield steel and America: A century of commercial and technological interdependence, 1830–1930.* Cambridge: Cambridge University Press.

Unger, R. W. 1978: *Dutch shipbuilding before 1800: shops and guilds.* Assen: Van Gorcum.

—— 1980: *The ship in the medieval economy, 600–1600.* London: Croom Helm.

—— 1981: Warships and cargo ships in medieval Europe. *Technology and Culture* 22, 233–52.

Van Der Wee, H. 1963: *The growth of the Antwerp market and the European economy.* The Hague: Martinus Nijhoff.

Van Houtte, J. A. and Van Buyten, L. 1977: The Low Countries. In Wilson and Parker 1977, 81–114.

Van Neck, A. 1979: *La révolution industrielle: Les débuts de la machine à vapeur dans l'industrie belge, 1800–1850.* Vol 2 Part 2 of *Histoire quantitative et développement de la Belgique.* (Brussels: Académie Royale de Belgique).

Verlinden, C. 1970: *The beginnings of modern colonization.* Ithaca: Cornell University Press.

—— 1972: From the Mediterranean to the Atlantic: Aspects of an economic shift (12th–18th century). *Journal of European Economic History* 1, 625–46.

Vetterli, W. A. 1951: The history of indigo. *Ciba Review* 85, 3066–71.

Von Weiher, S. 1980: The rise and development of electrical engineering and technology in Germany in the nineteenth century: A case study – Siemens and

Halske. In Okochi, A. and Uchida, H. (eds.), *Development and diffusion of technology* (Tokyo: Tokyo University Press), 23–44.

Wadsworth, A. P. and Mann, J. de L. 1931: *The cotton trade and industrial Lancashire 1600–1780.* Manchester: Manchester University Press.

Wake, C. H. H. 1979: The changing pattern of Europe's pepper and spice imports ca. 1400–1700. *Journal of European Economic History* 8, 361–403.

Wallace, A. F. C. 1982: *The social context of innovation.* Princeton: Princeton University Press.

Wallerstein, I. M. 1974: *The modern world-system: Capitalist agriculture and the origins of the European world-economy in the sixteenth century.* New York: Academic Press.

—— 1980: *The modern world-system: Mercantilism and the consolidation of the European world-economy, 1600–1750.* New York: Academic Press.

Walton, A. W. 1983: The persistence of French handicraft industries and the Crystal Palace Exhibition of 1851. Unpublished PhD dissertation, University of Wisconsin.

Walton, G. M. 1970: Obstacles to technical diffusion in ocean shipping, 1675–1775. *Explorations in Economic History* 8, 123–40.

Warren, K. 1980: *Chemical foundations: The alkali industry in Britain to 1926.* Oxford: Oxford University Press.

Webb, S. B. 1980: Tariffs, cartels, technology and growth in the German steel industry, 1879 to 1914. *Journal of Economic History* 40, 309–29.

Weinstein, B. 1983a: *The Amazon rubber boom, 1850–1920.* Stanford: Stanford University Press.

—— 1983b: Capital penetration and problems of labor in the Amazon rubber trade. *Radical History Review* 27, 121–40.

Weir, D. R. 1984: Life under pressure: France and England, 1670–1870. *Journal of Economic History* 44, 27–47.

Weissbach, L. S. 1982: Artisanal responses to artistic decline: The cabinet makers of Paris in the era of industrialization. *Journal of Social History* 16, 67–81.

Wensky, M. 1982: Women's guilds in Cologne in the later Middle Ages. *Journal of European Economic History* 11, 631–50.

Wertime, T. 1961: *The coming of the age of steel.* Leiden: Brill.

White, L. 1972: The expansion of technology, 500–1500. In Cipolla, C. M. (ed.), *The Fontana economic history of Europe* (Glasgow: Collins), vol. 1, 143–74.

Wiesner, M. E. 1986a: Spinsters and seamstresses: Women in cloth and clothing production. In Ferguson, M. W., Quilligan, M. and Vickers, N. J. (eds.), *Rewriting the Renaissance* (Chicago: University of Chicago Press), 191–205.

—— 1986b: *Working women in Renaissance Germany.* New Brunswick, NJ: Rutgers University Press.

—— 1987: Women's work in the changing city economy 1500–1650. In Boxer and Quataert 1987, 64–74.

Wiesner Wood, M. 1981: Paltry peddlars or essential merchants? Women in the distributive trades in early modern Nuremberg. *Sixteenth Century Journal* 12, 3–13.

Wilson, C. and Parker, G. (eds.) 1977: *An introduction to the sources of*

European economic history 1500–1800. London: Weidenfeld & Nicolson.

Wilson, R. G. 1973: The supremacy of the Yorkshire cloth industry in the eighteenth century. In Harte, N. B. and Ponting, K. G. (eds.), *Textile history and economic history* (Manchester: Manchester University Press), 225–46.

Wolf, E. 1982: *Europe and the people without history.* Berkeley: University of California Press.

Woodforde, J. 1970: *The story of the bicycle.* London: Routledge & Kegan Paul.

Woodruff, W. 1966. *The impact of western man.* London: Macmillan.

Woronoff, D. 1976: Le monde ouvrier de la sidérurgie ancienne: Note sur l'exemple français. *Le mouvement social* 97, 109–19.

—— 1984: *L'industrie sidérurgique en France pendant la Révolution et l'Empire.* Paris: Éditions de l'École des Hautes Études en Sciences Sociales.

Wright, G. 1971: An econometric study of cotton production and trade, 1830–1860. *Review of Economics and Statistics* 53, 111–20.

—— 1974: Cotton competition and the postbellum recovery of the American South. *Journal of Economic History* 34, 610–35.

Wrigley, E. A. 1962: *Industrial growth and population change.* Cambridge: Cambridge University Press.

—— 1967: A simple model of London's importance in changing English society and economy 1650–1750. *Past and Present* 37, 44–70.

—— 1969: *Population and history,* New York: McGraw-Hill.

—— 1972: The process of modernization and the Industrial Revolution in England. *Journal of Interdisciplinary History* 3, 225–59.

—— 1983: The growth of population in eighteenth-century England: A conundrum resolved. *Past and Present* 98, 121–50.

—— 1985: Urban growth and agricultural change: England and the Continent in the early modern period. *Journal of Interdisciplinary History* 15, 683–728.

—— 1986: Men on the land and men in the countryside: Employment in agriculture in early-nineteenth-century England. In Bonfield, L., Smith, R. M. and Wrightson, K. (eds.), *The world we have gained* (Oxford: Basil Blackwell), 295–336.

Wrigley, E. A. and Schofield, R. S. 1981: *The population history of England.* London: Edward Arnold.

Yamamura, K. and Kamiki, T. 1983: Silver mines and Sung coins – a monetary history of medieval and modern Japan in historical perspective. In Richards 1983b, 329–62.

Zimmeck, M. 1986: Jobs for the girls: The expansion of clerical work for women 1850–1914. In John, A. V. (ed.), *Unequal opportunities* (Oxford: Basil Blackwell), 153–77.

Index